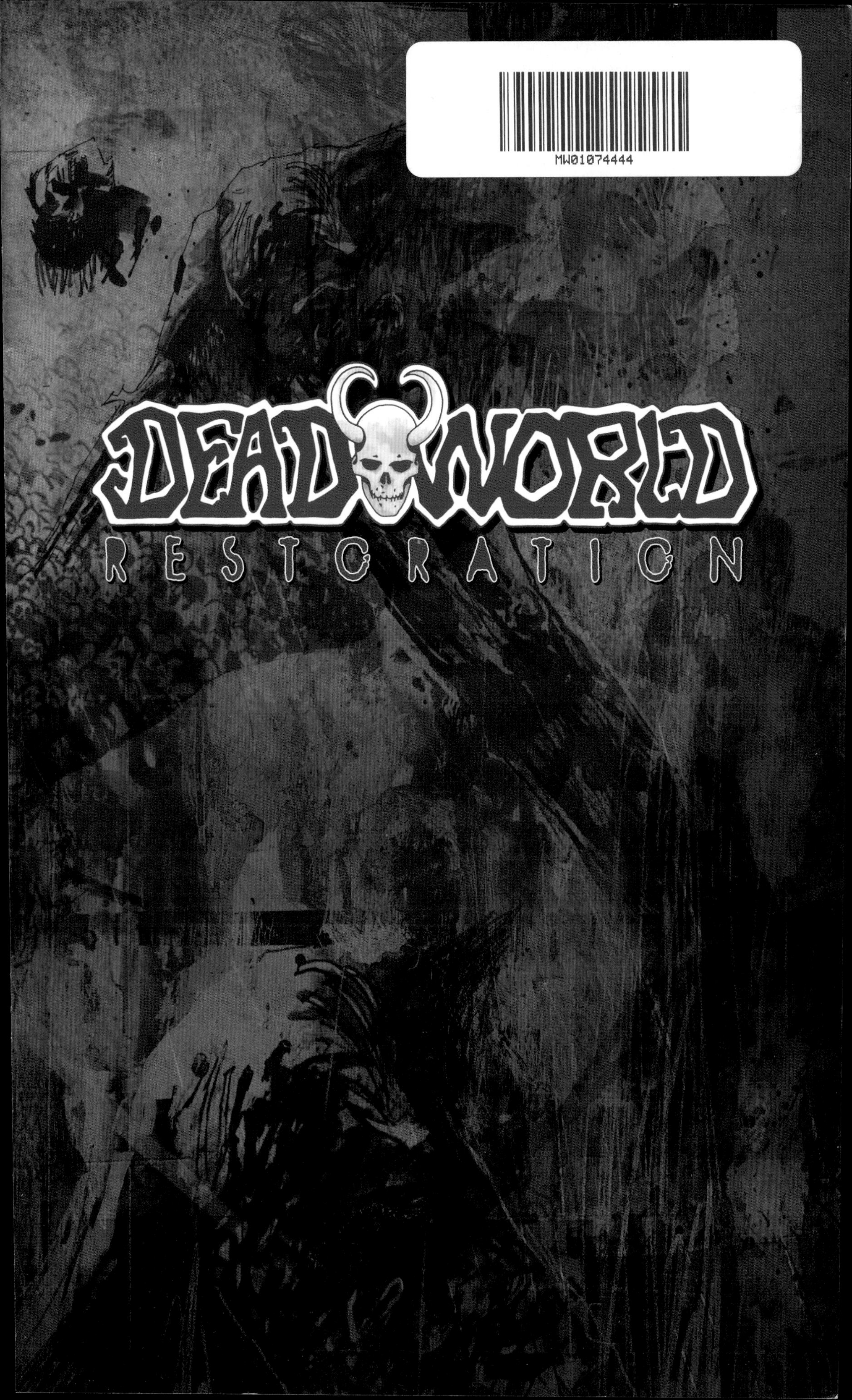
DEADWORLD
RESTORATION

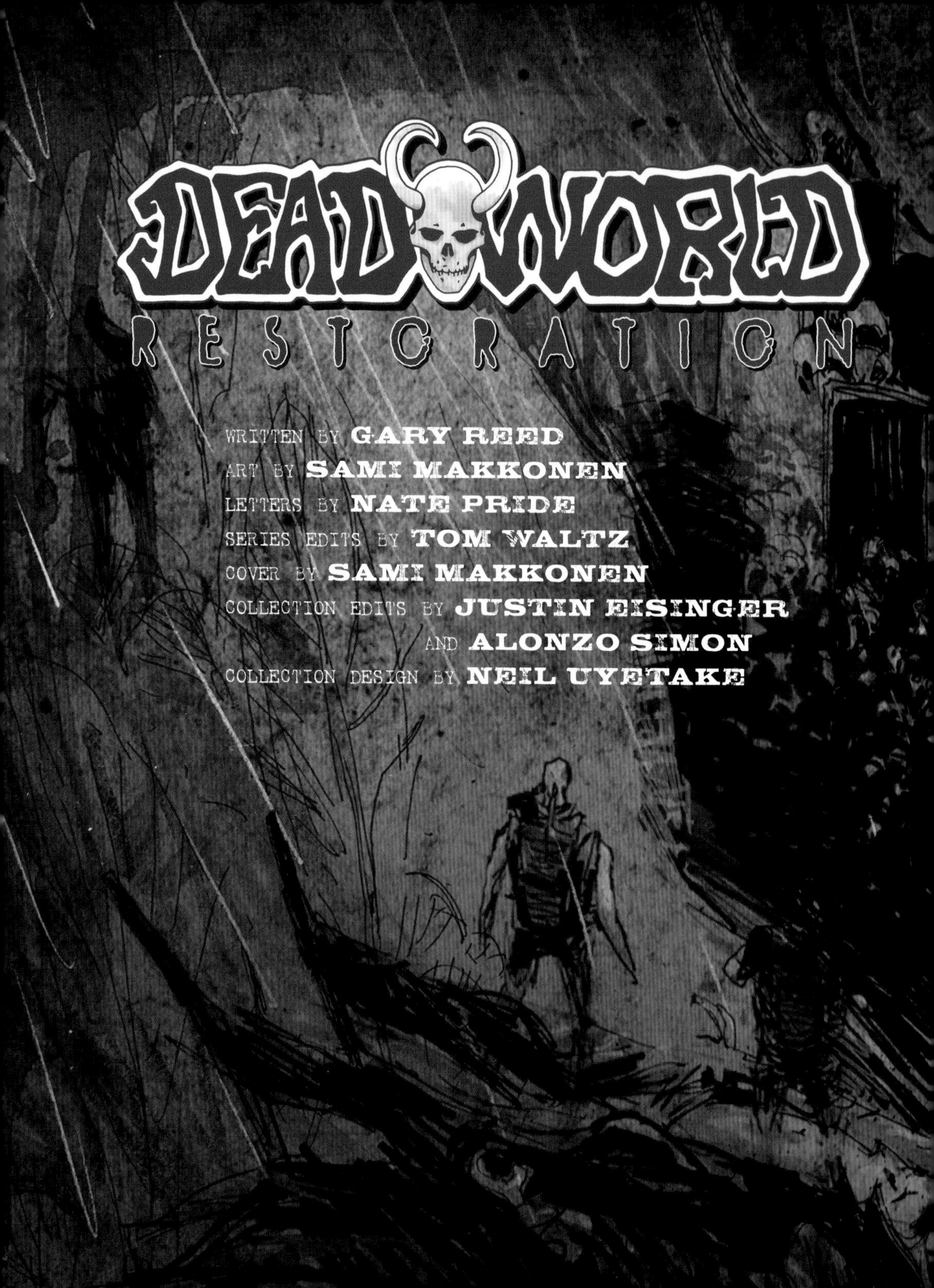

DEADWORLD

RESTORATION

WRITTEN BY **GARY REED**
ART BY **SAMI MAKKONEN**
LETTERS BY **NATE PRIDE**
SERIES EDITS BY **TOM WALTZ**
COVER BY **SAMI MAKKONEN**
COLLECTION EDITS BY **JUSTIN EISINGER**
AND **ALONZO SIMON**
COLLECTION DESIGN BY **NEIL UYETAKE**

ISBN: 978-1-61377-974-3

17 16 15 14 1 2 3 4

IDW®
www.IDWPUBLISHING.com
IDW founded by Ted Adams, Alex Garner, Kris Oprisko, and Robbie Robbins

Ted Adams, CEO & Publisher
Greg Goldstein, President & COO
Robbie Robbins, EVP/Sr. Graphic Artist
Chris Ryall, Chief Creative Officer/Editor-in-Chief
Matthew Ruzicka, CPA, Chief Financial Officer
Alan Payne, VP of Sales
Dirk Wood, VP of Marketing
Lorelei Bunjes, VP of Digital Services
Jeff Webber, VP of Digital Publishing & Business Development

Facebook: **facebook.com/idwpublishing**
Twitter: **@idwpublishing**
YouTube: **youtube.com/idwpublishing**
Instagram: **instagram.com/idwpublishing**
deviantART: **idwpublishing.deviantart.com**
Pinterest: **pinterest.com/idwpublishing/idw-staff-faves**

Originally published as DEADWORLD: RESTORATION issues #1–5.

FOREWORD

Another chapter in the *Deadworld* saga. As I continue to do these story arcs, primarily as mini-series, and then collected like this trade paperback, one might think that I'm taking a break between the arcs but actually I'm not. Something like *Deadworld*, which I accept is a big part of my writing career, is not something that stops and then starts when it's time to launch another mini. It's always in front of me.

Deadworld is an integral part of my writing "world." Sure, I have other "worlds" such as my teaching and my personal life and other projects that I'm working on, but *Deadworld* sometimes even intrudes in those areas. When I do my lectures on cellular respiration in my General Biology class and touch on the cessation of respiration leading into death and rigor mortis, I give a brief side excursion into the viability of zombies. Of course, the majority of students have no idea that after class I'm immersed in the zombie world, but occasionally a student stumbles across the connection. One time I had a student actually reading one of my graphic novels during a break in class and they never put it together that the Gary Reed they were reading was the same one gently nodding them to sleep during the endocrine lecture.

Now that *Restoration* is over (well, for me... not for you as I assume you're just starting off on this book), it seems that a deliberate plan has formed on how *Deadworld* is unfolding. Of course, I can't state that it is all some master plan, because it's not. I have a germ of an idea but as I'm writing the stories, they constantly shift into directions I didn't expect.

When I first took over *Deadworld*, decades ago (yes, decades), I felt obligated to keep the integrity of the series. Sure, I modified things and moved the story ahead but it wasn't until after I did the re-launch with Image Comics (*Requiem for the World*), that I really felt *Deadworld* was truly mine. By that, I mean, it had my voice. I could let go of the legacy of the past and even though I felt I should maintain the world, I was in a position to mold it more to my liking.

The last three story arcs could be seen as one larger one, although for each, I tried to give new readers an opportunity to come in and not feel lost. I don't know how successful that was but at the same time, I didn't want to sacrifice story for the "old" readers who have been here since the beginning.

Slaughterhouse, *War of the Dead*, and *Restoration* can be viewed as one long story line. They tie in with each other and build up to the climax at the end of this volume.

Of course, that climax is just a step towards the ultimate end, which to be honest, I don't exactly have worked out although I have a good idea now. But that's likely to change... again.

Gary Reed

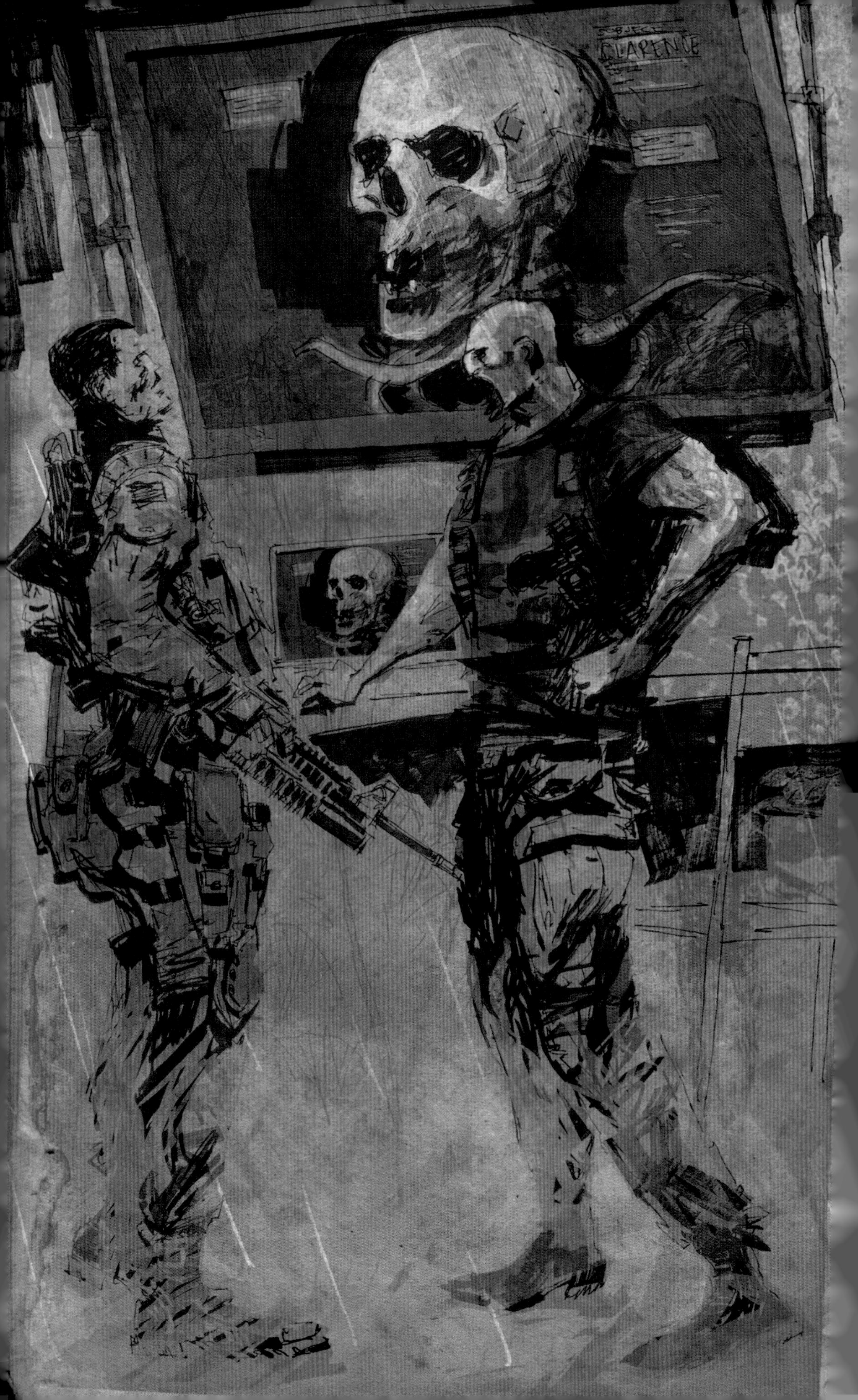
SUBJECT
CLARENCE

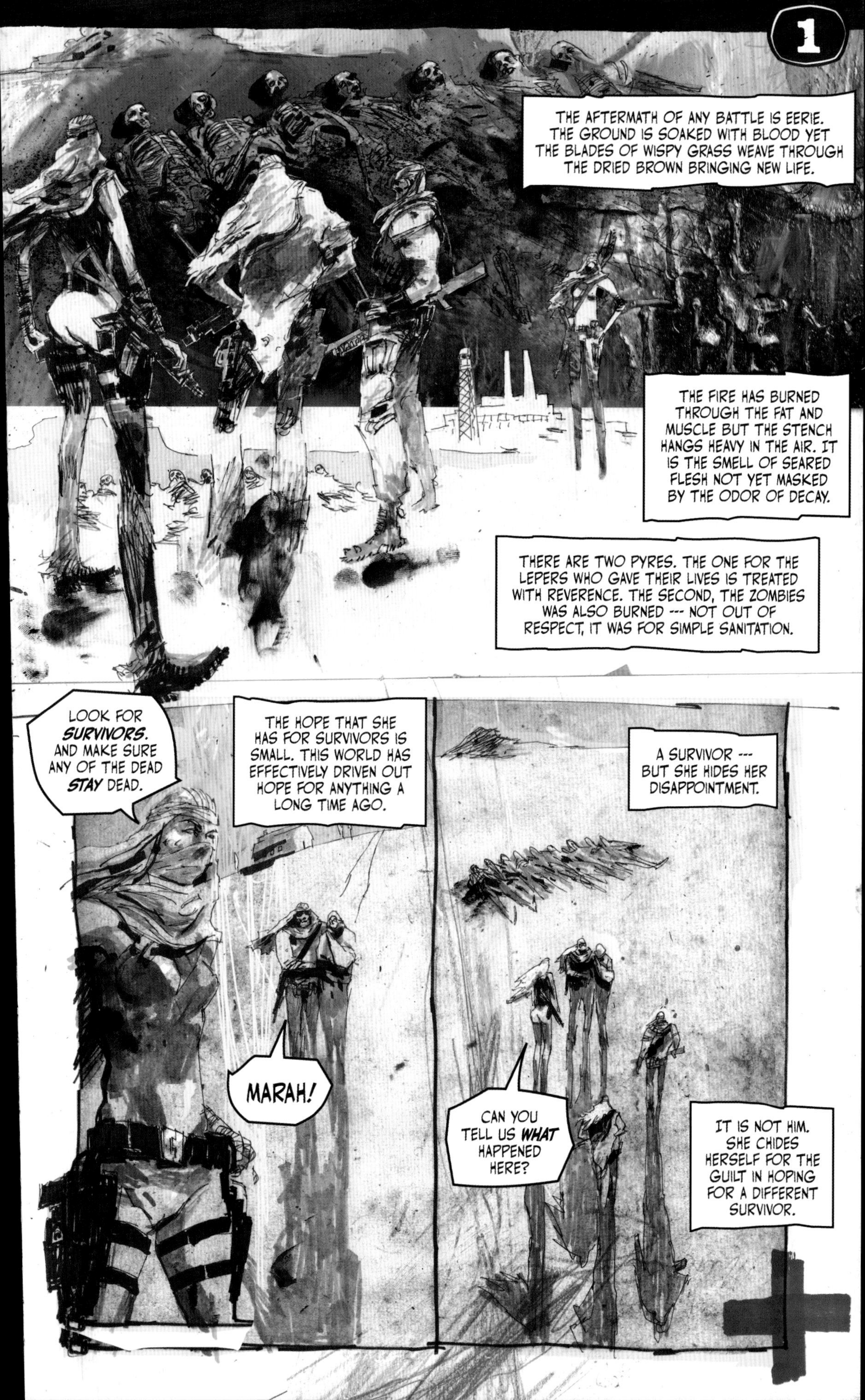
1
THE AFTERMATH OF ANY BATTLE IS EERIE. THE GROUND IS SOAKED WITH BLOOD YET THE BLADES OF WISPY GRASS WEAVE THROUGH THE DRIED BROWN BRINGING NEW LIFE.
THE FIRE HAS BURNED THROUGH THE FAT AND MUSCLE BUT THE STENCH HANGS HEAVY IN THE AIR. IT IS THE SMELL OF SEARED FLESH NOT YET MASKED BY THE ODOR OF DECAY.
THERE ARE TWO PYRES. THE ONE FOR THE LEPERS WHO GAVE THEIR LIVES IS TREATED WITH REVERENCE. THE SECOND, THE ZOMBIES WAS ALSO BURNED --- NOT OUT OF RESPECT, IT WAS FOR SIMPLE SANITATION.
LOOK FOR SURVIVORS. AND MAKE SURE ANY OF THE DEAD STAY DEAD.
THE HOPE THAT SHE HAS FOR SURVIVORS IS SMALL. THIS WORLD HAS EFFECTIVELY DRIVEN OUT HOPE FOR ANYTHING A LONG TIME AGO.
MARAH!
A SURVIVOR --- BUT SHE HIDES HER DISAPPOINTMENT.
CAN YOU TELL US WHAT HAPPENED HERE?
IT IS NOT HIM. SHE CHIDES HERSELF FOR THE GUILT IN HOPING FOR A DIFFERENT SURVIVOR.

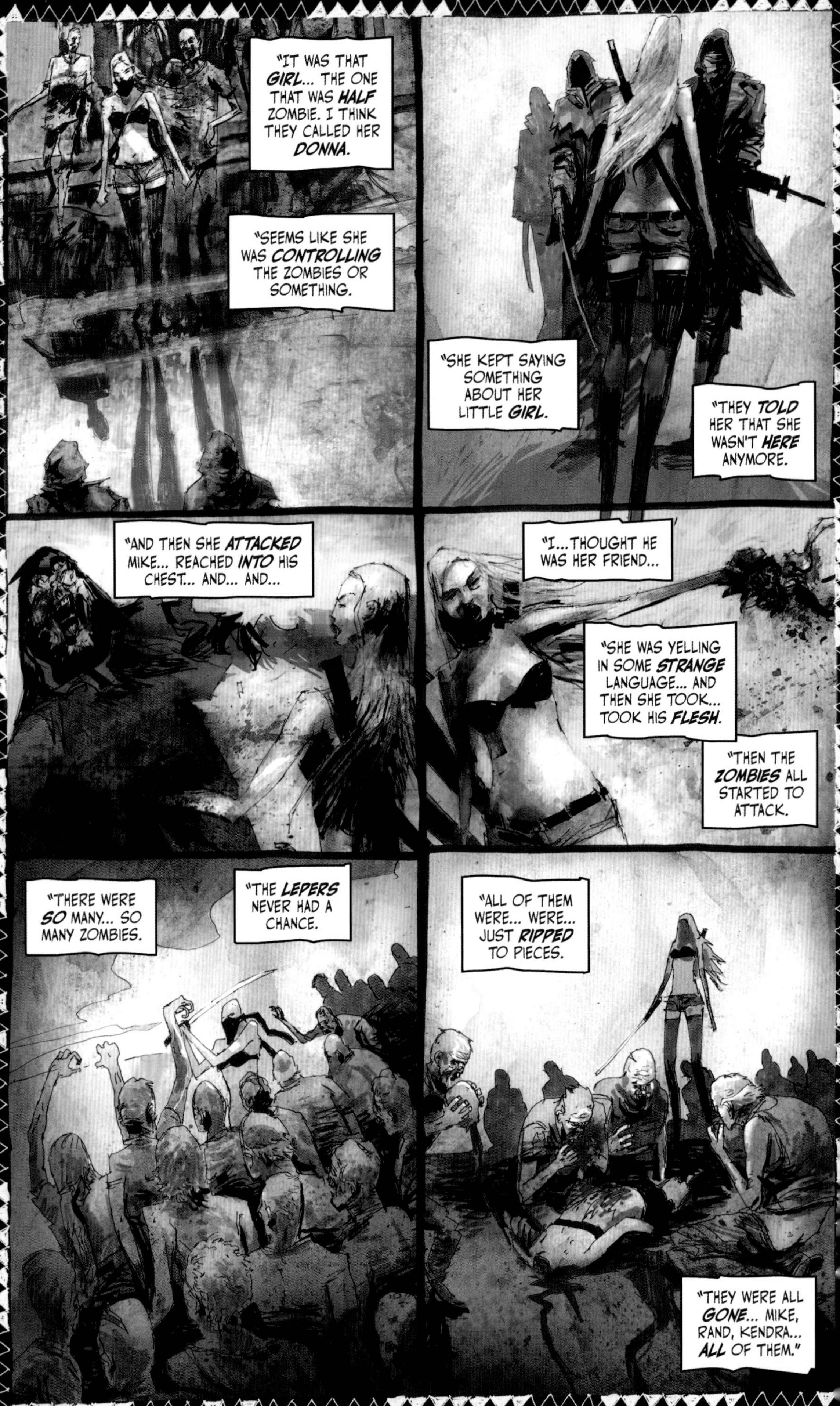
"IT WAS THAT GIRL... THE ONE THAT WAS HALF ZOMBIE. I THINK THEY CALLED HER DONNA.
"SEEMS LIKE SHE WAS CONTROLLING THE ZOMBIES OR SOMETHING.
"SHE KEPT SAYING SOMETHING ABOUT HER LITTLE GIRL.
"THEY TOLD HER THAT SHE WASN'T HERE ANYMORE.
"AND THEN SHE ATTACKED MIKE... REACHED INTO HIS CHEST... AND... AND...
"I...THOUGHT HE WAS HER FRIEND...
"SHE WAS YELLING IN SOME STRANGE LANGUAGE... AND THEN SHE TOOK... TOOK HIS FLESH.
"THEN THE ZOMBIES ALL STARTED TO ATTACK.
"THERE WERE SO MANY... SO MANY ZOMBIES.
"THE LEPERS NEVER HAD A CHANCE.
"ALL OF THEM WERE... WERE... JUST RIPPED TO PIECES.
"THEY WERE ALL GONE... MIKE, RAND, KENDRA... ALL OF THEM."

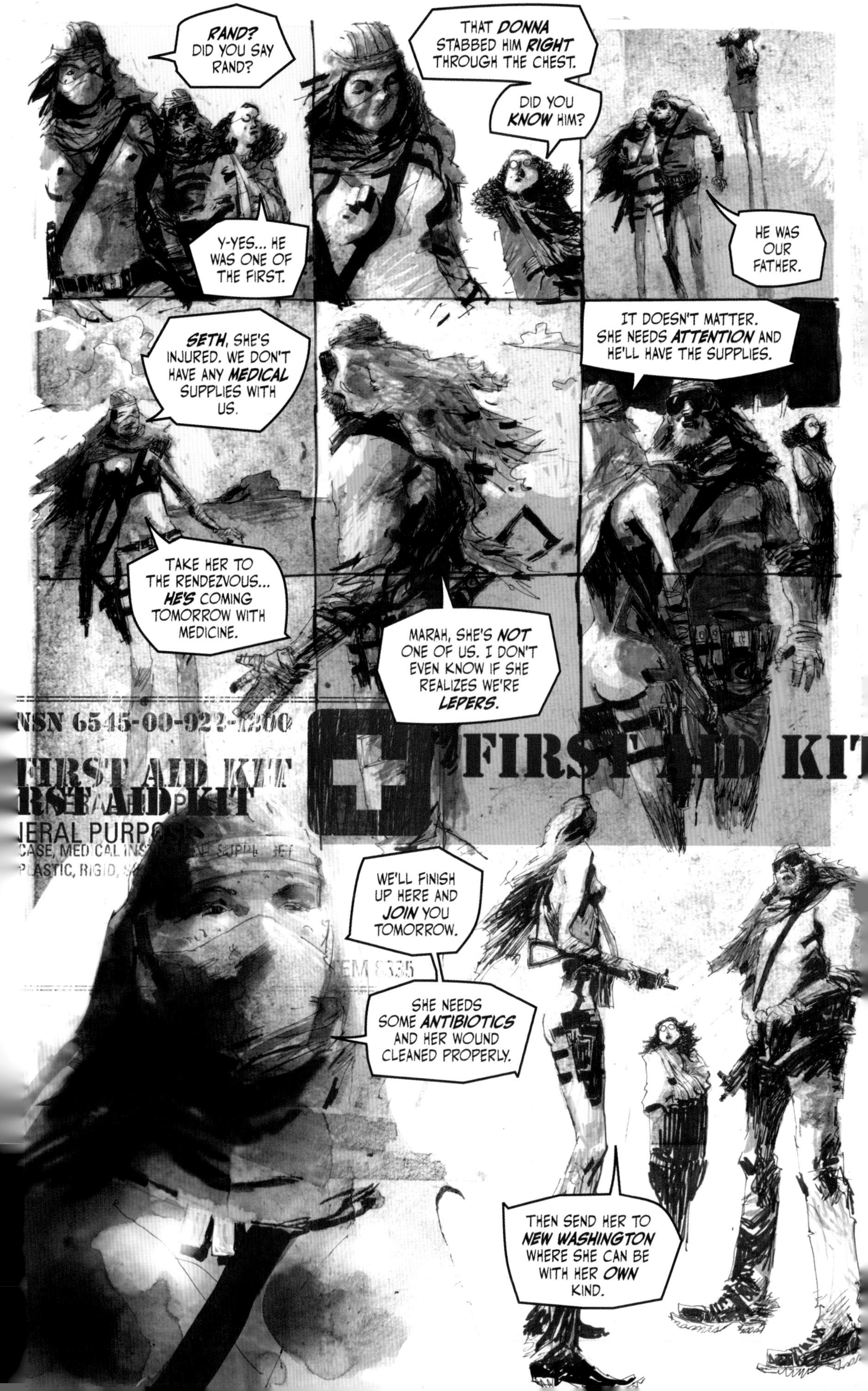
RAND? DID YOU SAY RAND?
Y-YES... HE WAS ONE OF THE FIRST.
THAT DONNA STABBED HIM RIGHT THROUGH THE CHEST.
DID YOU KNOW HIM?
HE WAS OUR FATHER.
SETH, SHE'S INJURED. WE DON'T HAVE ANY MEDICAL SUPPLIES WITH US.
TAKE HER TO THE RENDEZVOUS... HE'S COMING TOMORROW WITH MEDICINE.
IT DOESN'T MATTER. SHE NEEDS ATTENTION AND HE'LL HAVE THE SUPPLIES.
MARAH, SHE'S NOT ONE OF US. I DON'T EVEN KNOW IF SHE REALIZES WE'RE LEPERS.
NSN 6545-00-922-1200
FIRST AID KIT
FIRST AID KIT
WE'LL FINISH UP HERE AND JOIN YOU TOMORROW.
SHE NEEDS SOME ANTIBIOTICS AND HER WOUND CLEANED PROPERLY.
THEN SEND HER TO NEW WASHINGTON WHERE SHE CAN BE WITH HER OWN KIND.

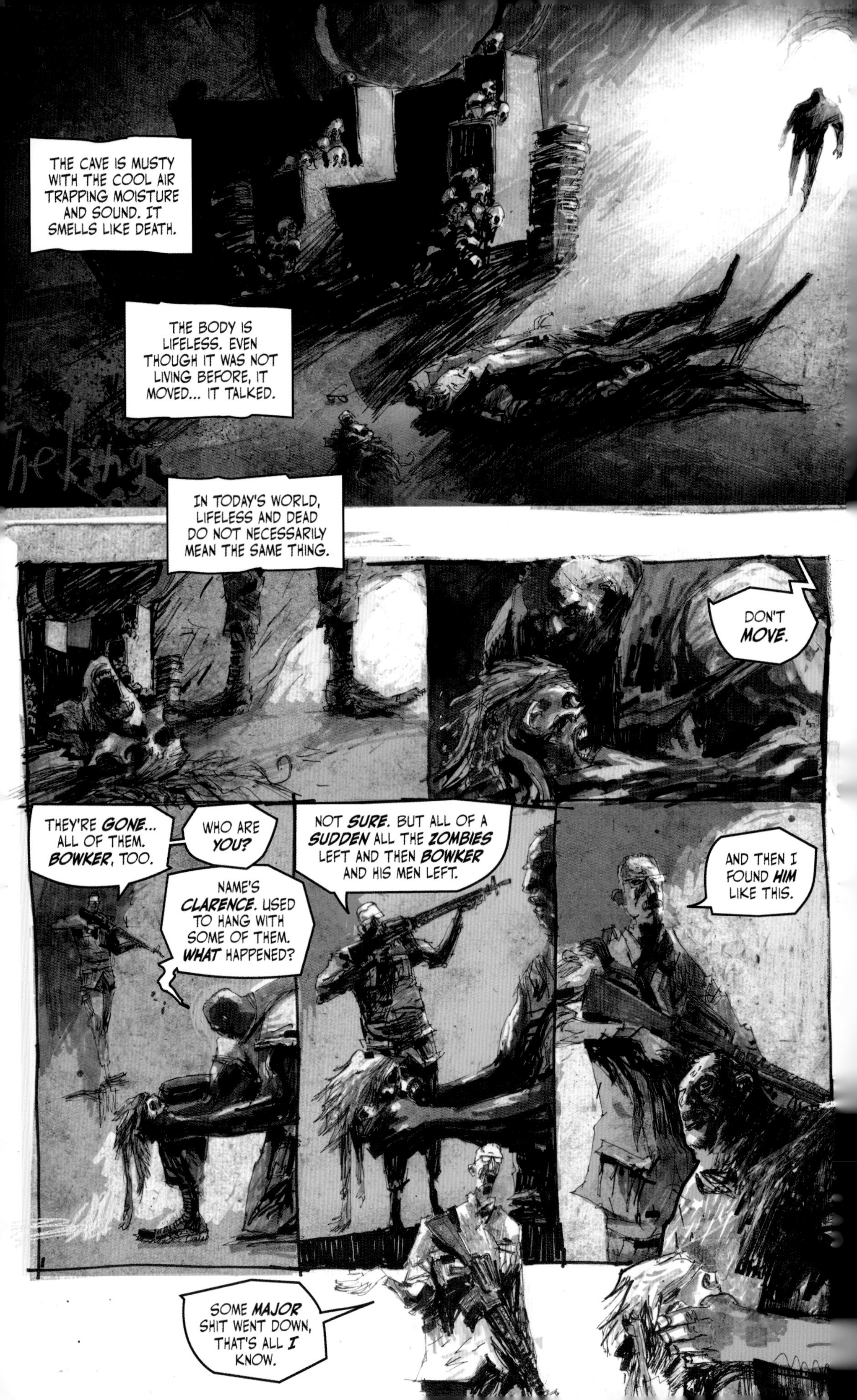
THE CAVE IS MUSTY WITH THE COOL AIR TRAPPING MOISTURE AND SOUND. IT SMELLS LIKE DEATH.
THE BODY IS LIFELESS. EVEN THOUGH IT WAS NOT LIVING BEFORE, IT MOVED... IT TALKED.
IN TODAY'S WORLD, LIFELESS AND DEAD DO NOT NECESSARILY MEAN THE SAME THING.
DON'T MOVE.
THEY'RE GONE... ALL OF THEM. BOWKER, TOO.
WHO ARE YOU?
NAME'S CLARENCE. USED TO HANG WITH SOME OF THEM. WHAT HAPPENED?
NOT SURE. BUT ALL OF A SUDDEN ALL THE ZOMBIES LEFT AND THEN BOWKER AND HIS MEN LEFT.
AND THEN I FOUND HIM LIKE THIS.
SOME MAJOR SHIT WENT DOWN, THAT'S ALL I KNOW.

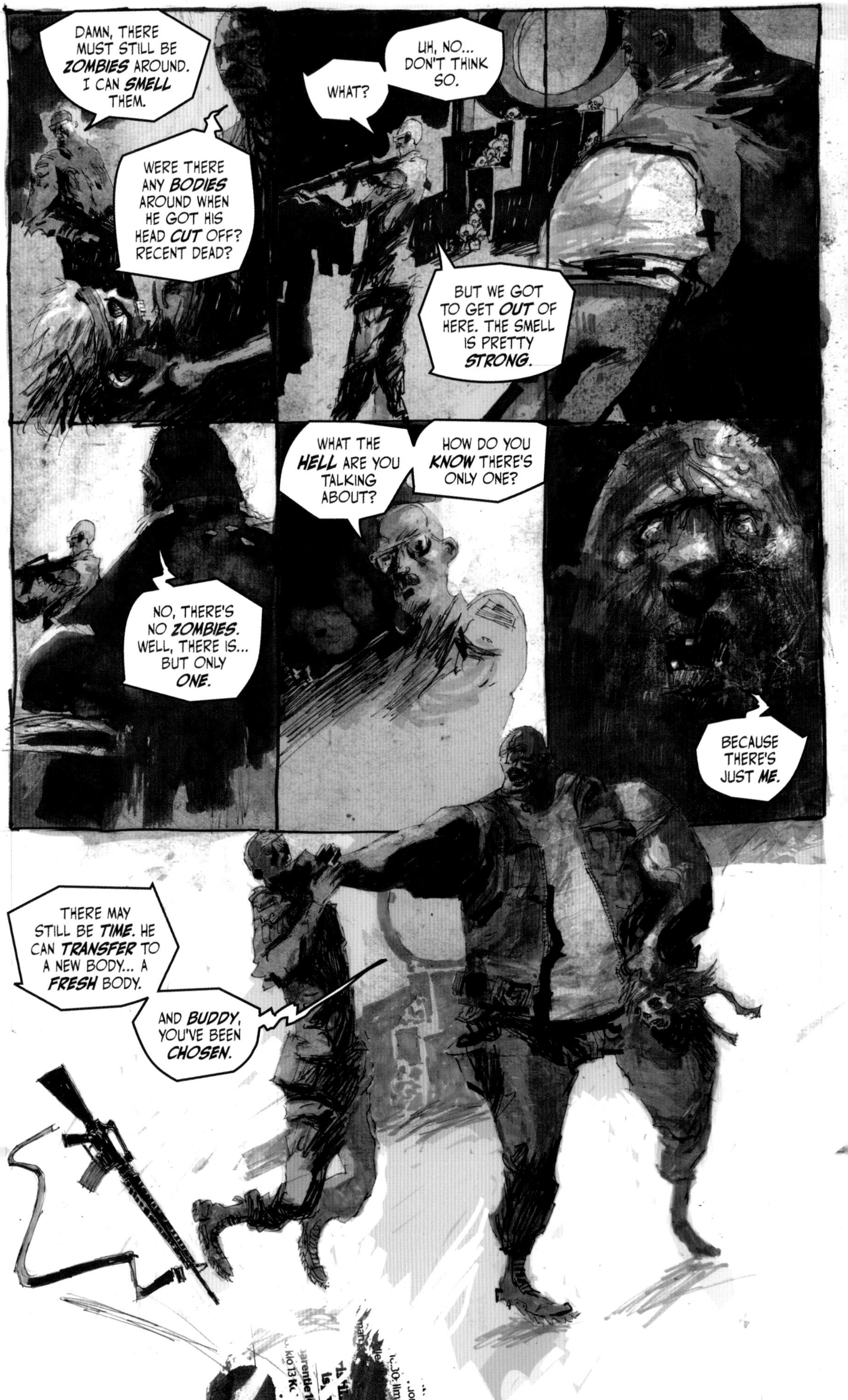

DAMN, THERE MUST STILL BE ZOMBIES AROUND. I CAN SMELL THEM.
WERE THERE ANY BODIES AROUND WHEN HE GOT HIS HEAD CUT OFF? RECENT DEAD?
WHAT?
UH, NO... DON'T THINK SO.
BUT WE GOT TO GET OUT OF HERE. THE SMELL IS PRETTY STRONG.
NO, THERE'S NO ZOMBIES. WELL, THERE IS... BUT ONLY ONE.
WHAT THE HELL ARE YOU TALKING ABOUT?
HOW DO YOU KNOW THERE'S ONLY ONE?
BECAUSE THERE'S JUST ME.
THERE MAY STILL BE TIME. HE CAN TRANSFER TO A NEW BODY... A FRESH BODY.
AND BUDDY, YOU'VE BEEN CHOSEN.

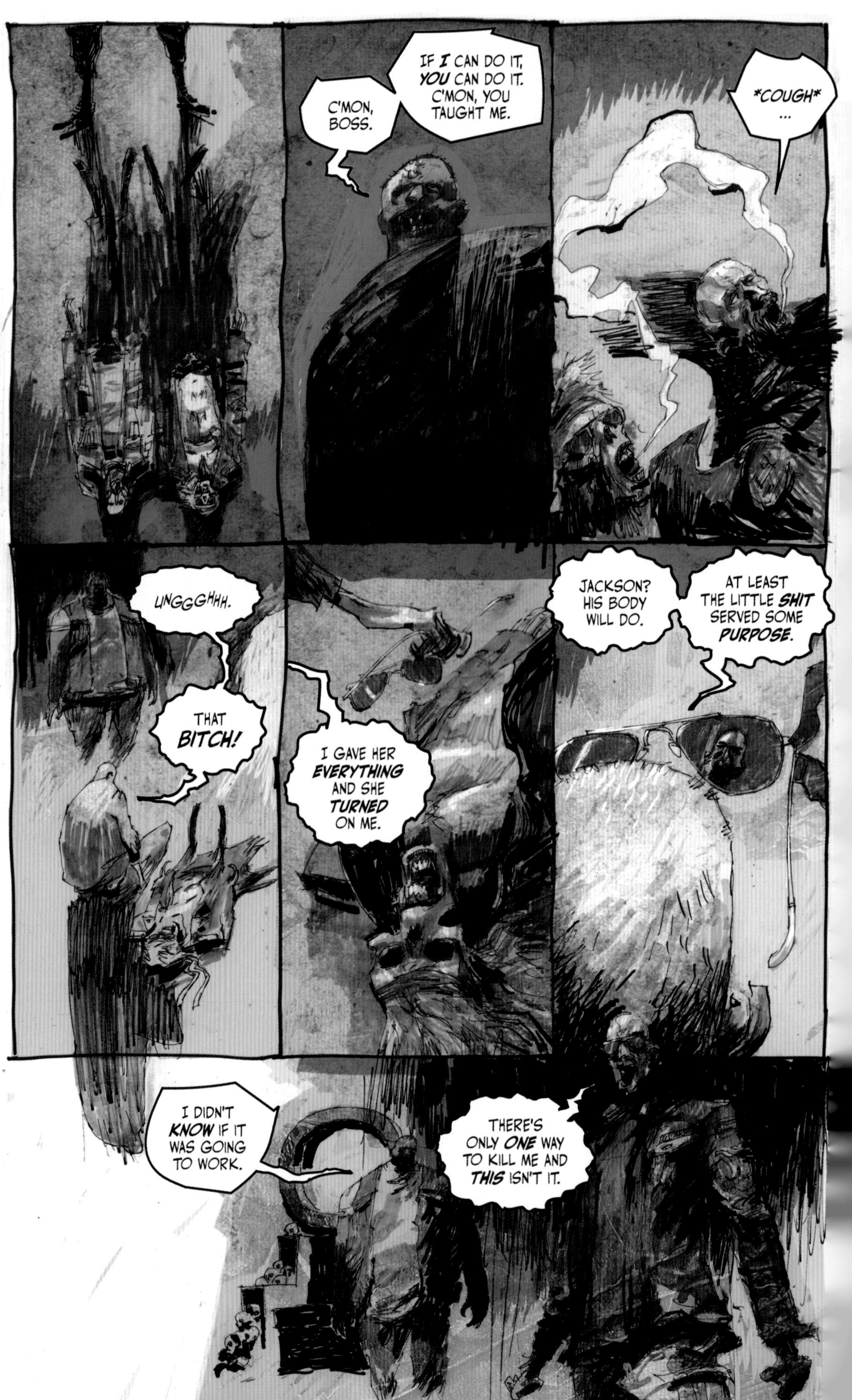
C'MON, BOSS.
IF I CAN DO IT, YOU CAN DO IT. C'MON, YOU TAUGHT ME.
COUGH ...
UNGGGHHH.
THAT BITCH!
I GAVE HER EVERYTHING AND SHE TURNED ON ME.
JACKSON? HIS BODY WILL DO.
AT LEAST THE LITTLE SHIT SERVED SOME PURPOSE.
I DIDN'T KNOW IF IT WAS GOING TO WORK.
THERE'S ONLY ONE WAY TO KILL ME AND THIS ISN'T IT.

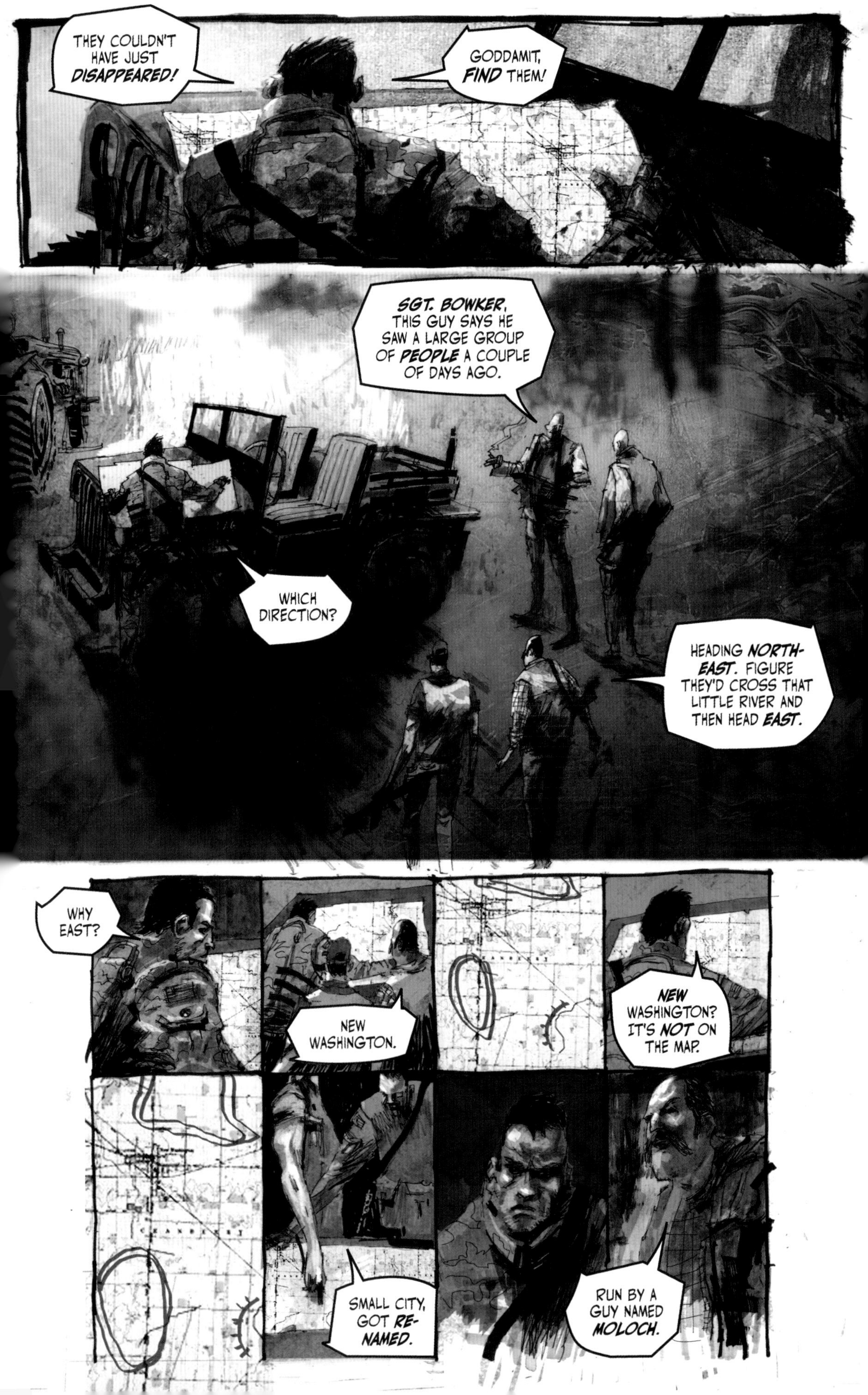

THEY COULDN'T HAVE JUST DISAPPEARED!
GODDAMIT, FIND THEM!
SGT. BOWKER, THIS GUY SAYS HE SAW A LARGE GROUP OF PEOPLE A COUPLE OF DAYS AGO.
WHICH DIRECTION?
HEADING NORTH-EAST. FIGURE THEY'D CROSS THAT LITTLE RIVER AND THEN HEAD EAST.
WHY EAST?
NEW WASHINGTON.
NEW WASHINGTON? IT'S NOT ON THE MAP.
SMALL CITY, GOT RE-NAMED.
RUN BY A GUY NAMED MOLOCH.

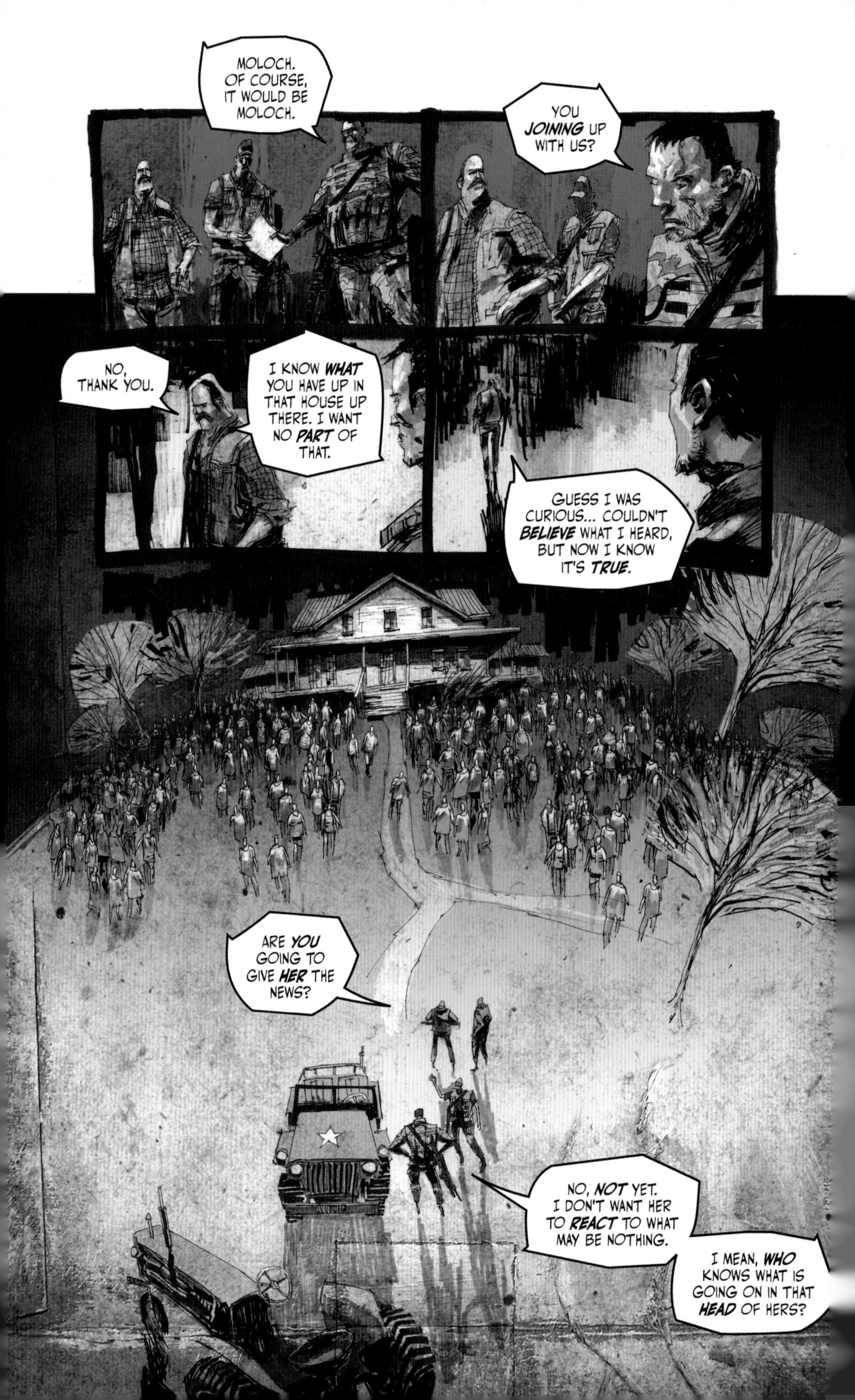
MOLOCH. OF COURSE, IT WOULD BE MOLOCH.
YOU JOINING UP WITH US?
NO, THANK YOU.
I KNOW WHAT YOU HAVE UP IN THAT HOUSE UP THERE. I WANT NO PART OF THAT.
GUESS I WAS CURIOUS... COULDN'T BELIEVE WHAT I HEARD, BUT NOW I KNOW IT'S TRUE.
ARE YOU GOING TO GIVE HER THE NEWS?
NO, NOT YET. I DON'T WANT HER TO REACT TO WHAT MAY BE NOTHING.
I MEAN, WHO KNOWS WHAT IS GOING ON IN THAT HEAD OF HERS?

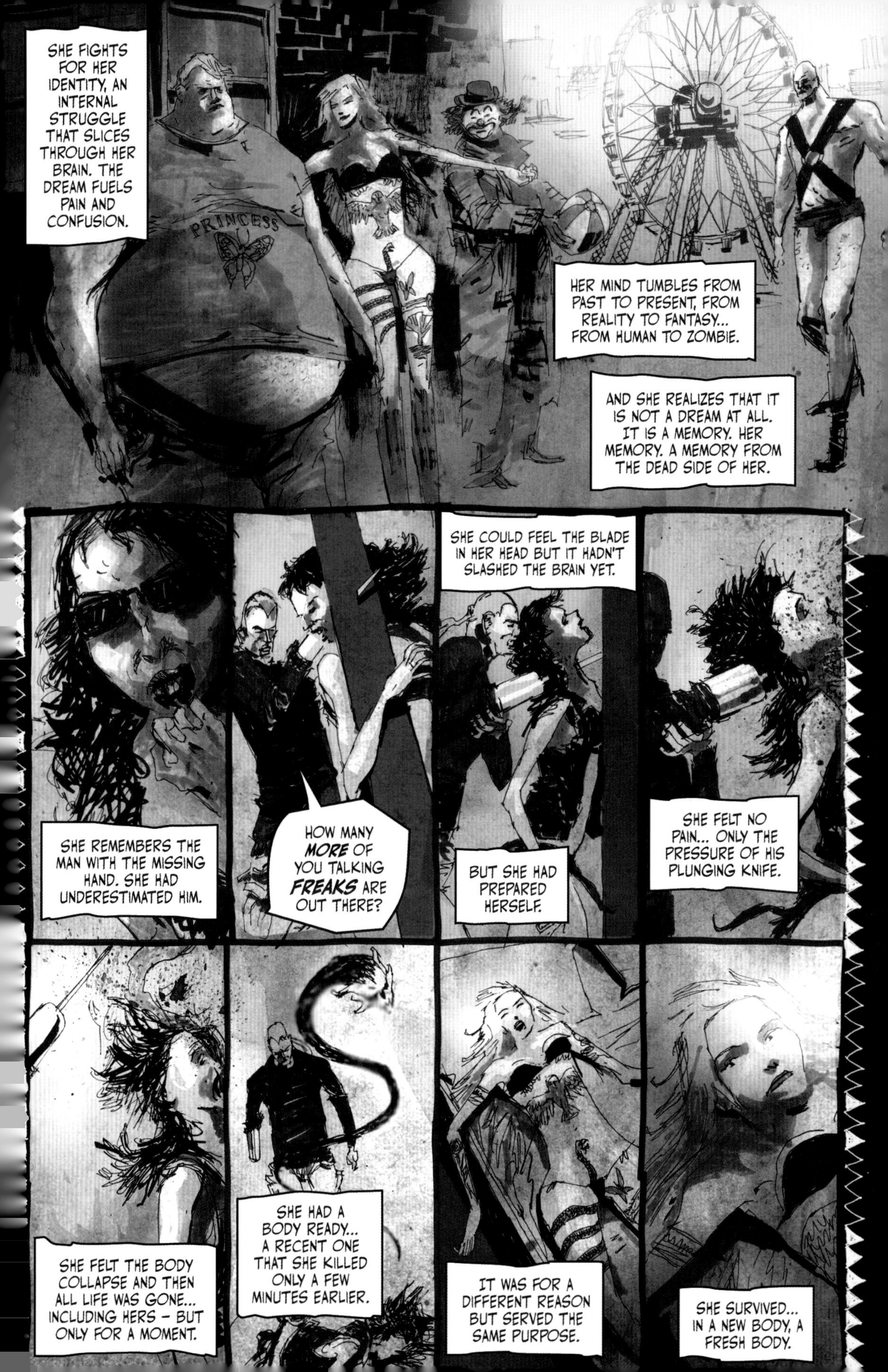
SHE FIGHTS FOR HER IDENTITY, AN INTERNAL STRUGGLE THAT SLICES THROUGH HER BRAIN. THE DREAM FUELS PAIN AND CONFUSION.
PRINCESS
HER MIND TUMBLES FROM PAST TO PRESENT, FROM REALITY TO FANTASY... FROM HUMAN TO ZOMBIE.
AND SHE REALIZES THAT IT IS NOT A DREAM AT ALL. IT IS A MEMORY. HER MEMORY. A MEMORY FROM THE DEAD SIDE OF HER.
SHE REMEMBERS THE MAN WITH THE MISSING HAND. SHE HAD UNDERESTIMATED HIM.
HOW MANY *MORE* OF YOU TALKING *FREAKS* ARE OUT THERE?
SHE COULD FEEL THE BLADE IN HER HEAD BUT IT HADN'T SLASHED THE BRAIN YET.
BUT SHE HAD PREPARED HERSELF.
SHE FELT NO PAIN... ONLY THE PRESSURE OF HIS PLUNGING KNIFE.
SHE FELT THE BODY COLLAPSE AND THEN ALL LIFE WAS GONE... INCLUDING HERS – BUT ONLY FOR A MOMENT.
SHE HAD A BODY READY... A RECENT ONE THAT SHE KILLED ONLY A FEW MINUTES EARLIER.
IT WAS FOR A DIFFERENT REASON BUT SERVED THE SAME PURPOSE.
SHE SURVIVED... IN A NEW BODY, A FRESH BODY.

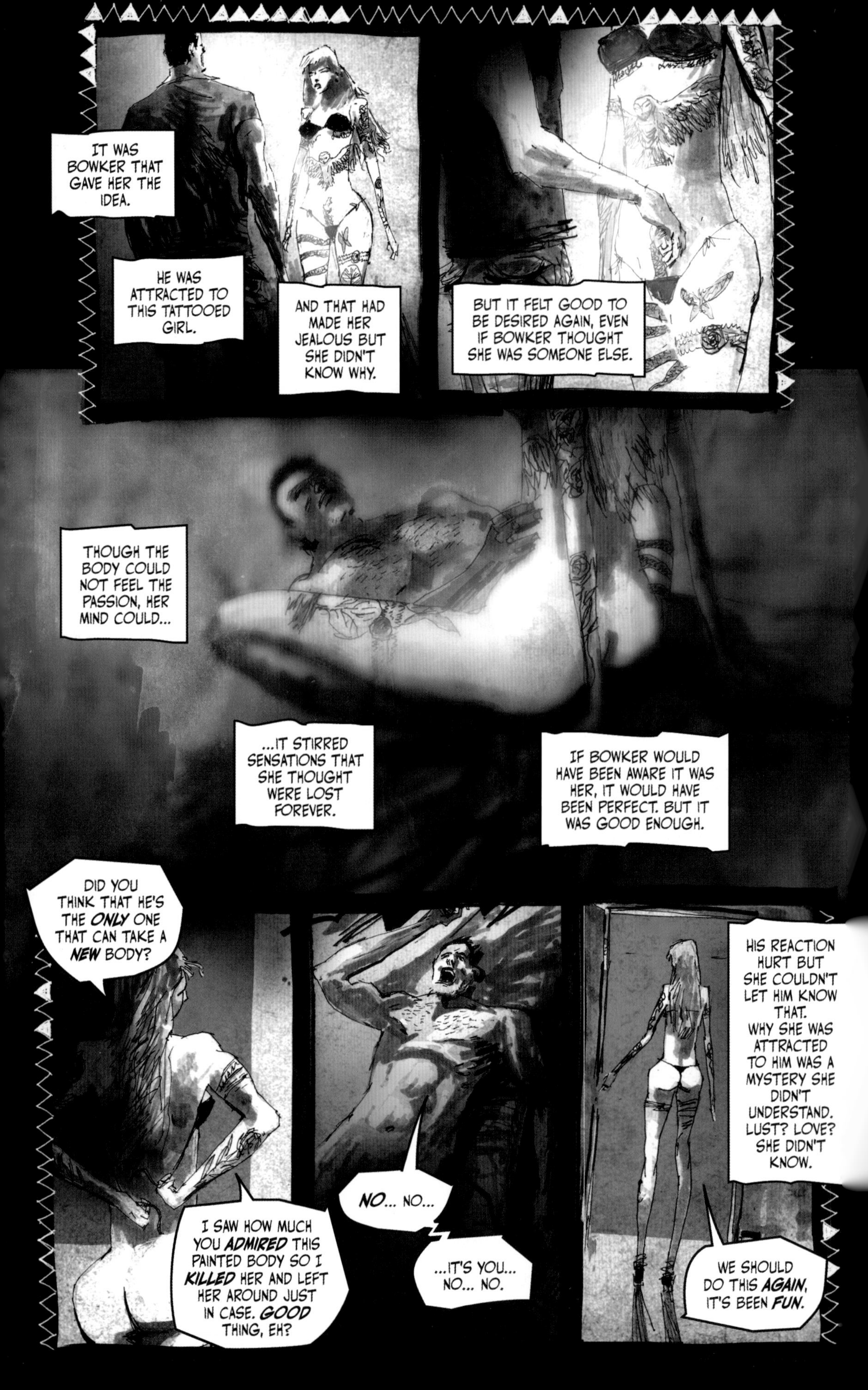
IT WAS BOWKER THAT GAVE HER THE IDEA.
HE WAS ATTRACTED TO THIS TATTOOED GIRL.
AND THAT HAD MADE HER JEALOUS BUT SHE DIDN'T KNOW WHY.
BUT IT FELT GOOD TO BE DESIRED AGAIN, EVEN IF BOWKER THOUGHT SHE WAS SOMEONE ELSE.
THOUGH THE BODY COULD NOT FEEL THE PASSION, HER MIND COULD...
...IT STIRRED SENSATIONS THAT SHE THOUGHT WERE LOST FOREVER.
IF BOWKER WOULD HAVE BEEN AWARE IT WAS HER, IT WOULD HAVE BEEN PERFECT. BUT IT WAS GOOD ENOUGH.
DID YOU THINK THAT HE'S THE *ONLY* ONE THAT CAN TAKE A *NEW* BODY?
I SAW HOW MUCH YOU *ADMIRED* THIS PAINTED BODY SO I *KILLED* HER AND LEFT HER AROUND JUST IN CASE. *GOOD* THING, EH?
NO... NO...
...IT'S YOU... NO... NO.
HIS REACTION HURT BUT SHE COULDN'T LET HIM KNOW THAT. WHY SHE WAS ATTRACTED TO HIM WAS A MYSTERY SHE DIDN'T UNDERSTAND. LUST? LOVE? SHE DIDN'T KNOW.
WE SHOULD DO THIS *AGAIN*, IT'S BEEN *FUN*.

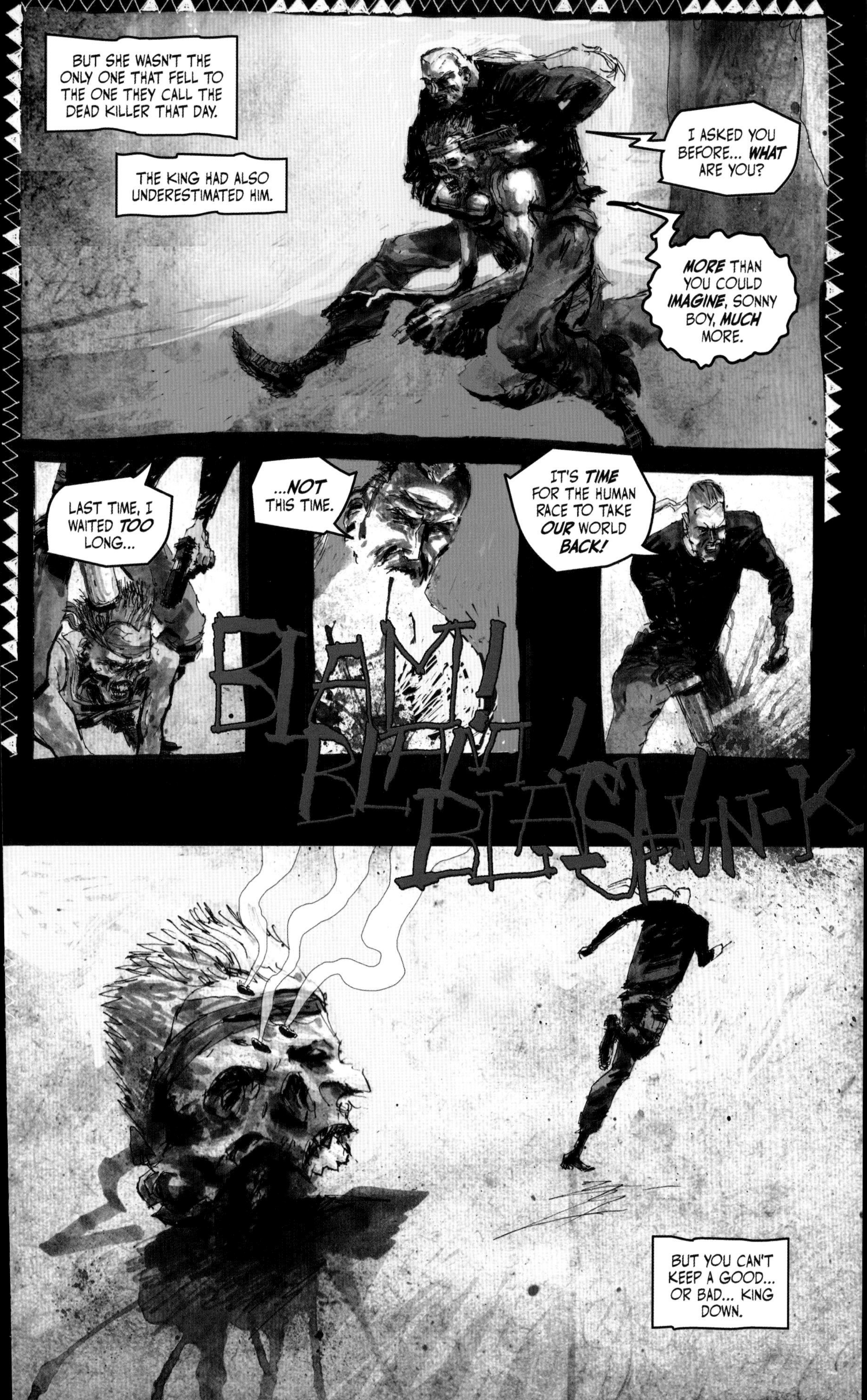
BUT SHE WASN'T THE ONLY ONE THAT FELL TO THE ONE THEY CALL THE DEAD KILLER THAT DAY.
THE KING HAD ALSO UNDERESTIMATED HIM.
I ASKED YOU BEFORE... *WHAT* ARE YOU?
MORE THAN YOU COULD *IMAGINE*, SONNY BOY, *MUCH* MORE.
LAST TIME, I WAITED *TOO* LONG...
...*NOT* THIS TIME.
IT'S *TIME* FOR THE HUMAN RACE TO TAKE *OUR* WORLD *BACK!*
BLAM! BLAM! BLAM! BLASHUN-K
BUT YOU CAN'T KEEP A GOOD... OR BAD... KING DOWN.

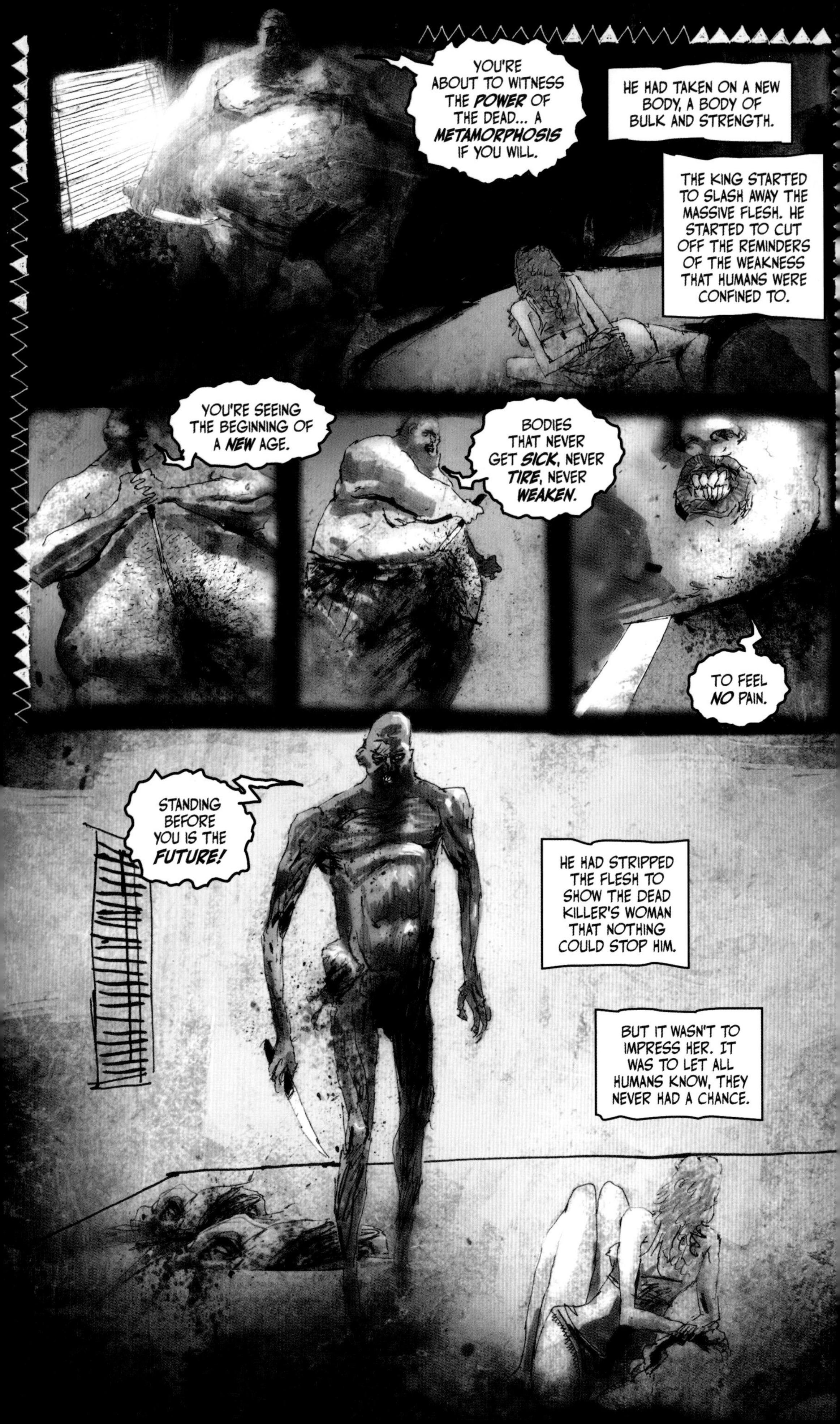
YOU'RE ABOUT TO WITNESS THE *POWER* OF THE DEAD... A *METAMORPHOSIS* IF YOU WILL.
HE HAD TAKEN ON A NEW BODY, A BODY OF BULK AND STRENGTH.
THE KING STARTED TO SLASH AWAY THE MASSIVE FLESH. HE STARTED TO CUT OFF THE REMINDERS OF THE WEAKNESS THAT HUMANS WERE CONFINED TO.
YOU'RE SEEING THE BEGINNING OF A *NEW* AGE.
BODIES THAT NEVER GET *SICK*, NEVER *TIRE*, NEVER *WEAKEN*.
TO FEEL *NO* PAIN.
STANDING BEFORE YOU IS THE *FUTURE!*
HE HAD STRIPPED THE FLESH TO SHOW THE DEAD KILLER'S WOMAN THAT NOTHING COULD STOP HIM.
BUT IT WASN'T TO IMPRESS HER. IT WAS TO LET ALL HUMANS KNOW, THEY NEVER HAD A CHANCE.

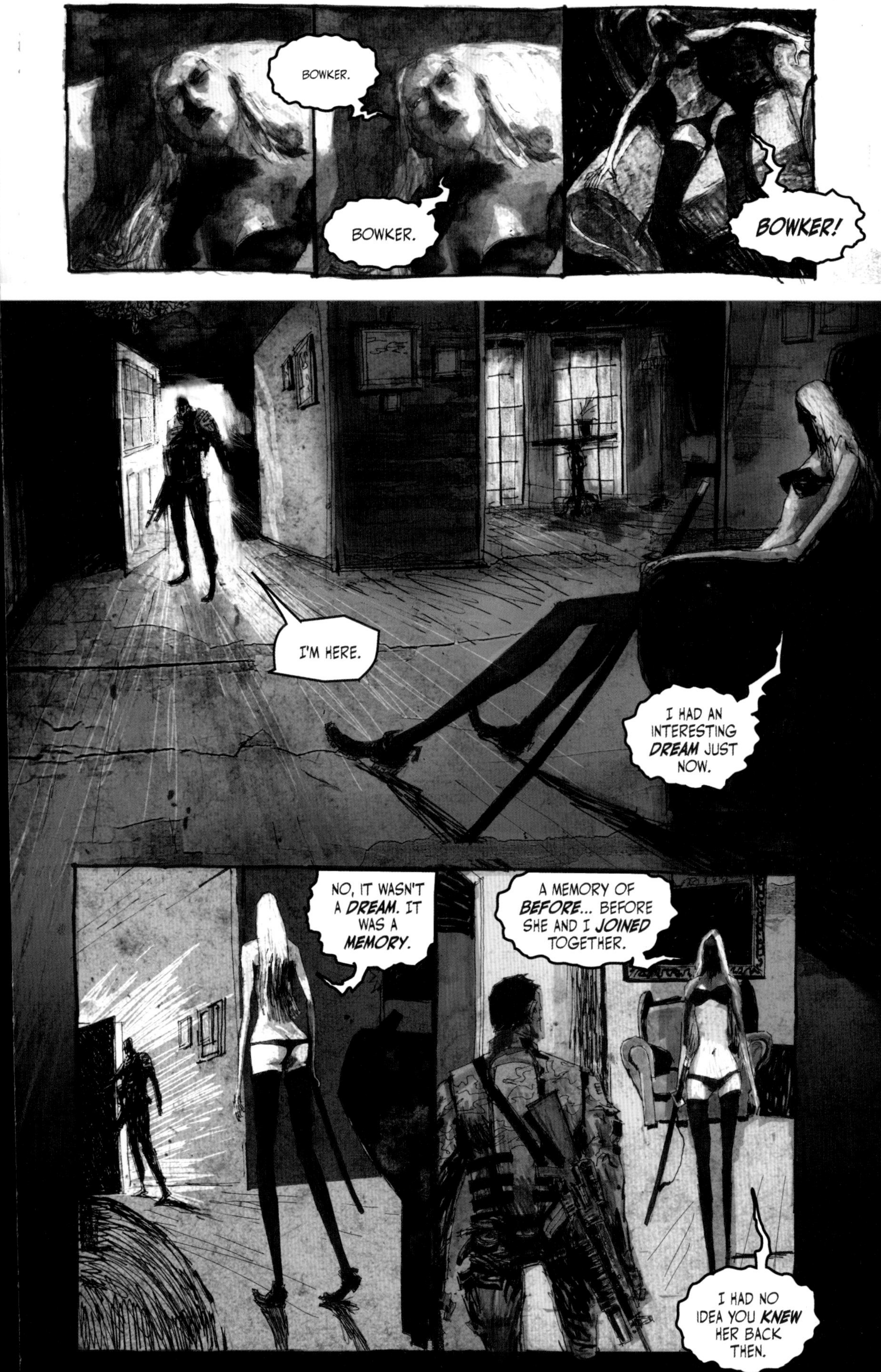
BOWKER.
BOWKER.
BOWKER!
I'M HERE.
I HAD AN INTERESTING DREAM JUST NOW.
NO, IT WASN'T A DREAM. IT WAS A MEMORY.
A MEMORY OF BEFORE... BEFORE SHE AND I JOINED TOGETHER.
I HAD NO IDEA YOU KNEW HER BACK THEN.

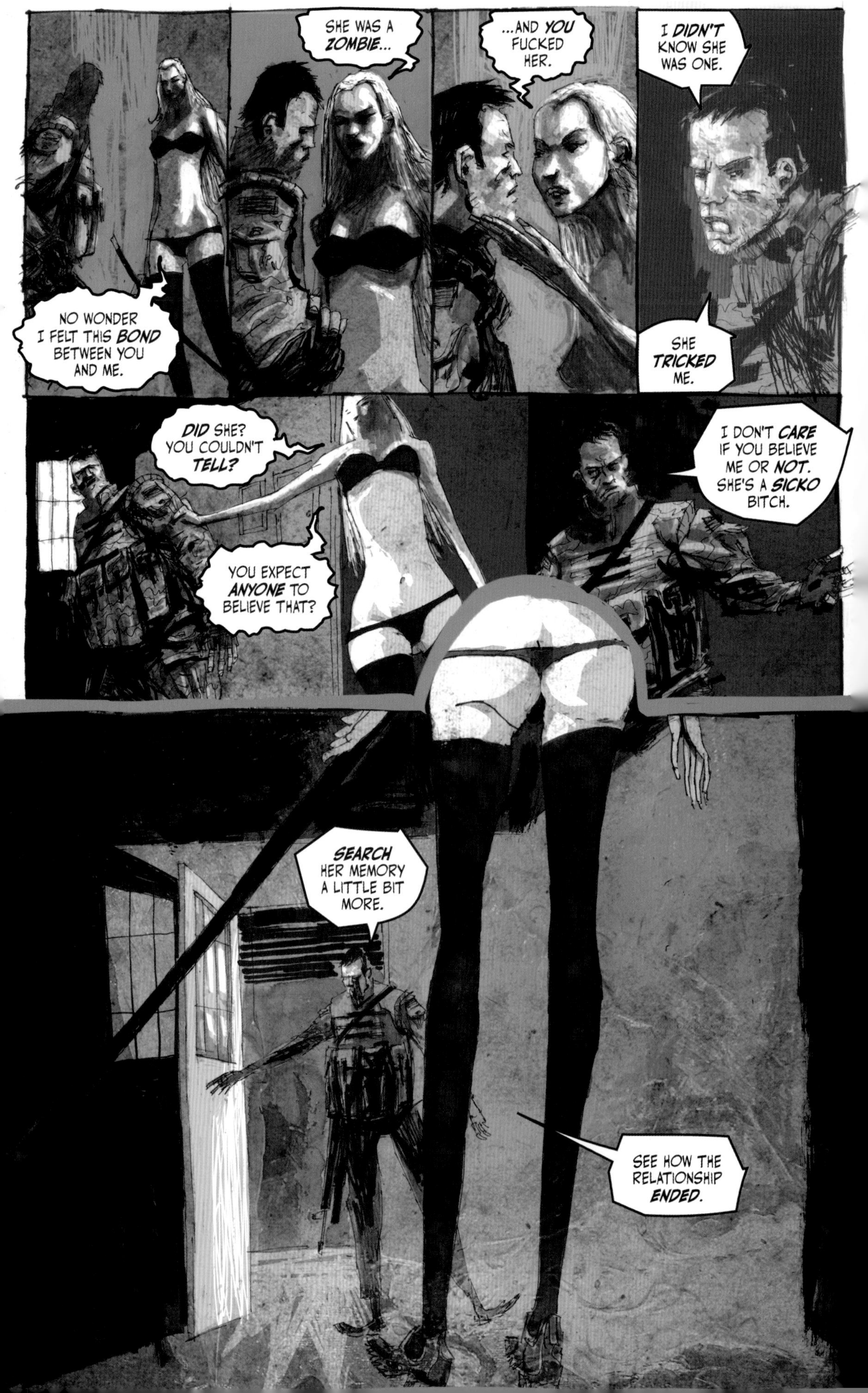
NO WONDER I FELT THIS BOND BETWEEN YOU AND ME.
SHE WAS A ZOMBIE...
...AND YOU FUCKED HER.
I DIDN'T KNOW SHE WAS ONE.
SHE TRICKED ME.
DID SHE? YOU COULDN'T TELL?
YOU EXPECT ANYONE TO BELIEVE THAT?
I DON'T CARE IF YOU BELIEVE ME OR NOT. SHE'S A SICKO BITCH.
SEARCH HER MEMORY A LITTLE BIT MORE.
SEE HOW THE RELATIONSHIP ENDED.

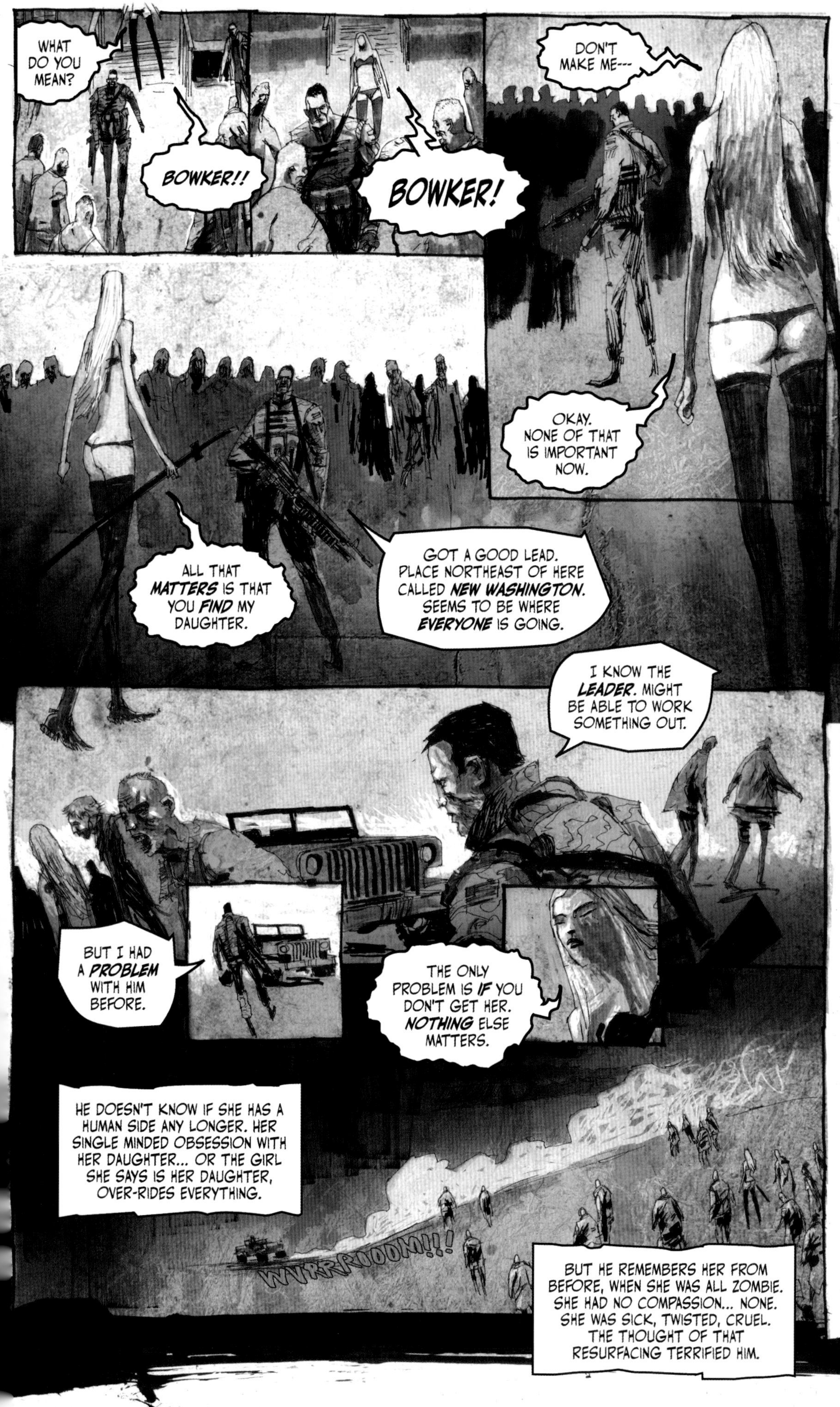
WHAT DO YOU MEAN?
BOWKER!!
BOWKER!
DON'T MAKE ME---
OKAY. NONE OF THAT IS IMPORTANT NOW.
ALL THAT MATTERS IS THAT YOU FIND MY DAUGHTER.
GOT A GOOD LEAD. PLACE NORTHEAST OF HERE CALLED NEW WASHINGTON. SEEMS TO BE WHERE EVERYONE IS GOING.
I KNOW THE LEADER. MIGHT BE ABLE TO WORK SOMETHING OUT.
BUT I HAD A PROBLEM WITH HIM BEFORE.
THE ONLY PROBLEM IS IF YOU DON'T GET HER. NOTHING ELSE MATTERS.
HE DOESN'T KNOW IF SHE HAS A HUMAN SIDE ANY LONGER. HER SINGLE MINDED OBSESSION WITH HER DAUGHTER... OR THE GIRL SHE SAYS IS HER DAUGHTER, OVER-RIDES EVERYTHING.
WVRRROOOM!!!
BUT HE REMEMBERS HER FROM BEFORE, WHEN SHE WAS ALL ZOMBIE. SHE HAD NO COMPASSION... NONE. SHE WAS SICK, TWISTED, CRUEL. THE THOUGHT OF THAT RESURFACING TERRIFIED HIM.

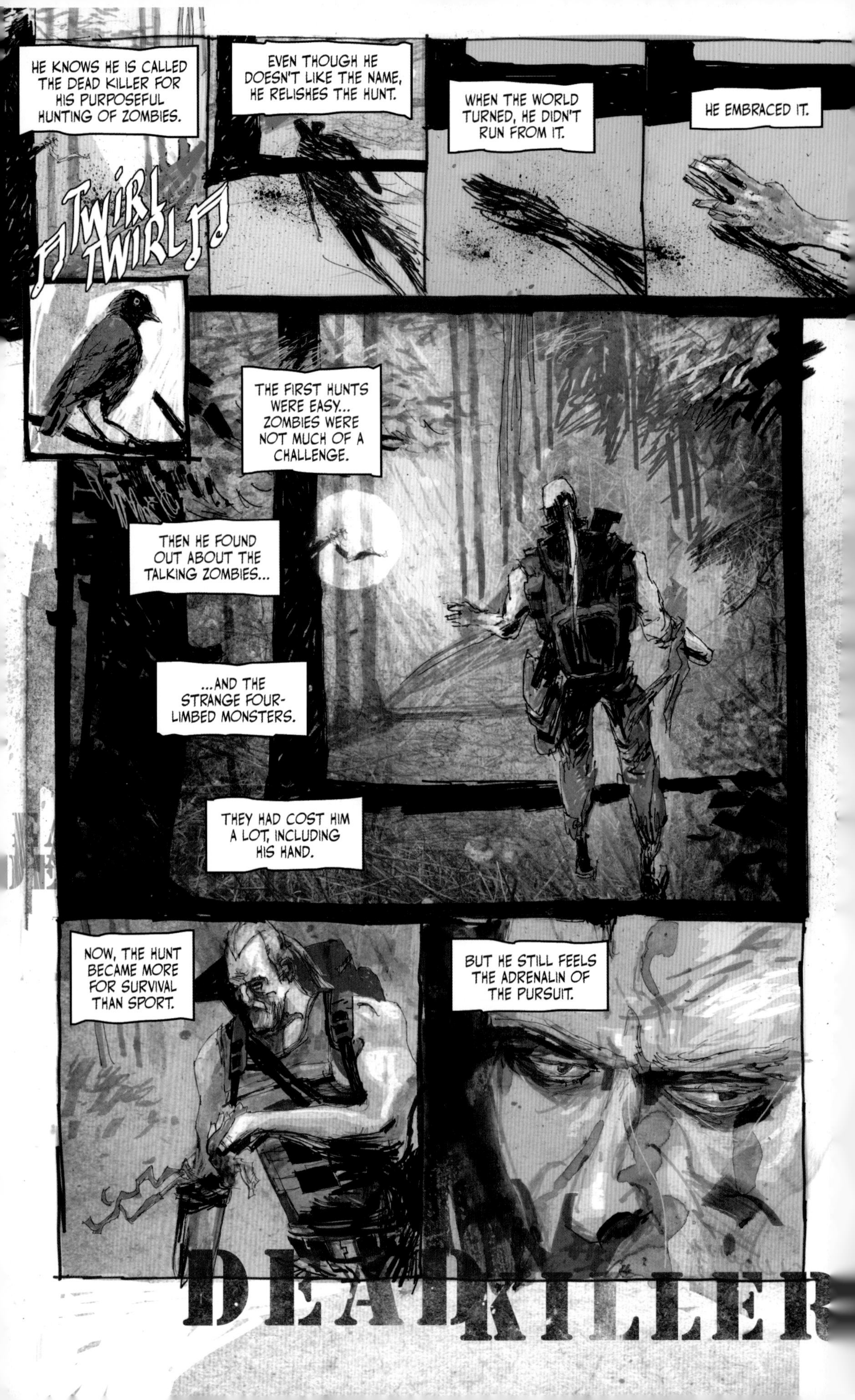
HE KNOWS HE IS CALLED THE DEAD KILLER FOR HIS PURPOSEFUL HUNTING OF ZOMBIES.
EVEN THOUGH HE DOESN'T LIKE THE NAME, HE RELISHES THE HUNT.
WHEN THE WORLD TURNED, HE DIDN'T RUN FROM IT.
HE EMBRACED IT.
TWIRL TWIRL
THE FIRST HUNTS WERE EASY... ZOMBIES WERE NOT MUCH OF A CHALLENGE.
THEN HE FOUND OUT ABOUT THE TALKING ZOMBIES...
...AND THE STRANGE FOUR-LIMBED MONSTERS.
THEY HAD COST HIM A LOT, INCLUDING HIS HAND.
NOW, THE HUNT BECAME MORE FOR SURVIVAL THAN SPORT.
BUT HE STILL FEELS THE ADRENALIN OF THE PURSUIT.
DEADKILLER

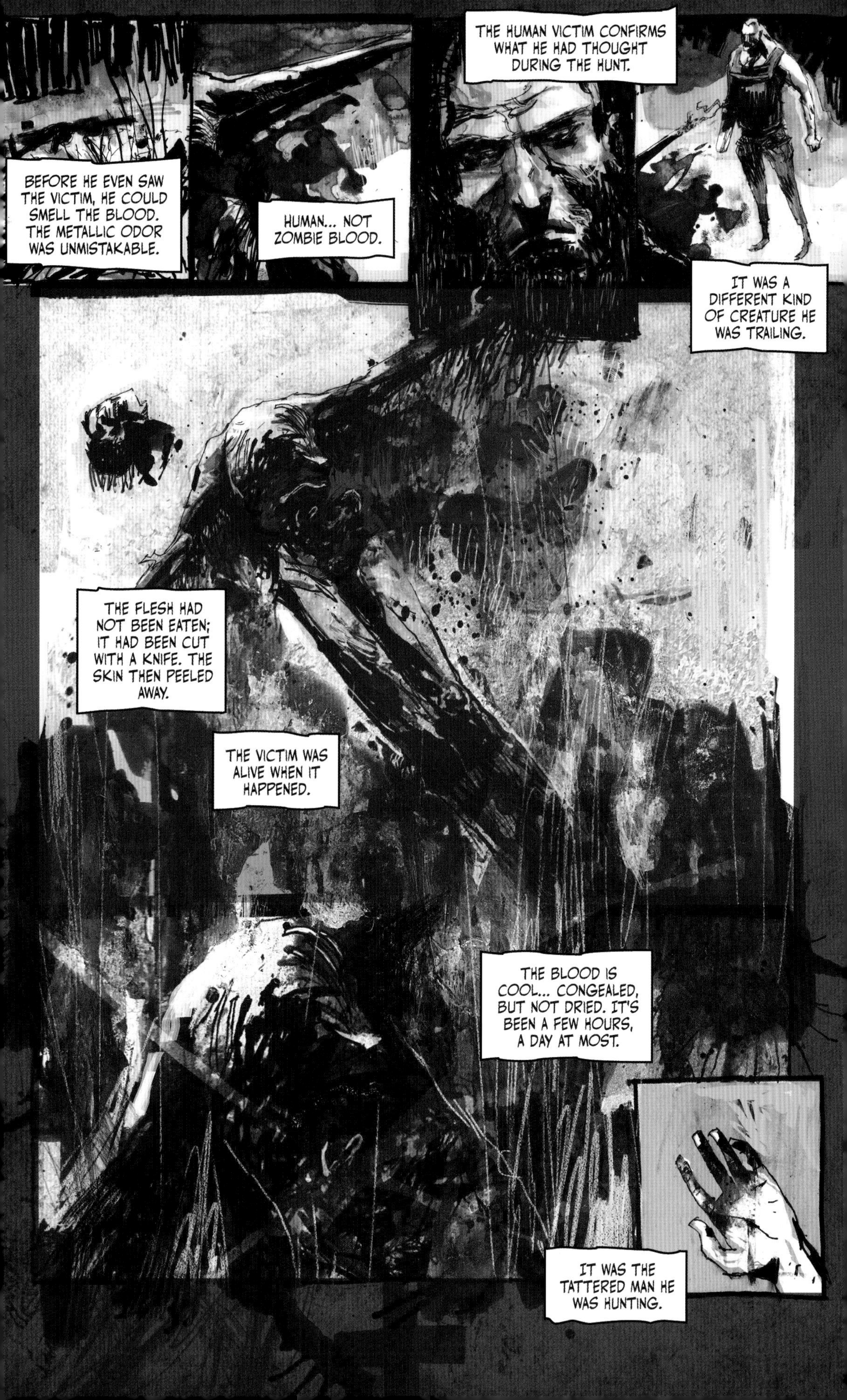
BEFORE HE EVEN SAW THE VICTIM, HE COULD SMELL THE BLOOD. THE METALLIC ODOR WAS UNMISTAKABLE.
HUMAN... NOT ZOMBIE BLOOD.
THE HUMAN VICTIM CONFIRMS WHAT HE HAD THOUGHT DURING THE HUNT.
IT WAS A DIFFERENT KIND OF CREATURE HE WAS TRAILING.
THE FLESH HAD NOT BEEN EATEN; IT HAD BEEN CUT WITH A KNIFE. THE SKIN THEN PEELED AWAY.
THE VICTIM WAS ALIVE WHEN IT HAPPENED.
THE BLOOD IS COOL... CONGEALED, BUT NOT DRIED. IT'S BEEN A FEW HOURS, A DAY AT MOST.
IT WAS THE TATTERED MAN HE WAS HUNTING.

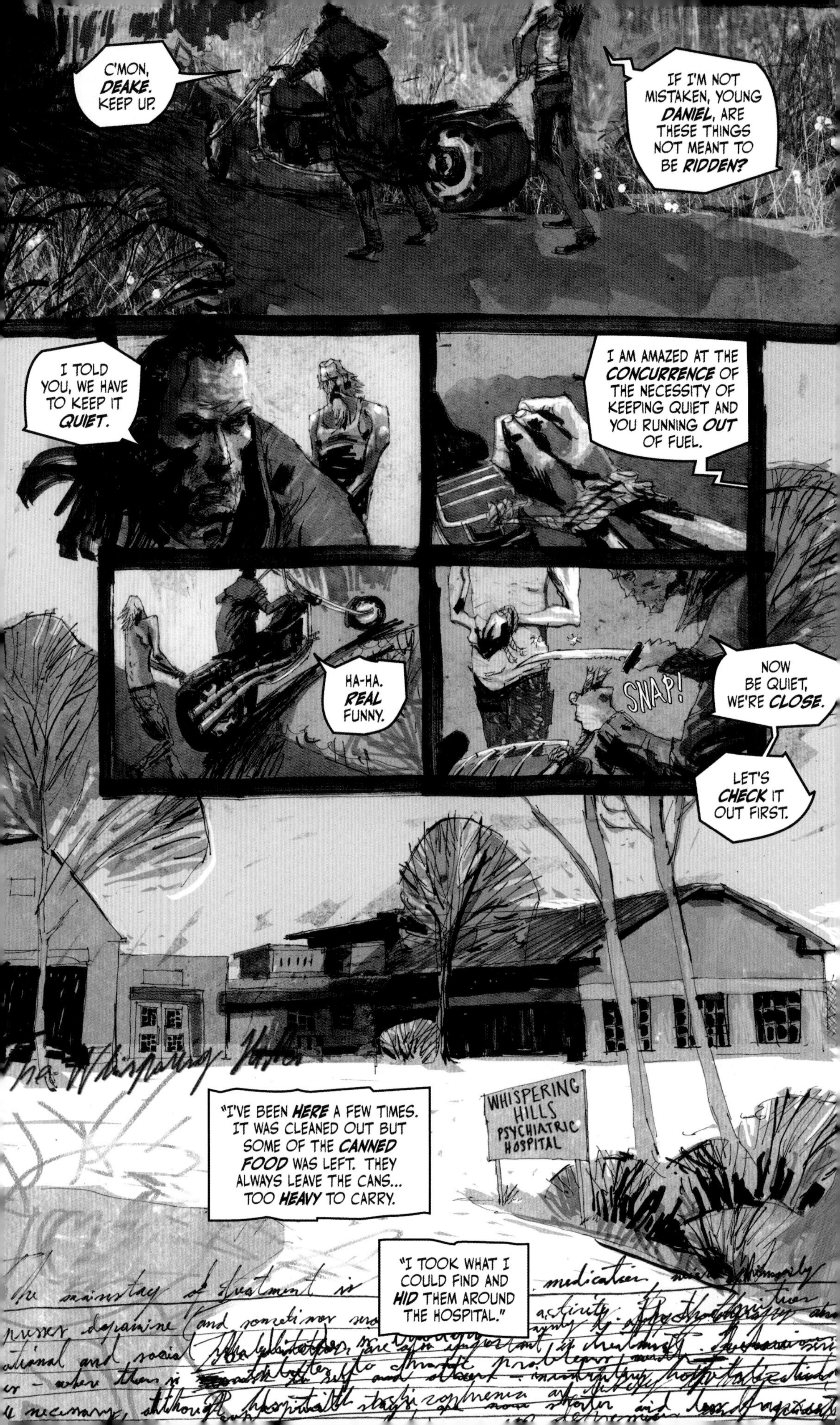

C'MON, DEAKE. KEEP UP.
IF I'M NOT MISTAKEN, YOUNG DANIEL, ARE THESE THINGS NOT MEANT TO BE RIDDEN?
I TOLD YOU, WE HAVE TO KEEP IT QUIET.
I AM AMAZED AT THE CONCURRENCE OF THE NECESSITY OF KEEPING QUIET AND YOU RUNNING OUT OF FUEL.
HA-HA. REAL FUNNY.
SNAP!
NOW BE QUIET, WE'RE CLOSE.
LET'S CHECK IT OUT FIRST.
"I'VE BEEN HERE A FEW TIMES. IT WAS CLEANED OUT BUT SOME OF THE CANNED FOOD WAS LEFT. THEY ALWAYS LEAVE THE CANS... TOO HEAVY TO CARRY.
WHISPERING HILLS PSYCHIATRIC HOSPITAL
"I TOOK WHAT I COULD FIND AND HID THEM AROUND THE HOSPITAL."

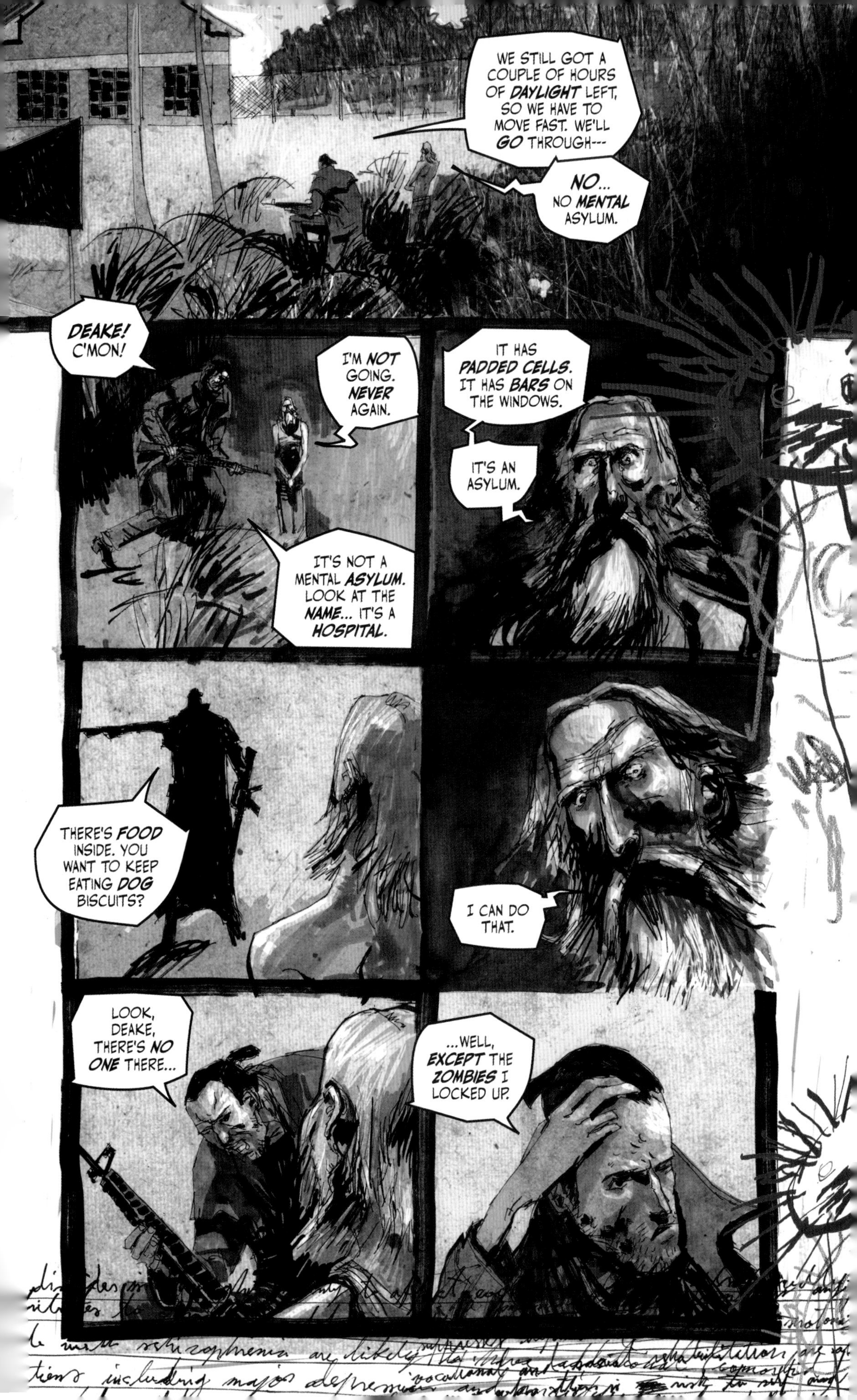
WE STILL GOT A COUPLE OF HOURS OF DAYLIGHT LEFT, SO WE HAVE TO MOVE FAST. WE'LL GO THROUGH---
NO... NO MENTAL ASYLUM.
DEAKE! C'MON!
I'M NOT GOING. NEVER AGAIN.
IT'S NOT A MENTAL ASYLUM. LOOK AT THE NAME... IT'S A HOSPITAL.
IT HAS PADDED CELLS. IT HAS BARS ON THE WINDOWS.
IT'S AN ASYLUM.
THERE'S FOOD INSIDE. YOU WANT TO KEEP EATING DOG BISCUITS?
I CAN DO THAT.
LOOK, DEAKE, THERE'S NO ONE THERE...
...WELL, EXCEPT THE ZOMBIES I LOCKED UP.

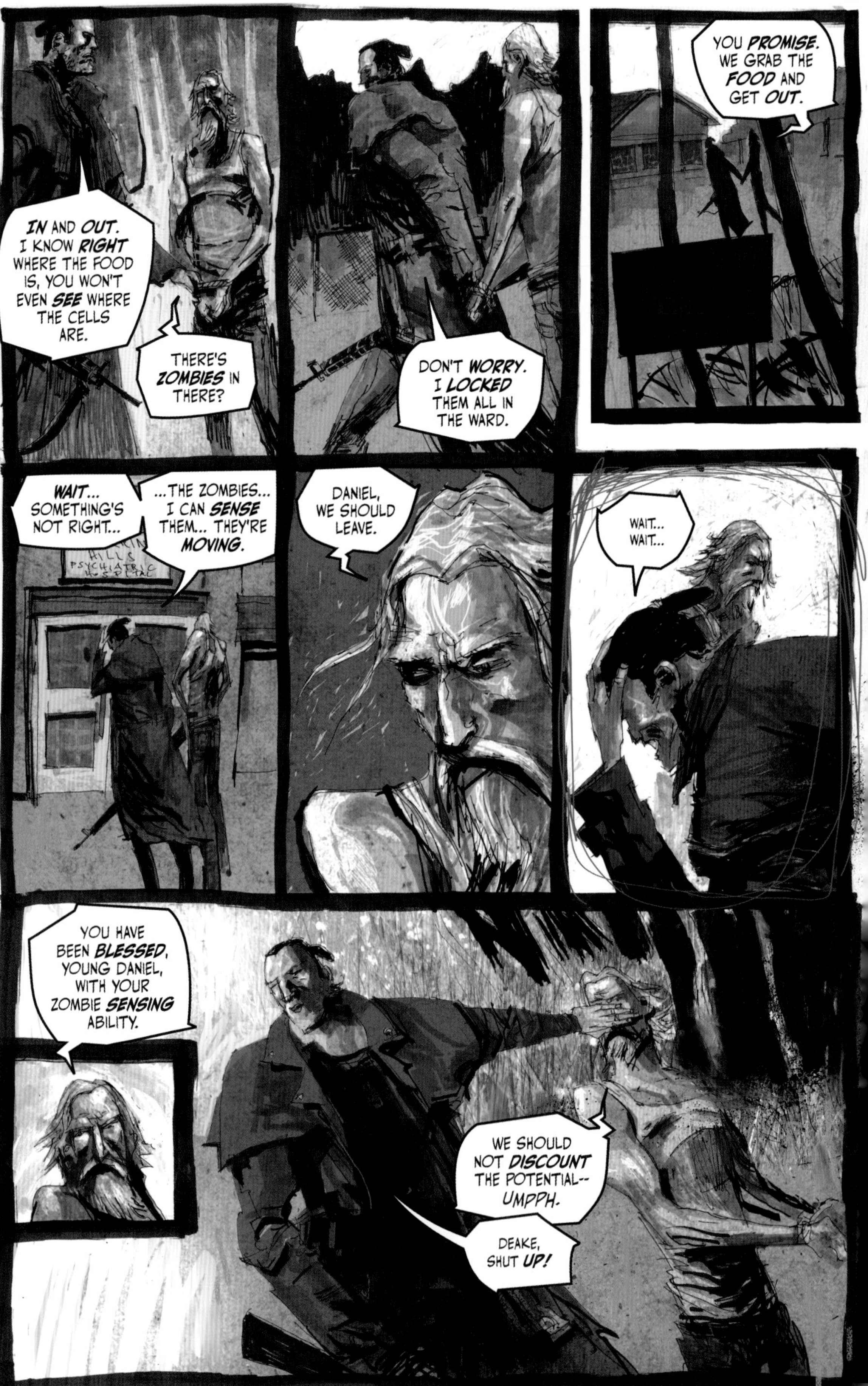
IN AND OUT. I KNOW RIGHT WHERE THE FOOD IS, YOU WON'T EVEN SEE WHERE THE CELLS ARE.
THERE'S ZOMBIES IN THERE?
DON'T WORRY. I LOCKED THEM ALL IN THE WARD.
YOU PROMISE. WE GRAB THE FOOD AND GET OUT.
WAIT... SOMETHING'S NOT RIGHT...
...THE ZOMBIES... I CAN SENSE THEM... THEY'RE MOVING.
DANIEL, WE SHOULD LEAVE.
WAIT... WAIT...
YOU HAVE BEEN BLESSED, YOUNG DANIEL, WITH YOUR ZOMBIE SENSING ABILITY.
WE SHOULD NOT DISCOUNT THE POTENTIAL-- UMPPH.
DEAKE, SHUT UP!

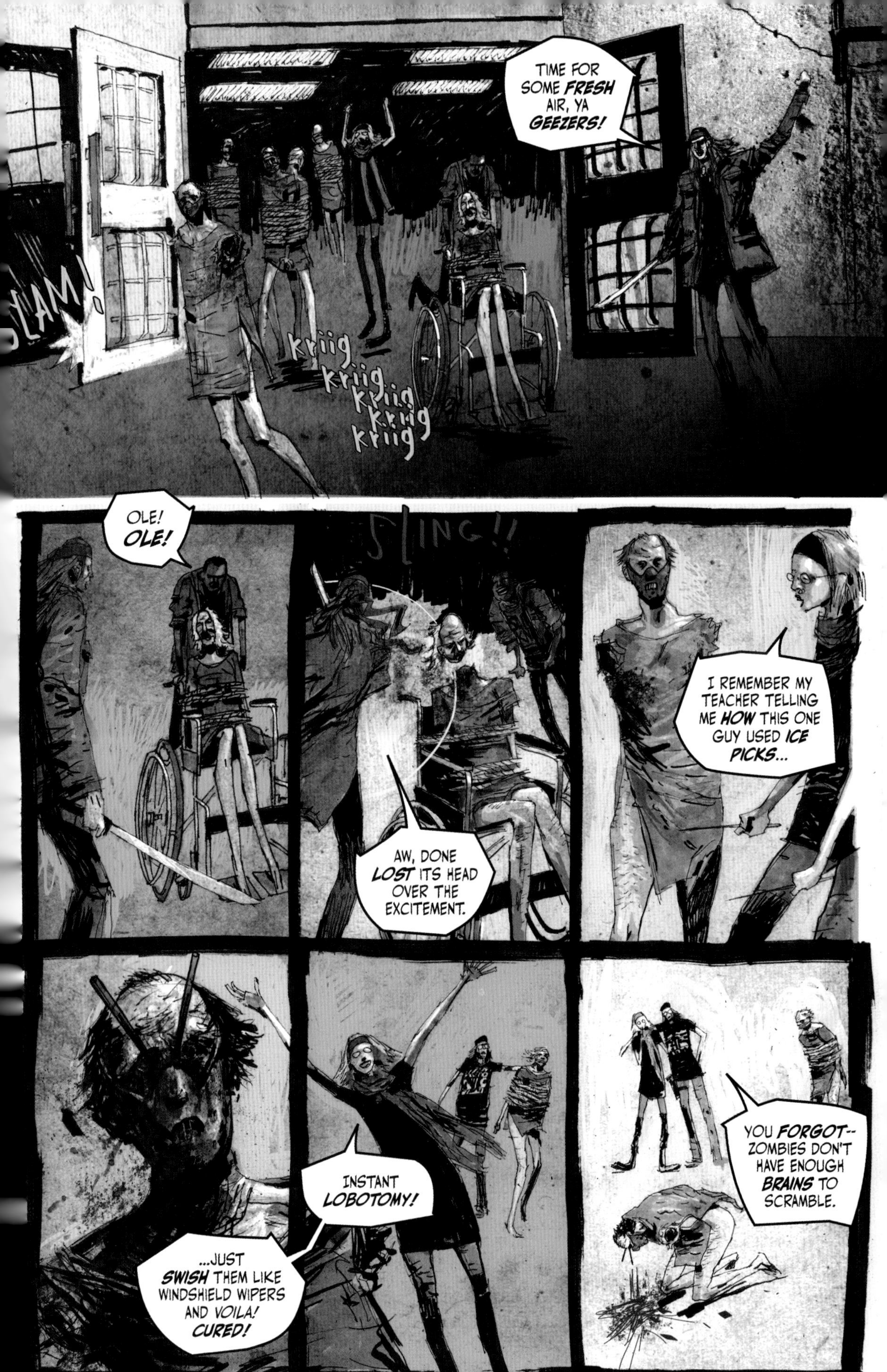
LAM!
kriig kriig kriig kriig kriig
TIME FOR SOME **FRESH** AIR, YA **GEEZERS!**
OLE! **OLE!**
SLING!!
AW, DONE **LOST** ITS HEAD OVER THE EXCITEMENT.
I REMEMBER MY TEACHER TELLING ME **HOW** THIS ONE GUY USED **ICE PICKS...**
...JUST **SWISH** THEM LIKE WINDSHIELD WIPERS AND **VOILA! CURED!**
INSTANT **LOBOTOMY!**
YOU **FORGOT**-- ZOMBIES DON'T HAVE ENOUGH **BRAINS** TO SCRAMBLE.

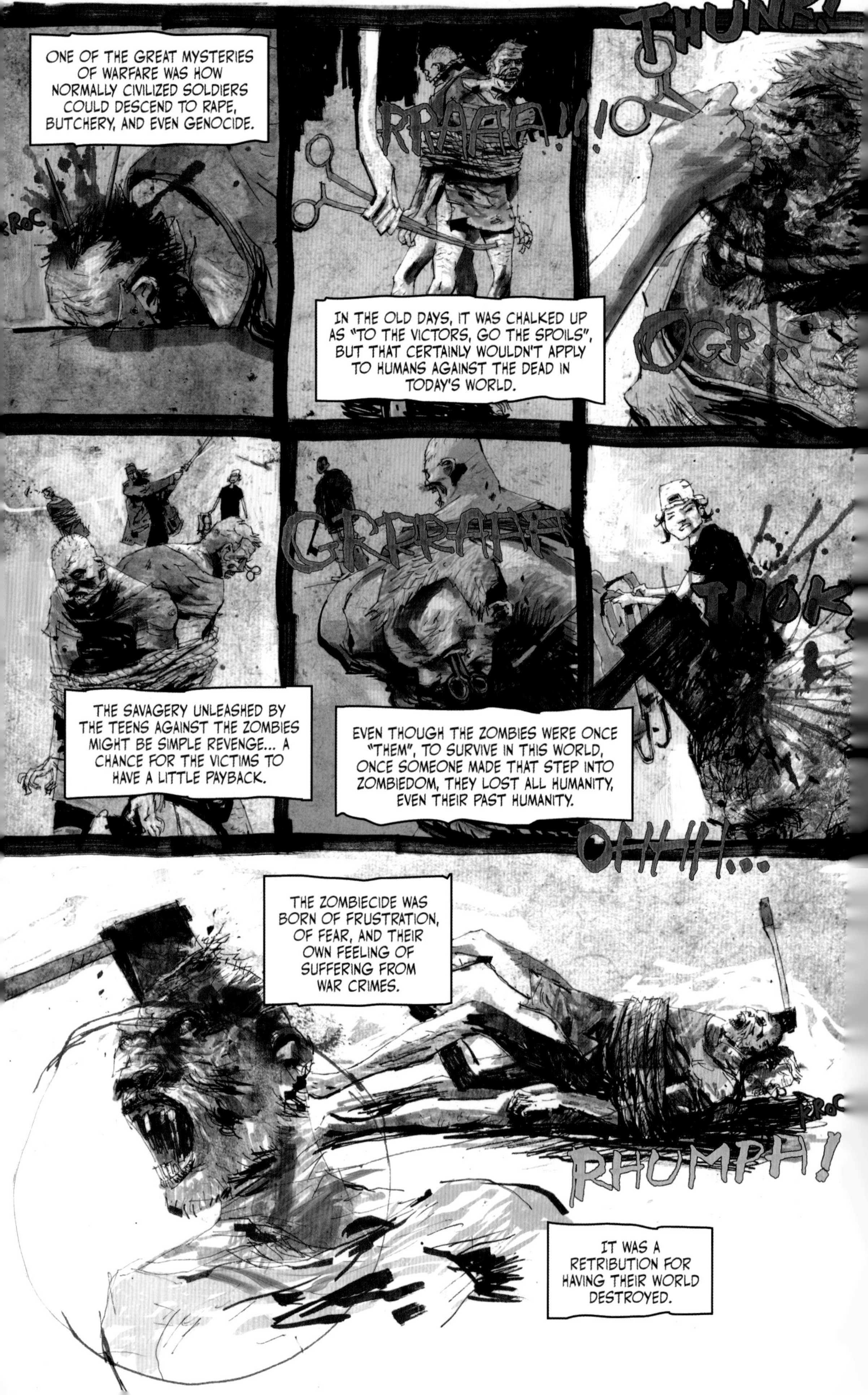
ONE OF THE GREAT MYSTERIES OF WARFARE WAS HOW NORMALLY CIVILIZED SOLDIERS COULD DESCEND TO RAPE, BUTCHERY, AND EVEN GENOCIDE.
IN THE OLD DAYS, IT WAS CHALKED UP AS "TO THE VICTORS, GO THE SPOILS", BUT THAT CERTAINLY WOULDN'T APPLY TO HUMANS AGAINST THE DEAD IN TODAY'S WORLD.
THUNK!
OGR...
THE SAVAGERY UNLEASHED BY THE TEENS AGAINST THE ZOMBIES MIGHT BE SIMPLE REVENGE... A CHANCE FOR THE VICTIMS TO HAVE A LITTLE PAYBACK.
EVEN THOUGH THE ZOMBIES WERE ONCE "THEM", TO SURVIVE IN THIS WORLD, ONCE SOMEONE MADE THAT STEP INTO ZOMBIEDOM, THEY LOST ALL HUMANITY, EVEN THEIR PAST HUMANITY.
THE ZOMBIECIDE WAS BORN OF FRUSTRATION, OF FEAR, AND THEIR OWN FEELING OF SUFFERING FROM WAR CRIMES.
KROC
RHUMPH!
IT WAS A RETRIBUTION FOR HAVING THEIR WORLD DESTROYED.

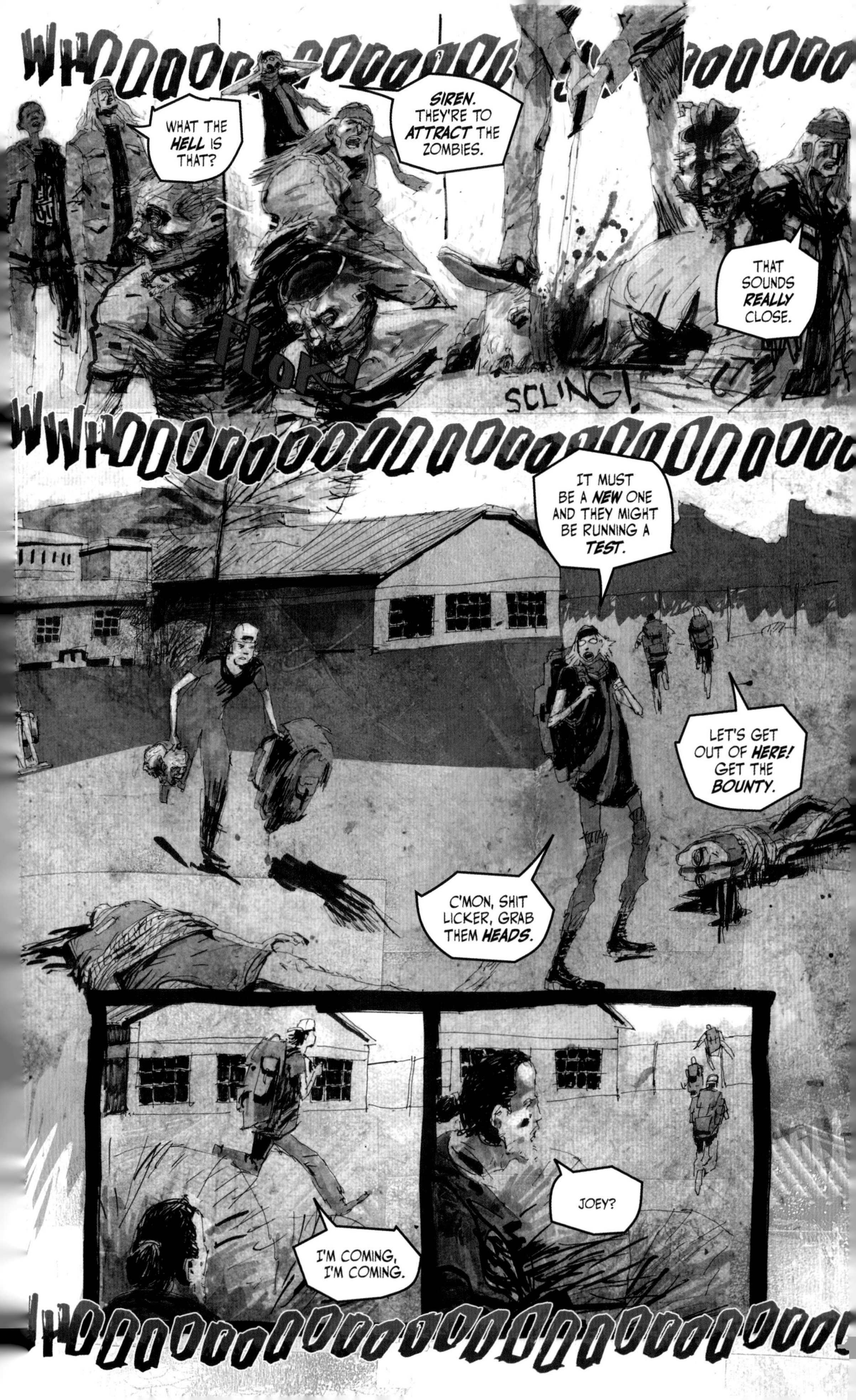
WHOOOOOOOOOOOOOOOOOOOOO
WHAT THE HELL IS THAT?
SIREN. THEY'RE TO ATTRACT THE ZOMBIES.
THAT SOUNDS REALLY CLOSE.
FLOK!
SCL'NG!
WWHOOOOOOOOOOOOOOOOOOOOOOOOOO
IT MUST BE A NEW ONE AND THEY MIGHT BE RUNNING A TEST.
LET'S GET OUT OF HERE! GET THE BOUNTY.
C'MON, SHIT LICKER, GRAB THEM HEADS.
I'M COMING, I'M COMING.
JOEY?
OOOOOOOOOOOOOOOOOOOOOOOOO

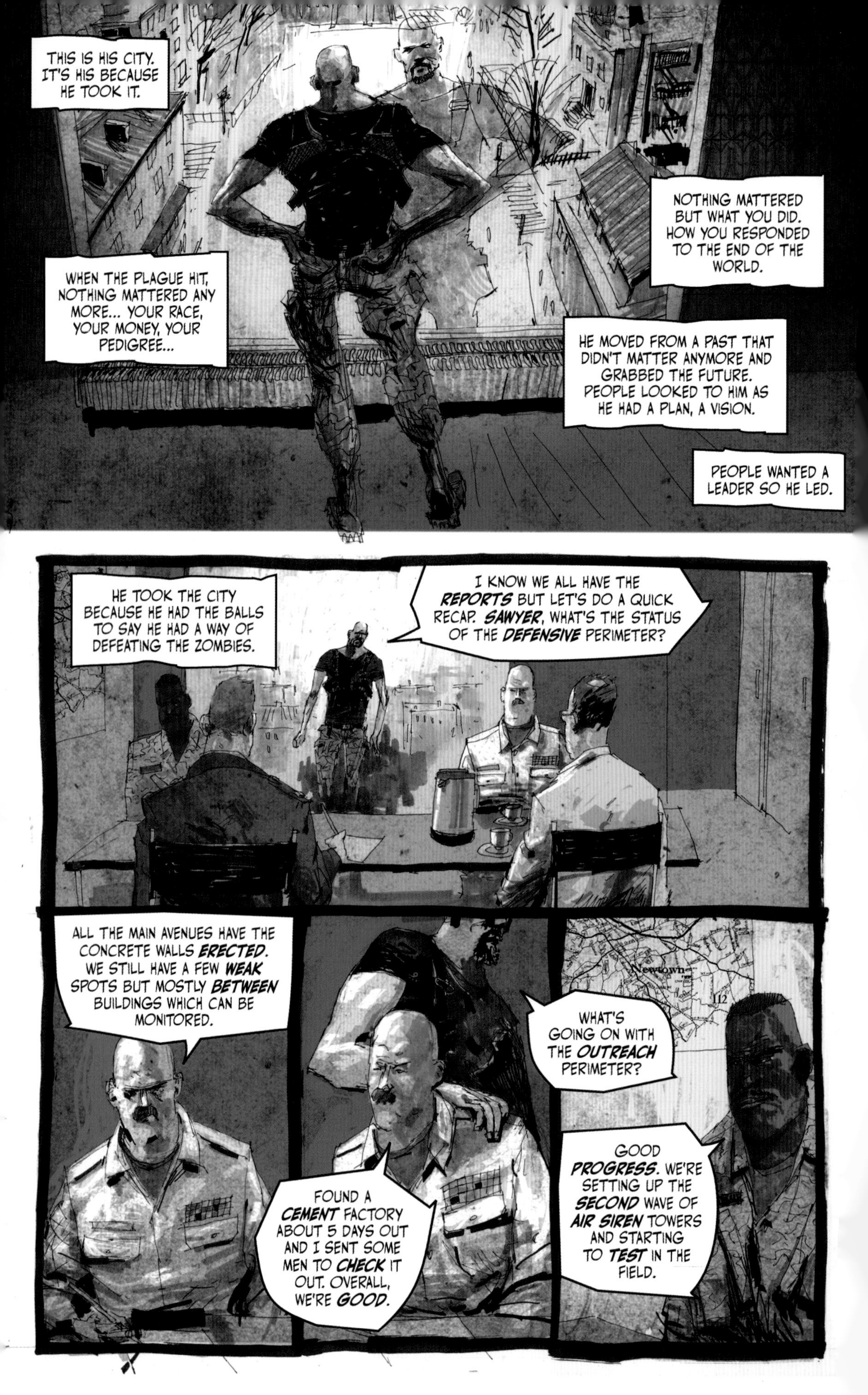
THIS IS HIS CITY. IT'S HIS BECAUSE HE TOOK IT.
WHEN THE PLAGUE HIT, NOTHING MATTERED ANY MORE... YOUR RACE, YOUR MONEY, YOUR PEDIGREE...
NOTHING MATTERED BUT WHAT YOU DID. HOW YOU RESPONDED TO THE END OF THE WORLD.
HE MOVED FROM A PAST THAT DIDN'T MATTER ANYMORE AND GRABBED THE FUTURE. PEOPLE LOOKED TO HIM AS HE HAD A PLAN, A VISION.
PEOPLE WANTED A LEADER SO HE LED.
HE TOOK THE CITY BECAUSE HE HAD THE BALLS TO SAY HE HAD A WAY OF DEFEATING THE ZOMBIES.
I KNOW WE ALL HAVE THE ***REPORTS*** BUT LET'S DO A QUICK RECAP. ***SAWYER***, WHAT'S THE STATUS OF THE ***DEFENSIVE*** PERIMETER?
ALL THE MAIN AVENUES HAVE THE CONCRETE WALLS ***ERECTED***. WE STILL HAVE A FEW ***WEAK*** SPOTS BUT MOSTLY ***BETWEEN*** BUILDINGS WHICH CAN BE MONITORED.
FOUND A ***CEMENT*** FACTORY ABOUT 5 DAYS OUT AND I SENT SOME MEN TO ***CHECK*** IT OUT. OVERALL, WE'RE ***GOOD***.
Newtown
112
WHAT'S GOING ON WITH THE ***OUTREACH*** PERIMETER?
GOOD ***PROGRESS***. WE'RE SETTING UP THE ***SECOND*** WAVE OF ***AIR SIREN*** TOWERS AND STARTING TO ***TEST*** IN THE FIELD.

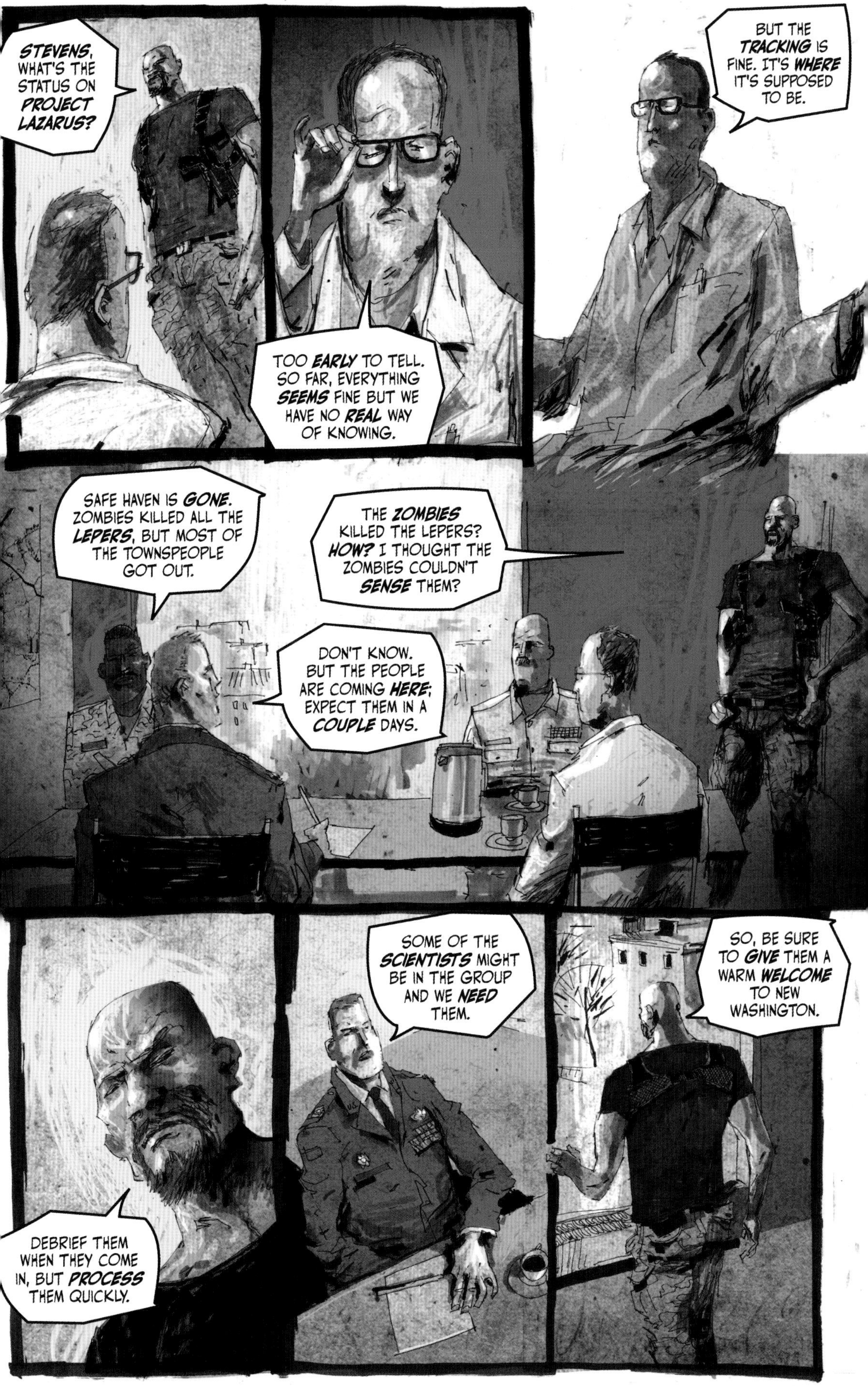

STEVENS, WHAT'S THE STATUS ON PROJECT LAZARUS?
TOO EARLY TO TELL. SO FAR, EVERYTHING SEEMS FINE BUT WE HAVE NO REAL WAY OF KNOWING.
BUT THE TRACKING IS FINE. IT'S WHERE IT'S SUPPOSED TO BE.
SAFE HAVEN IS GONE. ZOMBIES KILLED ALL THE LEPERS, BUT MOST OF THE TOWNSPEOPLE GOT OUT.
THE ZOMBIES KILLED THE LEPERS? HOW? I THOUGHT THE ZOMBIES COULDN'T SENSE THEM?
DON'T KNOW. BUT THE PEOPLE ARE COMING HERE; EXPECT THEM IN A COUPLE DAYS.
DEBRIEF THEM WHEN THEY COME IN, BUT PROCESS THEM QUICKLY.
SOME OF THE SCIENTISTS MIGHT BE IN THE GROUP AND WE NEED THEM.
SO, BE SURE TO GIVE THEM A WARM WELCOME TO NEW WASHINGTON.

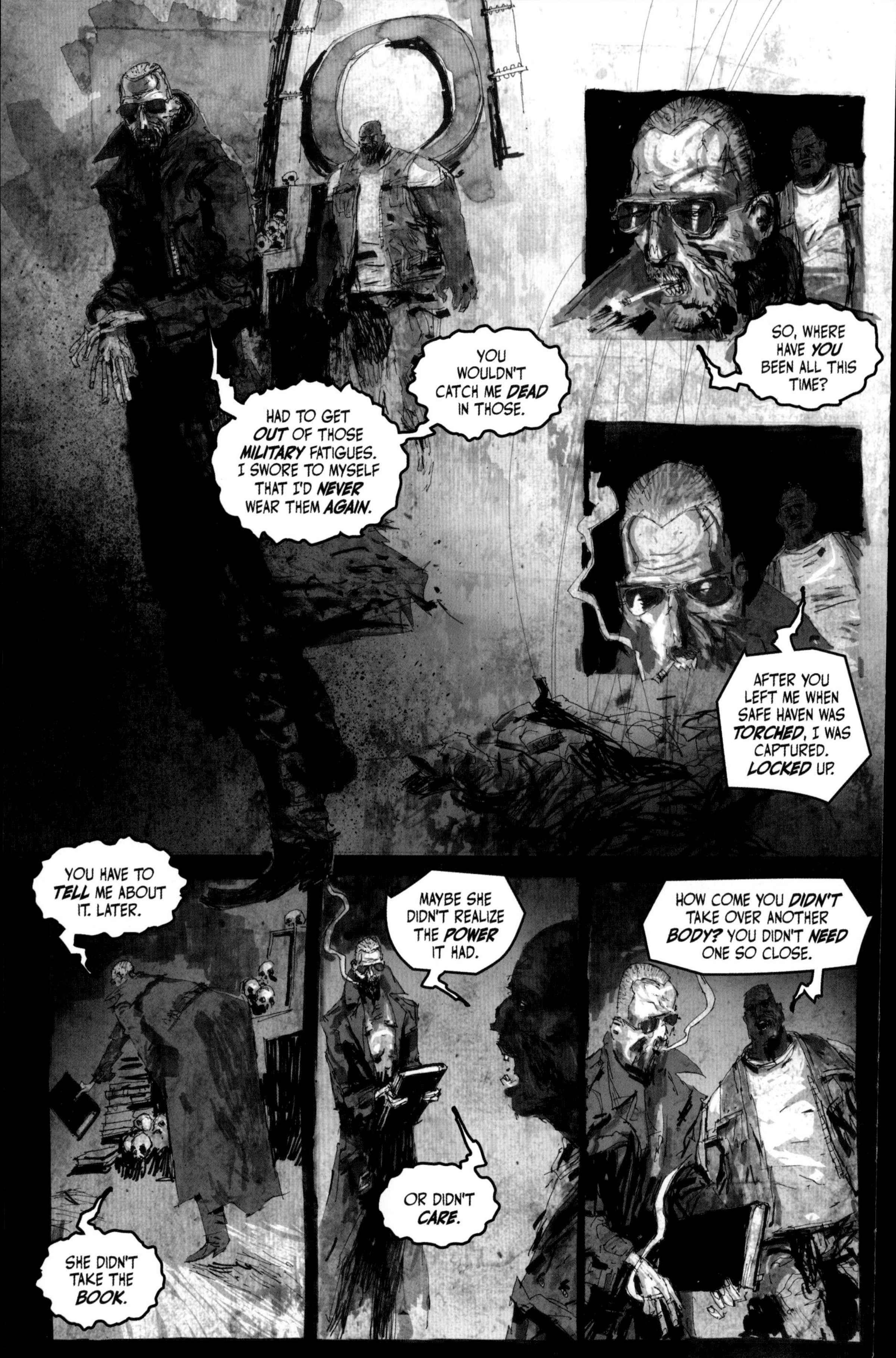
SO, WHERE HAVE YOU BEEN ALL THIS TIME?
YOU WOULDN'T CATCH ME DEAD IN THOSE.
HAD TO GET OUT OF THOSE MILITARY FATIGUES. I SWORE TO MYSELF THAT I'D NEVER WEAR THEM AGAIN.
AFTER YOU LEFT ME WHEN SAFE HAVEN WAS TORCHED, I WAS CAPTURED. LOCKED UP.
YOU HAVE TO TELL ME ABOUT IT. LATER.
SHE DIDN'T TAKE THE BOOK.
MAYBE SHE DIDN'T REALIZE THE POWER IT HAD.
OR DIDN'T CARE.
HOW COME YOU DIDN'T TAKE OVER ANOTHER BODY? YOU DIDN'T NEED ONE SO CLOSE.

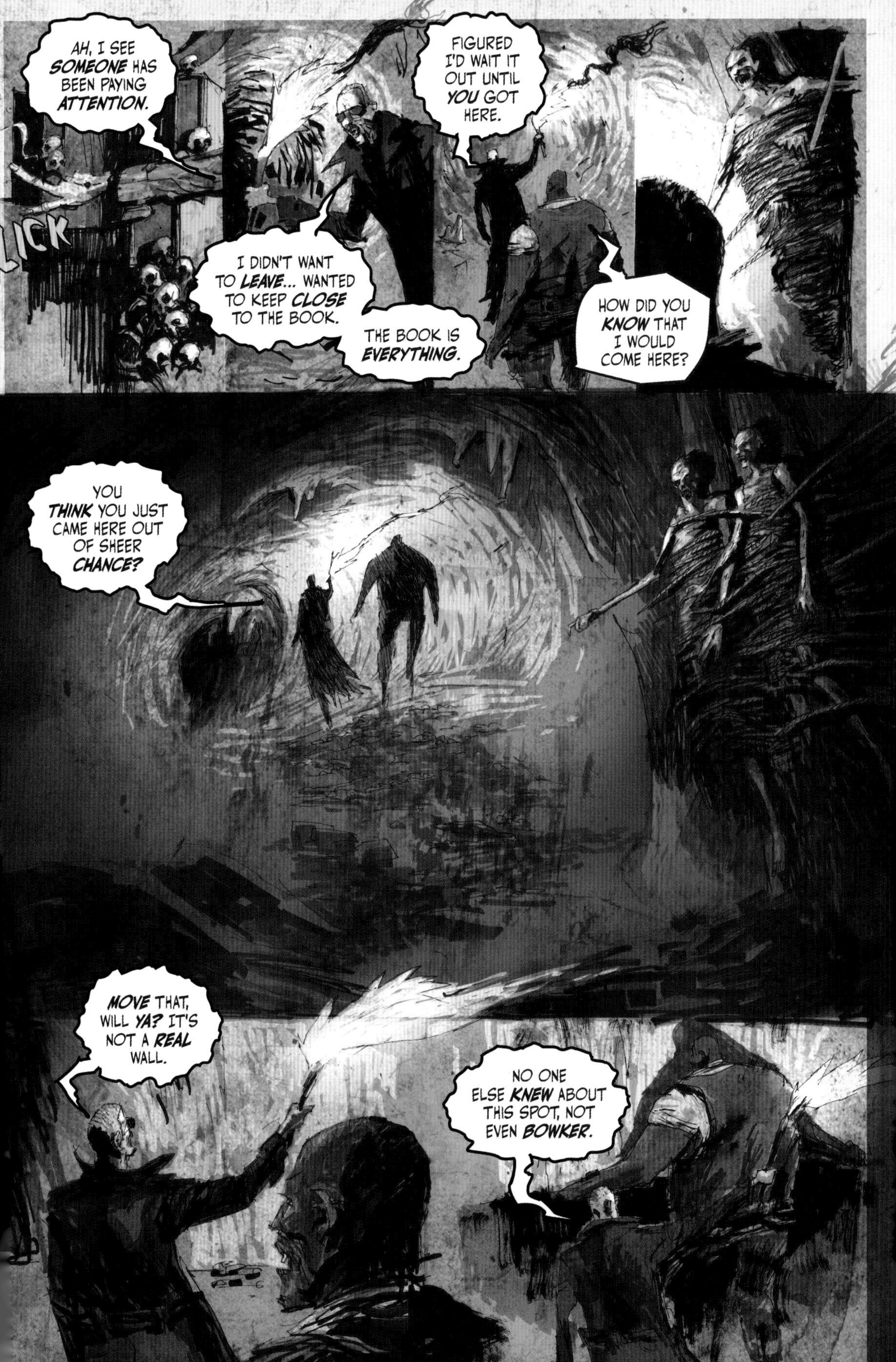
AH, I SEE SOMEONE HAS BEEN PAYING ATTENTION.
LICK
FIGURED I'D WAIT IT OUT UNTIL YOU GOT HERE.
I DIDN'T WANT TO LEAVE... WANTED TO KEEP CLOSE TO THE BOOK.
THE BOOK IS EVERYTHING.
HOW DID YOU KNOW THAT I WOULD COME HERE?
YOU THINK YOU JUST CAME HERE OUT OF SHEER CHANCE?
MOVE THAT, WILL YA? IT'S NOT A REAL WALL.
NO ONE ELSE KNEW ABOUT THIS SPOT, NOT EVEN BOWKER.

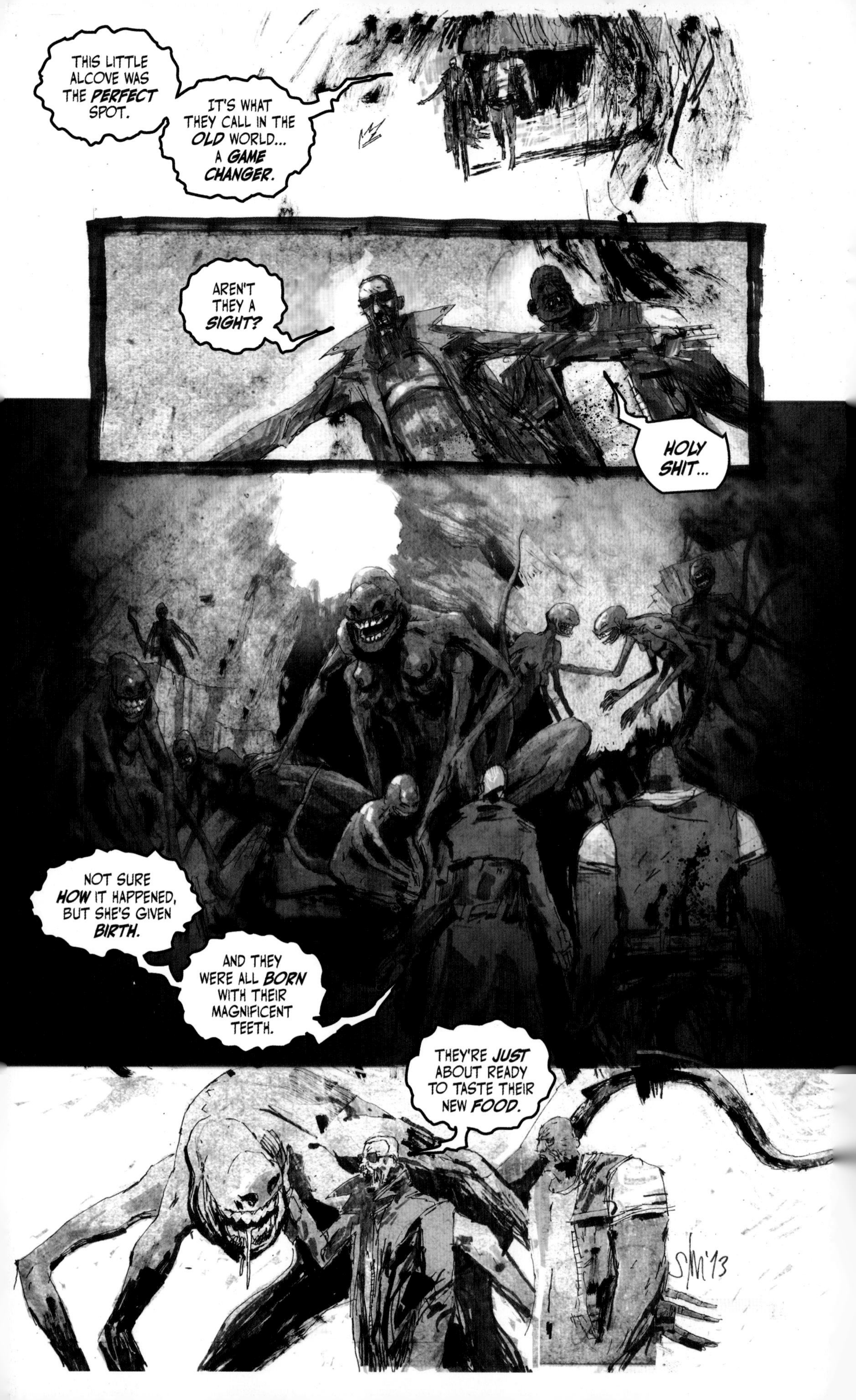

THIS LITTLE ALCOVE WAS THE PERFECT SPOT.
IT'S WHAT THEY CALL IN THE OLD WORLD... A GAME CHANGER.
AREN'T THEY A SIGHT?
HOLY SHIT...
NOT SURE HOW IT HAPPENED, BUT SHE'S GIVEN BIRTH.
AND THEY WERE ALL BORN WITH THEIR MAGNIFICENT TEETH.
THEY'RE JUST ABOUT READY TO TASTE THEIR NEW FOOD.
SM'13

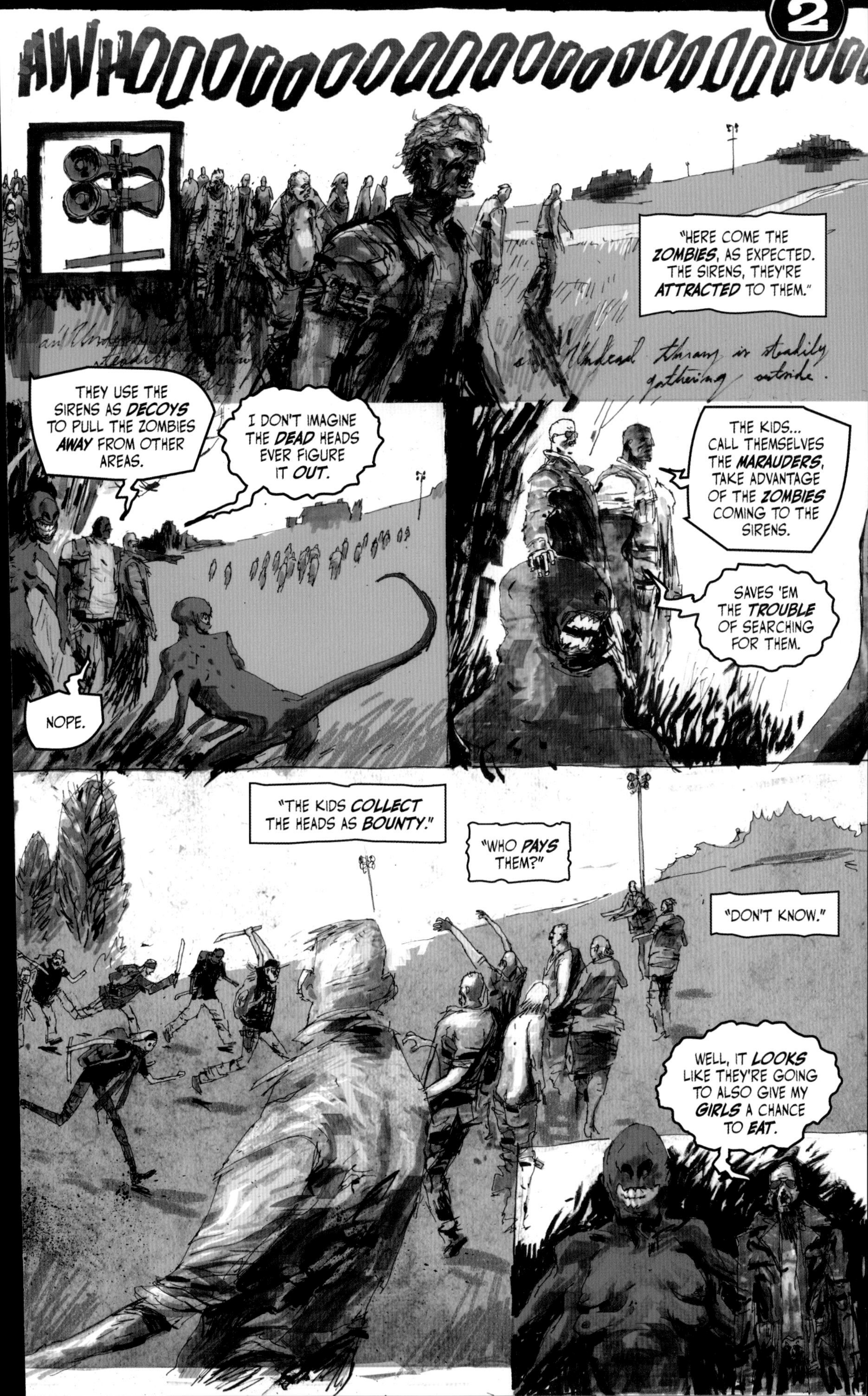

2
AWHOOOOOOOOOOOOOOOOOOOOOO
"HERE COME THE ZOMBIES, AS EXPECTED. THE SIRENS, THEY'RE ATTRACTED TO THEM."
an Undead throng is steadily gathering outside.
THEY USE THE SIRENS AS DECOYS TO PULL THE ZOMBIES AWAY FROM OTHER AREAS.
I DON'T IMAGINE THE DEAD HEADS EVER FIGURE IT OUT.
NOPE.
THE KIDS... CALL THEMSELVES THE MARAUDERS, TAKE ADVANTAGE OF THE ZOMBIES COMING TO THE SIRENS.
SAVES 'EM THE TROUBLE OF SEARCHING FOR THEM.
"THE KIDS COLLECT THE HEADS AS BOUNTY."
"WHO PAYS THEM?"
"DON'T KNOW."
WELL, IT LOOKS LIKE THEY'RE GOING TO ALSO GIVE MY GIRLS A CHANCE TO EAT.

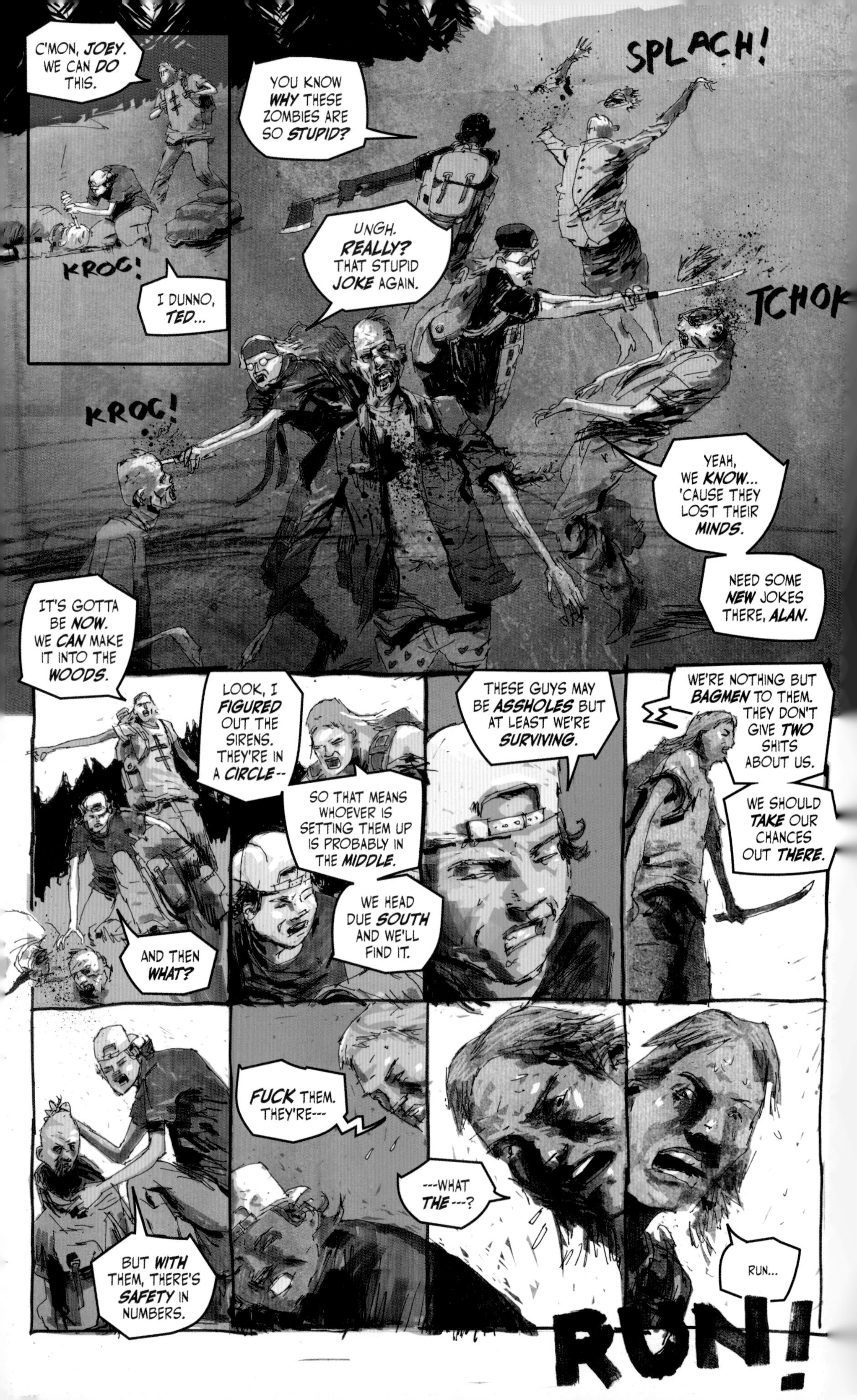

C'MON, JOEY. WE CAN DO THIS.
KROG!
I DUNNO, TED...
YOU KNOW WHY THESE ZOMBIES ARE SO STUPID?
SPLACH!
UNGH. REALLY? THAT STUPID JOKE AGAIN.
TCHOK
KROG!
YEAH, WE KNOW... 'CAUSE THEY LOST THEIR MINDS.
NEED SOME NEW JOKES THERE, ALAN.
IT'S GOTTA BE NOW. WE CAN MAKE IT INTO THE WOODS.
AND THEN WHAT?
LOOK, I FIGURED OUT THE SIRENS. THEY'RE IN A CIRCLE--
SO THAT MEANS WHOEVER IS SETTING THEM UP IS PROBABLY IN THE MIDDLE.
WE HEAD DUE SOUTH AND WE'LL FIND IT.
THESE GUYS MAY BE ASSHOLES BUT AT LEAST WE'RE SURVIVING.
WE'RE NOTHING BUT BAGMEN TO THEM. THEY DON'T GIVE TWO SHITS ABOUT US.
WE SHOULD TAKE OUR CHANCES OUT THERE.
BUT WITH THEM, THERE'S SAFETY IN NUMBERS.
FUCK THEM. THEY'RE---
---WHAT THE---?
RUN...
RUN!

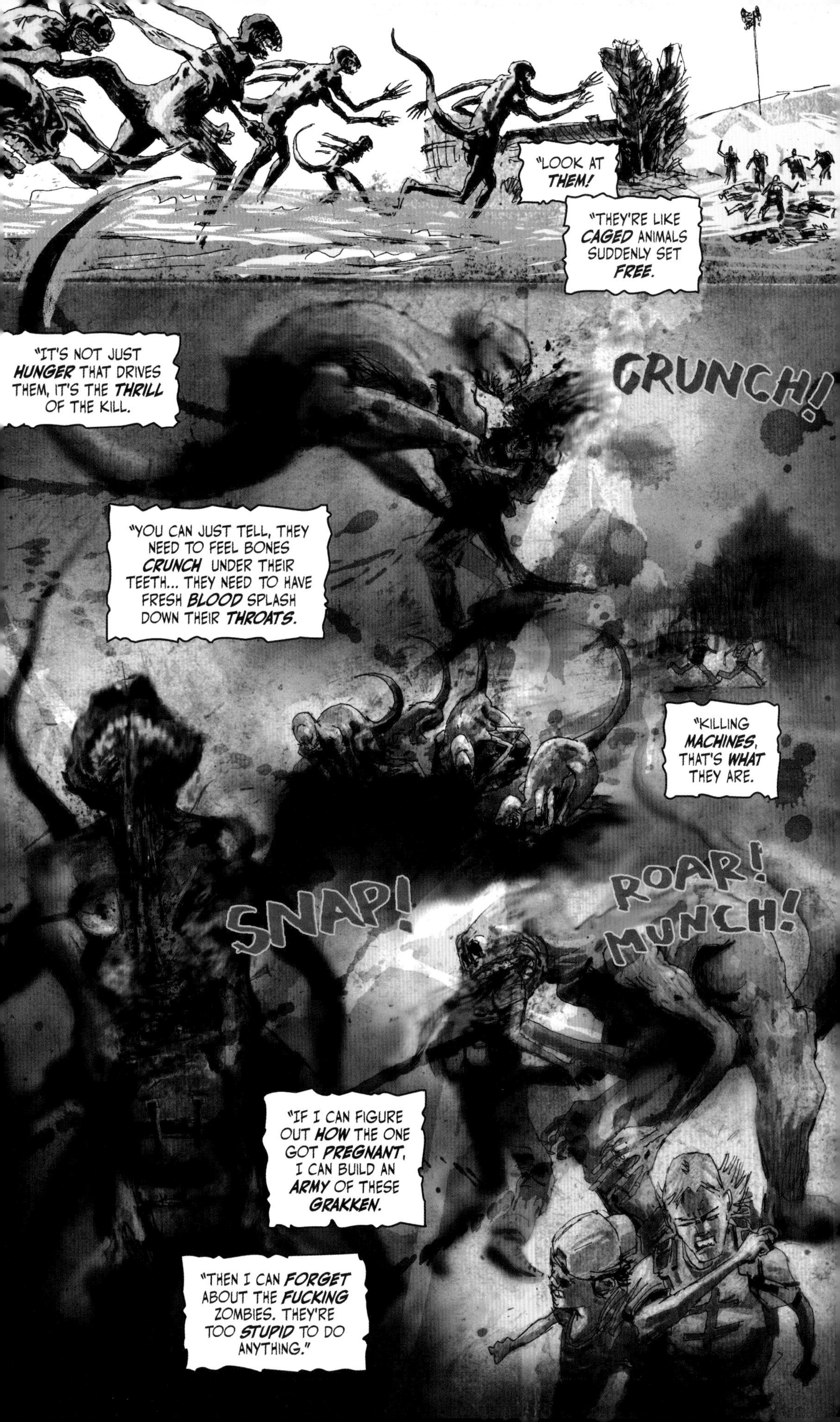
"LOOK AT THEM!
"THEY'RE LIKE CAGED ANIMALS SUDDENLY SET FREE.
"IT'S NOT JUST HUNGER THAT DRIVES THEM, IT'S THE THRILL OF THE KILL.
GRUNCH!
"YOU CAN JUST TELL, THEY NEED TO FEEL BONES CRUNCH UNDER THEIR TEETH... THEY NEED TO HAVE FRESH BLOOD SPLASH DOWN THEIR THROATS.
"KILLING MACHINES, THAT'S WHAT THEY ARE.
SNAP!
ROAR!
MUNCH!
"IF I CAN FIGURE OUT HOW THE ONE GOT PREGNANT, I CAN BUILD AN ARMY OF THESE GRAKKEN.
"THEN I CAN FORGET ABOUT THE FUCKING ZOMBIES. THEY'RE TOO STUPID TO DO ANYTHING."

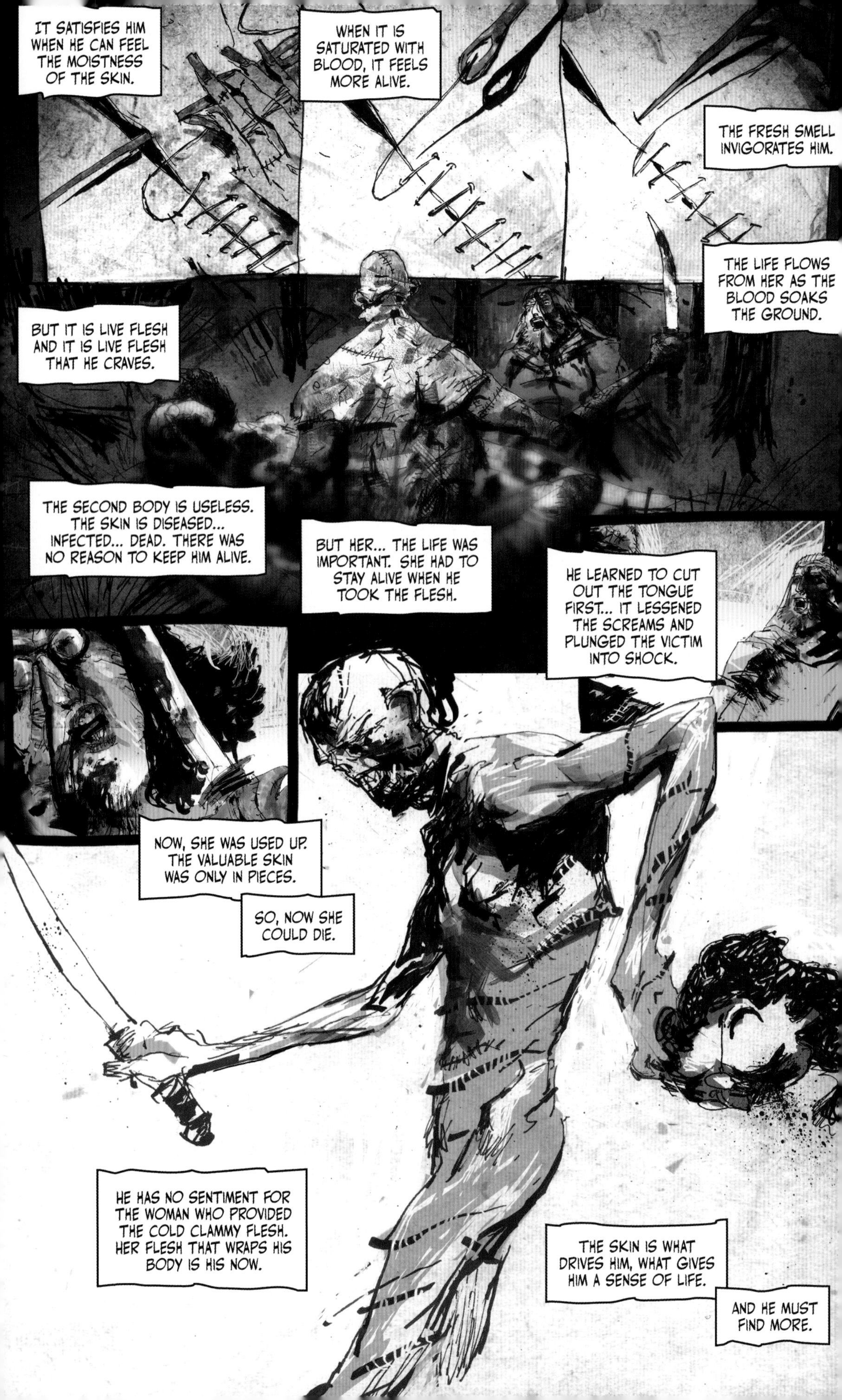
IT SATISFIES HIM WHEN HE CAN FEEL THE MOISTNESS OF THE SKIN.
WHEN IT IS SATURATED WITH BLOOD, IT FEELS MORE ALIVE.
THE FRESH SMELL INVIGORATES HIM.
THE LIFE FLOWS FROM HER AS THE BLOOD SOAKS THE GROUND.
BUT IT IS LIVE FLESH AND IT IS LIVE FLESH THAT HE CRAVES.
THE SECOND BODY IS USELESS. THE SKIN IS DISEASED... INFECTED... DEAD. THERE WAS NO REASON TO KEEP HIM ALIVE.
BUT HER... THE LIFE WAS IMPORTANT. SHE HAD TO STAY ALIVE WHEN HE TOOK THE FLESH.
HE LEARNED TO CUT OUT THE TONGUE FIRST... IT LESSENED THE SCREAMS AND PLUNGED THE VICTIM INTO SHOCK.
NOW, SHE WAS USED UP. THE VALUABLE SKIN WAS ONLY IN PIECES.
SO, NOW SHE COULD DIE.
HE HAS NO SENTIMENT FOR THE WOMAN WHO PROVIDED THE COLD CLAMMY FLESH. HER FLESH THAT WRAPS HIS BODY IS HIS NOW.
THE SKIN IS WHAT DRIVES HIM, WHAT GIVES HIM A SENSE OF LIFE.
AND HE MUST FIND MORE.

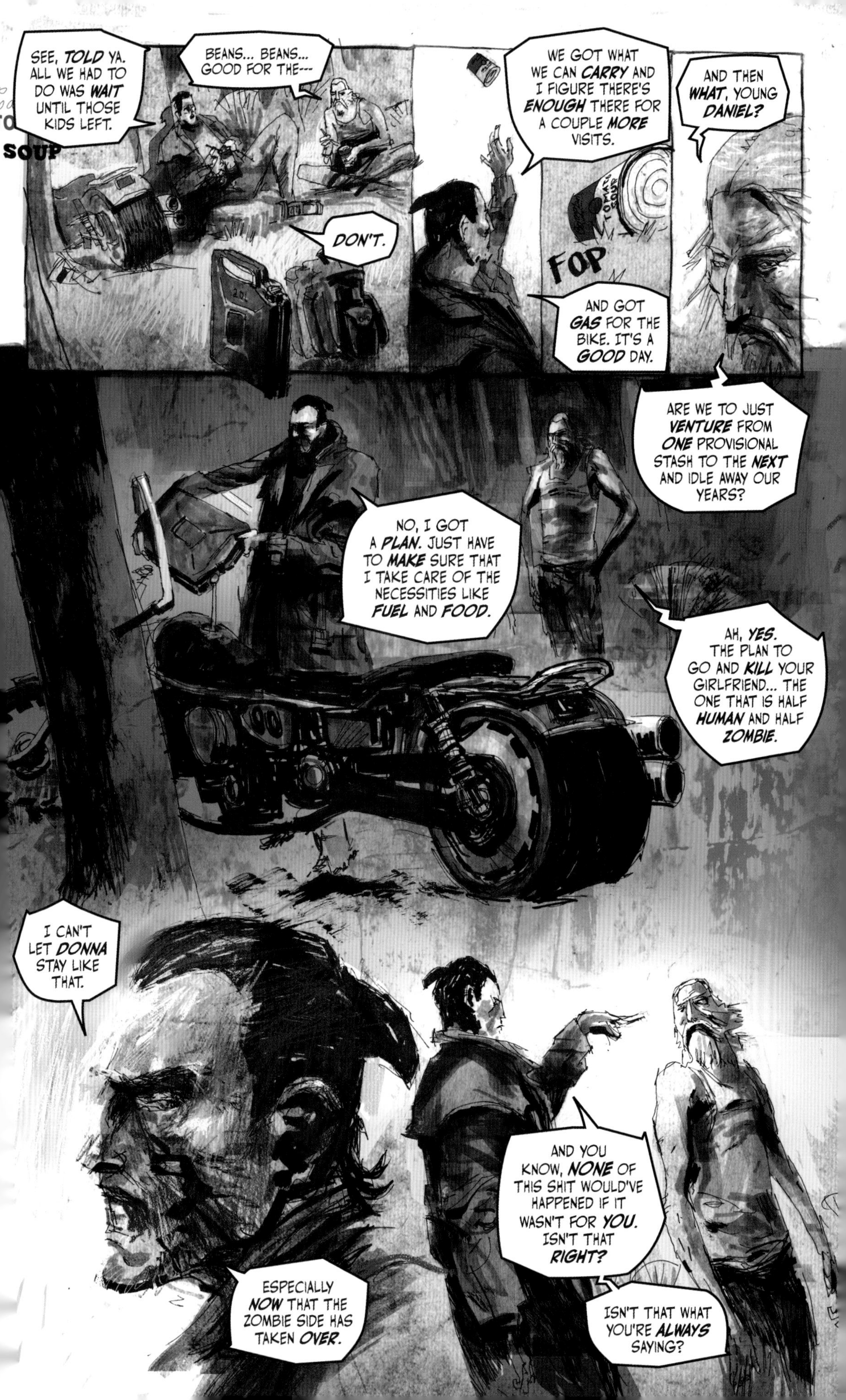
SEE, TOLD YA. ALL WE HAD TO DO WAS WAIT UNTIL THOSE KIDS LEFT.
BEANS... BEANS... GOOD FOR THE---
DON'T.
WE GOT WHAT WE CAN CARRY AND I FIGURE THERE'S ENOUGH THERE FOR A COUPLE MORE VISITS.
FOP
AND GOT GAS FOR THE BIKE. IT'S A GOOD DAY.
AND THEN WHAT, YOUNG DANIEL?
ARE WE TO JUST VENTURE FROM ONE PROVISIONAL STASH TO THE NEXT AND IDLE AWAY OUR YEARS?
NO, I GOT A PLAN. JUST HAVE TO MAKE SURE THAT I TAKE CARE OF THE NECESSITIES LIKE FUEL AND FOOD.
AH, YES. THE PLAN TO GO AND KILL YOUR GIRLFRIEND... THE ONE THAT IS HALF HUMAN AND HALF ZOMBIE.
I CAN'T LET DONNA STAY LIKE THAT.
ESPECIALLY NOW THAT THE ZOMBIE SIDE HAS TAKEN OVER.
AND YOU KNOW, NONE OF THIS SHIT WOULD'VE HAPPENED IF IT WASN'T FOR YOU. ISN'T THAT RIGHT?
ISN'T THAT WHAT YOU'RE ALWAYS SAYING?

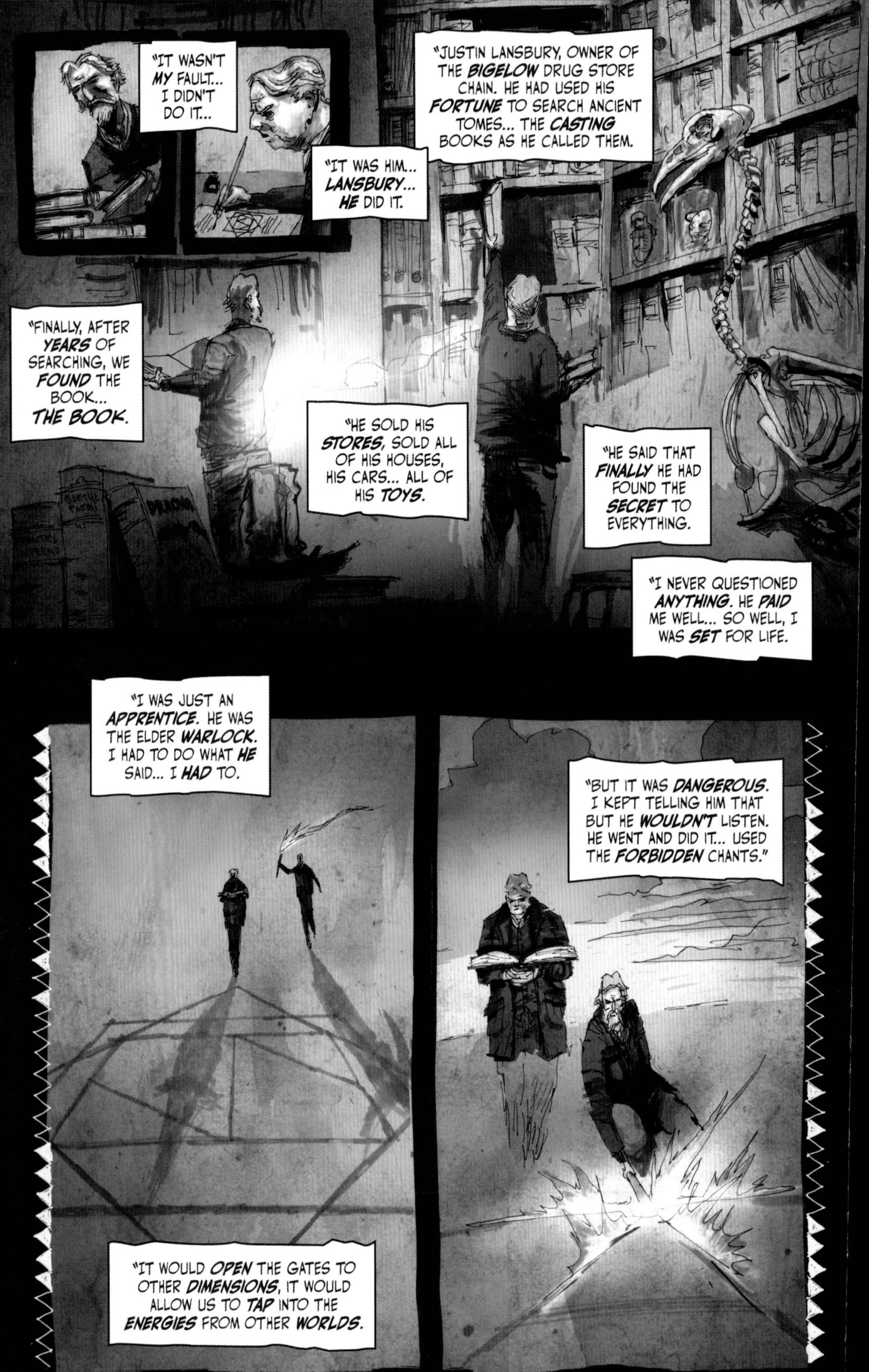
"IT WASN'T MY FAULT... I DIDN'T DO IT...
"IT WAS HIM... LANSBURY... HE DID IT.
"JUSTIN LANSBURY, OWNER OF THE BIGELOW DRUG STORE CHAIN. HE HAD USED HIS FORTUNE TO SEARCH ANCIENT TOMES... THE CASTING BOOKS AS HE CALLED THEM.
"FINALLY, AFTER YEARS OF SEARCHING, WE FOUND THE BOOK... THE BOOK.
"HE SOLD HIS STORES, SOLD ALL OF HIS HOUSES, HIS CARS... ALL OF HIS TOYS.
"HE SAID THAT FINALLY HE HAD FOUND THE SECRET TO EVERYTHING.
"I NEVER QUESTIONED ANYTHING. HE PAID ME WELL... SO WELL, I WAS SET FOR LIFE.
"I WAS JUST AN APPRENTICE. HE WAS THE ELDER WARLOCK. I HAD TO DO WHAT HE SAID... I HAD TO.
"IT WOULD OPEN THE GATES TO OTHER DIMENSIONS, IT WOULD ALLOW US TO TAP INTO THE ENERGIES FROM OTHER WORLDS.
"BUT IT WAS DANGEROUS. I KEPT TELLING HIM THAT BUT HE WOULDN'T LISTEN. HE WENT AND DID IT... USED THE FORBIDDEN CHANTS."

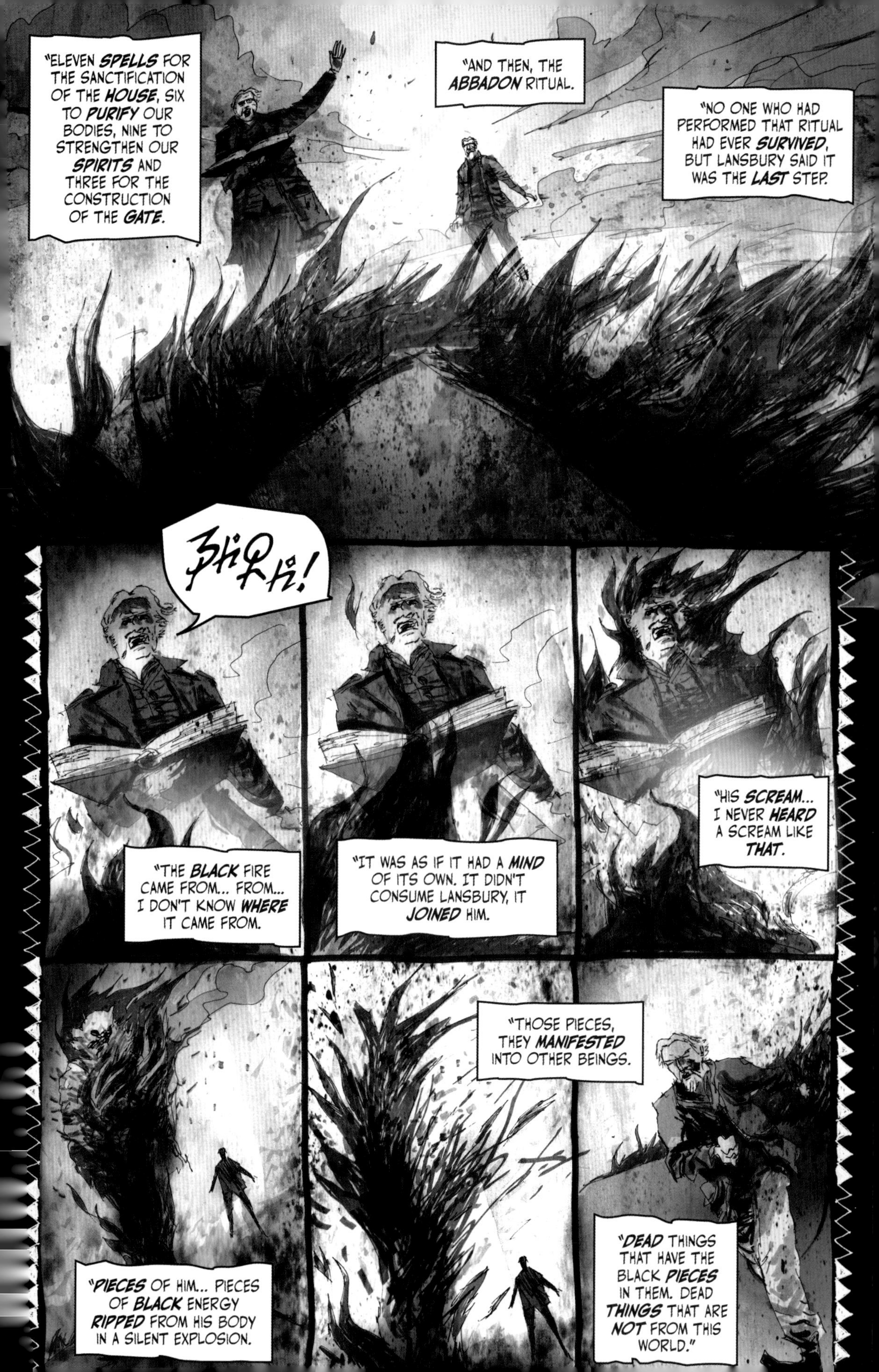
"ELEVEN SPELLS FOR THE SANCTIFICATION OF THE HOUSE, SIX TO PURIFY OUR BODIES, NINE TO STRENGTHEN OUR SPIRITS AND THREE FOR THE CONSTRUCTION OF THE GATE.
"AND THEN, THE ABBADON RITUAL.
"NO ONE WHO HAD PERFORMED THAT RITUAL HAD EVER SURVIVED, BUT LANSBURY SAID IT WAS THE LAST STEP.
"THE BLACK FIRE CAME FROM... FROM... I DON'T KNOW WHERE IT CAME FROM.
"IT WAS AS IF IT HAD A MIND OF ITS OWN. IT DIDN'T CONSUME LANSBURY, IT JOINED HIM.
"HIS SCREAM... I NEVER HEARD A SCREAM LIKE THAT.
"PIECES OF HIM... PIECES OF BLACK ENERGY RIPPED FROM HIS BODY IN A SILENT EXPLOSION.
"THOSE PIECES, THEY MANIFESTED INTO OTHER BEINGS.
"DEAD THINGS THAT HAVE THE BLACK PIECES IN THEM. DEAD THINGS THAT ARE NOT FROM THIS WORLD."

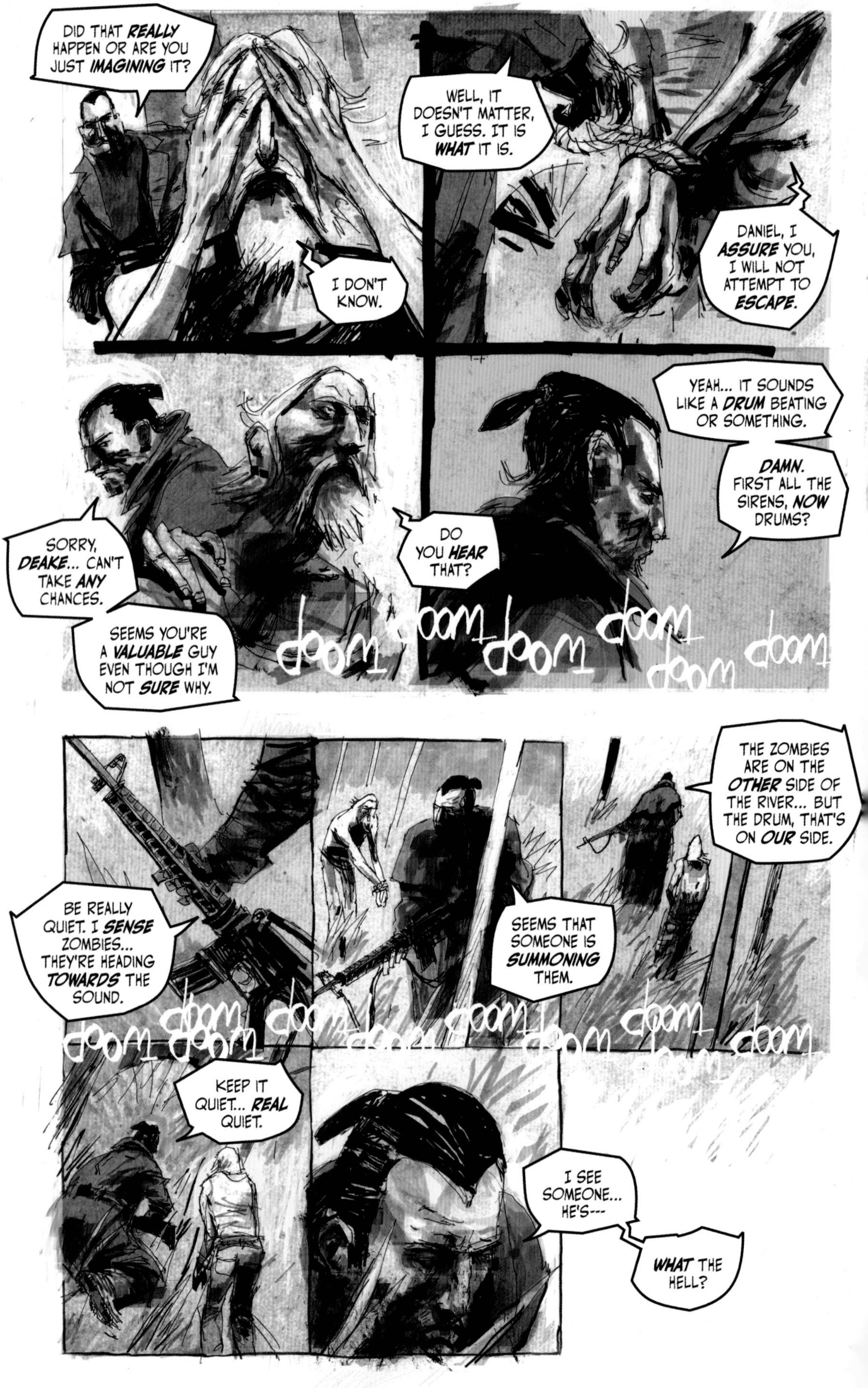
DID THAT REALLY HAPPEN OR ARE YOU JUST IMAGINING IT?
I DON'T KNOW.
WELL, IT DOESN'T MATTER, I GUESS. IT IS WHAT IT IS.
DANIEL, I ASSURE YOU, I WILL NOT ATTEMPT TO ESCAPE.
SORRY, DEAKE... CAN'T TAKE ANY CHANCES.
SEEMS YOU'RE A VALUABLE GUY EVEN THOUGH I'M NOT SURE WHY.
DO YOU HEAR THAT?
YEAH... IT SOUNDS LIKE A DRUM BEATING OR SOMETHING.
DAMN. FIRST ALL THE SIRENS, NOW DRUMS?
doom doom doom doom doom doom
BE REALLY QUIET. I SENSE ZOMBIES... THEY'RE HEADING TOWARDS THE SOUND.
SEEMS THAT SOMEONE IS SUMMONING THEM.
THE ZOMBIES ARE ON THE OTHER SIDE OF THE RIVER... BUT THE DRUM, THAT'S ON OUR SIDE.
doom doom doom doom doom doom doom doom
KEEP IT QUIET... REAL QUIET.
I SEE SOMEONE... HE'S---
WHAT THE HELL?

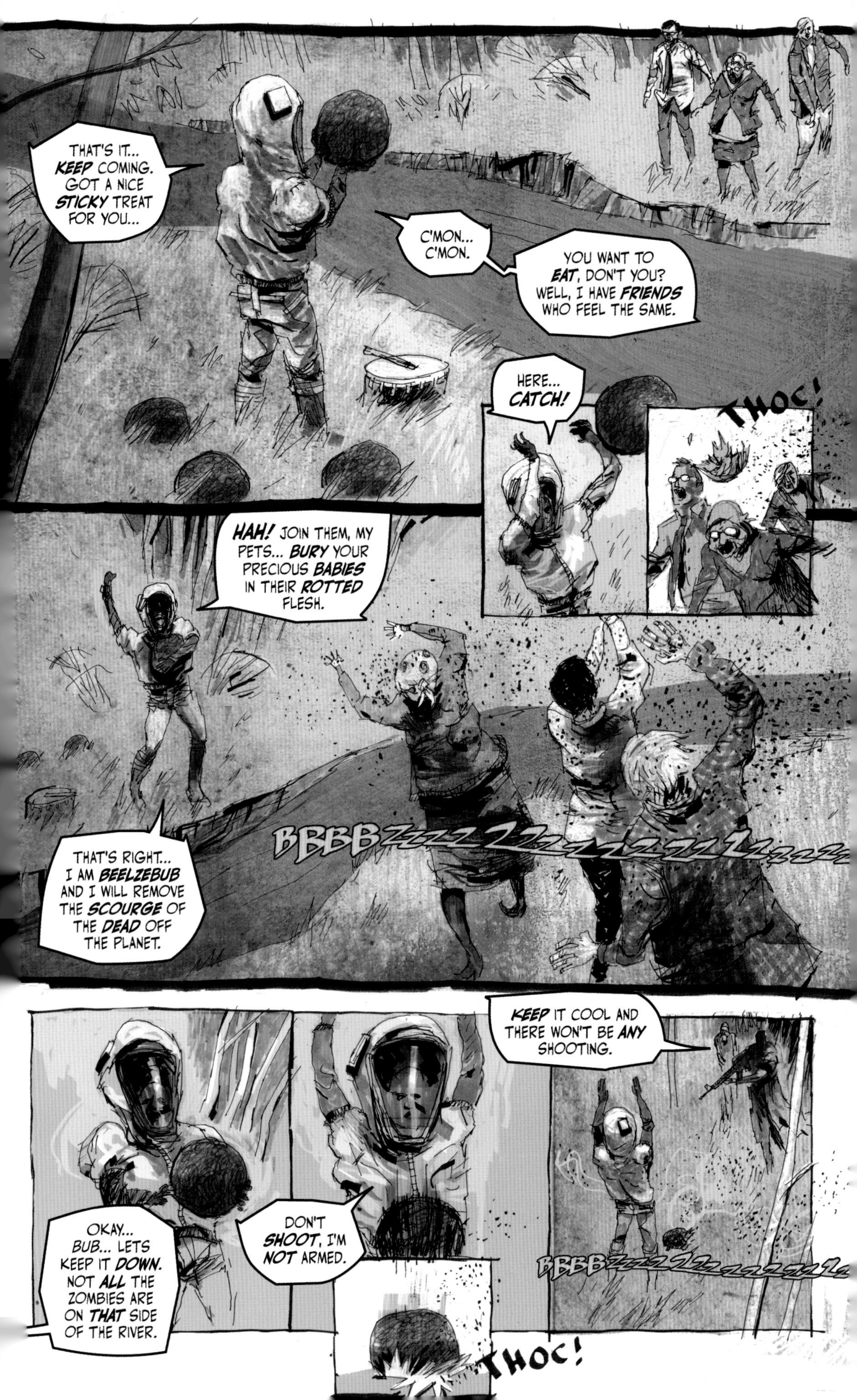
THAT'S IT... KEEP COMING. GOT A NICE STICKY TREAT FOR YOU...
C'MON... C'MON.
YOU WANT TO EAT, DON'T YOU? WELL, I HAVE FRIENDS WHO FEEL THE SAME.
HERE... CATCH!
THOC!
HAH! JOIN THEM, MY PETS... BURY YOUR PRECIOUS BABIES IN THEIR ROTTED FLESH.
BBBBZZZZZZZZZZZZZZZZ
THAT'S RIGHT... I AM BEELZEBUB AND I WILL REMOVE THE SCOURGE OF THE DEAD OFF THE PLANET.
OKAY... BUB... LETS KEEP IT DOWN. NOT ALL THE ZOMBIES ARE ON THAT SIDE OF THE RIVER.
DON'T SHOOT, I'M NOT ARMED.
KEEP IT COOL AND THERE WON'T BE ANY SHOOTING.
BBBBZZZZZZZZZZZZZZ
THOC!

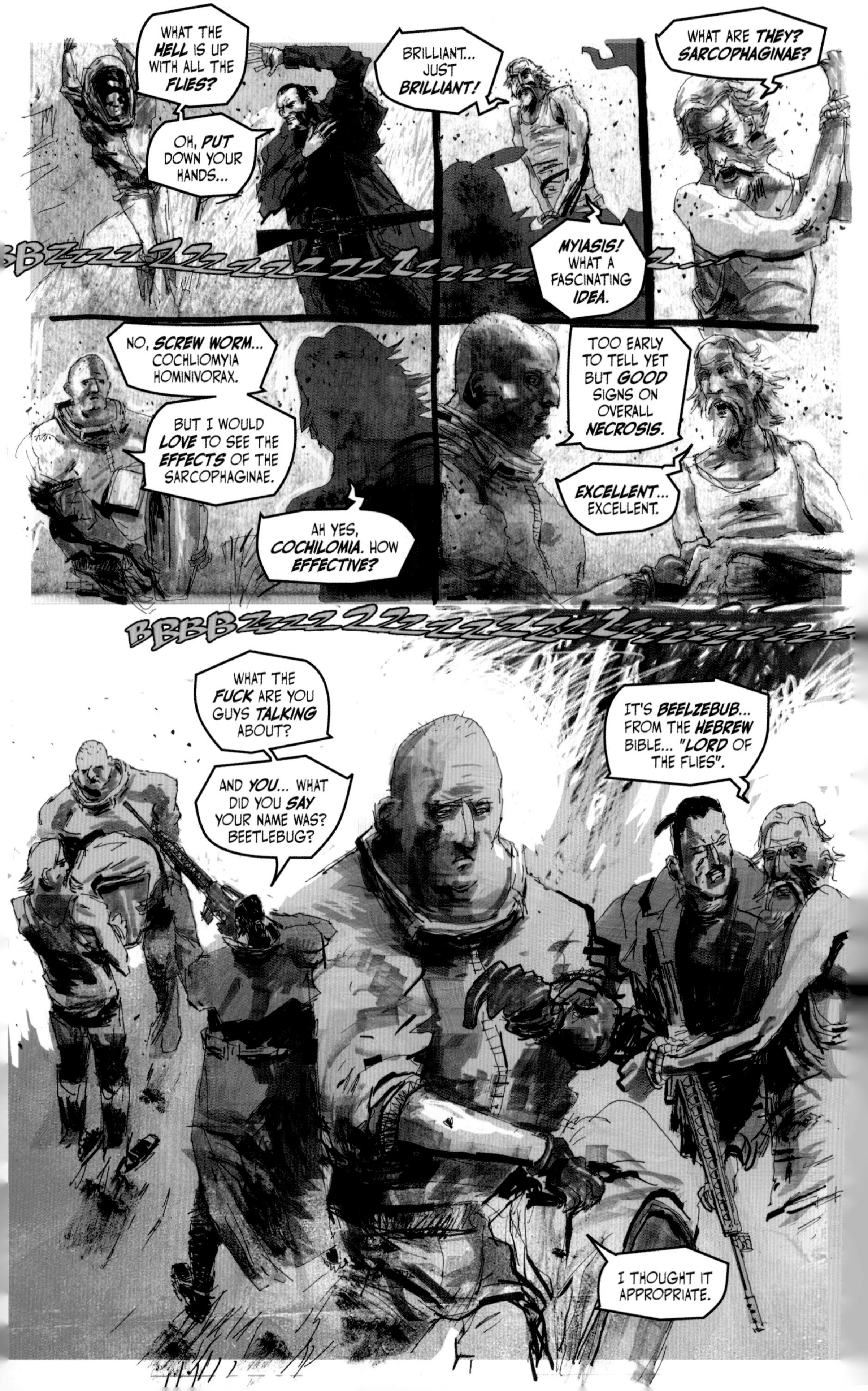
WHAT THE **HELL** IS UP WITH ALL THE **FLIES?**
OH, **PUT** DOWN YOUR HANDS...
BRILLIANT... JUST **BRILLIANT!**
WHAT ARE **THEY? SARCOPHAGINAE?**
MYIASIS! WHAT A FASCINATING **IDEA.**
NO, **SCREW WORM...** COCHLIOMYIA HOMINIVORAX.
BUT I WOULD **LOVE** TO SEE THE **EFFECTS** OF THE SARCOPHAGINAE.
AH YES, **COCHILOMIA.** HOW **EFFECTIVE?**
TOO EARLY TO TELL YET BUT **GOOD** SIGNS ON OVERALL **NECROSIS.**
EXCELLENT... EXCELLENT.
WHAT THE **FUCK** ARE YOU GUYS **TALKING** ABOUT?
AND **YOU...** WHAT DID YOU **SAY** YOUR NAME WAS? BEETLEBUG?
IT'S **BEELZEBUB...** FROM THE **HEBREW** BIBLE... "**LORD** OF THE FLIES".
I THOUGHT IT APPROPRIATE.

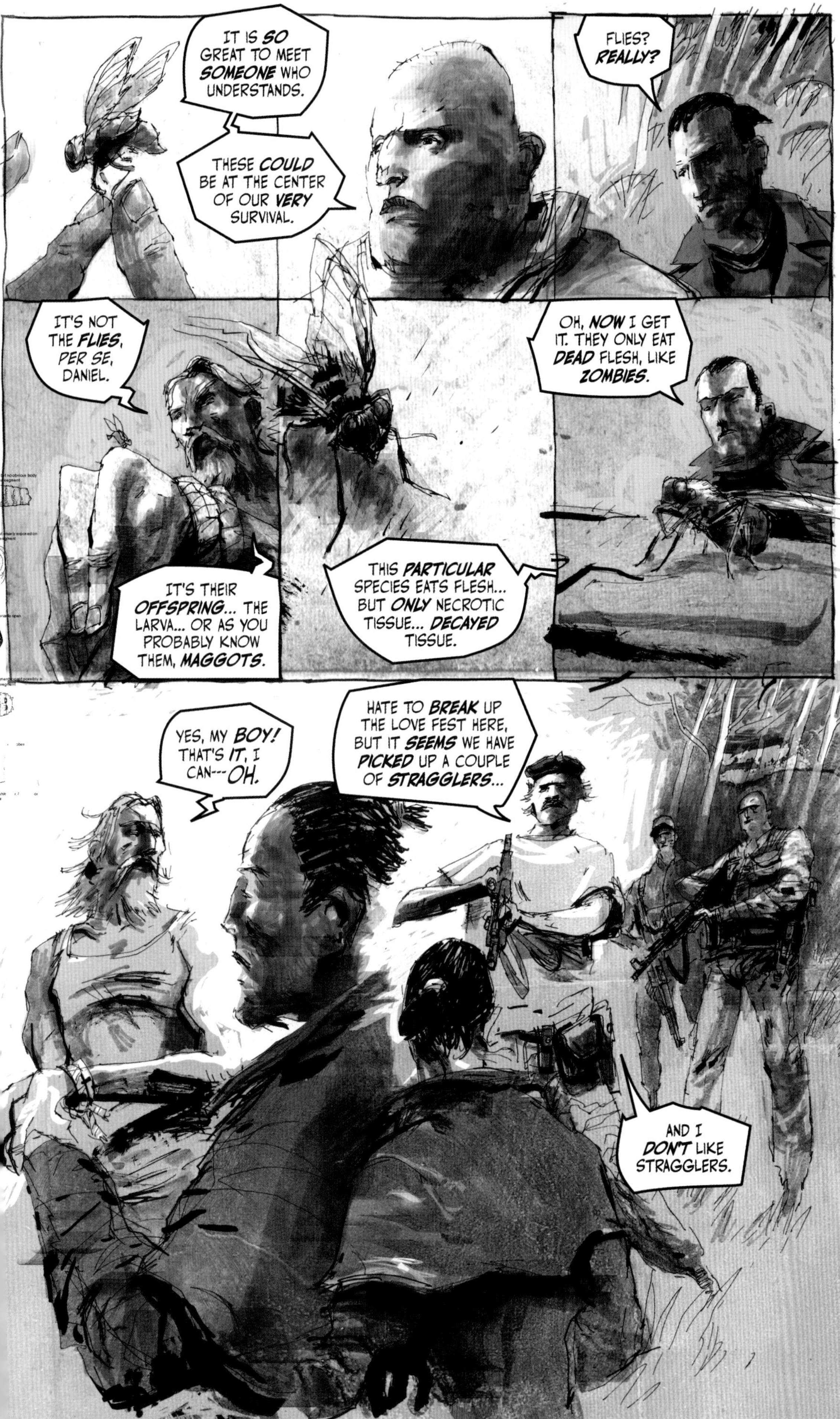
IT IS SO GREAT TO MEET SOMEONE WHO UNDERSTANDS.
THESE COULD BE AT THE CENTER OF OUR VERY SURVIVAL.
FLIES? REALLY?
IT'S NOT THE FLIES, PER SE, DANIEL.
IT'S THEIR OFFSPRING... THE LARVA... OR AS YOU PROBABLY KNOW THEM, MAGGOTS.
THIS PARTICULAR SPECIES EATS FLESH... BUT ONLY NECROTIC TISSUE... DECAYED TISSUE.
OH, NOW I GET IT. THEY ONLY EAT DEAD FLESH, LIKE ZOMBIES.
YES, MY BOY! THAT'S IT, I CAN---OH.
HATE TO BREAK UP THE LOVE FEST HERE, BUT IT SEEMS WE HAVE PICKED UP A COUPLE OF STRAGGLERS...
AND I DON'T LIKE STRAGGLERS.

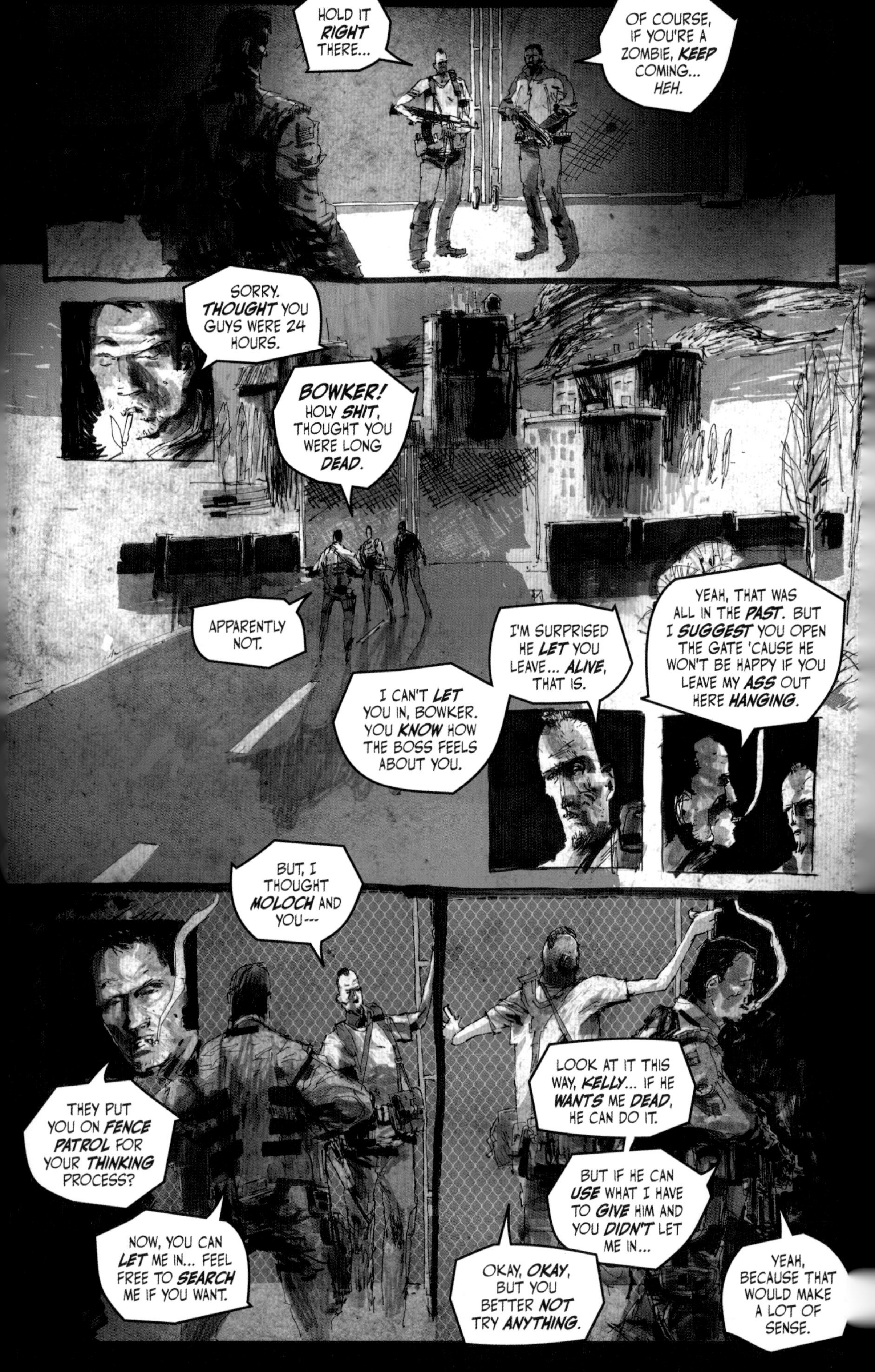
HOLD IT RIGHT THERE...
OF COURSE, IF YOU'RE A ZOMBIE, KEEP COMING... HEH.
SORRY. THOUGHT YOU GUYS WERE 24 HOURS.
BOWKER! HOLY SHIT, THOUGHT YOU WERE LONG DEAD.
APPARENTLY NOT.
I CAN'T LET YOU IN, BOWKER. YOU KNOW HOW THE BOSS FEELS ABOUT YOU.
I'M SURPRISED HE LET YOU LEAVE... ALIVE, THAT IS.
YEAH, THAT WAS ALL IN THE PAST. BUT I SUGGEST YOU OPEN THE GATE 'CAUSE HE WON'T BE HAPPY IF YOU LEAVE MY ASS OUT HERE HANGING.
BUT, I THOUGHT MOLOCH AND YOU---
THEY PUT YOU ON FENCE PATROL FOR YOUR THINKING PROCESS?
NOW, YOU CAN LET ME IN... FEEL FREE TO SEARCH ME IF YOU WANT.
LOOK AT IT THIS WAY, KELLY... IF HE WANTS ME DEAD, HE CAN DO IT.
BUT IF HE CAN USE WHAT I HAVE TO GIVE HIM AND YOU DIDN'T LET ME IN...
OKAY, OKAY, BUT YOU BETTER NOT TRY ANYTHING.
YEAH, BECAUSE THAT WOULD MAKE A LOT OF SENSE.

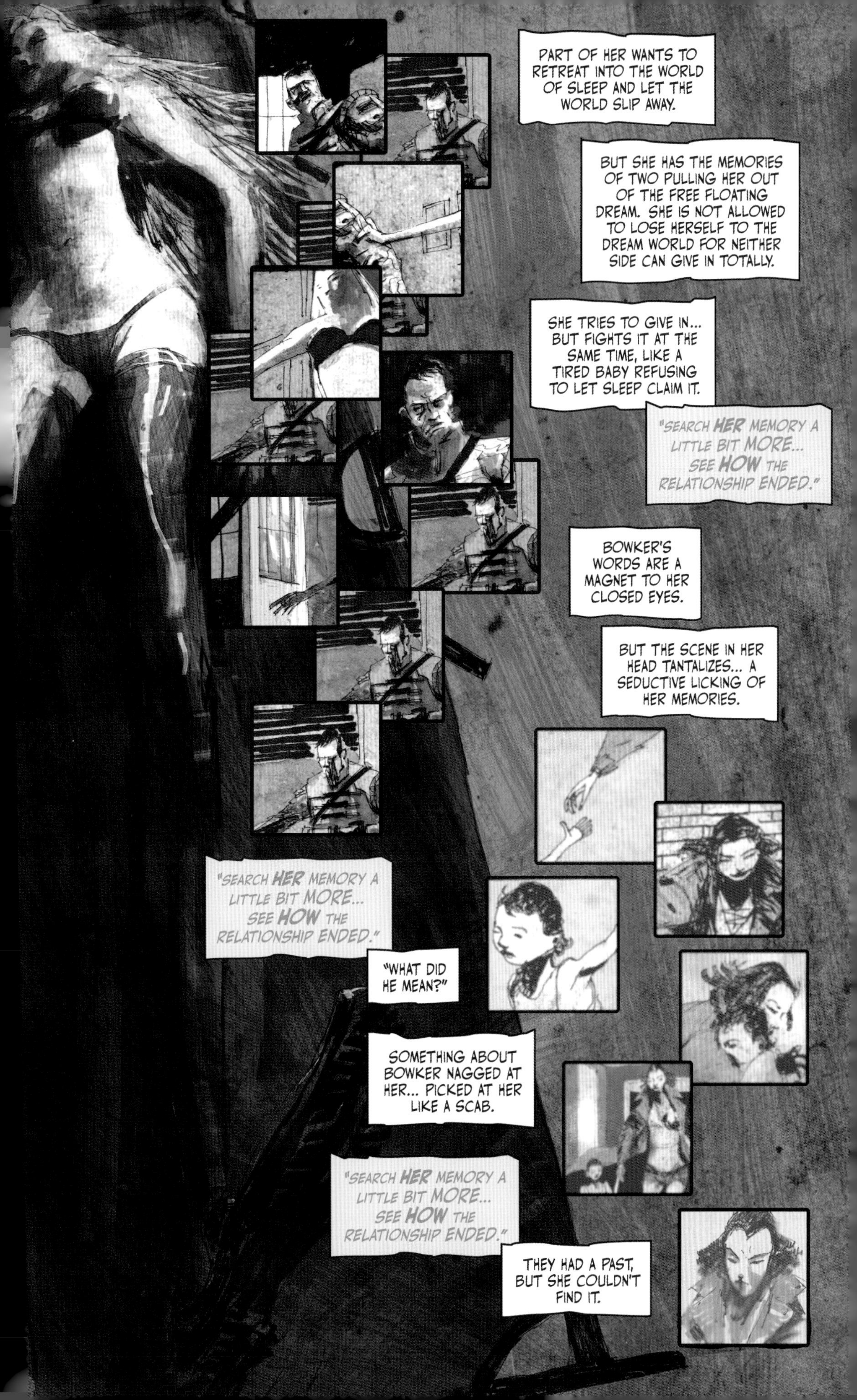
PART OF HER WANTS TO RETREAT INTO THE WORLD OF SLEEP AND LET THE WORLD SLIP AWAY.
BUT SHE HAS THE MEMORIES OF TWO PULLING HER OUT OF THE FREE FLOATING DREAM. SHE IS NOT ALLOWED TO LOSE HERSELF TO THE DREAM WORLD FOR NEITHER SIDE CAN GIVE IN TOTALLY.
SHE TRIES TO GIVE IN... BUT FIGHTS IT AT THE SAME TIME, LIKE A TIRED BABY REFUSING TO LET SLEEP CLAIM IT.
"SEARCH HER MEMORY A LITTLE BIT MORE... SEE HOW THE RELATIONSHIP ENDED."
BOWKER'S WORDS ARE A MAGNET TO HER CLOSED EYES.
BUT THE SCENE IN HER HEAD TANTALIZES... A SEDUCTIVE LICKING OF HER MEMORIES.
"SEARCH HER MEMORY A LITTLE BIT MORE... SEE HOW THE RELATIONSHIP ENDED."
"WHAT DID HE MEAN?"
SOMETHING ABOUT BOWKER NAGGED AT HER... PICKED AT HER LIKE A SCAB.
"SEARCH HER MEMORY A LITTLE BIT MORE... SEE HOW THE RELATIONSHIP ENDED."
THEY HAD A PAST, BUT SHE COULDN'T FIND IT.

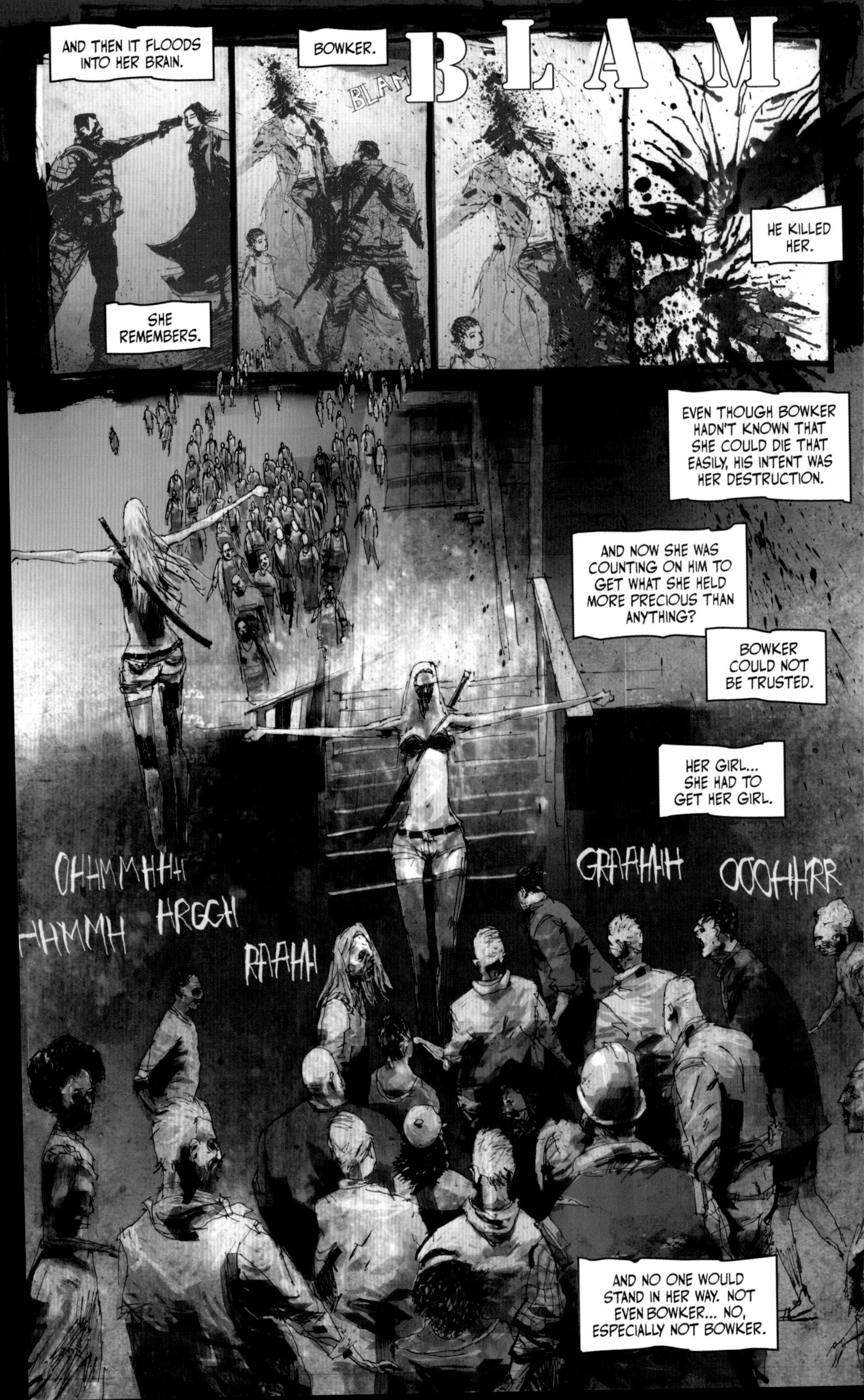
AND THEN IT FLOODS INTO HER BRAIN.
SHE REMEMBERS.
BOWKER.
BLAM
BLAM
HE KILLED HER.
EVEN THOUGH BOWKER HADN'T KNOWN THAT SHE COULD DIE THAT EASILY, HIS INTENT WAS HER DESTRUCTION.
AND NOW SHE WAS COUNTING ON HIM TO GET WHAT SHE HELD MORE PRECIOUS THAN ANYTHING?
BOWKER COULD NOT BE TRUSTED.
HER GIRL... SHE HAD TO GET HER GIRL.
OHHMMHHH
HHMMH
HRGGH
RAAHH
GRAAHH
OOOHHRR
AND NO ONE WOULD STAND IN HER WAY. NOT EVEN BOWKER... NO, ESPECIALLY NOT BOWKER.

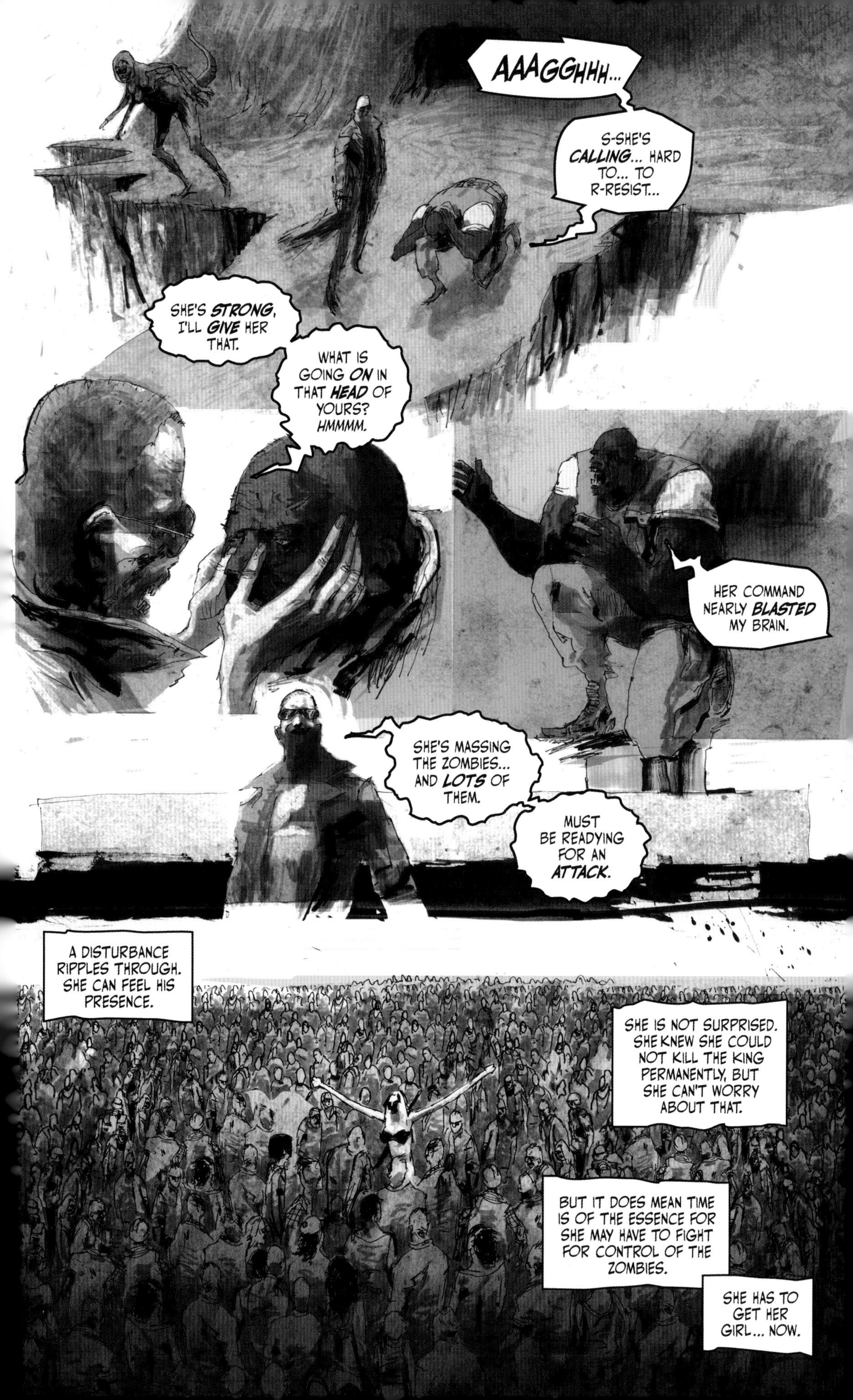
AAAGGHHH...
S-SHE'S CALLING... HARD TO... TO R-RESIST...
SHE'S STRONG, I'LL GIVE HER THAT.
WHAT IS GOING ON IN THAT HEAD OF YOURS? HMMMM.
HER COMMAND NEARLY BLASTED MY BRAIN.
SHE'S MASSING THE ZOMBIES... AND LOTS OF THEM.
MUST BE READYING FOR AN ATTACK.
A DISTURBANCE RIPPLES THROUGH. SHE CAN FEEL HIS PRESENCE.
SHE IS NOT SURPRISED. SHE KNEW SHE COULD NOT KILL THE KING PERMANENTLY, BUT SHE CAN'T WORRY ABOUT THAT.
BUT IT DOES MEAN TIME IS OF THE ESSENCE FOR SHE MAY HAVE TO FIGHT FOR CONTROL OF THE ZOMBIES.
SHE HAS TO GET HER GIRL... NOW.

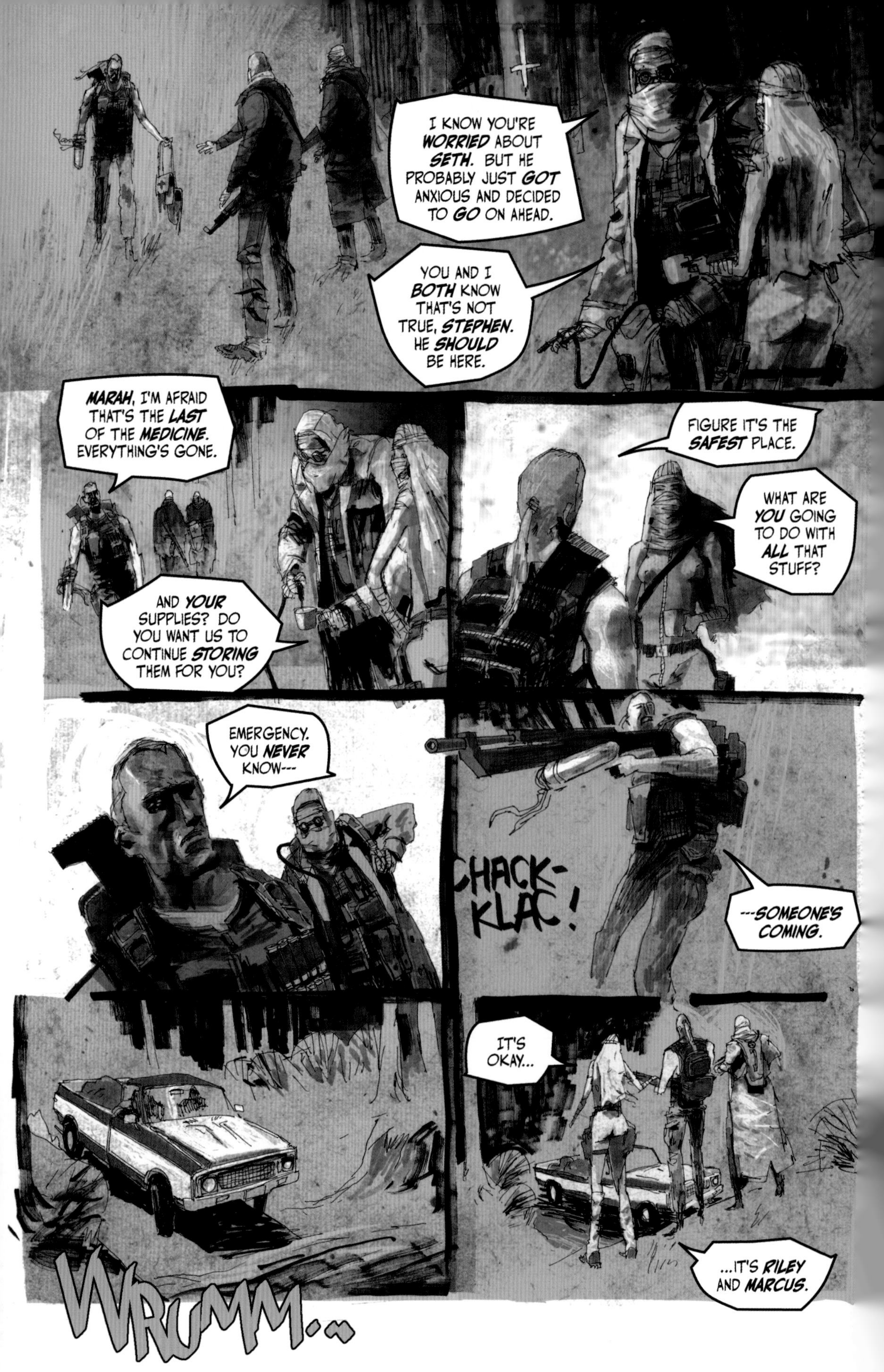
I KNOW YOU'RE WORRIED ABOUT SETH. BUT HE PROBABLY JUST GOT ANXIOUS AND DECIDED TO GO ON AHEAD.
YOU AND I BOTH KNOW THAT'S NOT TRUE, STEPHEN. HE SHOULD BE HERE.
MARAH, I'M AFRAID THAT'S THE LAST OF THE MEDICINE. EVERYTHING'S GONE.
AND YOUR SUPPLIES? DO YOU WANT US TO CONTINUE STORING THEM FOR YOU?
FIGURE IT'S THE SAFEST PLACE.
WHAT ARE YOU GOING TO DO WITH ALL THAT STUFF?
EMERGENCY. YOU NEVER KNOW---
CHACK-KLAC!
---SOMEONE'S COMING.
WRUMM..
IT'S OKAY...
...IT'S RILEY AND MARCUS.

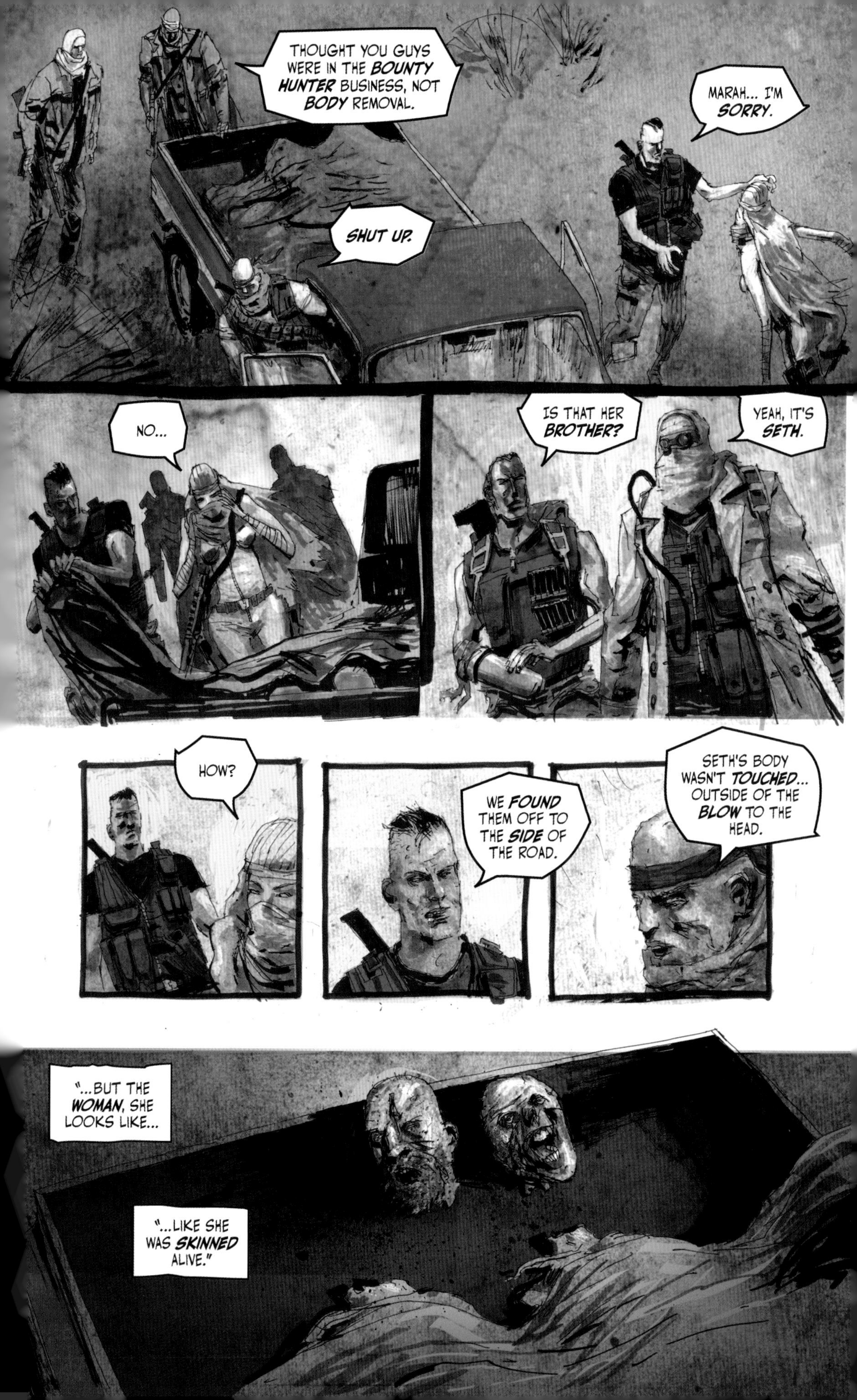
THOUGHT YOU GUYS WERE IN THE BOUNTY HUNTER BUSINESS, NOT BODY REMOVAL.
SHUT UP.
MARAH... I'M SORRY.
NO...
IS THAT HER BROTHER?
YEAH, IT'S SETH.
HOW?
WE FOUND THEM OFF TO THE SIDE OF THE ROAD.
SETH'S BODY WASN'T TOUCHED... OUTSIDE OF THE BLOW TO THE HEAD.
"...BUT THE WOMAN, SHE LOOKS LIKE...
"...LIKE SHE WAS SKINNED ALIVE."

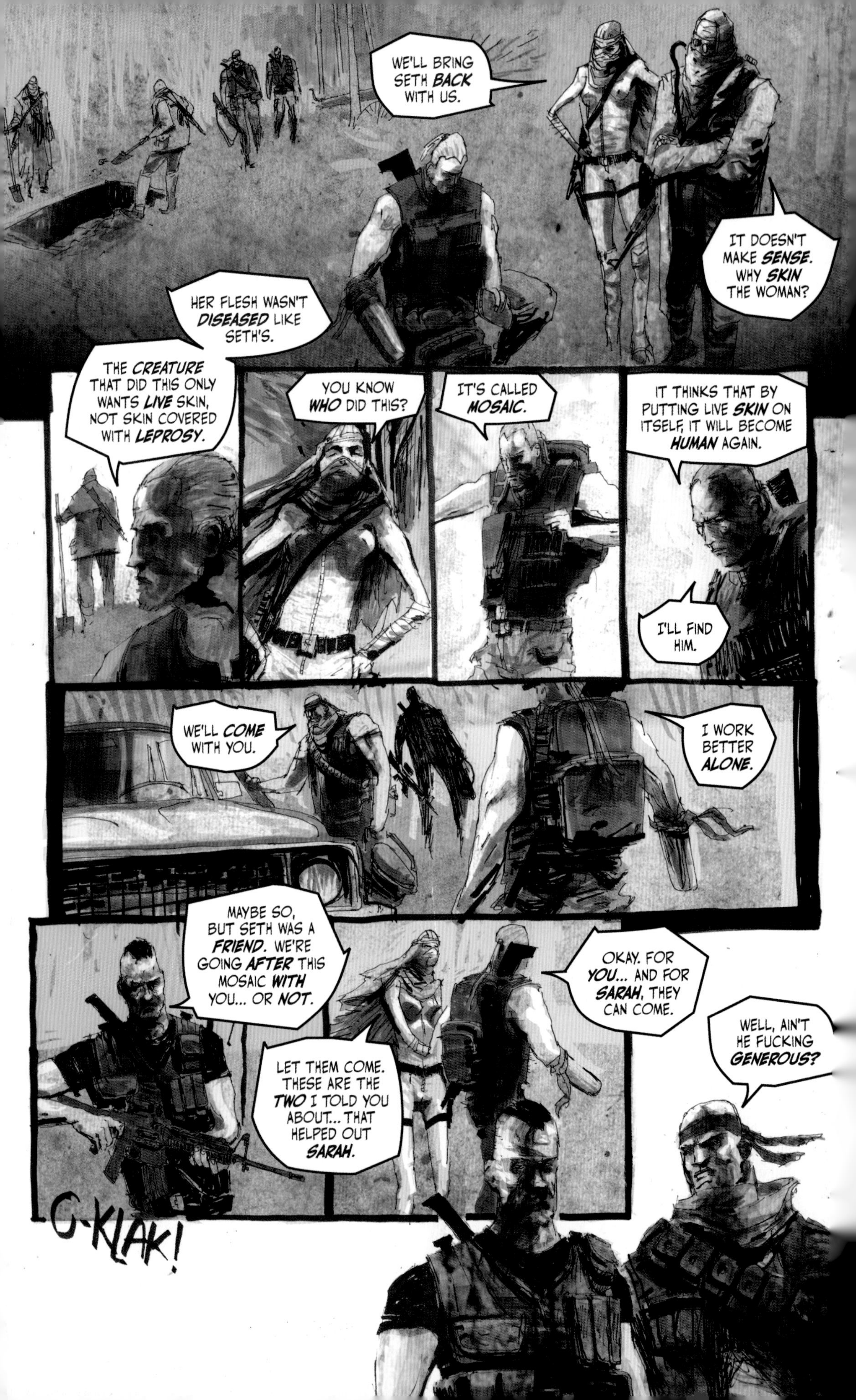
WE'LL BRING SETH BACK WITH US.
IT DOESN'T MAKE SENSE. WHY SKIN THE WOMAN?
HER FLESH WASN'T DISEASED LIKE SETH'S.
THE CREATURE THAT DID THIS ONLY WANTS LIVE SKIN, NOT SKIN COVERED WITH LEPROSY.
YOU KNOW WHO DID THIS?
IT'S CALLED MOSAIC.
IT THINKS THAT BY PUTTING LIVE SKIN ON ITSELF, IT WILL BECOME HUMAN AGAIN.
I'LL FIND HIM.
WE'LL COME WITH YOU.
I WORK BETTER ALONE.
MAYBE SO, BUT SETH WAS A FRIEND. WE'RE GOING AFTER THIS MOSAIC WITH YOU... OR NOT.
C-KLAK!
LET THEM COME. THESE ARE THE TWO I TOLD YOU ABOUT... THAT HELPED OUT SARAH.
OKAY. FOR YOU... AND FOR SARAH, THEY CAN COME.
WELL, AIN'T HE FUCKING GENEROUS?

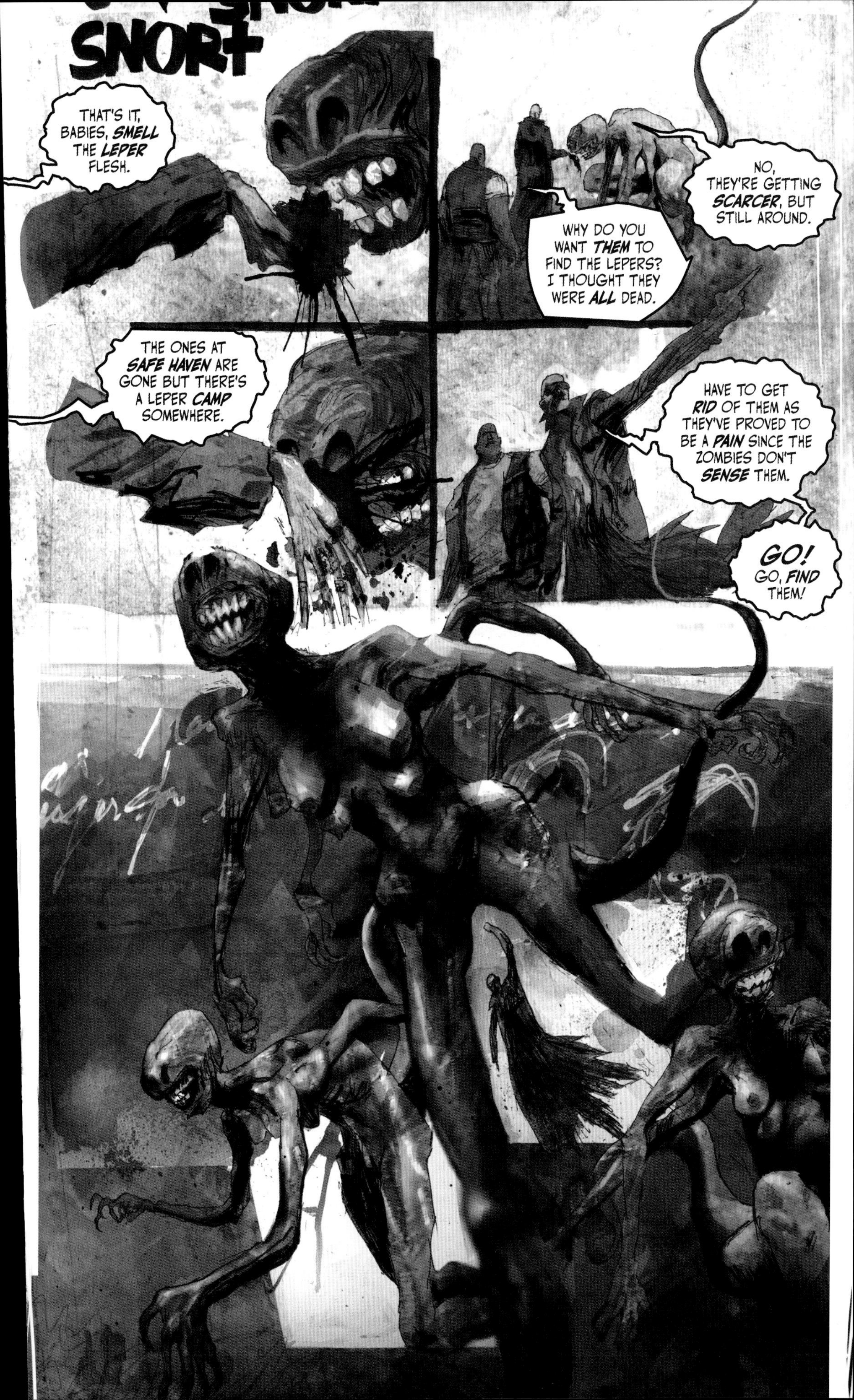
SNORT
THAT'S IT, BABIES, SMELL THE LEPER FLESH.
WHY DO YOU WANT THEM TO FIND THE LEPERS? I THOUGHT THEY WERE ALL DEAD.
NO, THEY'RE GETTING SCARCER, BUT STILL AROUND.
THE ONES AT SAFE HAVEN ARE GONE BUT THERE'S A LEPER CAMP SOMEWHERE.
HAVE TO GET RID OF THEM AS THEY'VE PROVED TO BE A PAIN SINCE THE ZOMBIES DON'T SENSE THEM.
GO! GO, FIND THEM!

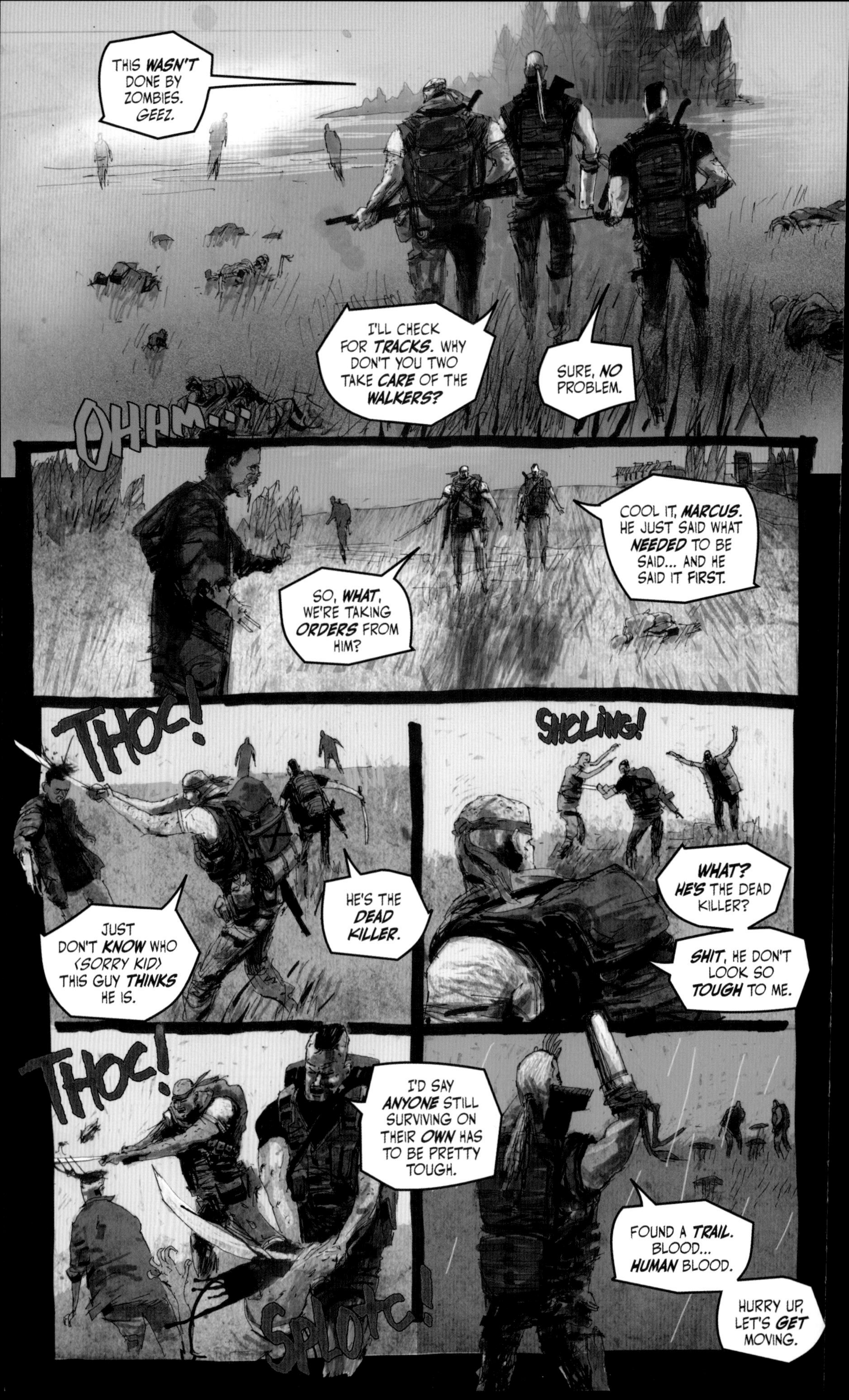
THIS WASN'T DONE BY ZOMBIES. GEEZ.
I'LL CHECK FOR TRACKS. WHY DON'T YOU TWO TAKE CARE OF THE WALKERS?
SURE, NO PROBLEM.
OHHM...
SO, WHAT, WE'RE TAKING ORDERS FROM HIM?
COOL IT, MARCUS. HE JUST SAID WHAT NEEDED TO BE SAID... AND HE SAID IT FIRST.
THOC!
JUST DON'T KNOW WHO (SORRY KID) THIS GUY THINKS HE IS.
HE'S THE DEAD KILLER.
SHCLING!
WHAT? HE'S THE DEAD KILLER?
SHIT, HE DON'T LOOK SO TOUGH TO ME.
THOC!
I'D SAY ANYONE STILL SURVIVING ON THEIR OWN HAS TO BE PRETTY TOUGH.
SPLOTC!
FOUND A TRAIL. BLOOD... HUMAN BLOOD.
HURRY UP, LET'S GET MOVING.

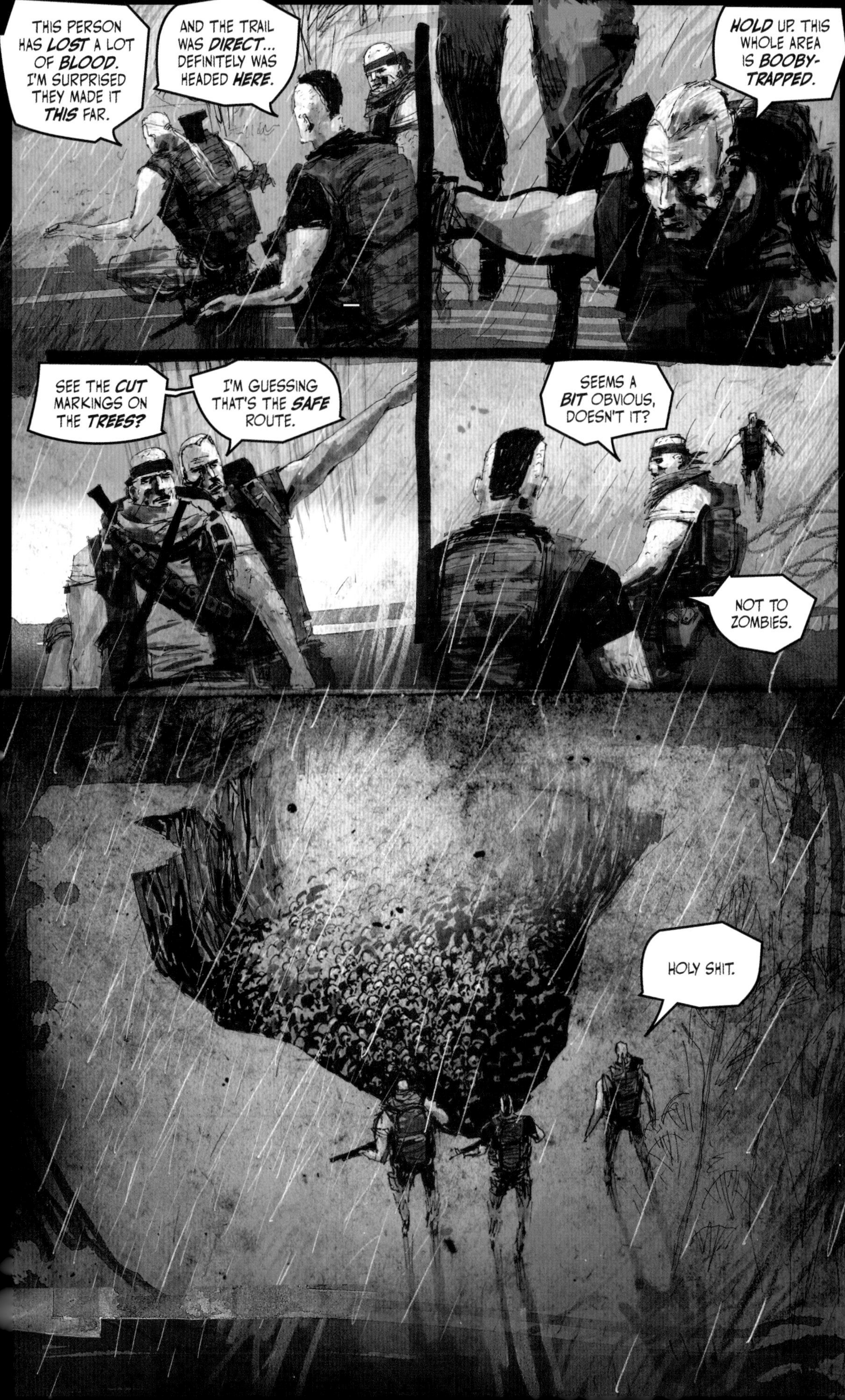

THIS PERSON HAS LOST A LOT OF BLOOD. I'M SURPRISED THEY MADE IT THIS FAR.
AND THE TRAIL WAS DIRECT... DEFINITELY WAS HEADED HERE.
HOLD UP. THIS WHOLE AREA IS BOOBY-TRAPPED.
SEE THE CUT MARKINGS ON THE TREES?
I'M GUESSING THAT'S THE SAFE ROUTE.
SEEMS A BIT OBVIOUS, DOESN'T IT?
NOT TO ZOMBIES.
HOLY SHIT.

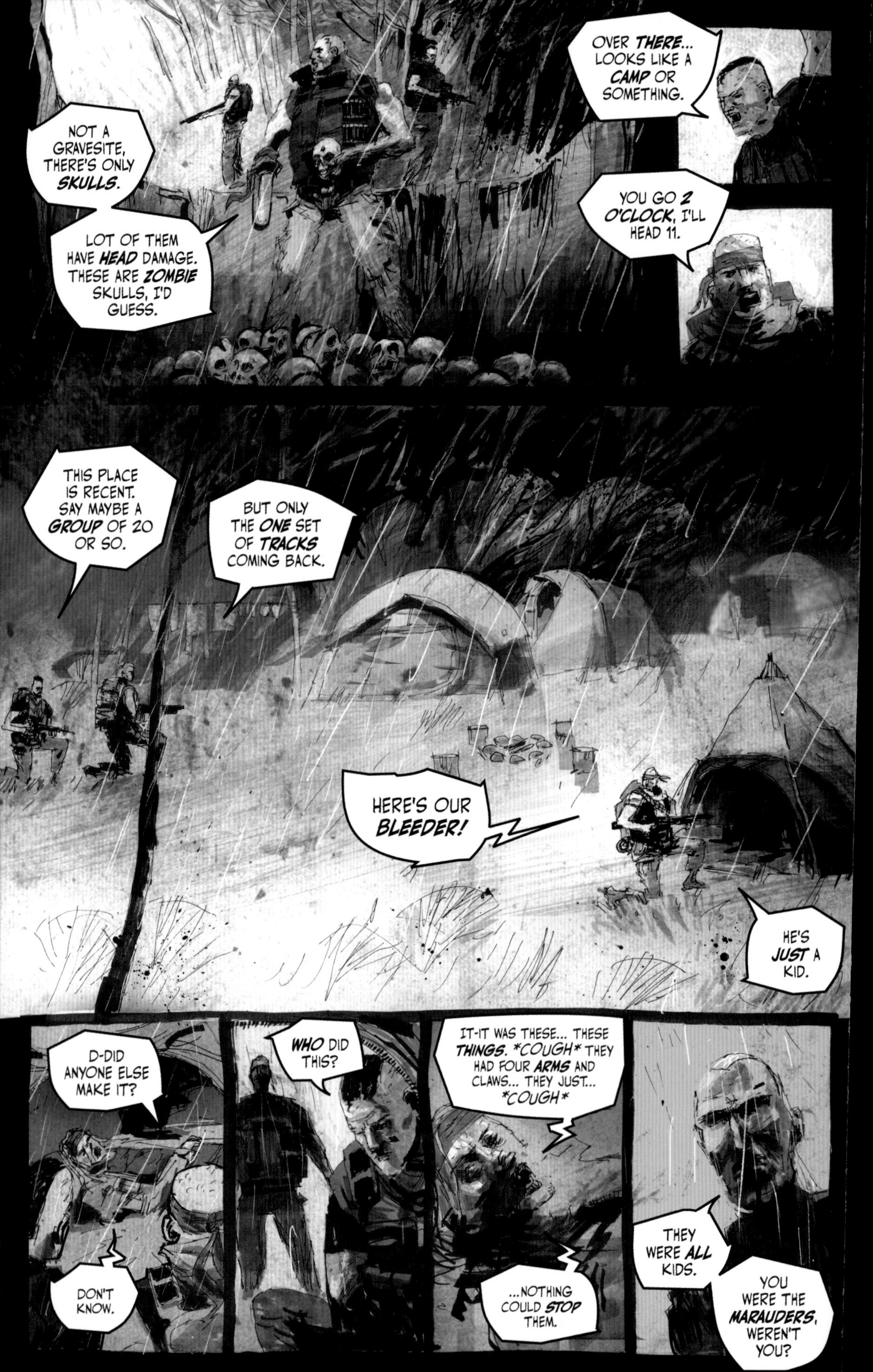
NOT A GRAVESITE, THERE'S ONLY SKULLS.
LOT OF THEM HAVE HEAD DAMAGE. THESE ARE ZOMBIE SKULLS, I'D GUESS.
OVER THERE... LOOKS LIKE A CAMP OR SOMETHING.
YOU GO 2 O'CLOCK, I'LL HEAD 11.
THIS PLACE IS RECENT. SAY MAYBE A GROUP OF 20 OR SO.
BUT ONLY THE ONE SET OF TRACKS COMING BACK.
HERE'S OUR BLEEDER!
HE'S JUST A KID.
D-DID ANYONE ELSE MAKE IT?
DON'T KNOW.
WHO DID THIS?
IT-IT WAS THESE... THESE THINGS. *COUGH* THEY HAD FOUR ARMS AND CLAWS... THEY JUST... *COUGH*
...NOTHING COULD STOP THEM.
THEY WERE ALL KIDS.
YOU WERE THE MARAUDERS, WEREN'T YOU?

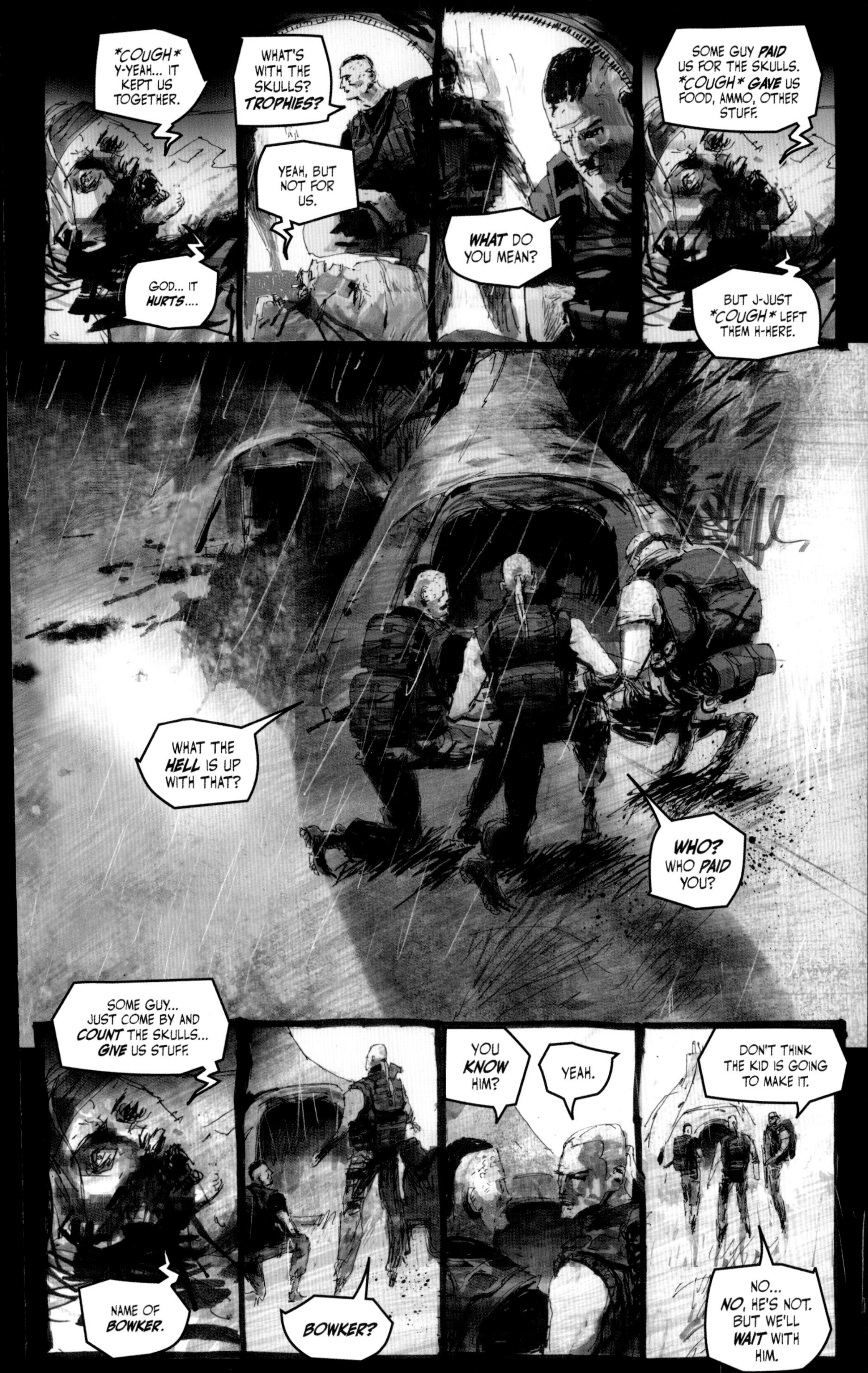
COUGH Y-YEAH... IT KEPT US TOGETHER.
GOD... IT HURTS....
WHAT'S WITH THE SKULLS? TROPHIES?
YEAH, BUT NOT FOR US.
WHAT DO YOU MEAN?
SOME GUY PAID US FOR THE SKULLS. *COUGH* GAVE US FOOD, AMMO, OTHER STUFF.
BUT J-JUST *COUGH* LEFT THEM H-HERE.
WHAT THE HELL IS UP WITH THAT?
WHO? WHO PAID YOU?
SOME GUY... JUST COME BY AND COUNT THE SKULLS... GIVE US STUFF.
NAME OF BOWKER.
BOWKER?
YOU KNOW HIM?
YEAH.
DON'T THINK THE KID IS GOING TO MAKE IT.
NO... NO, HE'S NOT. BUT WE'LL WAIT WITH HIM.

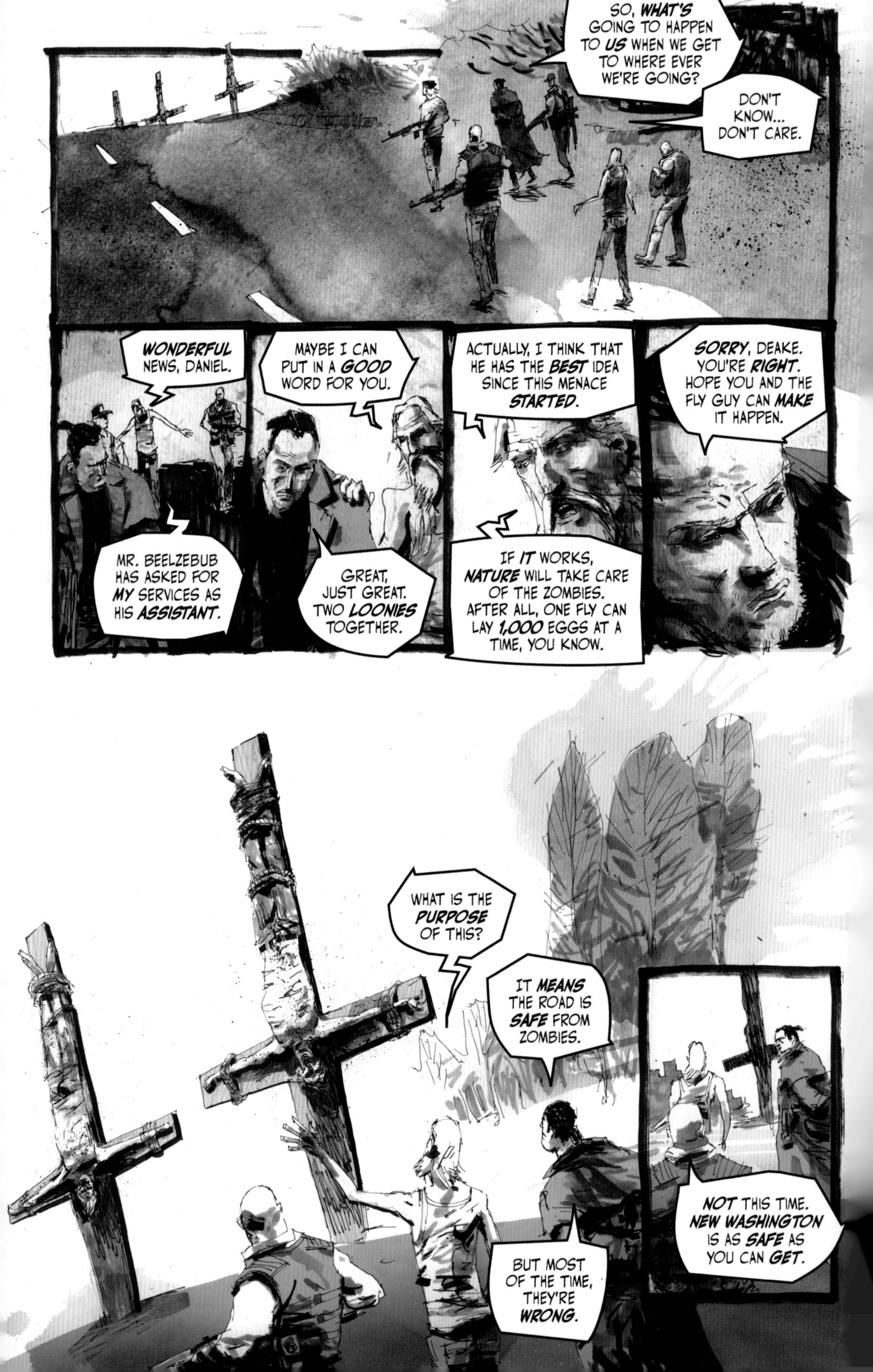

SO, WHAT'S GOING TO HAPPEN TO US WHEN WE GET TO WHERE EVER WE'RE GOING?
DON'T KNOW... DON'T CARE.
WONDERFUL NEWS, DANIEL.
MR. BEELZEBUB HAS ASKED FOR MY SERVICES AS HIS ASSISTANT.
MAYBE I CAN PUT IN A GOOD WORD FOR YOU.
GREAT, JUST GREAT. TWO LOONIES TOGETHER.
ACTUALLY, I THINK THAT HE HAS THE BEST IDEA SINCE THIS MENACE STARTED.
IF IT WORKS, NATURE WILL TAKE CARE OF THE ZOMBIES. AFTER ALL, ONE FLY CAN LAY 1,000 EGGS AT A TIME, YOU KNOW.
SORRY, DEAKE. YOU'RE RIGHT. HOPE YOU AND THE FLY GUY CAN MAKE IT HAPPEN.
WHAT IS THE PURPOSE OF THIS?
IT MEANS THE ROAD IS SAFE FROM ZOMBIES.
BUT MOST OF THE TIME, THEY'RE WRONG.
NOT THIS TIME. NEW WASHINGTON IS AS SAFE AS YOU CAN GET.

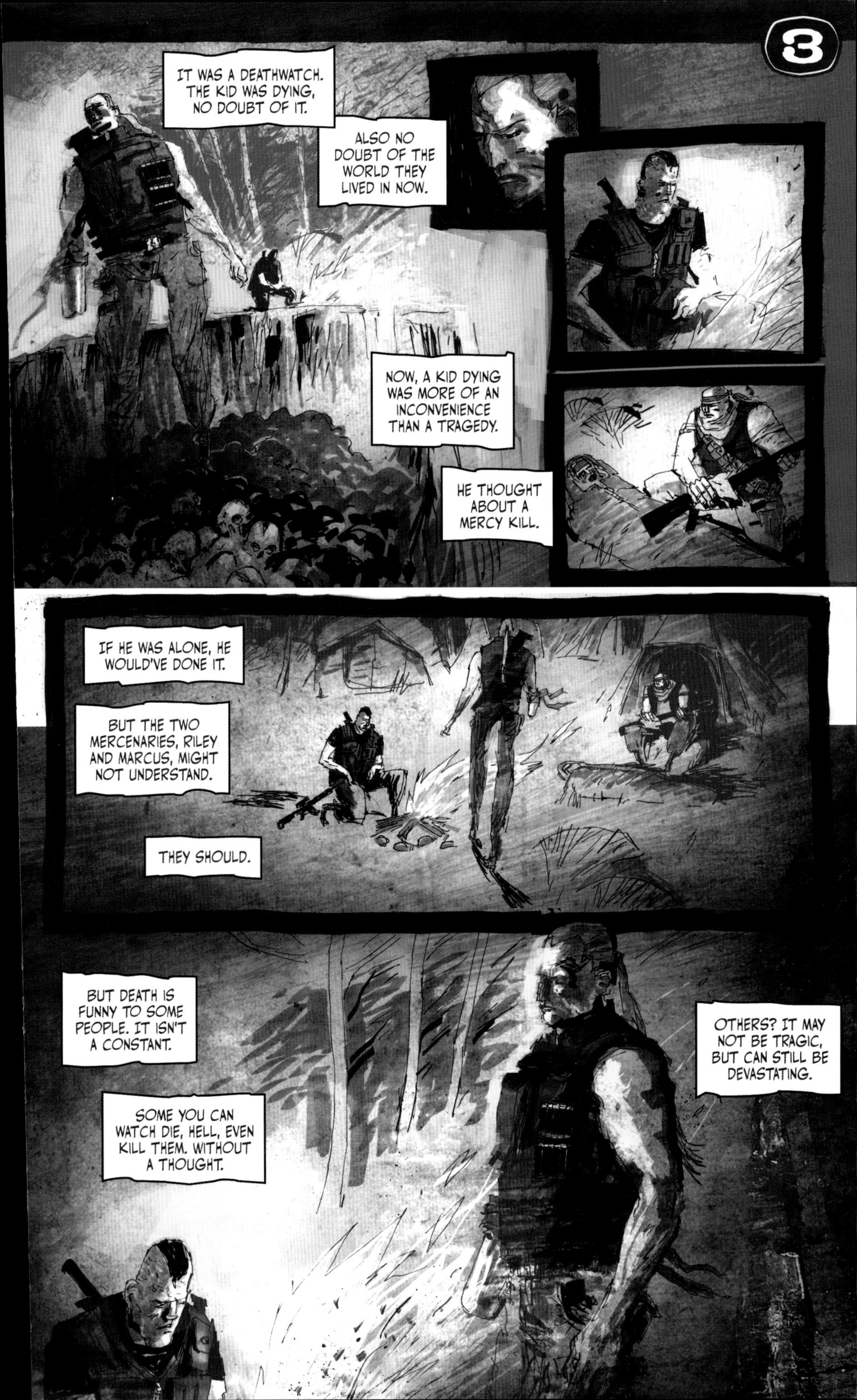
3
IT WAS A DEATHWATCH. THE KID WAS DYING, NO DOUBT OF IT.
ALSO NO DOUBT OF THE WORLD THEY LIVED IN NOW.
NOW, A KID DYING WAS MORE OF AN INCONVENIENCE THAN A TRAGEDY.
HE THOUGHT ABOUT A MERCY KILL.
IF HE WAS ALONE, HE WOULD'VE DONE IT.
BUT THE TWO MERCENARIES, RILEY AND MARCUS, MIGHT NOT UNDERSTAND.
THEY SHOULD.
BUT DEATH IS FUNNY TO SOME PEOPLE. IT ISN'T A CONSTANT.
SOME YOU CAN WATCH DIE, HELL, EVEN KILL THEM. WITHOUT A THOUGHT.
OTHERS? IT MAY NOT BE TRAGIC, BUT CAN STILL BE DEVASTATING.

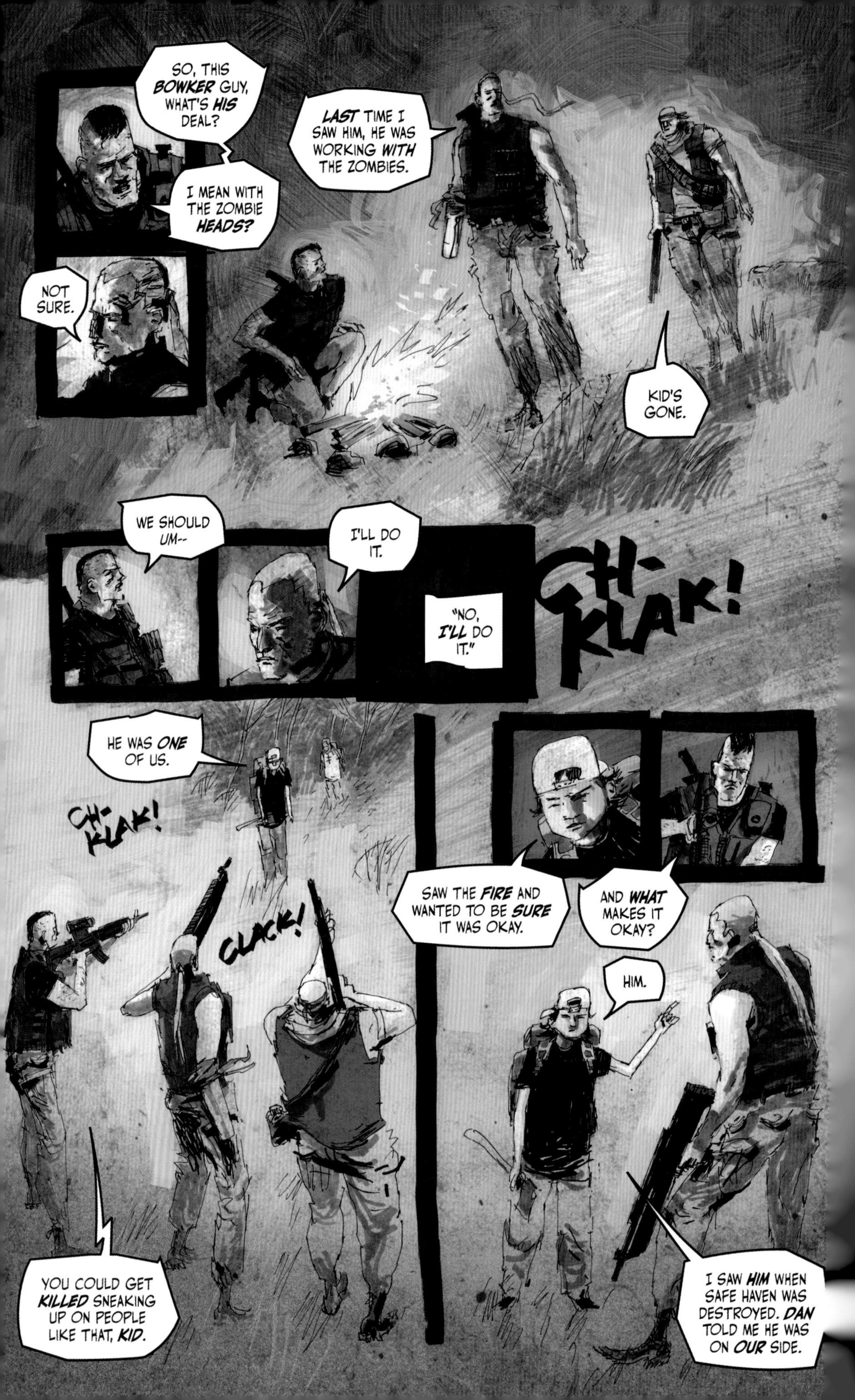

SO, THIS BOWKER GUY, WHAT'S HIS DEAL?
I MEAN WITH THE ZOMBIE HEADS?
LAST TIME I SAW HIM, HE WAS WORKING WITH THE ZOMBIES.
NOT SURE.
KID'S GONE.
WE SHOULD UM--
I'LL DO IT.
"NO, I'LL DO IT."
CH-KLAK!
HE WAS ONE OF US.
CH-KLAK!
CLACK!
YOU COULD GET KILLED SNEAKING UP ON PEOPLE LIKE THAT, KID.
SAW THE FIRE AND WANTED TO BE SURE IT WAS OKAY.
AND WHAT MAKES IT OKAY?
HIM.
I SAW HIM WHEN SAFE HAVEN WAS DESTROYED. DAN TOLD ME HE WAS ON OUR SIDE.

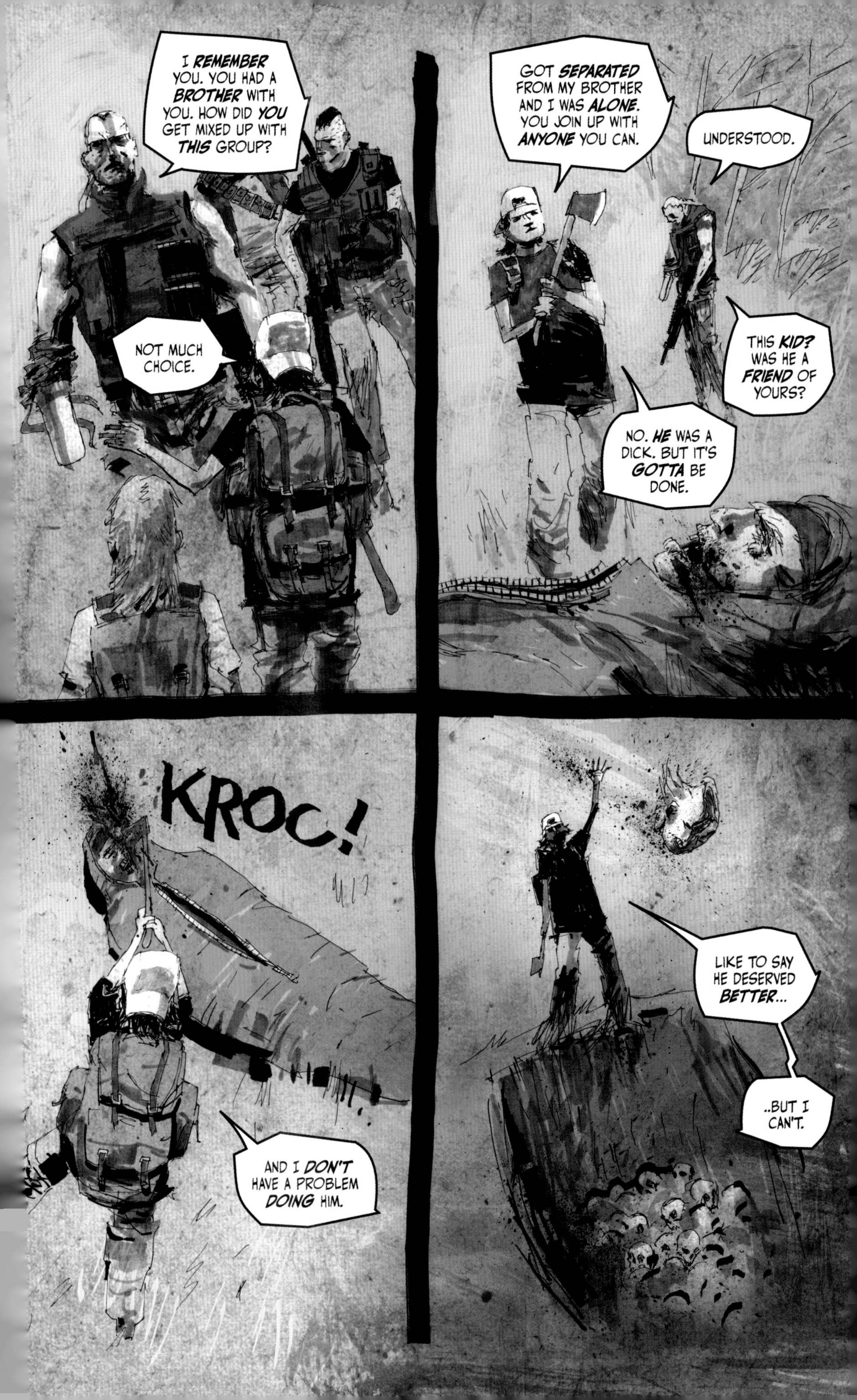
I REMEMBER YOU. YOU HAD A BROTHER WITH YOU. HOW DID YOU GET MIXED UP WITH THIS GROUP?
NOT MUCH CHOICE.
GOT SEPARATED FROM MY BROTHER AND I WAS ALONE. YOU JOIN UP WITH ANYONE YOU CAN.
UNDERSTOOD.
THIS KID? WAS HE A FRIEND OF YOURS?
NO. HE WAS A DICK. BUT IT'S GOTTA BE DONE.
KROC!
AND I DON'T HAVE A PROBLEM DOING HIM.
LIKE TO SAY HE DESERVED BETTER...
..BUT I CAN'T.

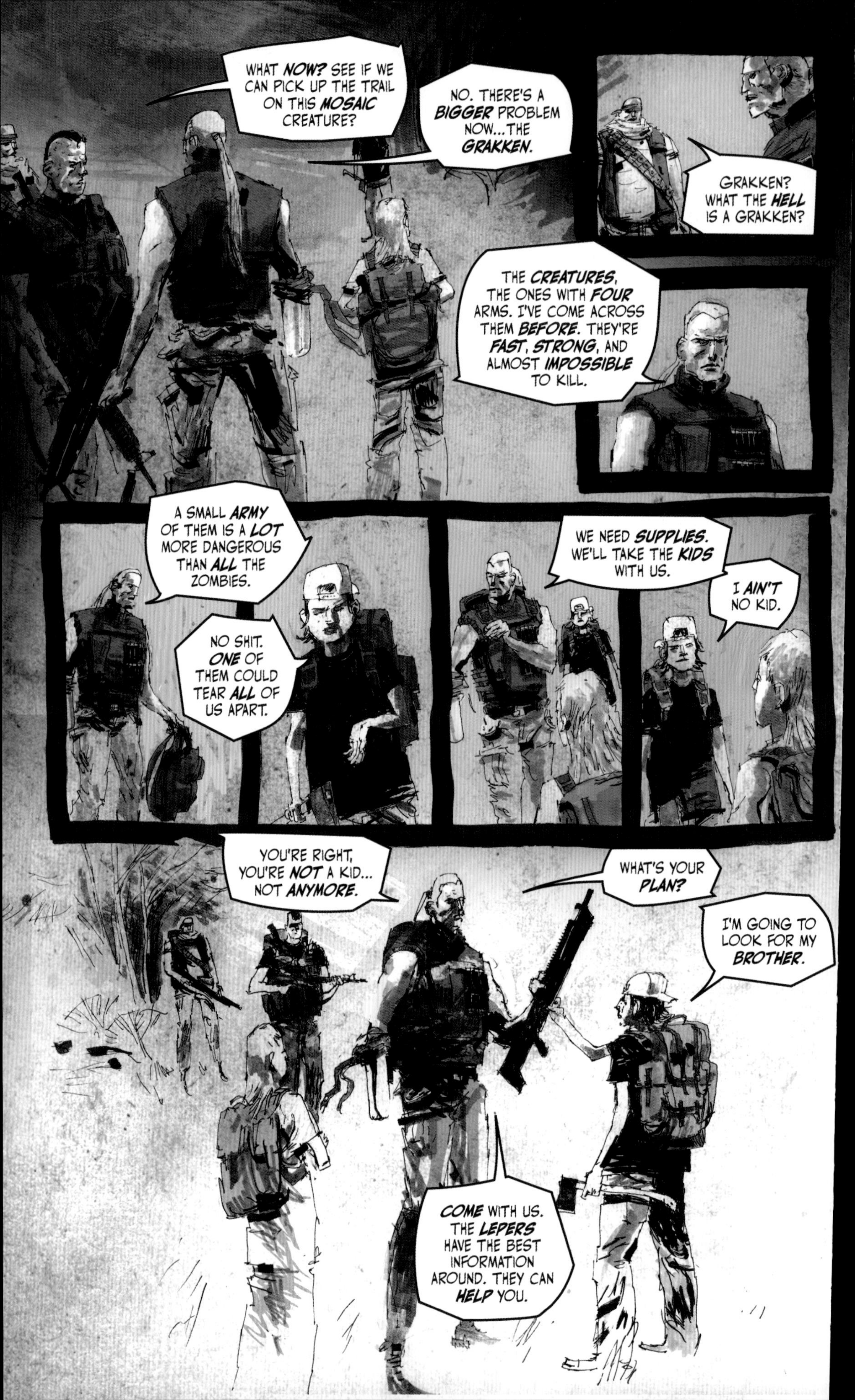
WHAT NOW? SEE IF WE CAN PICK UP THE TRAIL ON THIS MOSAIC CREATURE?
NO. THERE'S A BIGGER PROBLEM NOW...THE GRAKKEN.
GRAKKEN? WHAT THE HELL IS A GRAKKEN?
THE CREATURES, THE ONES WITH FOUR ARMS. I'VE COME ACROSS THEM BEFORE. THEY'RE FAST, STRONG, AND ALMOST IMPOSSIBLE TO KILL.
A SMALL ARMY OF THEM IS A LOT MORE DANGEROUS THAN ALL THE ZOMBIES.
NO SHIT. ONE OF THEM COULD TEAR ALL OF US APART.
WE NEED SUPPLIES. WE'LL TAKE THE KIDS WITH US.
I AIN'T NO KID.
YOU'RE RIGHT, YOU'RE NOT A KID... NOT ANYMORE.
WHAT'S YOUR PLAN?
I'M GOING TO LOOK FOR MY BROTHER.
COME WITH US. THE LEPERS HAVE THE BEST INFORMATION AROUND. THEY CAN HELP YOU.

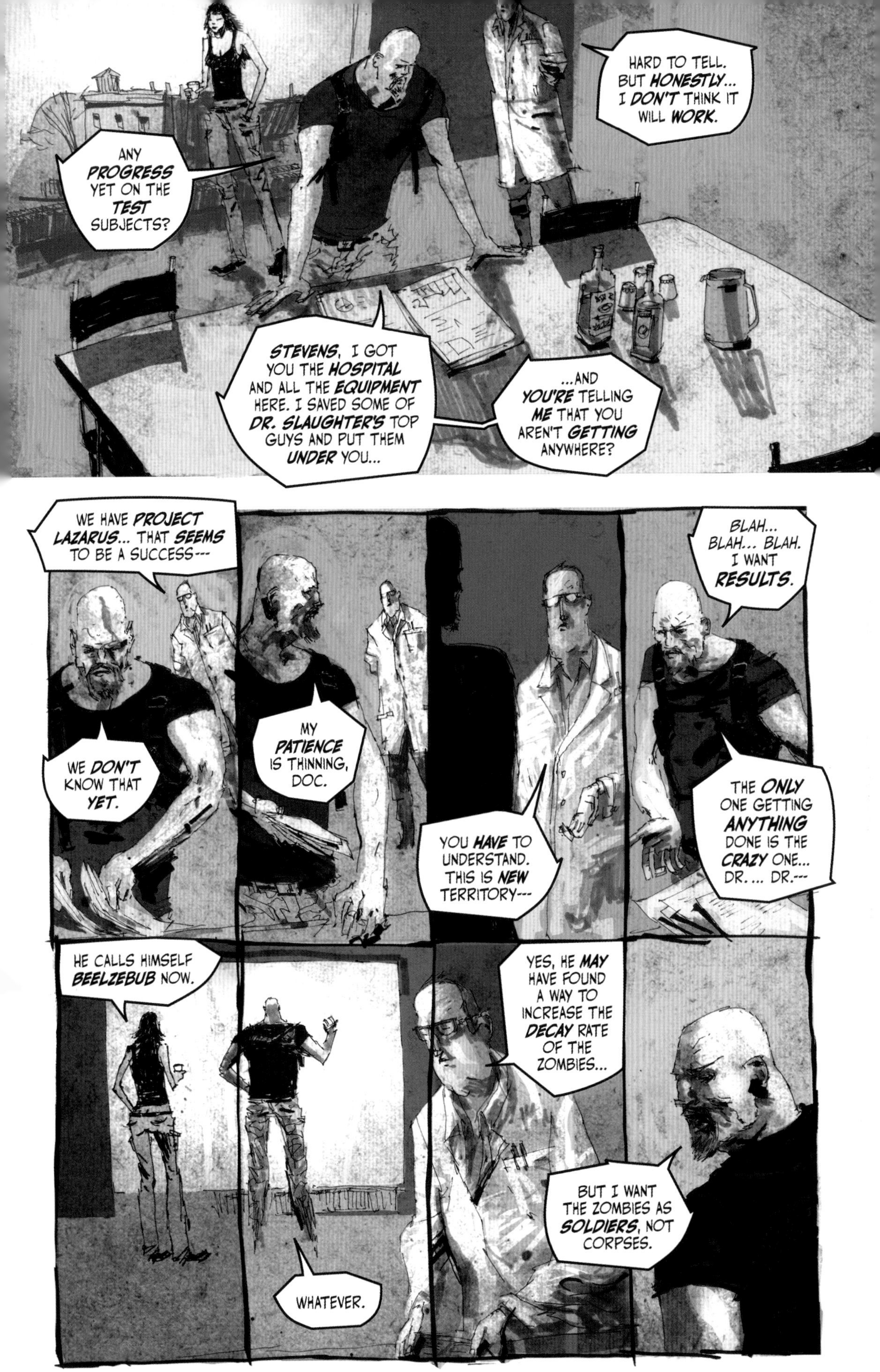
ANY PROGRESS YET ON THE TEST SUBJECTS?
HARD TO TELL. BUT HONESTLY... I DON'T THINK IT WILL WORK.
STEVENS, I GOT YOU THE HOSPITAL AND ALL THE EQUIPMENT HERE. I SAVED SOME OF DR. SLAUGHTER'S TOP GUYS AND PUT THEM UNDER YOU...
...AND YOU'RE TELLING ME THAT YOU AREN'T GETTING ANYWHERE?
WE HAVE PROJECT LAZARUS... THAT SEEMS TO BE A SUCCESS---
WE DON'T KNOW THAT YET.
MY PATIENCE IS THINNING, DOC.
YOU HAVE TO UNDERSTAND. THIS IS NEW TERRITORY---
BLAH... BLAH... BLAH. I WANT RESULTS.
THE ONLY ONE GETTING ANYTHING DONE IS THE CRAZY ONE... DR. ... DR.---
HE CALLS HIMSELF BEELZEBUB NOW.
WHATEVER.
YES, HE MAY HAVE FOUND A WAY TO INCREASE THE DECAY RATE OF THE ZOMBIES...
BUT I WANT THE ZOMBIES AS SOLDIERS, NOT CORPSES.

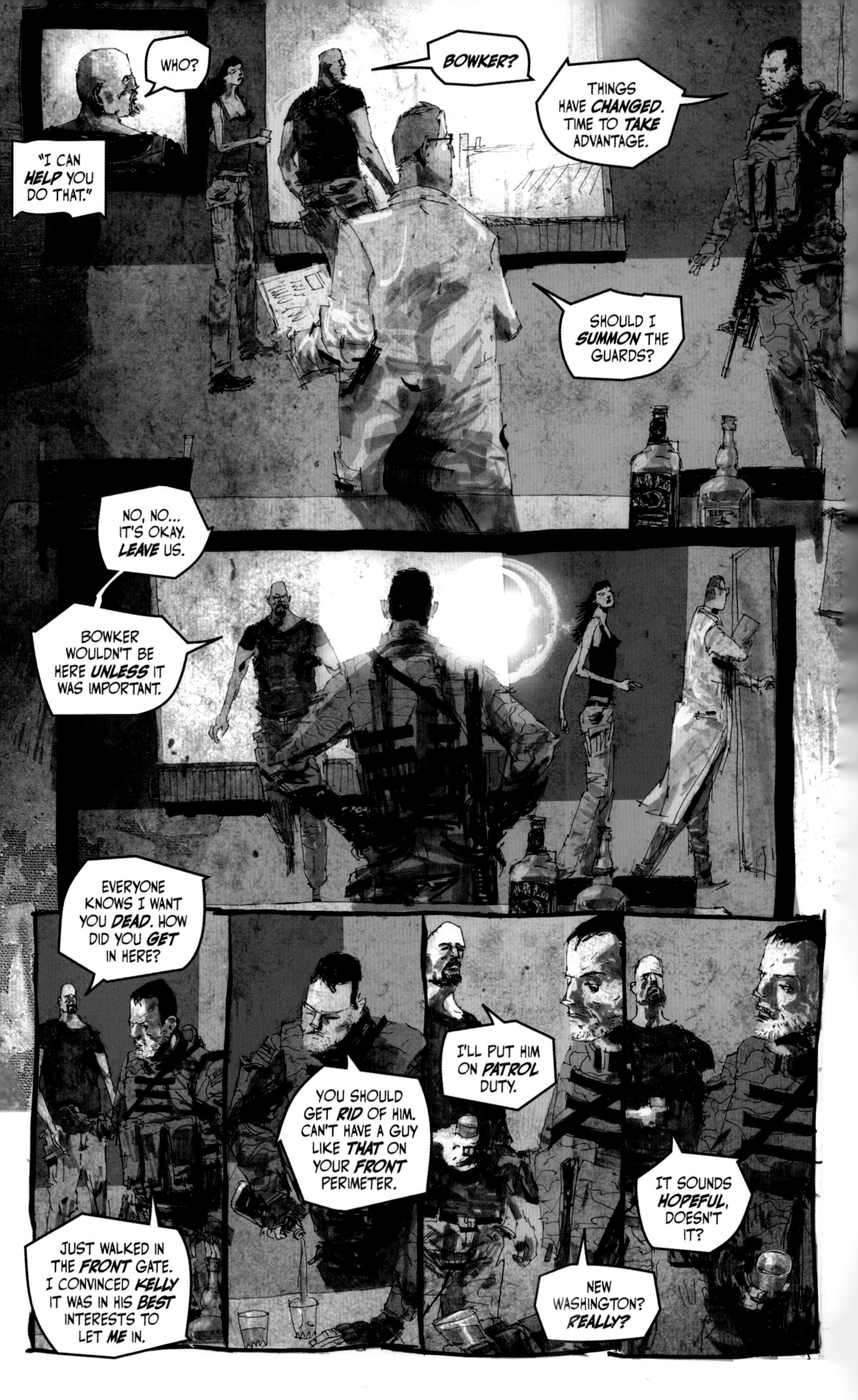
WHO?
"I CAN HELP YOU DO THAT."
BOWKER?
THINGS HAVE CHANGED. TIME TO TAKE ADVANTAGE.
SHOULD I SUMMON THE GUARDS?
NO, NO... IT'S OKAY. LEAVE US.
BOWKER WOULDN'T BE HERE UNLESS IT WAS IMPORTANT.
EVERYONE KNOWS I WANT YOU DEAD. HOW DID YOU GET IN HERE?
JUST WALKED IN THE FRONT GATE. I CONVINCED KELLY IT WAS IN HIS BEST INTERESTS TO LET ME IN.
YOU SHOULD GET RID OF HIM. CAN'T HAVE A GUY LIKE THAT ON YOUR FRONT PERIMETER.
I'LL PUT HIM ON PATROL DUTY.
NEW WASHINGTON? REALLY?
IT SOUNDS HOPEFUL, DOESN'T IT?

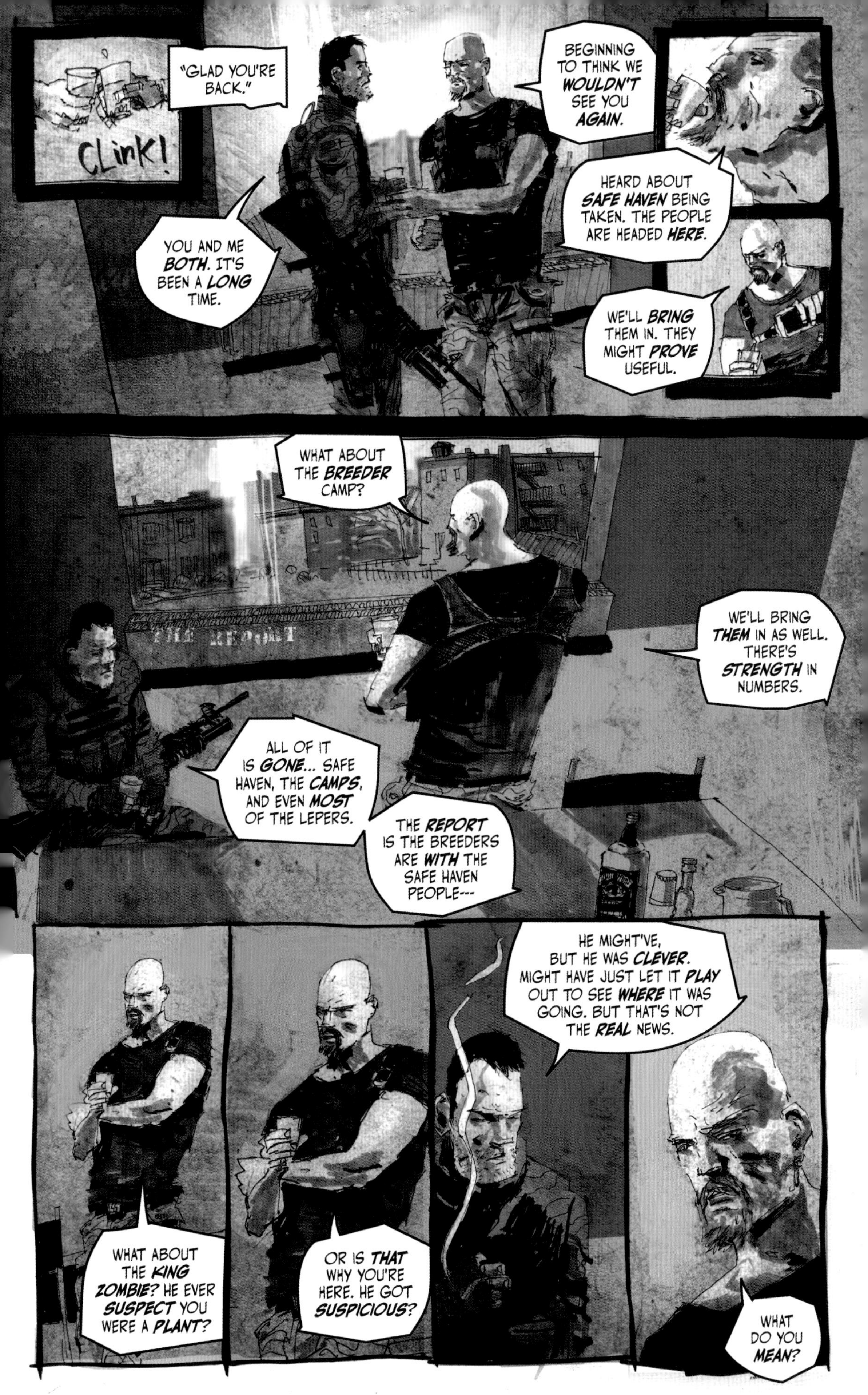
CLINK!
"GLAD YOU'RE BACK."
BEGINNING TO THINK WE WOULDN'T SEE YOU AGAIN.
YOU AND ME BOTH. IT'S BEEN A LONG TIME.
HEARD ABOUT SAFE HAVEN BEING TAKEN. THE PEOPLE ARE HEADED HERE.
WE'LL BRING THEM IN. THEY MIGHT PROVE USEFUL.
WHAT ABOUT THE BREEDER CAMP?
THE REPORT
WE'LL BRING THEM IN AS WELL. THERE'S STRENGTH IN NUMBERS.
ALL OF IT IS GONE... SAFE HAVEN, THE CAMPS, AND EVEN MOST OF THE LEPERS.
THE REPORT IS THE BREEDERS ARE WITH THE SAFE HAVEN PEOPLE---
WHAT ABOUT THE KING ZOMBIE? HE EVER SUSPECT YOU WERE A PLANT?
OR IS THAT WHY YOU'RE HERE. HE GOT SUSPICIOUS?
HE MIGHT'VE, BUT HE WAS CLEVER. MIGHT HAVE JUST LET IT PLAY OUT TO SEE WHERE IT WAS GOING. BUT THAT'S NOT THE REAL NEWS.
WHAT DO YOU MEAN?

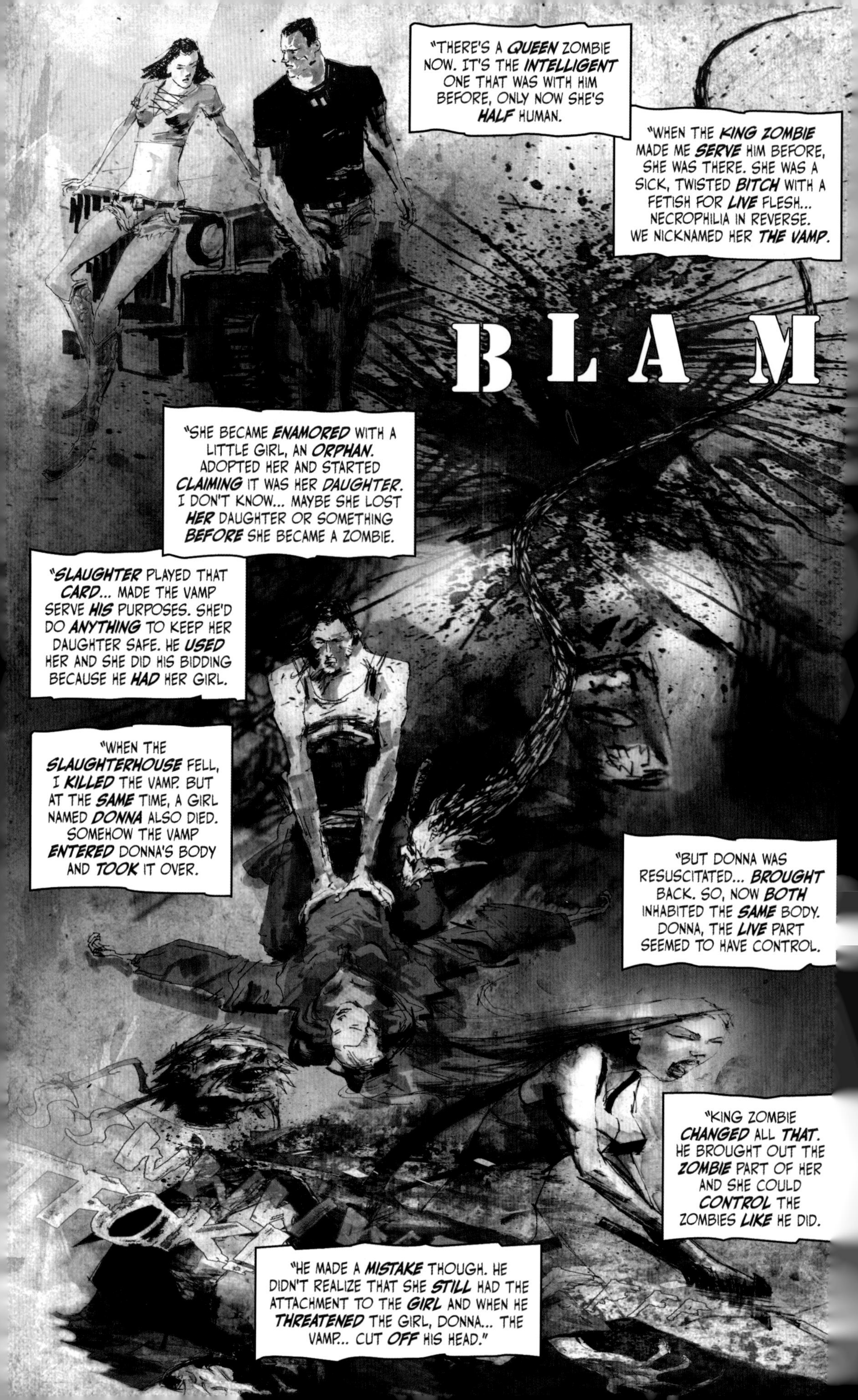
"THERE'S A QUEEN ZOMBIE NOW. IT'S THE INTELLIGENT ONE THAT WAS WITH HIM BEFORE, ONLY NOW SHE'S HALF HUMAN.
"WHEN THE KING ZOMBIE MADE ME SERVE HIM BEFORE, SHE WAS THERE. SHE WAS A SICK, TWISTED BITCH WITH A FETISH FOR LIVE FLESH... NECROPHILIA IN REVERSE. WE NICKNAMED HER THE VAMP.
BLAM
"SHE BECAME ENAMORED WITH A LITTLE GIRL, AN ORPHAN. ADOPTED HER AND STARTED CLAIMING IT WAS HER DAUGHTER. I DON'T KNOW... MAYBE SHE LOST HER DAUGHTER OR SOMETHING BEFORE SHE BECAME A ZOMBIE.
"SLAUGHTER PLAYED THAT CARD... MADE THE VAMP SERVE HIS PURPOSES. SHE'D DO ANYTHING TO KEEP HER DAUGHTER SAFE. HE USED HER AND SHE DID HIS BIDDING BECAUSE HE HAD HER GIRL.
"WHEN THE SLAUGHTERHOUSE FELL, I KILLED THE VAMP. BUT AT THE SAME TIME, A GIRL NAMED DONNA ALSO DIED. SOMEHOW THE VAMP ENTERED DONNA'S BODY AND TOOK IT OVER.
"BUT DONNA WAS RESUSCITATED... BROUGHT BACK. SO, NOW BOTH INHABITED THE SAME BODY. DONNA, THE LIVE PART SEEMED TO HAVE CONTROL.
"KING ZOMBIE CHANGED ALL THAT. HE BROUGHT OUT THE ZOMBIE PART OF HER AND SHE COULD CONTROL THE ZOMBIES LIKE HE DID.
"HE MADE A MISTAKE THOUGH. HE DIDN'T REALIZE THAT SHE STILL HAD THE ATTACHMENT TO THE GIRL AND WHEN HE THREATENED THE GIRL, DONNA... THE VAMP... CUT OFF HIS HEAD."

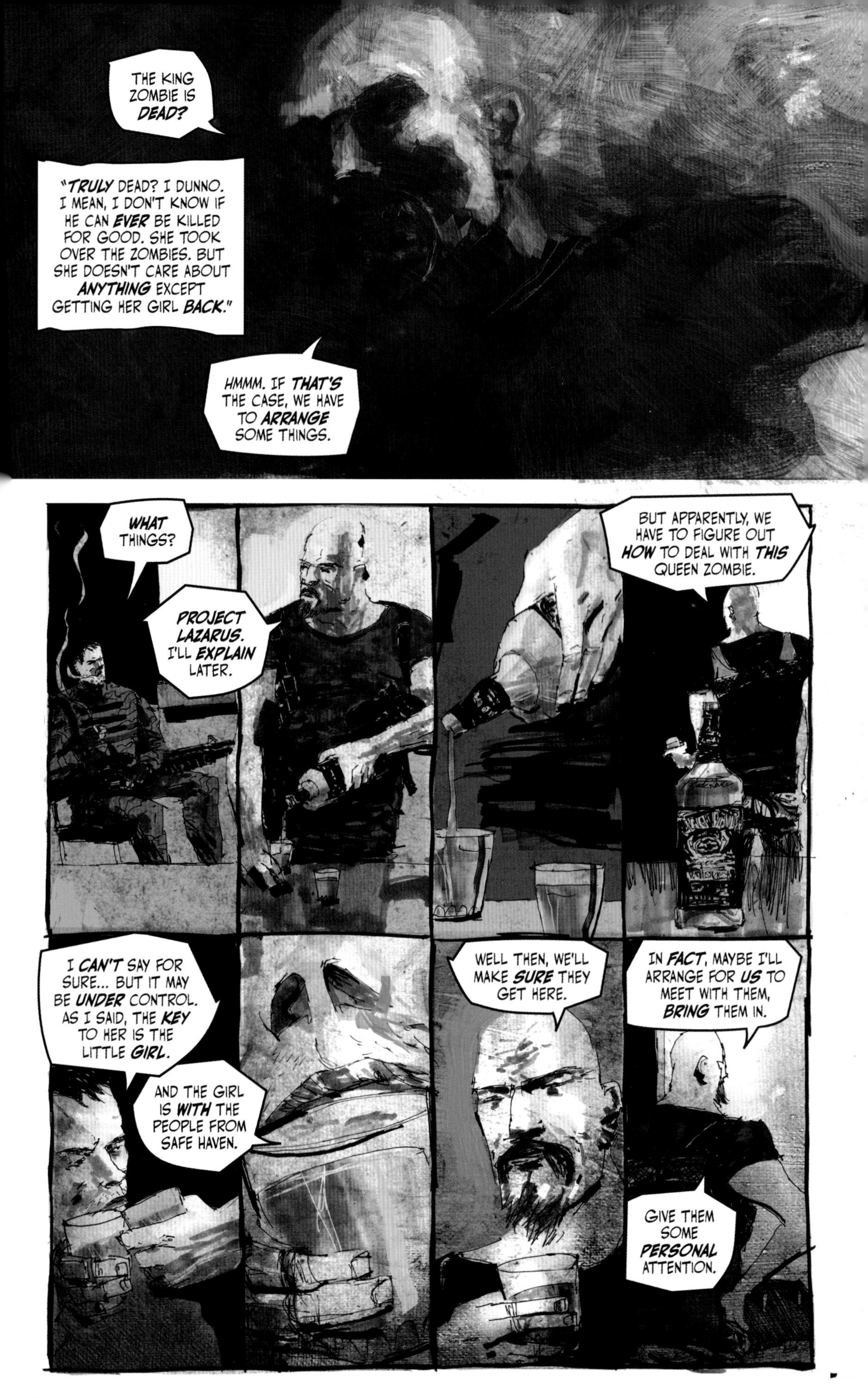
THE KING ZOMBIE IS DEAD?
"TRULY DEAD? I DUNNO. I MEAN, I DON'T KNOW IF HE CAN EVER BE KILLED FOR GOOD. SHE TOOK OVER THE ZOMBIES. BUT SHE DOESN'T CARE ABOUT ANYTHING EXCEPT GETTING HER GIRL BACK."
HMMM. IF THAT'S THE CASE, WE HAVE TO ARRANGE SOME THINGS.
WHAT THINGS?
PROJECT LAZARUS. I'LL EXPLAIN LATER.
BUT APPARENTLY, WE HAVE TO FIGURE OUT HOW TO DEAL WITH THIS QUEEN ZOMBIE.
I CAN'T SAY FOR SURE... BUT IT MAY BE UNDER CONTROL. AS I SAID, THE KEY TO HER IS THE LITTLE GIRL.
AND THE GIRL IS WITH THE PEOPLE FROM SAFE HAVEN.
WELL THEN, WE'LL MAKE SURE THEY GET HERE.
IN FACT, MAYBE I'LL ARRANGE FOR US TO MEET WITH THEM, BRING THEM IN.
GIVE THEM SOME PERSONAL ATTENTION.

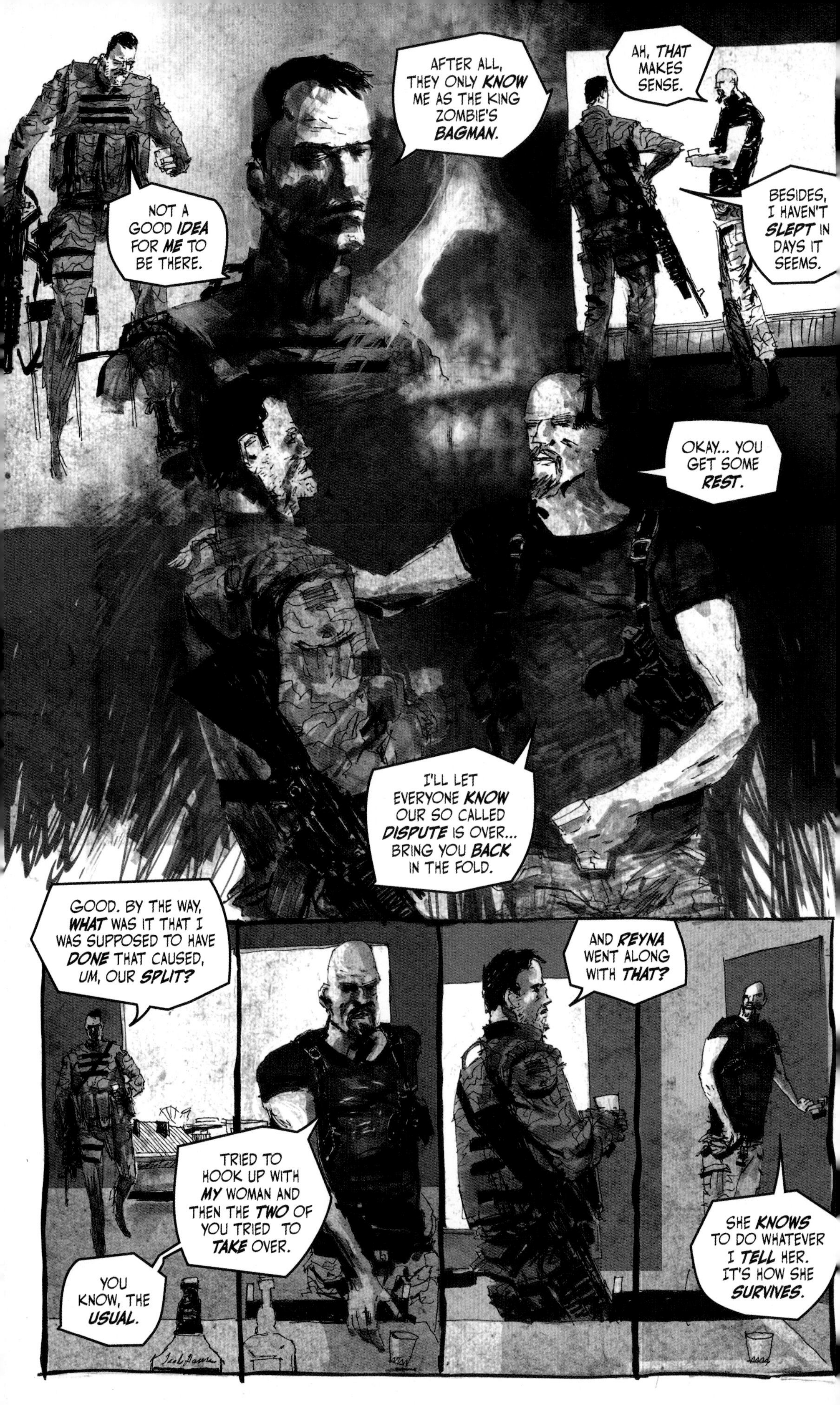
NOT A GOOD IDEA FOR ME TO BE THERE.
AFTER ALL, THEY ONLY KNOW ME AS THE KING ZOMBIE'S BAGMAN.
AH, THAT MAKES SENSE.
BESIDES, I HAVEN'T SLEPT IN DAYS IT SEEMS.
OKAY... YOU GET SOME REST.
I'LL LET EVERYONE KNOW OUR SO CALLED DISPUTE IS OVER... BRING YOU BACK IN THE FOLD.
GOOD. BY THE WAY, WHAT WAS IT THAT I WAS SUPPOSED TO HAVE DONE THAT CAUSED, UM, OUR SPLIT?
TRIED TO HOOK UP WITH MY WOMAN AND THEN THE TWO OF YOU TRIED TO TAKE OVER.
YOU KNOW, THE USUAL.
AND REYNA WENT ALONG WITH THAT?
SHE KNOWS TO DO WHATEVER I TELL HER. IT'S HOW SHE SURVIVES.

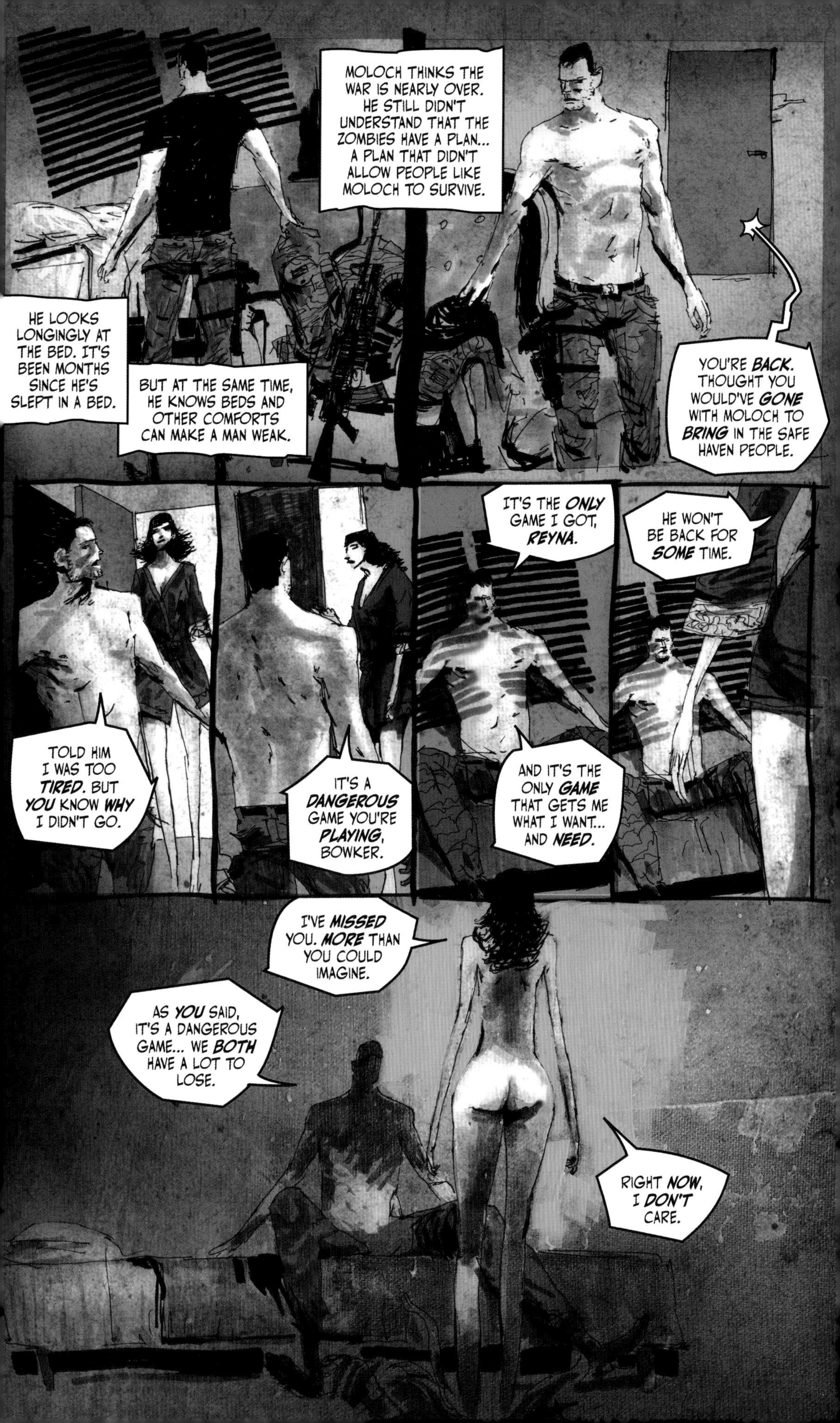

MOLOCH THINKS THE WAR IS NEARLY OVER. HE STILL DIDN'T UNDERSTAND THAT THE ZOMBIES HAVE A PLAN... A PLAN THAT DIDN'T ALLOW PEOPLE LIKE MOLOCH TO SURVIVE.
HE LOOKS LONGINGLY AT THE BED. IT'S BEEN MONTHS SINCE HE'S SLEPT IN A BED.
BUT AT THE SAME TIME, HE KNOWS BEDS AND OTHER COMFORTS CAN MAKE A MAN WEAK.
YOU'RE **BACK**. THOUGHT YOU WOULD'VE **GONE** WITH MOLOCH TO **BRING** IN THE SAFE HAVEN PEOPLE.
TOLD HIM I WAS TOO **TIRED**. BUT **YOU** KNOW **WHY** I DIDN'T GO.
IT'S A **DANGEROUS** GAME YOU'RE **PLAYING**, BOWKER.
IT'S THE **ONLY** GAME I GOT, **REYNA**.
AND IT'S THE ONLY **GAME** THAT GETS ME WHAT I WANT... AND **NEED**.
HE WON'T BE BACK FOR **SOME** TIME.
I'VE **MISSED** YOU. **MORE** THAN YOU COULD IMAGINE.
AS **YOU** SAID, IT'S A DANGEROUS GAME... WE **BOTH** HAVE A LOT TO LOSE.
RIGHT **NOW**, I **DON'T** CARE.

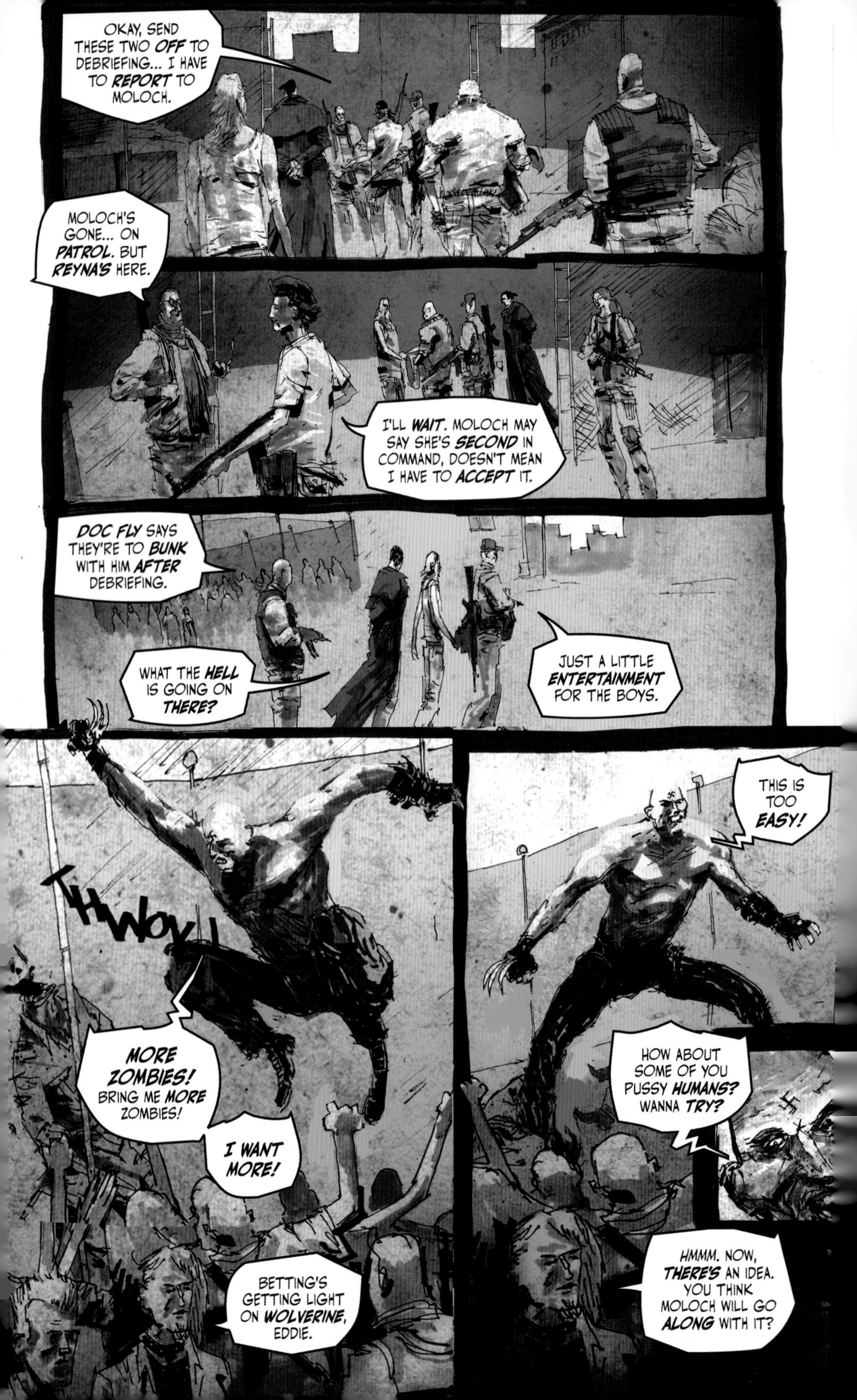

OKAY, SEND THESE TWO OFF TO DEBRIEFING... I HAVE TO REPORT TO MOLOCH.
MOLOCH'S GONE... ON PATROL. BUT REYNA'S HERE.
I'LL WAIT. MOLOCH MAY SAY SHE'S SECOND IN COMMAND, DOESN'T MEAN I HAVE TO ACCEPT IT.
DOC FLY SAYS THEY'RE TO BUNK WITH HIM AFTER DEBRIEFING.
WHAT THE HELL IS GOING ON THERE?
JUST A LITTLE ENTERTAINMENT FOR THE BOYS.
THWOK!
MORE ZOMBIES! BRING ME MORE ZOMBIES!
I WANT MORE!
BETTING'S GETTING LIGHT ON WOLVERINE, EDDIE.
THIS IS TOO EASY!
HOW ABOUT SOME OF YOU PUSSY HUMANS? WANNA TRY?
HMMM. NOW, THERE'S AN IDEA. YOU THINK MOLOCH WILL GO ALONG WITH IT?

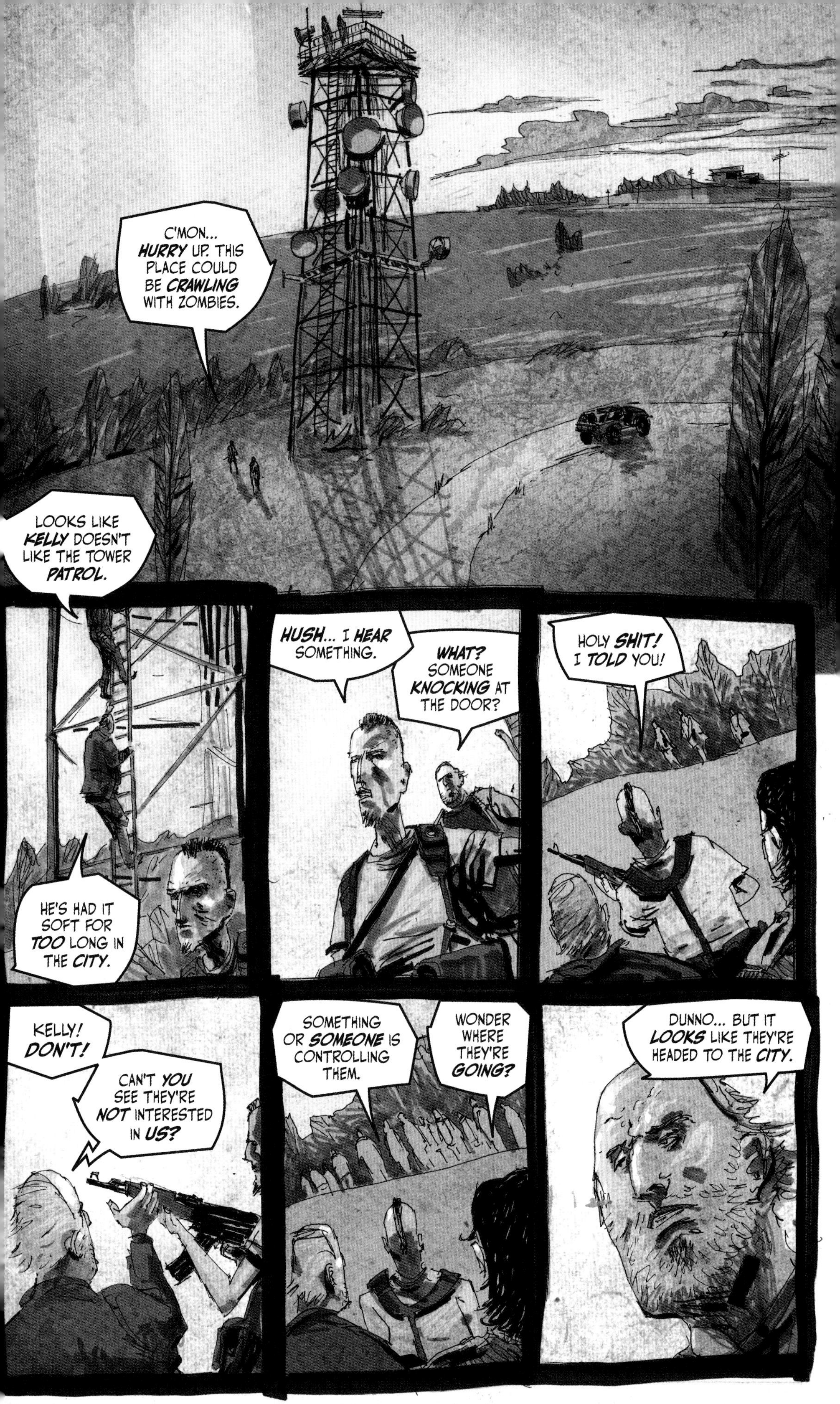
C'MON... HURRY UP. THIS PLACE COULD BE CRAWLING WITH ZOMBIES.
LOOKS LIKE KELLY DOESN'T LIKE THE TOWER PATROL.
HE'S HAD IT SOFT FOR TOO LONG IN THE CITY.
HUSH... I HEAR SOMETHING.
WHAT? SOMEONE KNOCKING AT THE DOOR?
HOLY SHIT! I TOLD YOU!
KELLY! DON'T!
CAN'T YOU SEE THEY'RE NOT INTERESTED IN US?
SOMETHING OR SOMEONE IS CONTROLLING THEM.
WONDER WHERE THEY'RE GOING?
DUNNO... BUT IT LOOKS LIKE THEY'RE HEADED TO THE CITY.

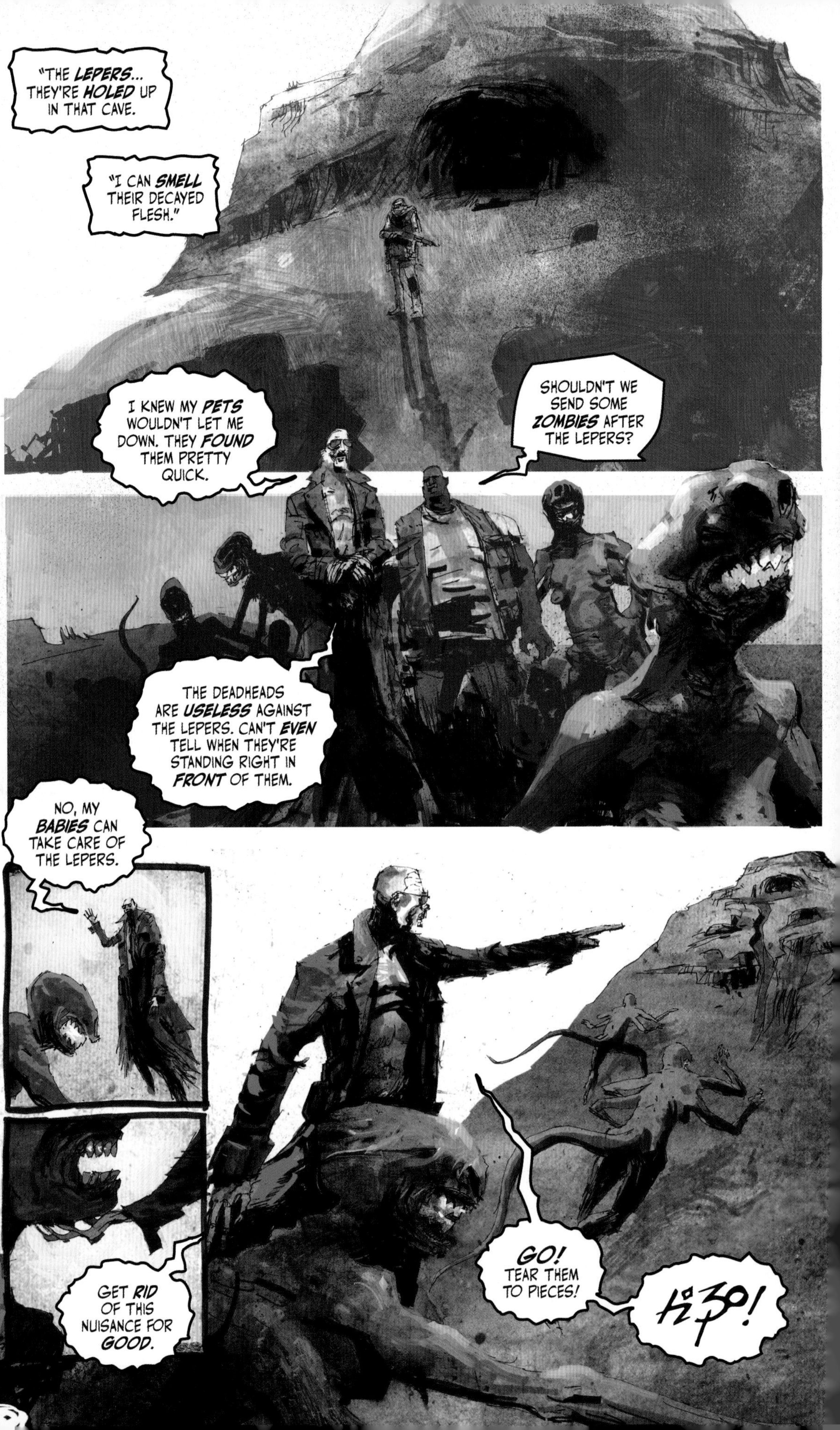
"THE LEPERS... THEY'RE HOLED UP IN THAT CAVE.
"I CAN SMELL THEIR DECAYED FLESH."
I KNEW MY PETS WOULDN'T LET ME DOWN. THEY FOUND THEM PRETTY QUICK.
SHOULDN'T WE SEND SOME ZOMBIES AFTER THE LEPERS?
THE DEADHEADS ARE USELESS AGAINST THE LEPERS. CAN'T EVEN TELL WHEN THEY'RE STANDING RIGHT IN FRONT OF THEM.
NO, MY BABIES CAN TAKE CARE OF THE LEPERS.
GET RID OF THIS NUISANCE FOR GOOD.
GO! TEAR THEM TO PIECES!

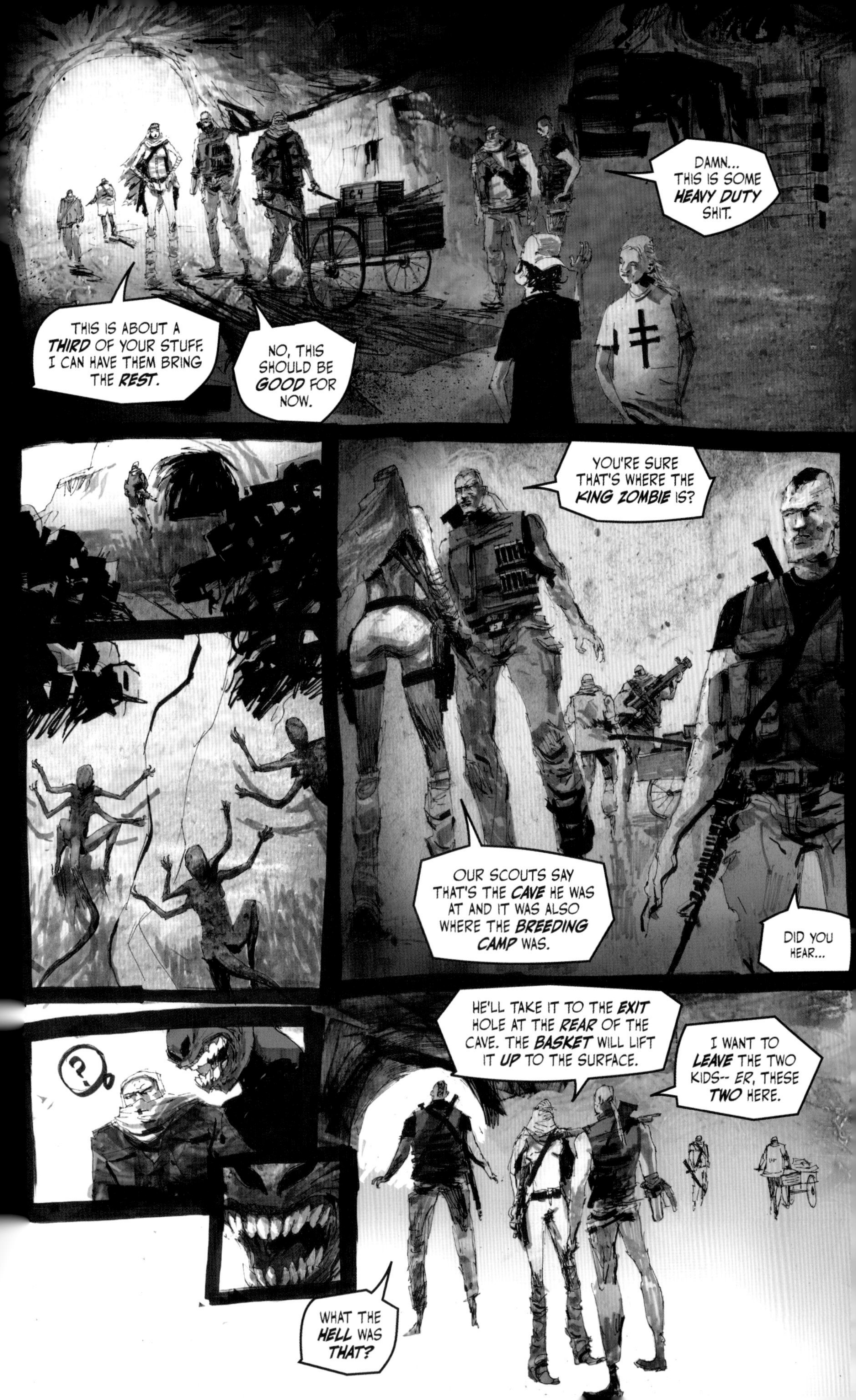
DAMN... THIS IS SOME HEAVY DUTY SHIT.
THIS IS ABOUT A THIRD OF YOUR STUFF. I CAN HAVE THEM BRING THE REST.
NO, THIS SHOULD BE GOOD FOR NOW.
YOU'RE SURE THAT'S WHERE THE KING ZOMBIE IS?
OUR SCOUTS SAY THAT'S THE CAVE HE WAS AT AND IT WAS ALSO WHERE THE BREEDING CAMP WAS.
DID YOU HEAR...
?
HE'LL TAKE IT TO THE EXIT HOLE AT THE REAR OF THE CAVE. THE BASKET WILL LIFT IT UP TO THE SURFACE.
I WANT TO LEAVE THE TWO KIDS-- ER, THESE TWO HERE.
WHAT THE HELL WAS THAT?

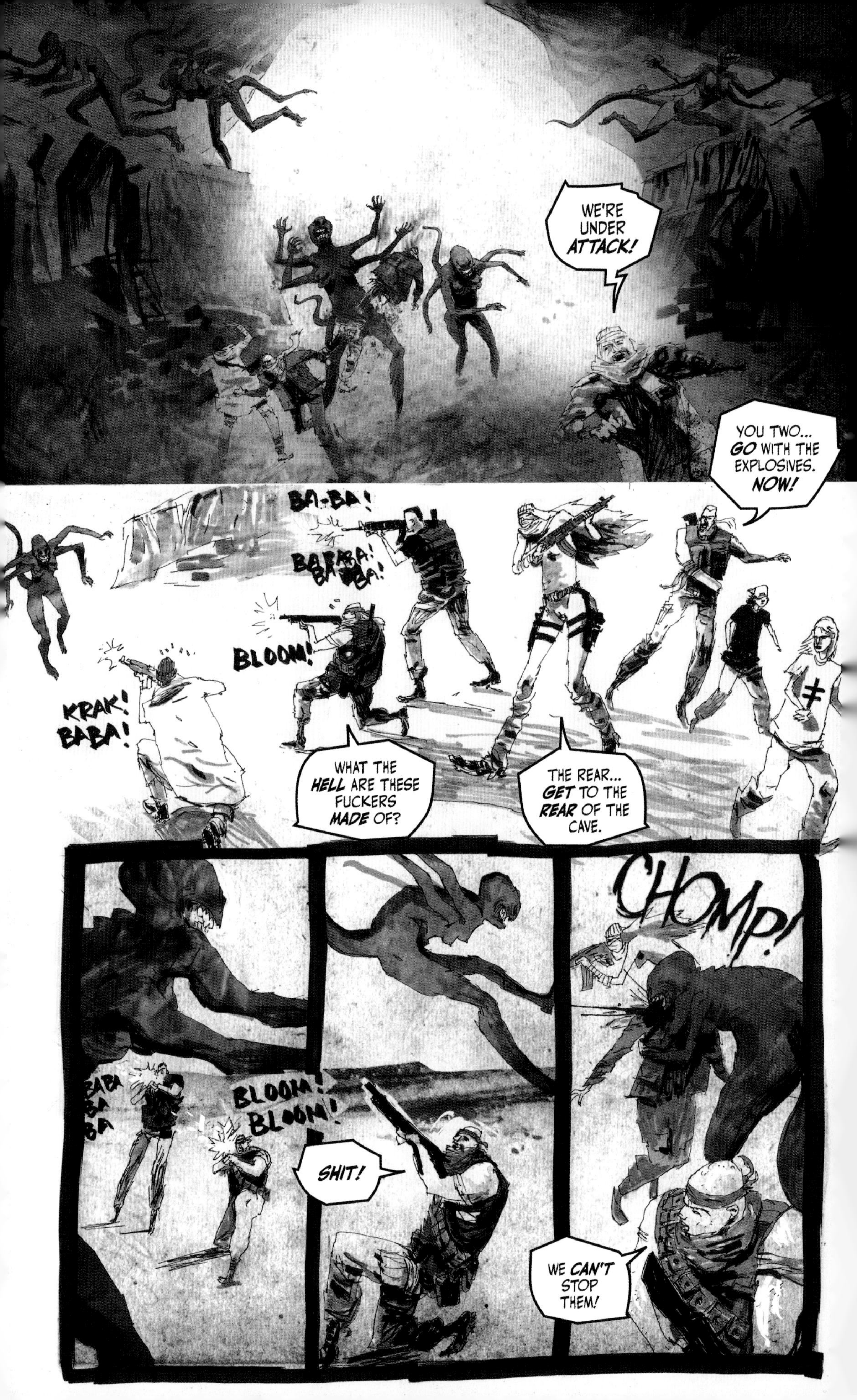
WE'RE UNDER ATTACK!
YOU TWO... GO WITH THE EXPLOSIVES. NOW!
BA-BA!
BABABA! BABABA!
BLOOM!
KRAK! BABA!
WHAT THE HELL ARE THESE FUCKERS MADE OF?
THE REAR... GET TO THE REAR OF THE CAVE.
BABA BA BA
BLOOM! BLOOM!
SHIT!
CHOMP!
WE CAN'T STOP THEM!

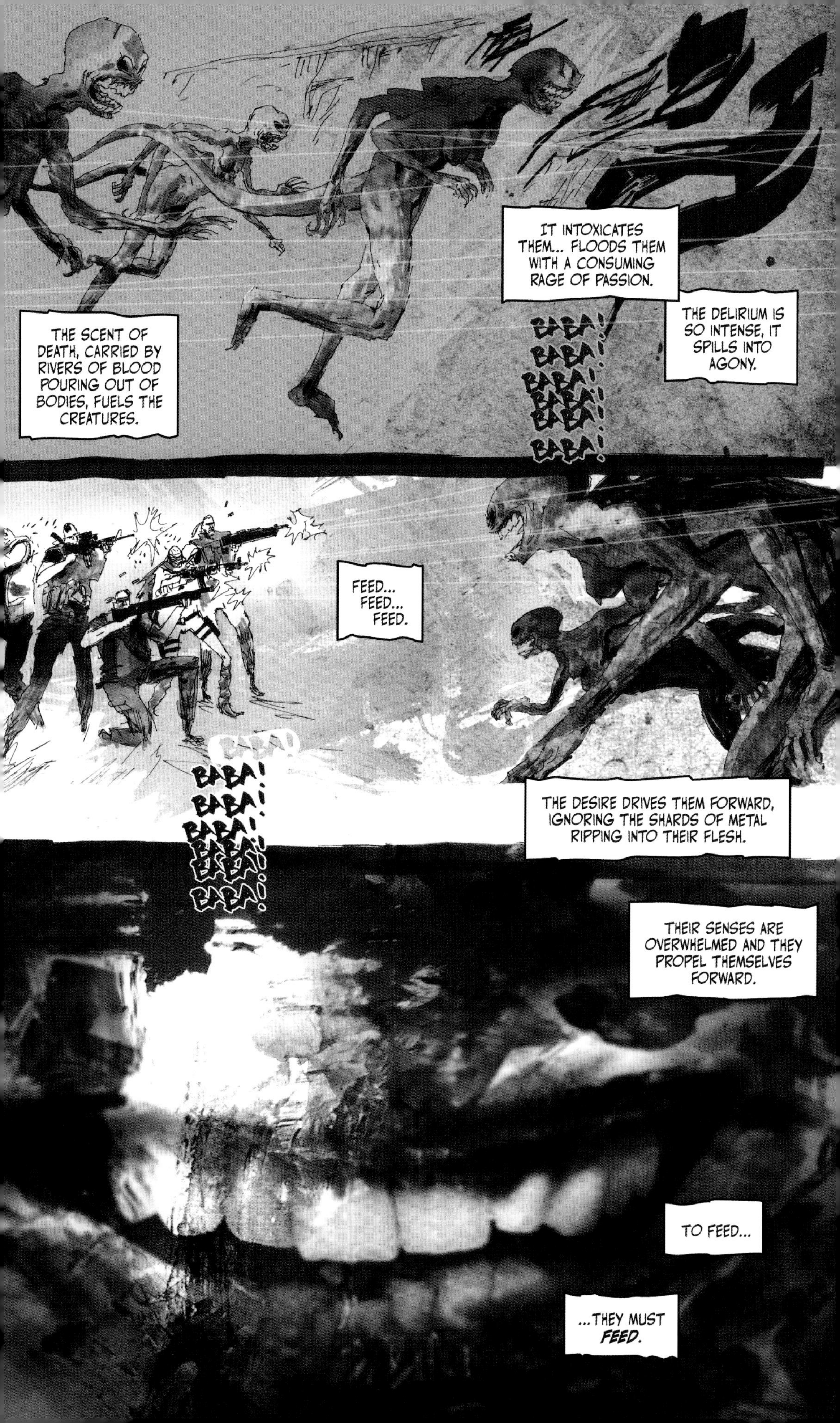
THE SCENT OF DEATH, CARRIED BY RIVERS OF BLOOD POURING OUT OF BODIES, FUELS THE CREATURES.
IT INTOXICATES THEM... FLOODS THEM WITH A CONSUMING RAGE OF PASSION.
BABA! BABA! BABA! BABA! BABA! BABA!
THE DELIRIUM IS SO INTENSE, IT SPILLS INTO AGONY.
FEED... FEED... FEED.
BABA! BABA! BABA! BABA! BABA! BABA! BABA!
THE DESIRE DRIVES THEM FORWARD, IGNORING THE SHARDS OF METAL RIPPING INTO THEIR FLESH.
THEIR SENSES ARE OVERWHELMED AND THEY PROPEL THEMSELVES FORWARD.
TO FEED...
...THEY MUST *FEED*.

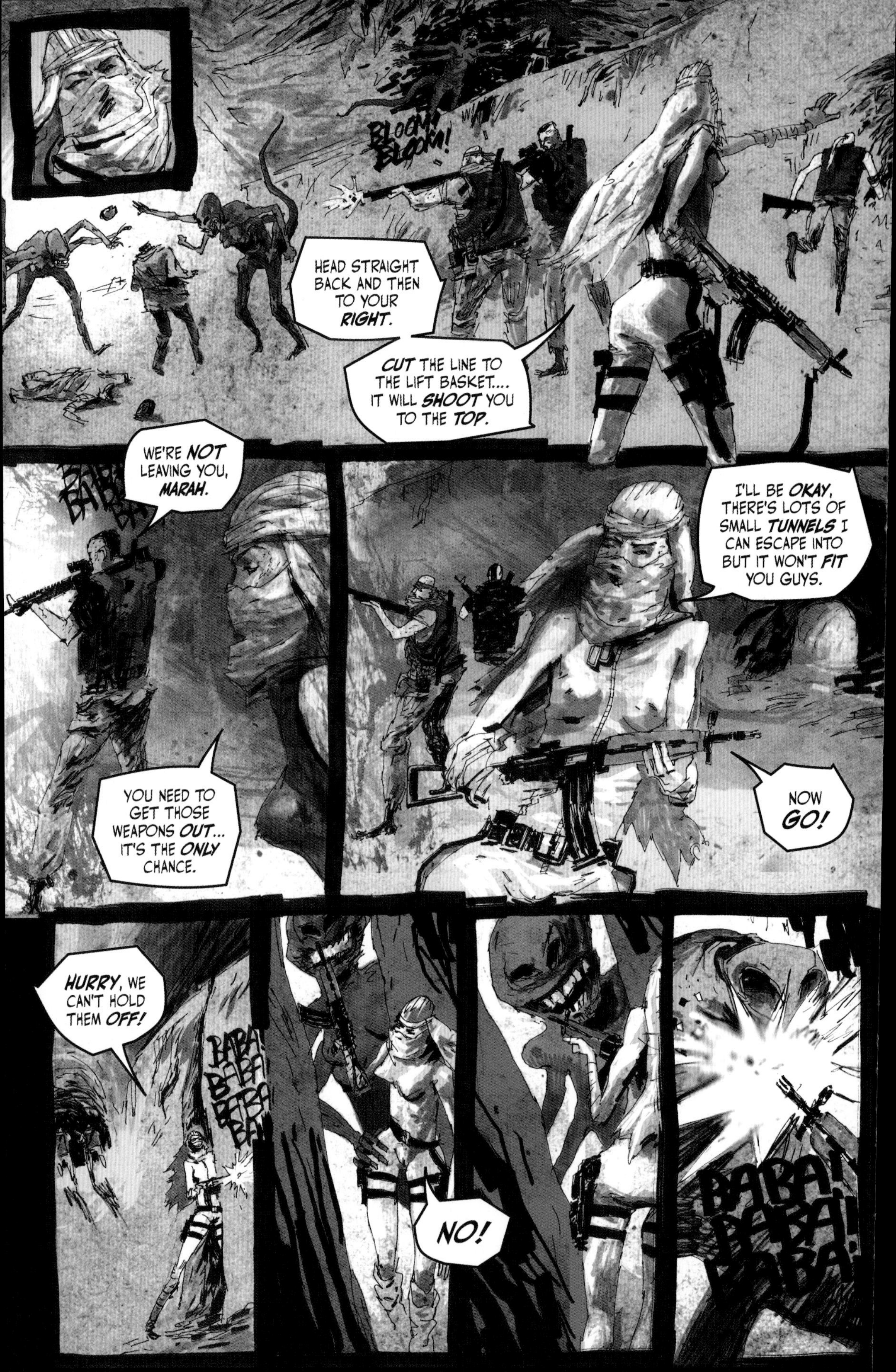

BLOOM! BLOOM!
HEAD STRAIGHT BACK AND THEN TO YOUR *RIGHT*.
CUT THE LINE TO THE LIFT BASKET.... IT WILL *SHOOT* YOU TO THE *TOP*.
WE'RE *NOT* LEAVING YOU, *MARAH*.
YOU NEED TO GET THOSE WEAPONS *OUT*... IT'S THE *ONLY* CHANCE.
I'LL BE *OKAY*, THERE'S LOTS OF SMALL *TUNNELS* I CAN ESCAPE INTO BUT IT WON'T *FIT* YOU GUYS.
NOW *GO!*
HURRY, WE CAN'T HOLD THEM *OFF!*
NO!
BABA! BABA! BABA!

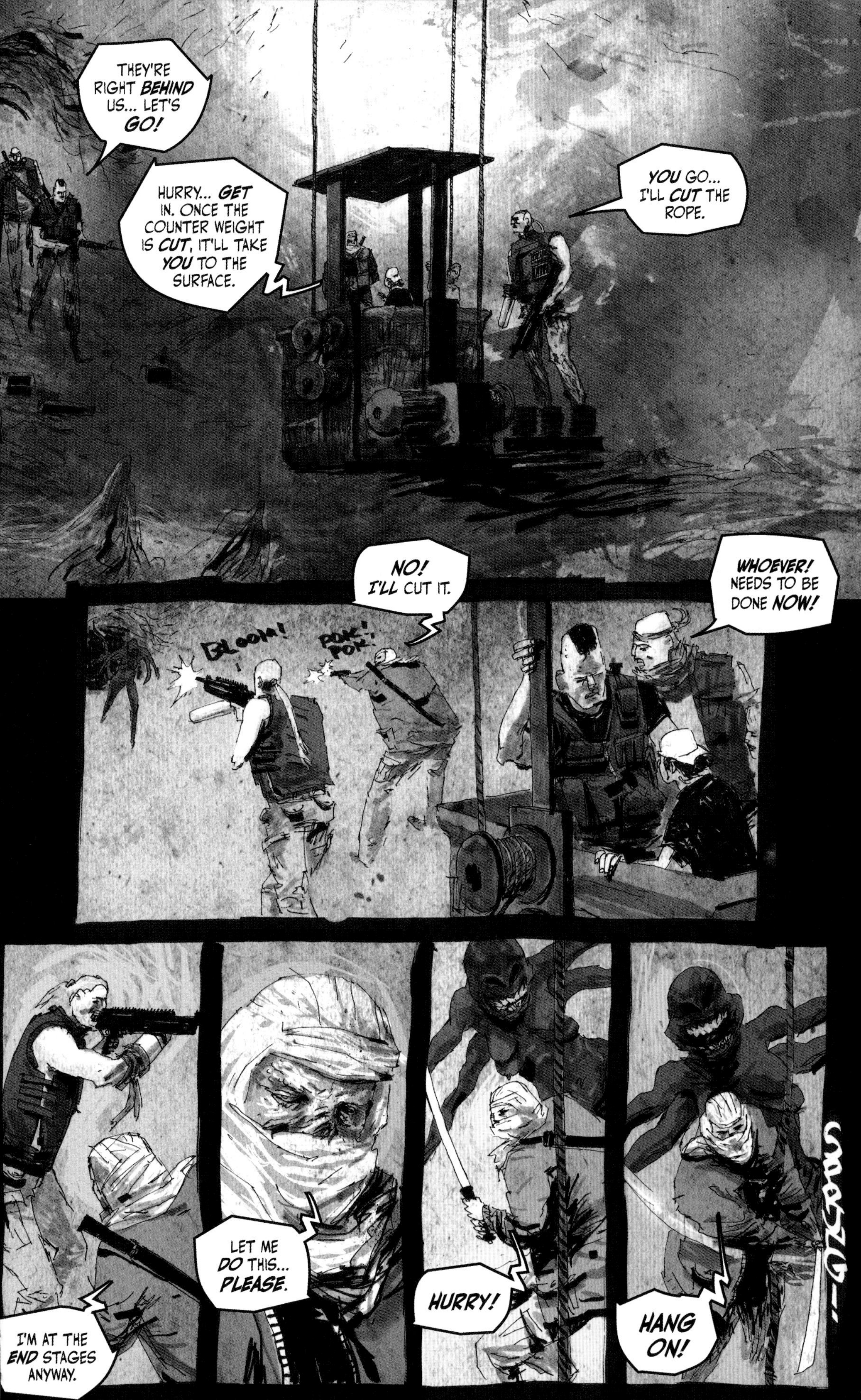
THEY'RE RIGHT **BEHIND** US... LET'S **GO!**
HURRY... **GET** IN. ONCE THE COUNTER WEIGHT IS **CUT**, IT'LL TAKE **YOU** TO THE SURFACE.
YOU GO... I'LL **CUT** THE ROPE.
BLOOM!
POK! POK!
NO! I'LL CUT IT.
WHOEVER! NEEDS TO BE DONE **NOW!**
I'M AT THE **END** STAGES ANYWAY.
LET ME **DO** THIS... **PLEASE.**
HURRY!
HANG ON!

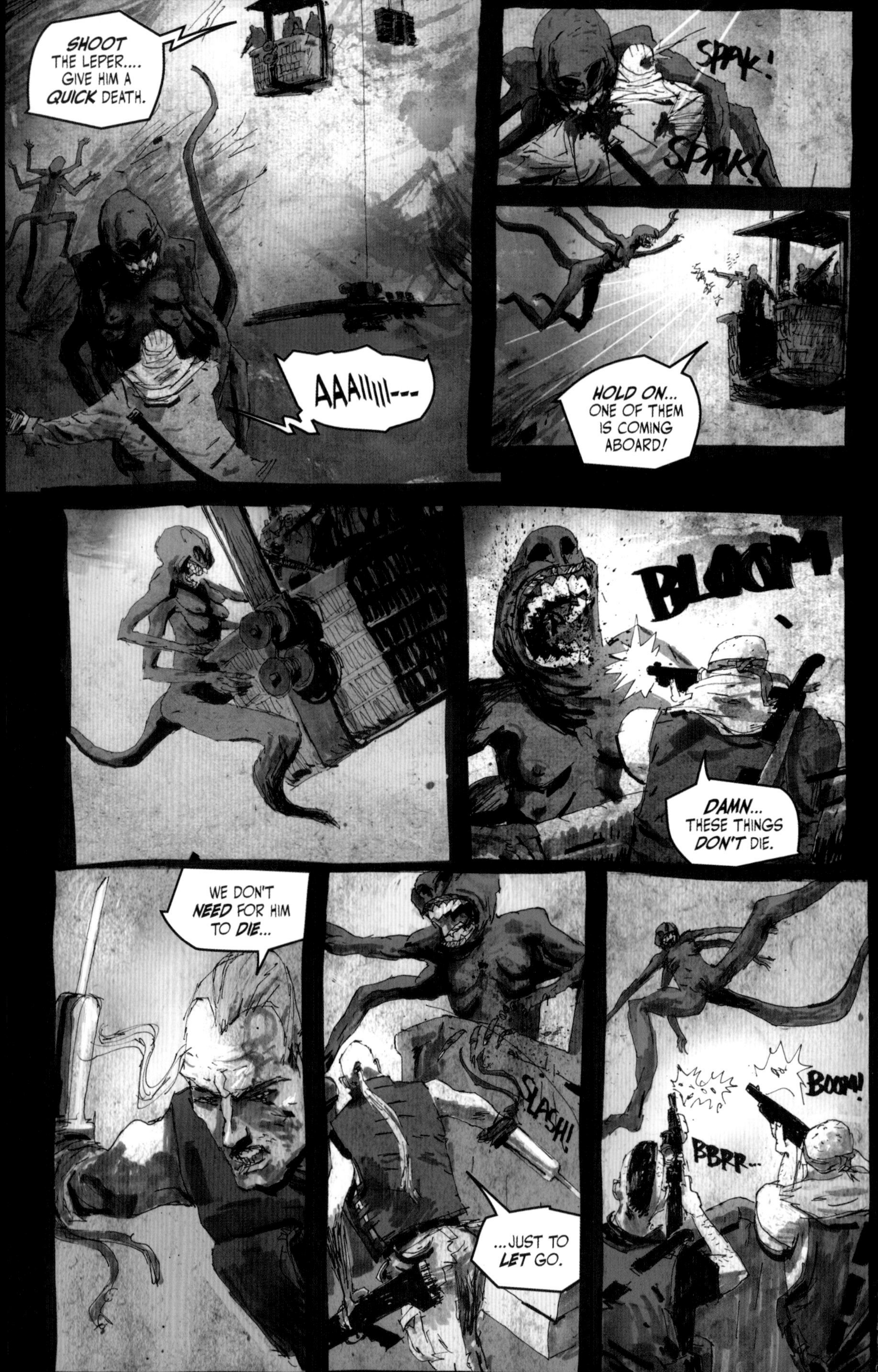
SHOOT THE LEPER.... GIVE HIM A QUICK DEATH.
AAAIIIII---
SPPAK!
SPPAK!
HOLD ON... ONE OF THEM IS COMING ABOARD!
BLOOM
DAMN... THESE THINGS DON'T DIE.
WE DON'T NEED FOR HIM TO DIE...
SLASH!
...JUST TO LET GO.
BOOM!
BBRR...

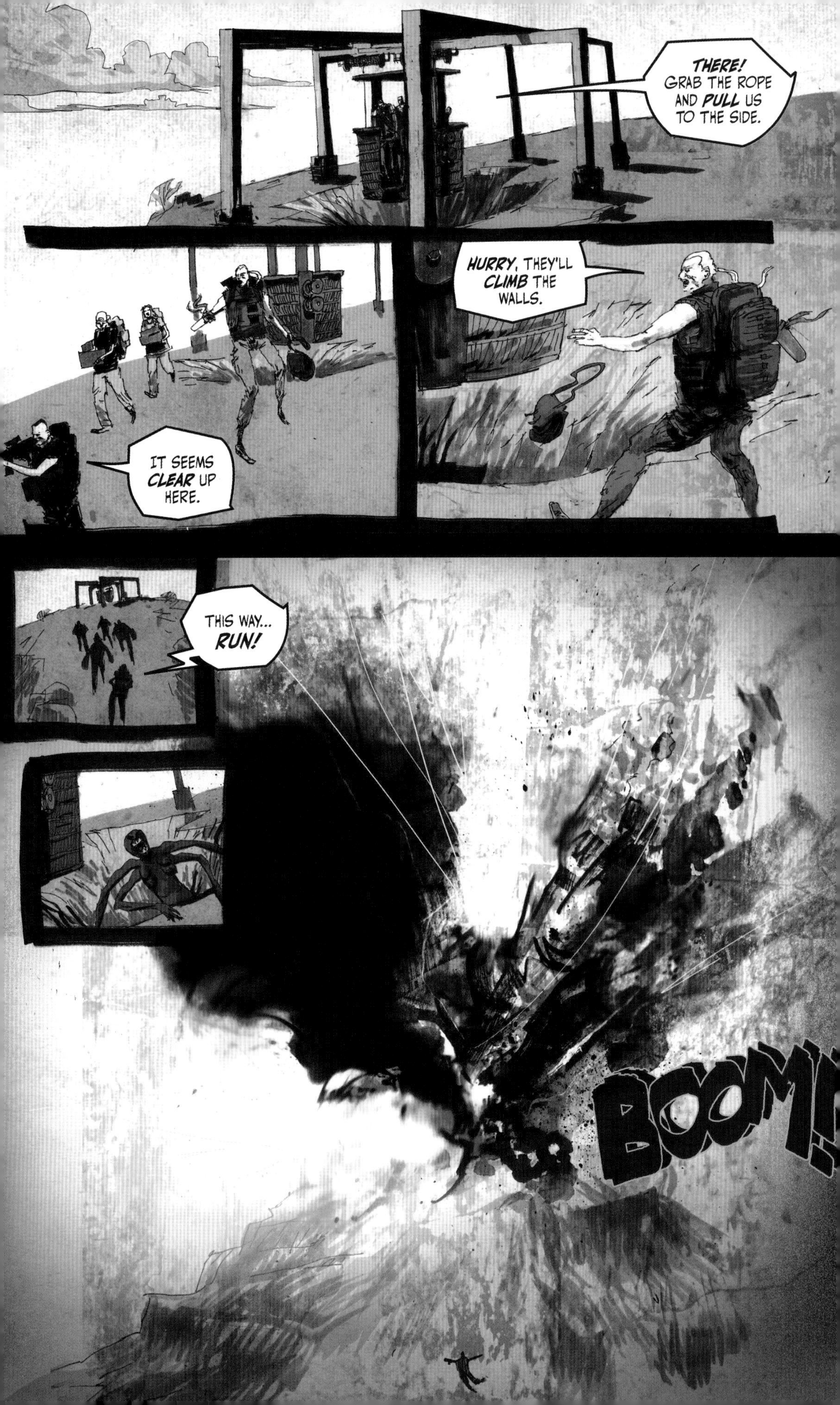
THERE! GRAB THE ROPE AND PULL US TO THE SIDE.
IT SEEMS CLEAR UP HERE.
HURRY, THEY'LL CLIMB THE WALLS.
THIS WAY... RUN!
BOOM!!

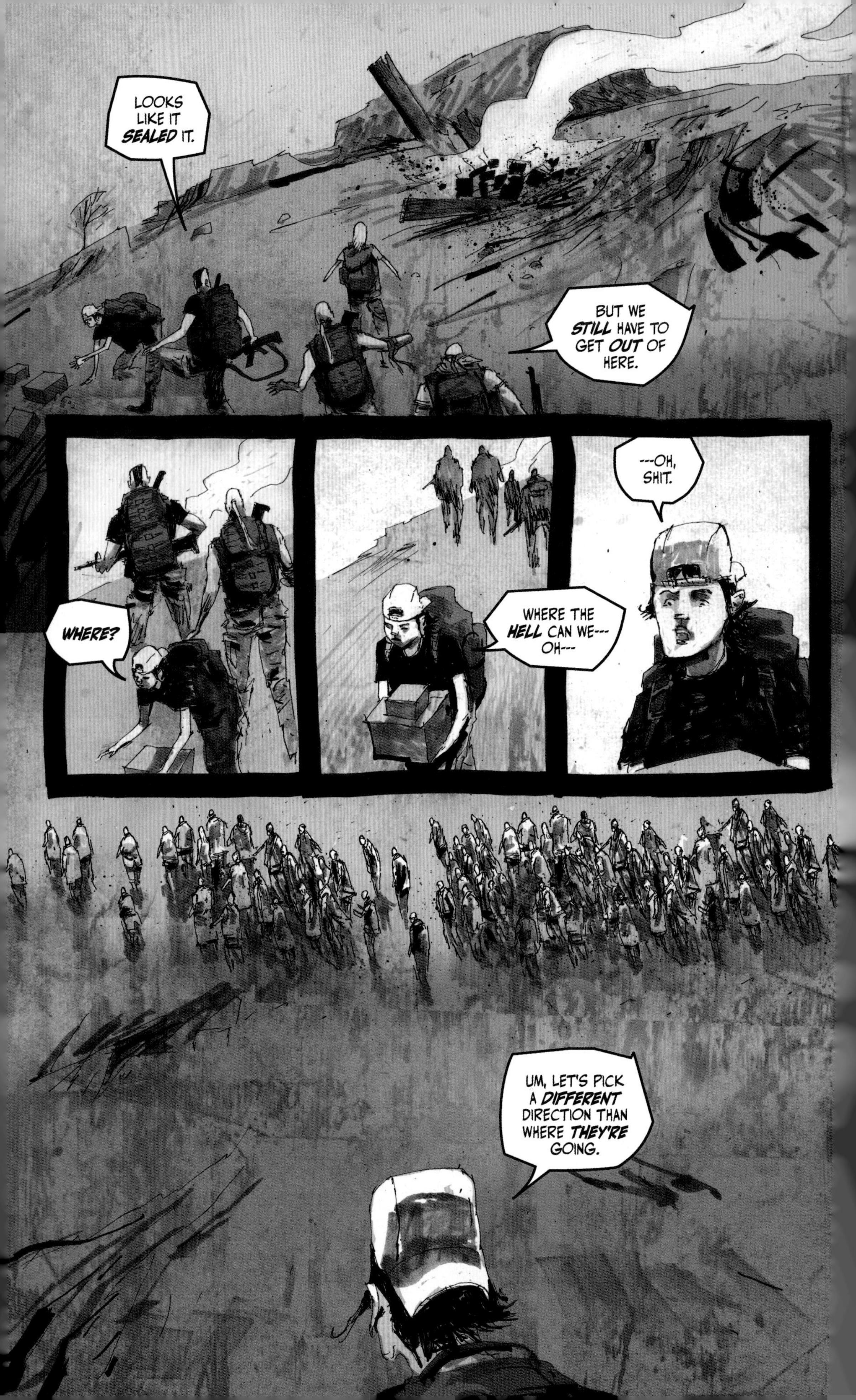
LOOKS LIKE IT SEALED IT.
BUT WE STILL HAVE TO GET OUT OF HERE.
WHERE?
WHERE THE HELL CAN WE--- OH---
---OH, SHIT.
UM, LET'S PICK A DIFFERENT DIRECTION THAN WHERE THEY'RE GOING.

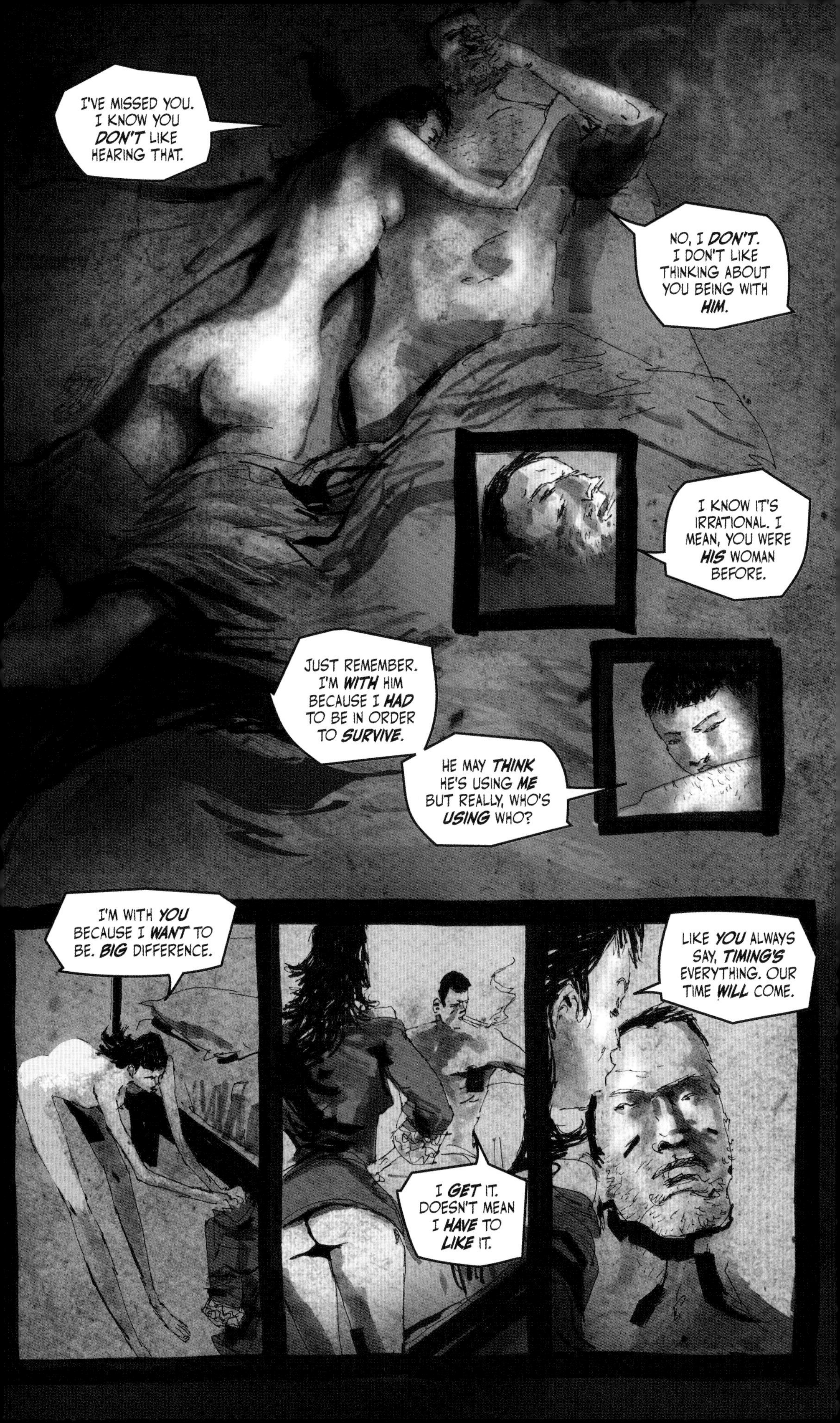
I'VE MISSED YOU. I KNOW YOU DON'T LIKE HEARING THAT.
NO, I DON'T. I DON'T LIKE THINKING ABOUT YOU BEING WITH HIM.
I KNOW IT'S IRRATIONAL. I MEAN, YOU WERE HIS WOMAN BEFORE.
JUST REMEMBER. I'M WITH HIM BECAUSE I HAD TO BE IN ORDER TO SURVIVE.
HE MAY THINK HE'S USING ME BUT REALLY, WHO'S USING WHO?
I'M WITH YOU BECAUSE I WANT TO BE. BIG DIFFERENCE.
I GET IT. DOESN'T MEAN I HAVE TO LIKE IT.
LIKE YOU ALWAYS SAY, TIMING'S EVERYTHING. OUR TIME WILL COME.

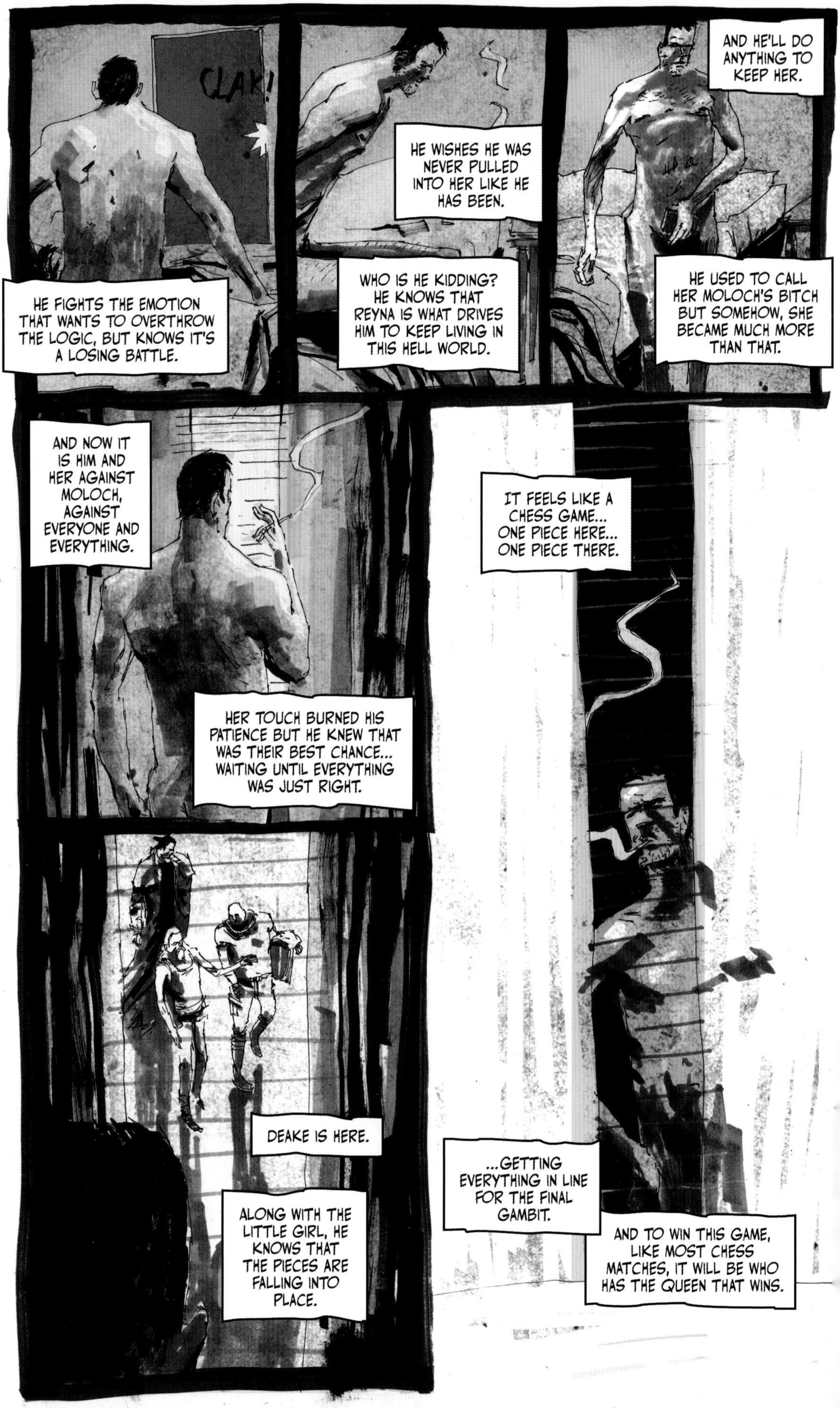
CLAK!
HE FIGHTS THE EMOTION THAT WANTS TO OVERTHROW THE LOGIC, BUT KNOWS IT'S A LOSING BATTLE.
HE WISHES HE WAS NEVER PULLED INTO HER LIKE HE HAS BEEN.
WHO IS HE KIDDING? HE KNOWS THAT REYNA IS WHAT DRIVES HIM TO KEEP LIVING IN THIS HELL WORLD.
AND HE'LL DO ANYTHING TO KEEP HER.
HE USED TO CALL HER MOLOCH'S BITCH BUT SOMEHOW, SHE BECAME MUCH MORE THAN THAT.
AND NOW IT IS HIM AND HER AGAINST MOLOCH, AGAINST EVERYONE AND EVERYTHING.
HER TOUCH BURNED HIS PATIENCE BUT HE KNEW THAT WAS THEIR BEST CHANCE... WAITING UNTIL EVERYTHING WAS JUST RIGHT.
DEAKE IS HERE.
ALONG WITH THE LITTLE GIRL, HE KNOWS THAT THE PIECES ARE FALLING INTO PLACE.
IT FEELS LIKE A CHESS GAME... ONE PIECE HERE... ONE PIECE THERE.
...GETTING EVERYTHING IN LINE FOR THE FINAL GAMBIT.
AND TO WIN THIS GAME, LIKE MOST CHESS MATCHES, IT WILL BE WHO HAS THE QUEEN THAT WINS.

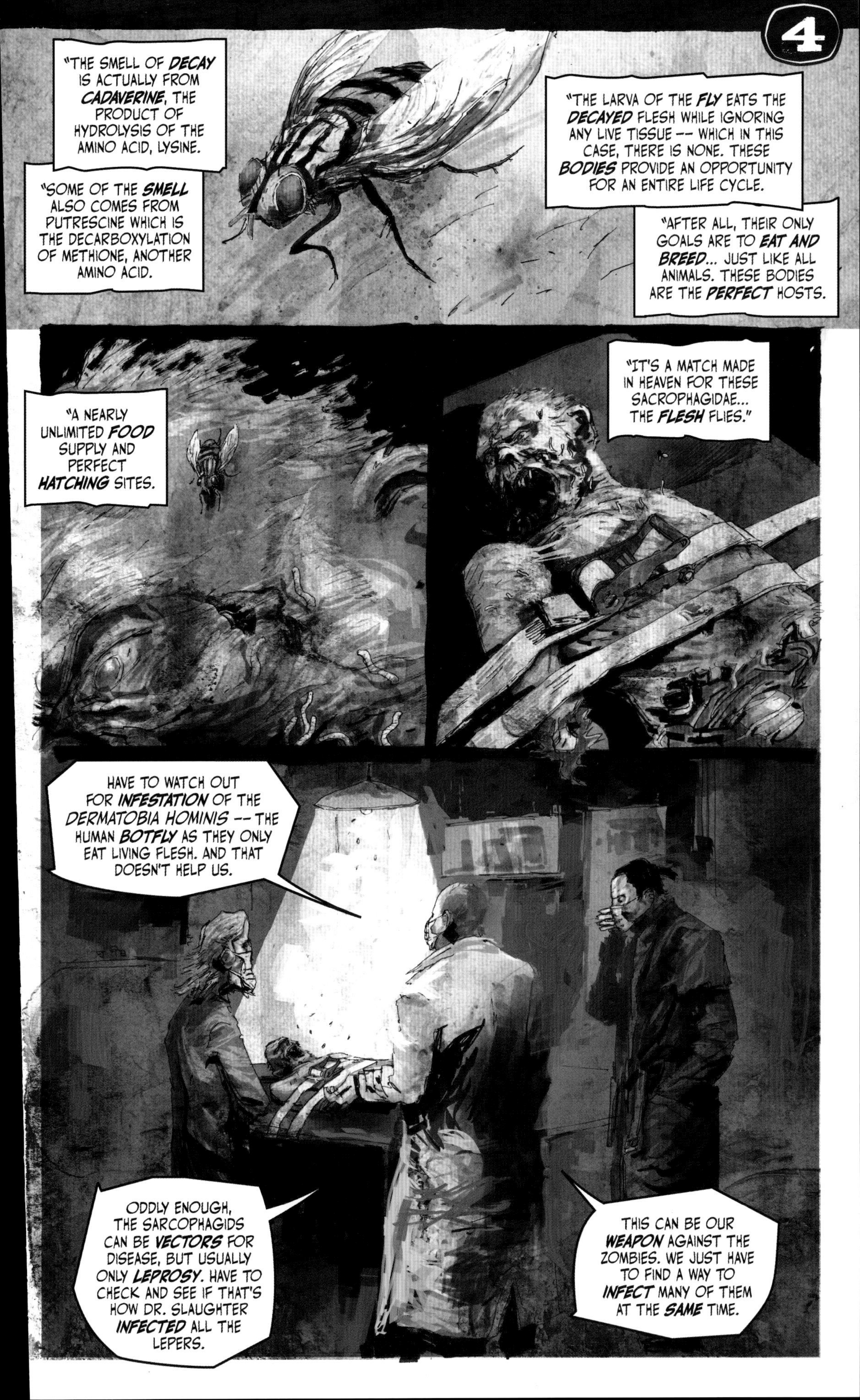
4
"THE SMELL OF DECAY IS ACTUALLY FROM CADAVERINE, THE PRODUCT OF HYDROLYSIS OF THE AMINO ACID, LYSINE.
"SOME OF THE SMELL ALSO COMES FROM PUTRESCINE WHICH IS THE DECARBOXYLATION OF METHIONE, ANOTHER AMINO ACID.
"THE LARVA OF THE FLY EATS THE DECAYED FLESH WHILE IGNORING ANY LIVE TISSUE -- WHICH IN THIS CASE, THERE IS NONE. THESE BODIES PROVIDE AN OPPORTUNITY FOR AN ENTIRE LIFE CYCLE.
"AFTER ALL, THEIR ONLY GOALS ARE TO EAT AND BREED... JUST LIKE ALL ANIMALS. THESE BODIES ARE THE PERFECT HOSTS.
"A NEARLY UNLIMITED FOOD SUPPLY AND PERFECT HATCHING SITES.
"IT'S A MATCH MADE IN HEAVEN FOR THESE SACROPHAGIDAE... THE FLESH FLIES."
HAVE TO WATCH OUT FOR INFESTATION OF THE DERMATOBIA HOMINIS -- THE HUMAN BOTFLY AS THEY ONLY EAT LIVING FLESH. AND THAT DOESN'T HELP US.
ODDLY ENOUGH, THE SARCOPHAGIDS CAN BE VECTORS FOR DISEASE, BUT USUALLY ONLY LEPROSY. HAVE TO CHECK AND SEE IF THAT'S HOW DR. SLAUGHTER INFECTED ALL THE LEPERS.
THIS CAN BE OUR WEAPON AGAINST THE ZOMBIES. WE JUST HAVE TO FIND A WAY TO INFECT MANY OF THEM AT THE SAME TIME.

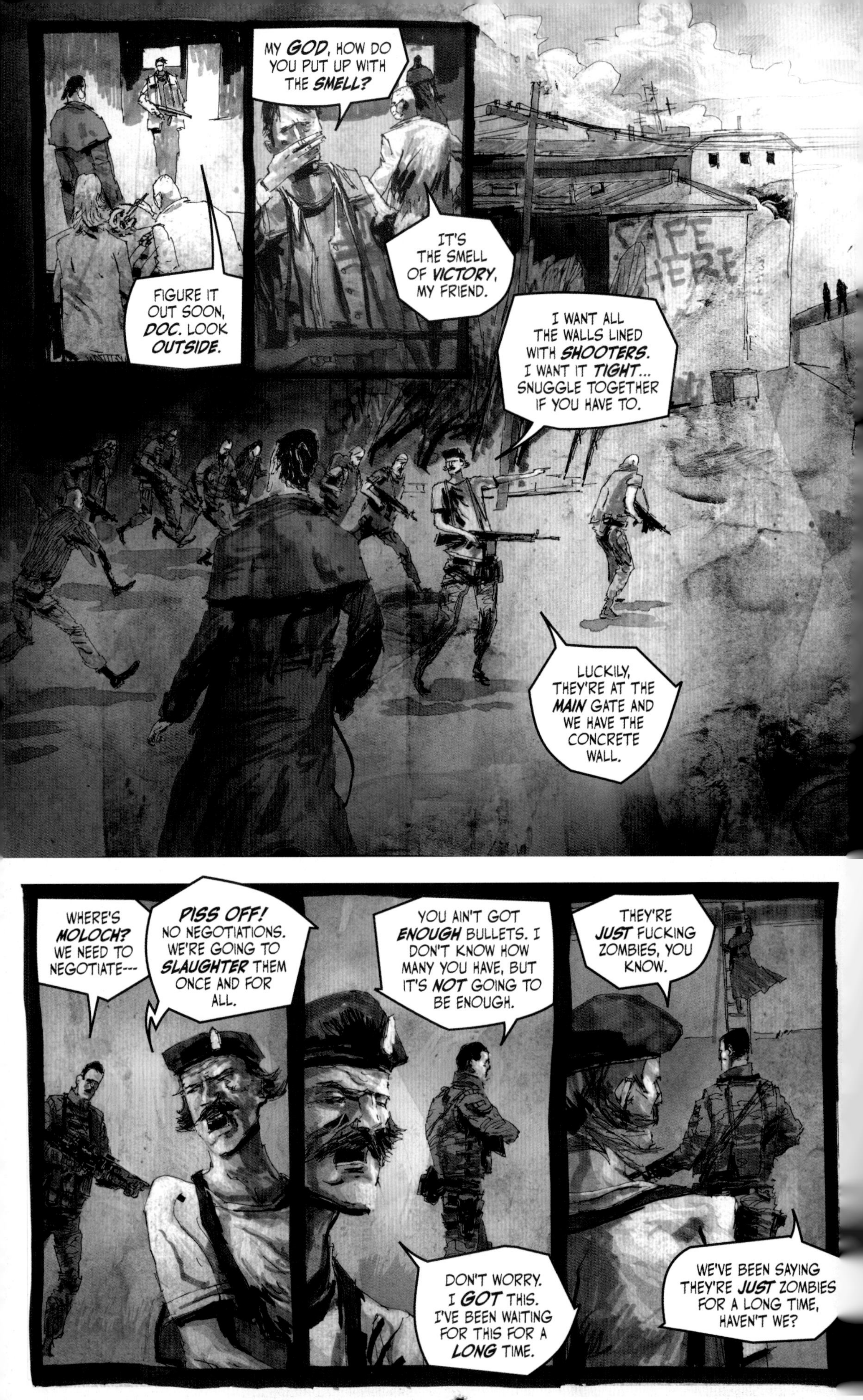
FIGURE IT OUT SOON, DOC. LOOK OUTSIDE.
MY GOD, HOW DO YOU PUT UP WITH THE SMELL?
IT'S THE SMELL OF VICTORY, MY FRIEND.
I WANT ALL THE WALLS LINED WITH SHOOTERS. I WANT IT TIGHT... SNUGGLE TOGETHER IF YOU HAVE TO.
LUCKILY, THEY'RE AT THE MAIN GATE AND WE HAVE THE CONCRETE WALL.
WHERE'S MOLOCH? WE NEED TO NEGOTIATE---
PISS OFF! NO NEGOTIATIONS. WE'RE GOING TO SLAUGHTER THEM ONCE AND FOR ALL.
YOU AIN'T GOT ENOUGH BULLETS. I DON'T KNOW HOW MANY YOU HAVE, BUT IT'S NOT GOING TO BE ENOUGH.
DON'T WORRY. I GOT THIS. I'VE BEEN WAITING FOR THIS FOR A LONG TIME.
THEY'RE JUST FUCKING ZOMBIES, YOU KNOW.
WE'VE BEEN SAYING THEY'RE JUST ZOMBIES FOR A LONG TIME, HAVEN'T WE?

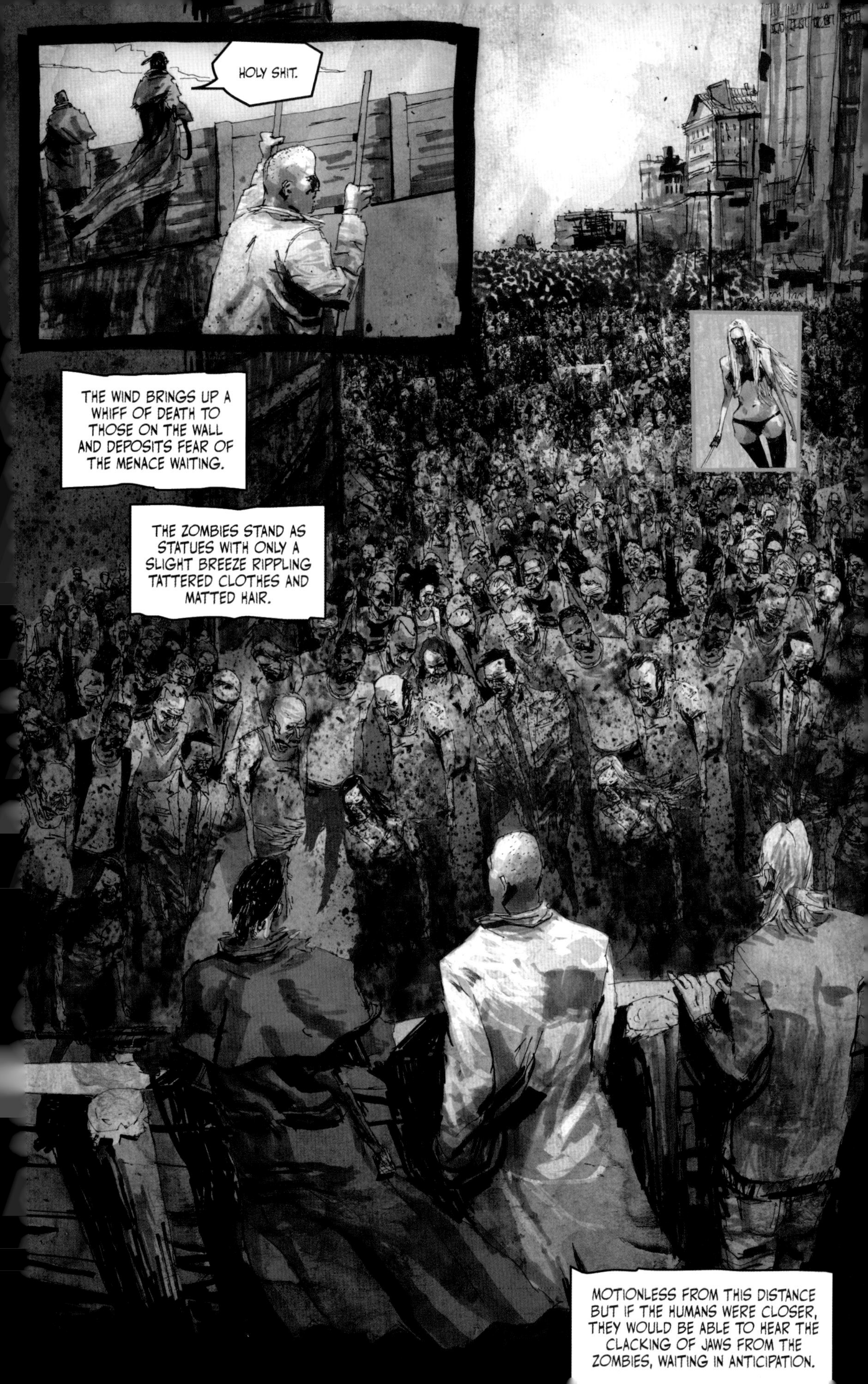
HOLY SHIT.
THE WIND BRINGS UP A WHIFF OF DEATH TO THOSE ON THE WALL AND DEPOSITS FEAR OF THE MENACE WAITING.
THE ZOMBIES STAND AS STATUES WITH ONLY A SLIGHT BREEZE RIPPLING TATTERED CLOTHES AND MATTED HAIR.
MOTIONLESS FROM THIS DISTANCE BUT IF THE HUMANS WERE CLOSER, THEY WOULD BE ABLE TO HEAR THE CLACKING OF JAWS FROM THE ZOMBIES, WAITING IN ANTICIPATION.

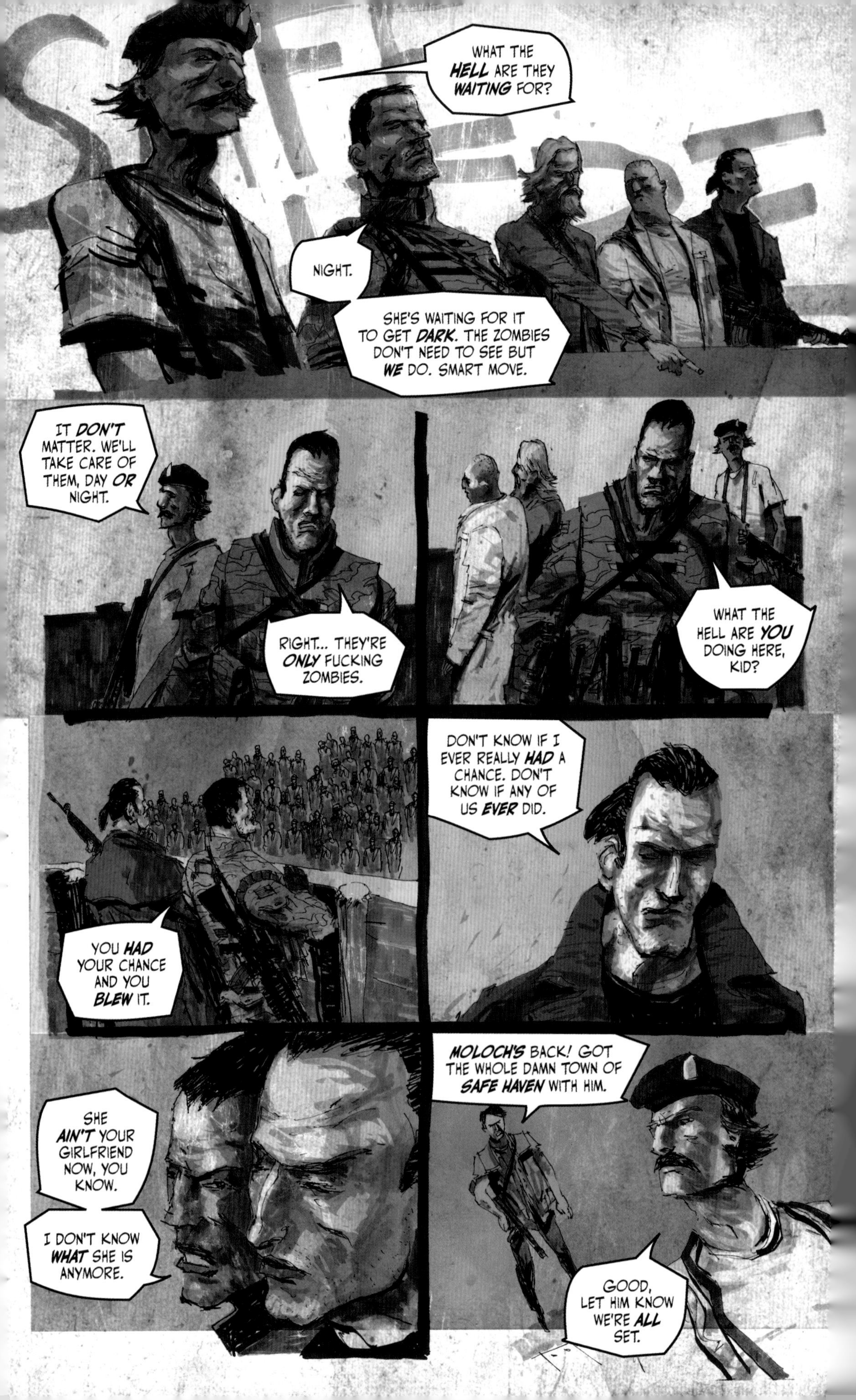
WHAT THE HELL ARE THEY WAITING FOR?
NIGHT.
SHE'S WAITING FOR IT TO GET DARK. THE ZOMBIES DON'T NEED TO SEE BUT WE DO. SMART MOVE.
IT DON'T MATTER. WE'LL TAKE CARE OF THEM, DAY OR NIGHT.
RIGHT... THEY'RE ONLY FUCKING ZOMBIES.
WHAT THE HELL ARE YOU DOING HERE, KID?
DON'T KNOW IF I EVER REALLY HAD A CHANCE. DON'T KNOW IF ANY OF US EVER DID.
YOU HAD YOUR CHANCE AND YOU BLEW IT.
SHE AIN'T YOUR GIRLFRIEND NOW, YOU KNOW.
I DON'T KNOW WHAT SHE IS ANYMORE.
MOLOCH'S BACK! GOT THE WHOLE DAMN TOWN OF SAFE HAVEN WITH HIM.
GOOD, LET HIM KNOW WE'RE ALL SET.

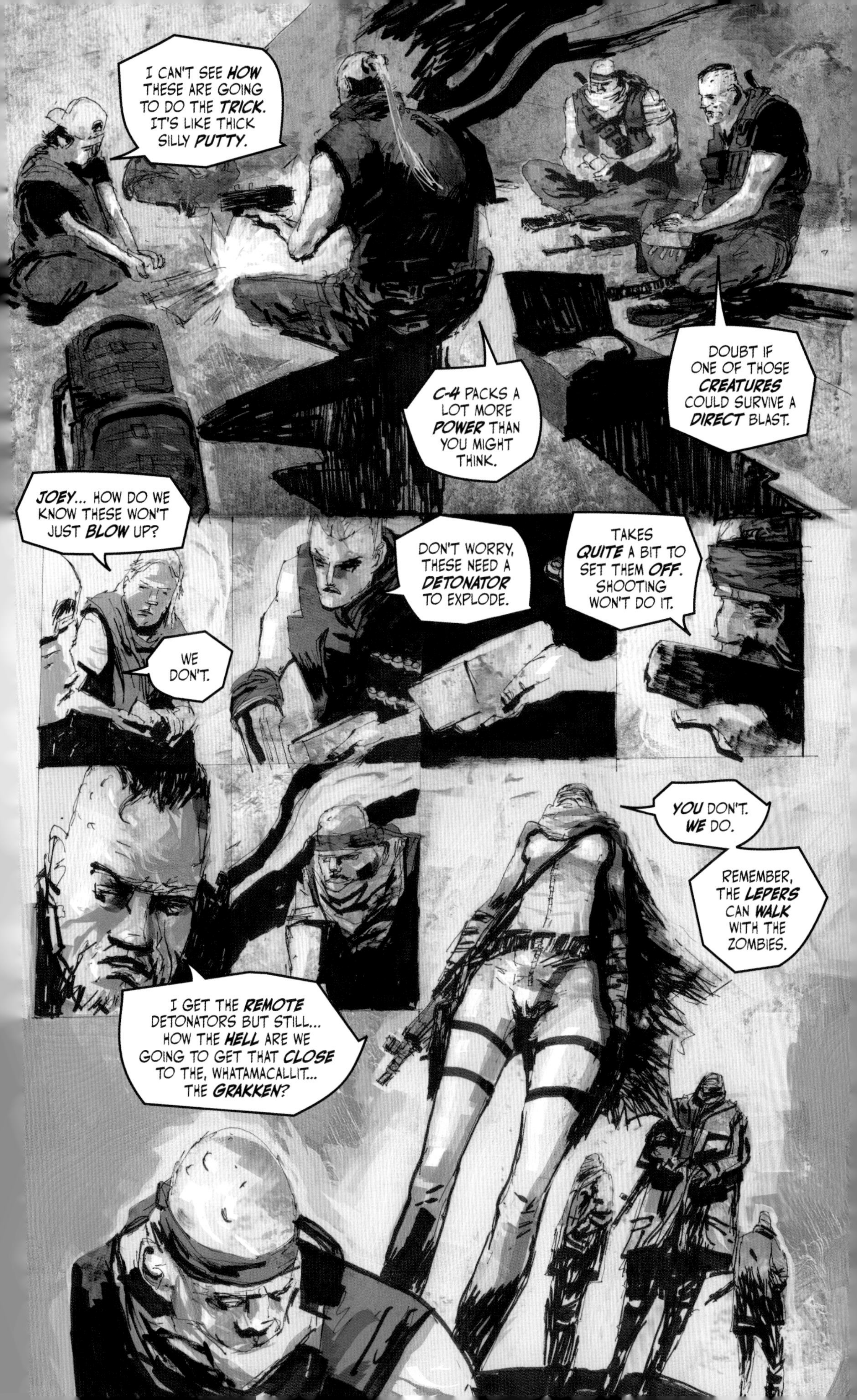
I CAN'T SEE HOW THESE ARE GOING TO DO THE TRICK. IT'S LIKE THICK SILLY PUTTY.
C-4 PACKS A LOT MORE POWER THAN YOU MIGHT THINK.
DOUBT IF ONE OF THOSE CREATURES COULD SURVIVE A DIRECT BLAST.
JOEY... HOW DO WE KNOW THESE WON'T JUST BLOW UP?
WE DON'T.
DON'T WORRY, THESE NEED A DETONATOR TO EXPLODE.
TAKES QUITE A BIT TO SET THEM OFF. SHOOTING WON'T DO IT.
YOU DON'T. WE DO.
REMEMBER, THE LEPERS CAN WALK WITH THE ZOMBIES.
I GET THE REMOTE DETONATORS BUT STILL... HOW THE HELL ARE WE GOING TO GET THAT CLOSE TO THE, WHATAMACALLIT... THE GRAKKEN?

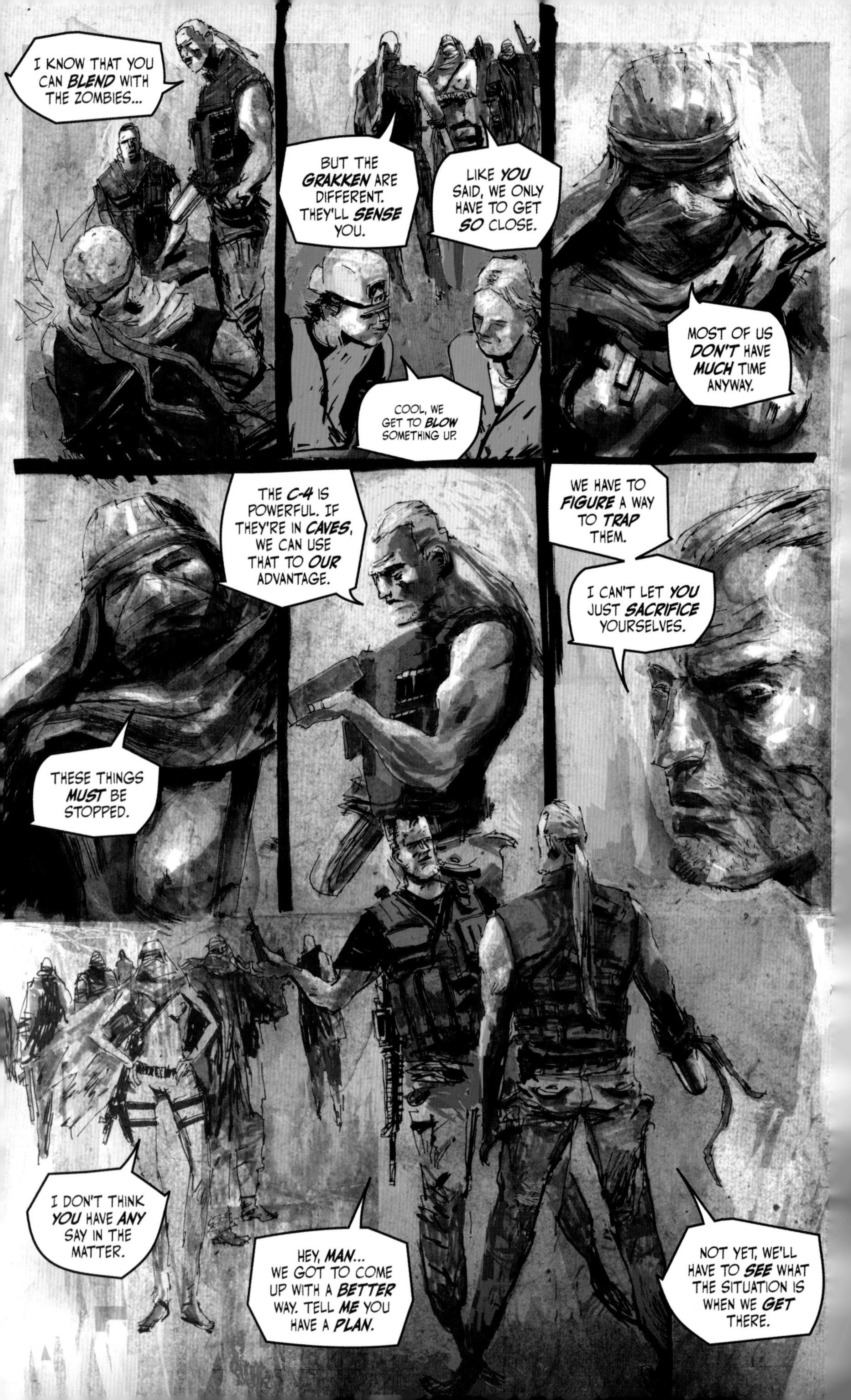
I KNOW THAT YOU CAN BLEND WITH THE ZOMBIES...
BUT THE GRAKKEN ARE DIFFERENT. THEY'LL SENSE YOU.
LIKE YOU SAID, WE ONLY HAVE TO GET SO CLOSE.
COOL, WE GET TO BLOW SOMETHING UP.
MOST OF US DON'T HAVE MUCH TIME ANYWAY.
THESE THINGS MUST BE STOPPED.
THE C-4 IS POWERFUL. IF THEY'RE IN CAVES, WE CAN USE THAT TO OUR ADVANTAGE.
WE HAVE TO FIGURE A WAY TO TRAP THEM.
I CAN'T LET YOU JUST SACRIFICE YOURSELVES.
I DON'T THINK YOU HAVE ANY SAY IN THE MATTER.
HEY, MAN... WE GOT TO COME UP WITH A BETTER WAY. TELL ME YOU HAVE A PLAN.
NOT YET, WE'LL HAVE TO SEE WHAT THE SITUATION IS WHEN WE GET THERE.

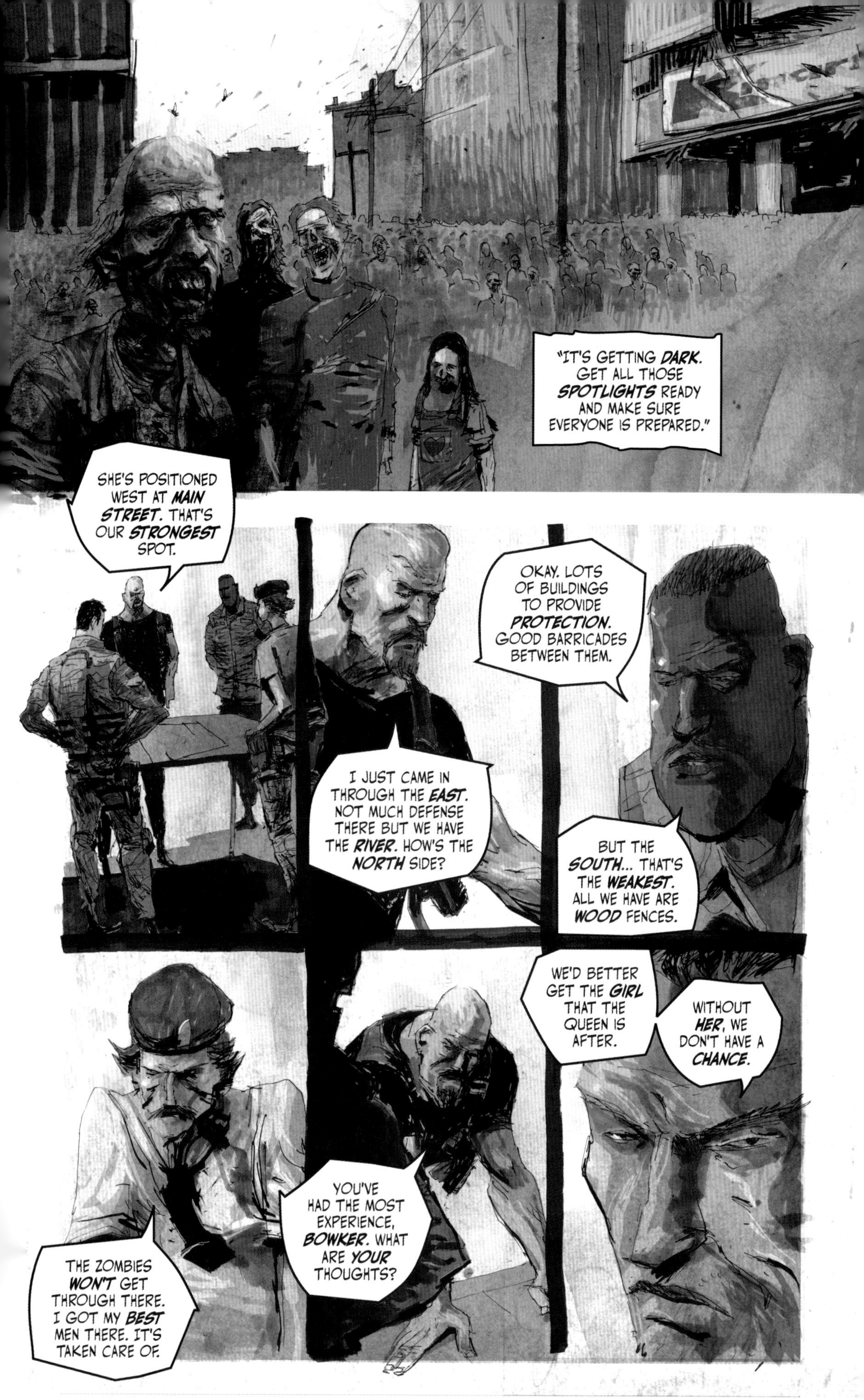
"IT'S GETTING DARK. GET ALL THOSE SPOTLIGHTS READY AND MAKE SURE EVERYONE IS PREPARED."
SHE'S POSITIONED WEST AT MAIN STREET. THAT'S OUR STRONGEST SPOT.
I JUST CAME IN THROUGH THE EAST. NOT MUCH DEFENSE THERE BUT WE HAVE THE RIVER. HOW'S THE NORTH SIDE?
OKAY. LOTS OF BUILDINGS TO PROVIDE PROTECTION. GOOD BARRICADES BETWEEN THEM.
BUT THE SOUTH... THAT'S THE WEAKEST. ALL WE HAVE ARE WOOD FENCES.
THE ZOMBIES WON'T GET THROUGH THERE. I GOT MY BEST MEN THERE. IT'S TAKEN CARE OF.
YOU'VE HAD THE MOST EXPERIENCE, BOWKER. WHAT ARE YOUR THOUGHTS?
WE'D BETTER GET THE GIRL THAT THE QUEEN IS AFTER.
WITHOUT HER, WE DON'T HAVE A CHANCE.

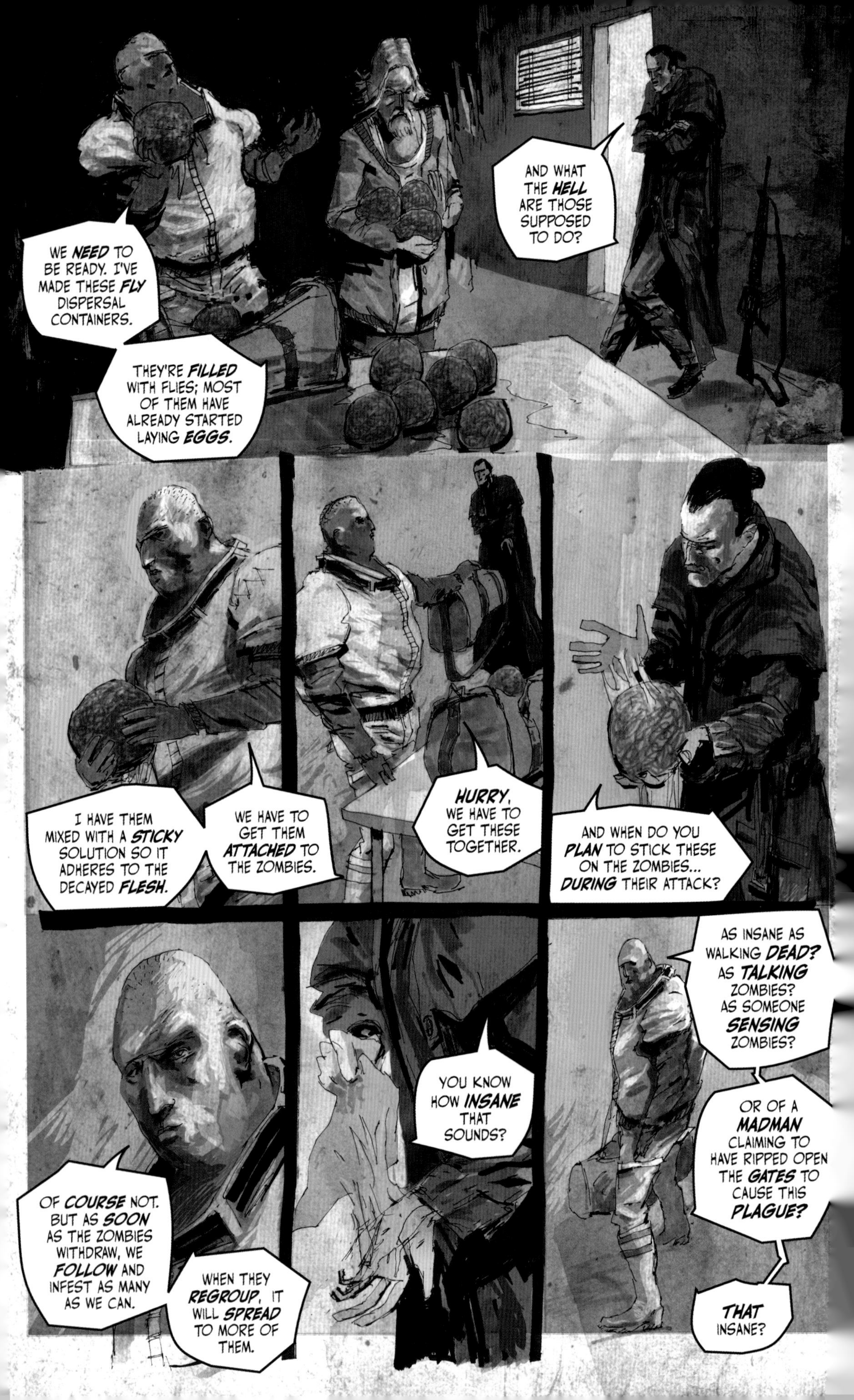
WE NEED TO BE READY. I'VE MADE THESE FLY DISPERSAL CONTAINERS.
THEY'RE FILLED WITH FLIES; MOST OF THEM HAVE ALREADY STARTED LAYING EGGS.
AND WHAT THE HELL ARE THOSE SUPPOSED TO DO?
I HAVE THEM MIXED WITH A STICKY SOLUTION SO IT ADHERES TO THE DECAYED FLESH.
WE HAVE TO GET THEM ATTACHED TO THE ZOMBIES.
HURRY, WE HAVE TO GET THESE TOGETHER.
AND WHEN DO YOU PLAN TO STICK THESE ON THE ZOMBIES... DURING THEIR ATTACK?
OF COURSE NOT. BUT AS SOON AS THE ZOMBIES WITHDRAW, WE FOLLOW AND INFEST AS MANY AS WE CAN.
WHEN THEY REGROUP, IT WILL SPREAD TO MORE OF THEM.
YOU KNOW HOW INSANE THAT SOUNDS?
AS INSANE AS WALKING DEAD? AS TALKING ZOMBIES? AS SOMEONE SENSING ZOMBIES?
OR OF A MADMAN CLAIMING TO HAVE RIPPED OPEN THE GATES TO CAUSE THIS PLAGUE?
THAT INSANE?

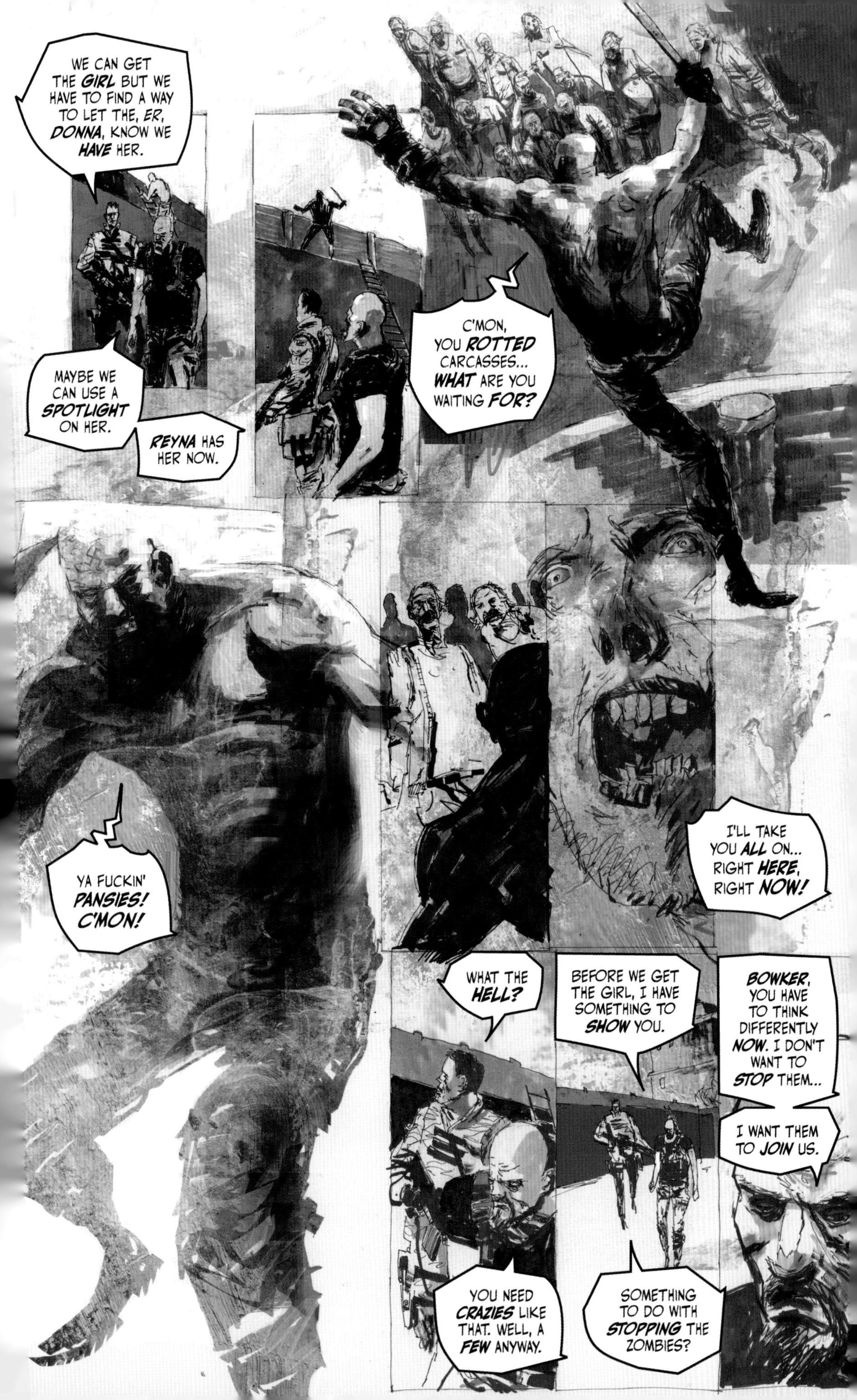
WE CAN GET THE GIRL BUT WE HAVE TO FIND A WAY TO LET THE, ER, DONNA, KNOW WE HAVE HER.
MAYBE WE CAN USE A SPOTLIGHT ON HER.
REYNA HAS HER NOW.
C'MON, YOU ROTTED CARCASSES... WHAT ARE YOU WAITING FOR?
YA FUCKIN' PANSIES! C'MON!
I'LL TAKE YOU ALL ON... RIGHT HERE, RIGHT NOW!
WHAT THE HELL?
YOU NEED CRAZIES LIKE THAT. WELL, A FEW ANYWAY.
BEFORE WE GET THE GIRL, I HAVE SOMETHING TO SHOW YOU.
SOMETHING TO DO WITH STOPPING THE ZOMBIES?
BOWKER, YOU HAVE TO THINK DIFFERENTLY NOW. I DON'T WANT TO STOP THEM...
I WANT THEM TO JOIN US.

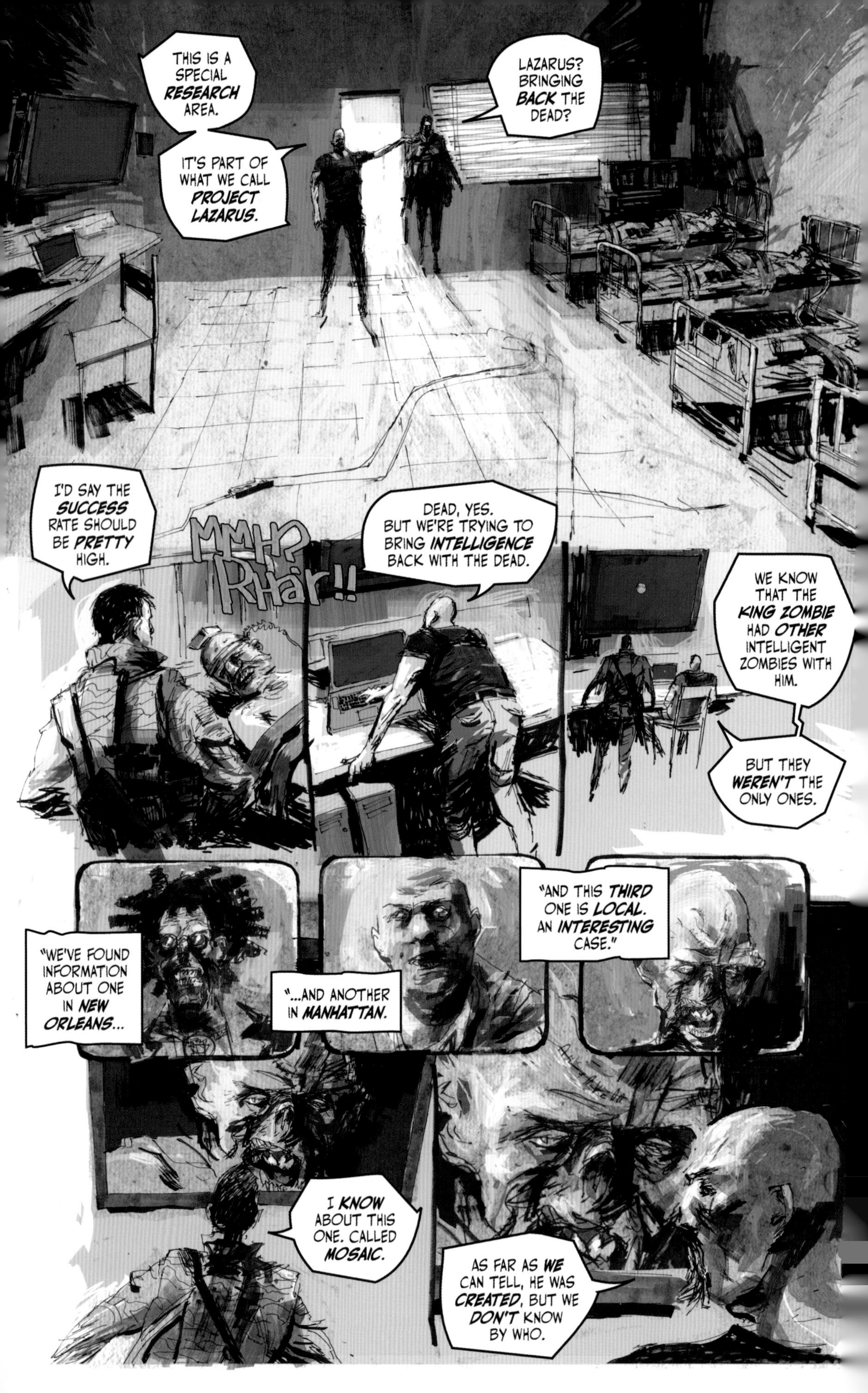
THIS IS A SPECIAL RESEARCH AREA.
IT'S PART OF WHAT WE CALL PROJECT LAZARUS.
LAZARUS? BRINGING BACK THE DEAD?
I'D SAY THE SUCCESS RATE SHOULD BE PRETTY HIGH.
MMH? RHAR!!
DEAD, YES. BUT WE'RE TRYING TO BRING INTELLIGENCE BACK WITH THE DEAD.
WE KNOW THAT THE KING ZOMBIE HAD OTHER INTELLIGENT ZOMBIES WITH HIM.
BUT THEY WEREN'T THE ONLY ONES.
"WE'VE FOUND INFORMATION ABOUT ONE IN NEW ORLEANS...
"...AND ANOTHER IN MANHATTAN.
"AND THIS THIRD ONE IS LOCAL. AN INTERESTING CASE."
I KNOW ABOUT THIS ONE. CALLED MOSAIC.
AS FAR AS WE CAN TELL, HE WAS CREATED, BUT WE DON'T KNOW BY WHO.

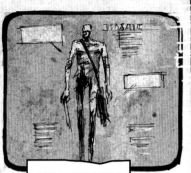

"HIS INTELLIGENCE IS *LIMITED* AND HE ATTEMPTS TO *CAPTURE* LIFE.

"HE TAKES THE *SKIN* OFF THE LIVING TO *SEW* ONTO HIS BODY."

I'VE *SEEN* HIS TAILORING UP CLOSE.

"LIMITED" IS THE *KEY* WORD FOR HIS INTELLIGENCE.

BUT HE'S *NOT* THE ONE OF INTEREST.

LET ME SHOW YOU PROJECT LAZARUS *PRIME.*

HE SOMEHOW *TRANSFERRED* INTO THIS BODY WHEN *SLAUGHTER'S* TOWN FELL.

WE *CAPTURED* HIM.

"THIS WAS *ONE* OF THE KING ZOMBIE'S *GROUP.*"

"IN CAPTIVITY FOR *MONTHS*, WE SUBJECTED HIM TO *PSYCHOLOGICAL* TESTS.

"AFTER ALL, IF HE HAD *HUMAN* INTELLIGENCE...

"...IT *STANDS* TO REASON, HE HAD HUMAN *ATTRIBUTES.*

"AND THAT ALLOWED US TO *BRAINWASH* HIM.

"HE IS NOW *OURS.*"

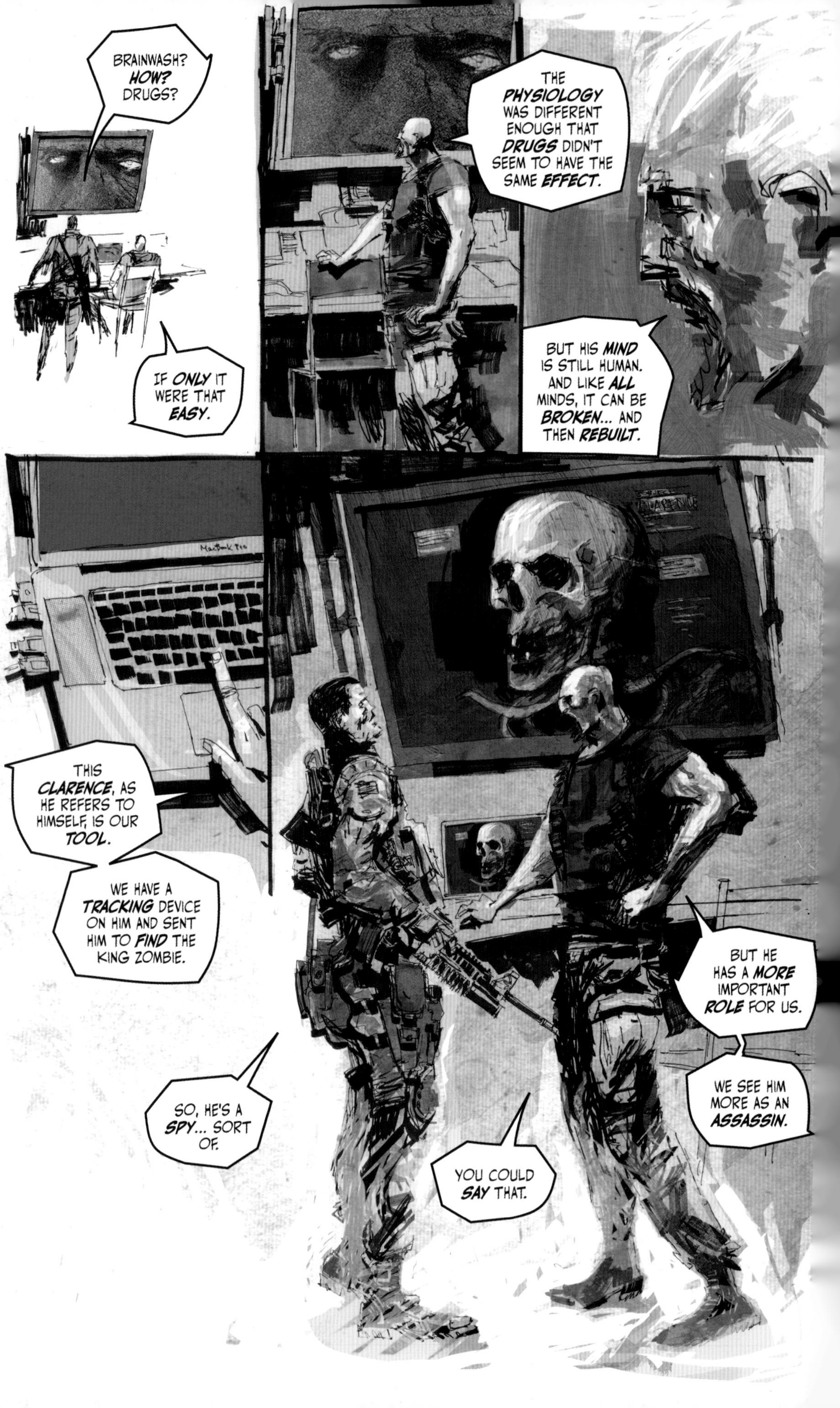
BRAINWASH? HOW? DRUGS?
IF ONLY IT WERE THAT EASY.
THE PHYSIOLOGY WAS DIFFERENT ENOUGH THAT DRUGS DIDN'T SEEM TO HAVE THE SAME EFFECT.
BUT HIS MIND IS STILL HUMAN. AND LIKE ALL MINDS, IT CAN BE BROKEN... AND THEN REBUILT.
MacBook Pro
THIS CLARENCE, AS HE REFERS TO HIMSELF, IS OUR TOOL.
WE HAVE A TRACKING DEVICE ON HIM AND SENT HIM TO FIND THE KING ZOMBIE.
BUT HE HAS A MORE IMPORTANT ROLE FOR US.
WE SEE HIM MORE AS AN ASSASSIN.
SO, HE'S A SPY... SORT OF.
YOU COULD SAY THAT.

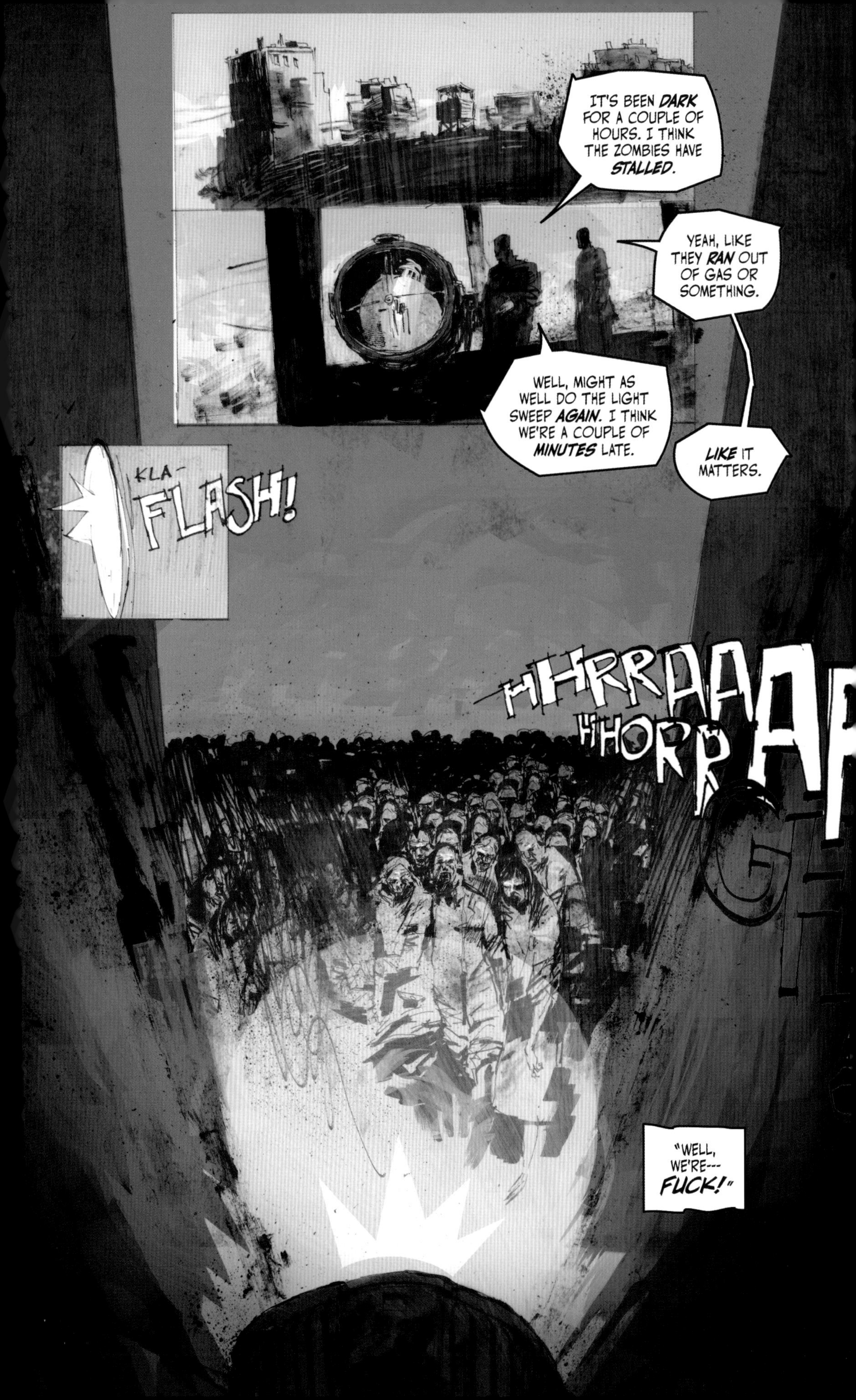
IT'S BEEN DARK FOR A COUPLE OF HOURS. I THINK THE ZOMBIES HAVE STALLED.
YEAH, LIKE THEY RAN OUT OF GAS OR SOMETHING.
WELL, MIGHT AS WELL DO THE LIGHT SWEEP AGAIN. I THINK WE'RE A COUPLE OF MINUTES LATE.
LIKE IT MATTERS.
KLA-FLASH!
HHRRAAA
HHORR
"WELL, WE'RE--- FUCK!"

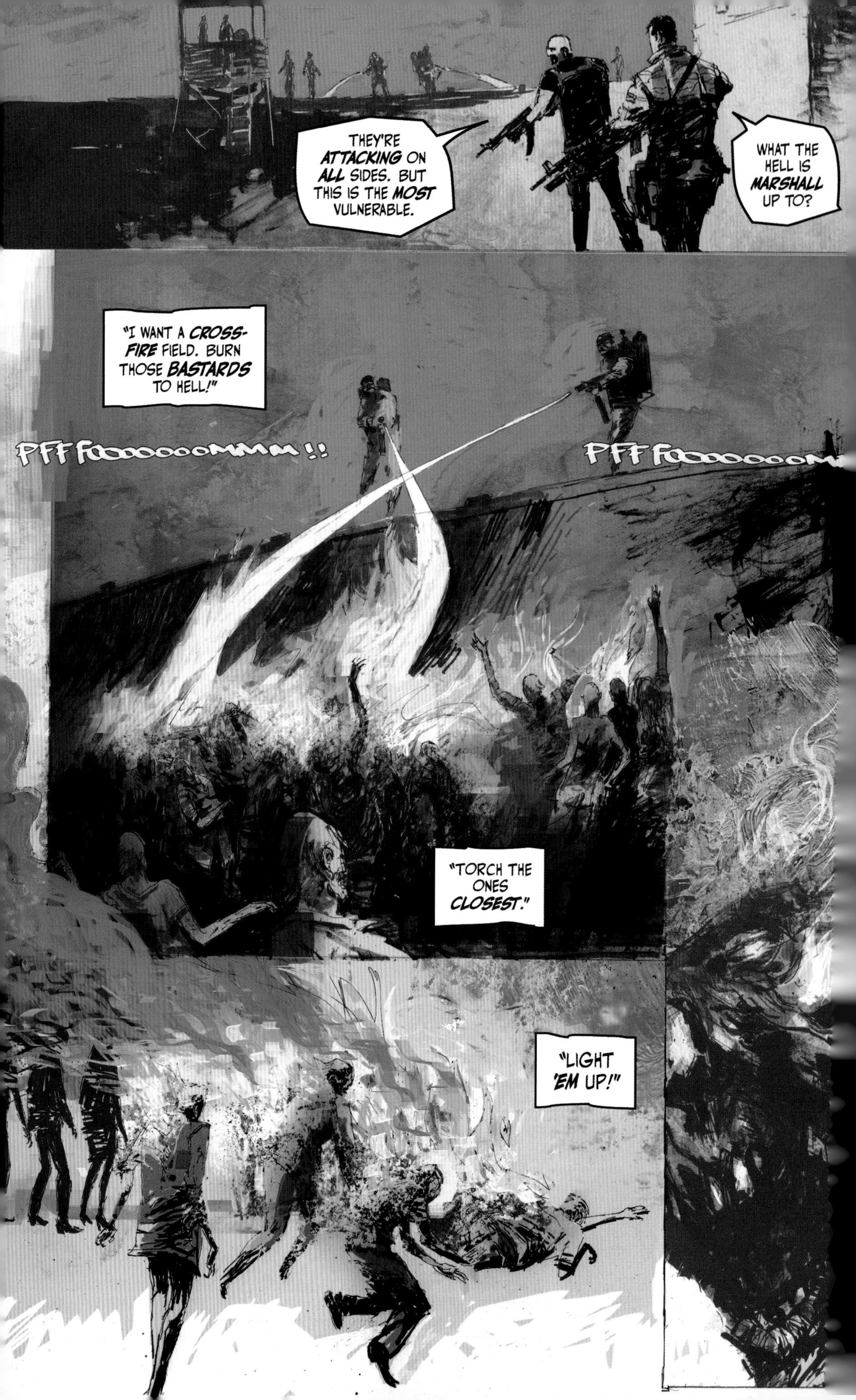
THEY'RE ATTACKING ON ALL SIDES. BUT THIS IS THE MOST VULNERABLE.
WHAT THE HELL IS MARSHALL UP TO?
"I WANT A CROSS-FIRE FIELD. BURN THOSE BASTARDS TO HELL!"
PFFFOOOOOOOMMMM!!
PFFFOOOOOOOOM
"TORCH THE ONES CLOSEST."
"LIGHT 'EM UP!"

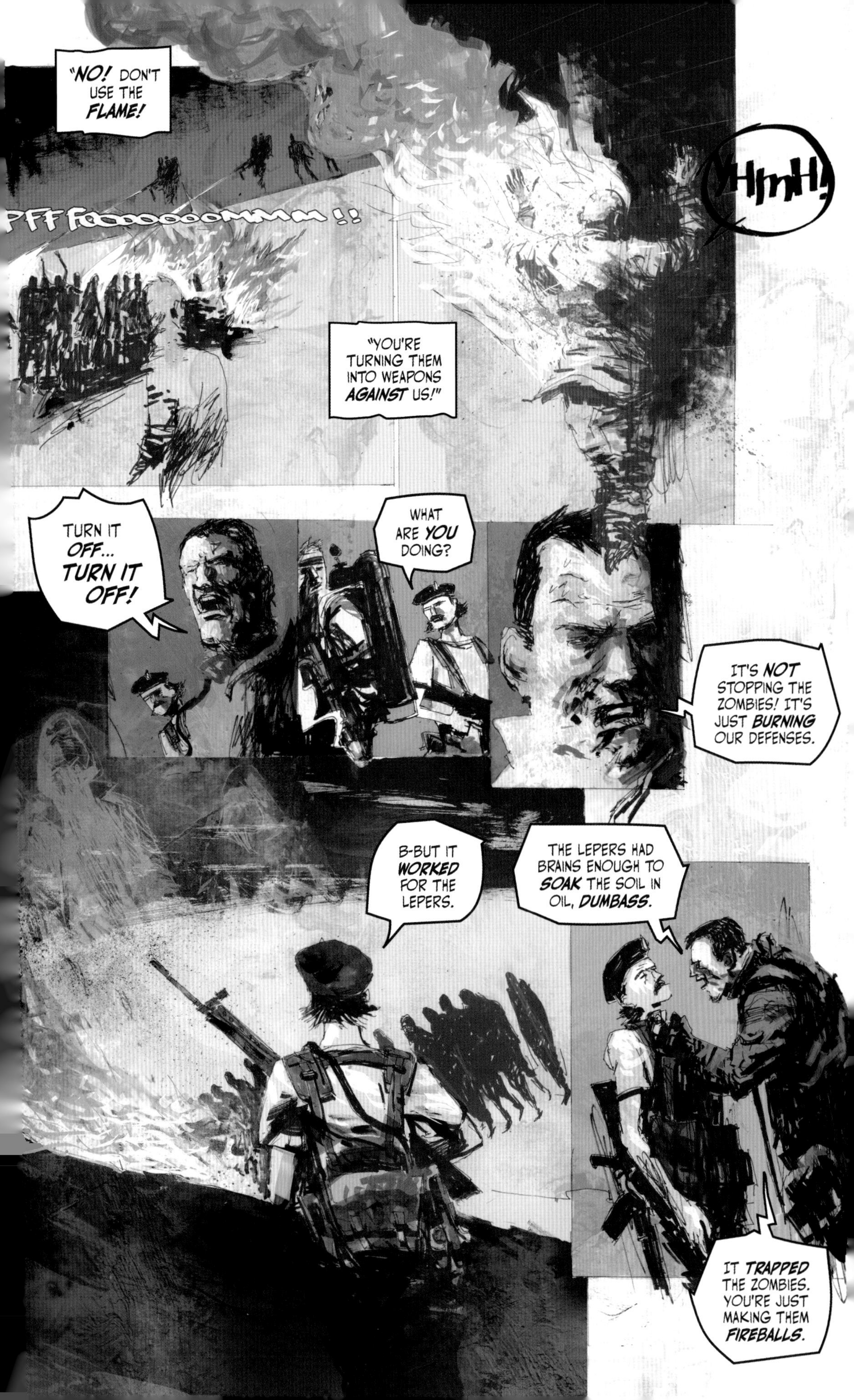
"NO! DON'T USE THE FLAME!
PFFFOOOOOOMMMM!!
YHMH!
"YOU'RE TURNING THEM INTO WEAPONS AGAINST US!"
TURN IT OFF... TURN IT OFF!
WHAT ARE YOU DOING?
IT'S NOT STOPPING THE ZOMBIES! IT'S JUST BURNING OUR DEFENSES.
B-BUT IT WORKED FOR THE LEPERS.
THE LEPERS HAD BRAINS ENOUGH TO SOAK THE SOIL IN OIL, DUMBASS.
IT TRAPPED THE ZOMBIES. YOU'RE JUST MAKING THEM FIREBALLS.

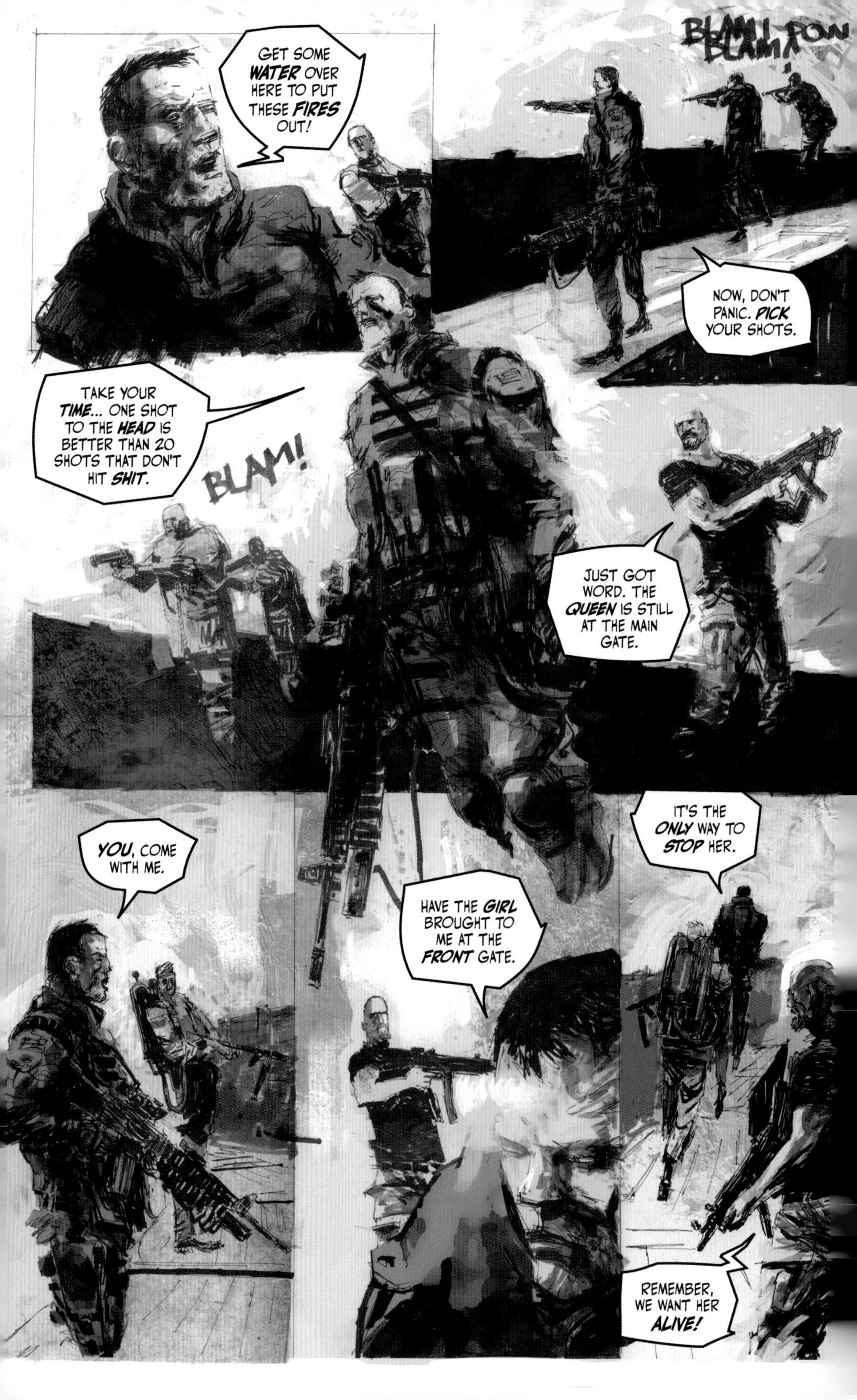

GET SOME WATER OVER HERE TO PUT THESE FIRES OUT!
NOW, DON'T PANIC. PICK YOUR SHOTS.
TAKE YOUR TIME... ONE SHOT TO THE HEAD IS BETTER THAN 20 SHOTS THAT DON'T HIT SHIT.
BLAM!
JUST GOT WORD. THE QUEEN IS STILL AT THE MAIN GATE.
YOU, COME WITH ME.
HAVE THE GIRL BROUGHT TO ME AT THE FRONT GATE.
IT'S THE ONLY WAY TO STOP HER.
REMEMBER, WE WANT HER ALIVE!

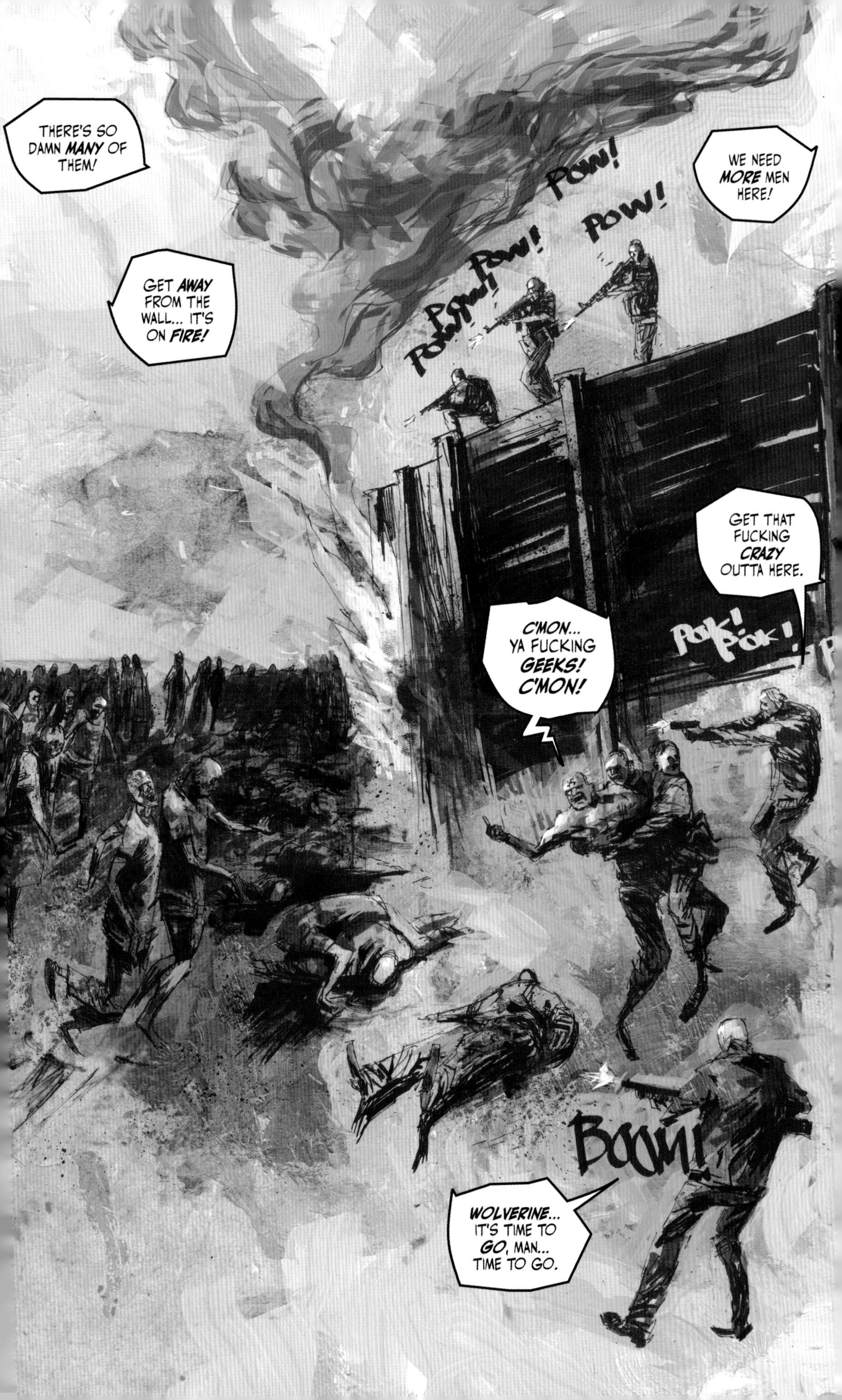
THERE'S SO DAMN MANY OF THEM!
WE NEED MORE MEN HERE!
POW!
POW!
POW!
GET AWAY FROM THE WALL... IT'S ON FIRE!
GET THAT FUCKING CRAZY OUTTA HERE.
C'MON... YA FUCKING GEEKS! C'MON!
POK! POK!
BOOM!
WOLVERINE... IT'S TIME TO GO, MAN... TIME TO GO.

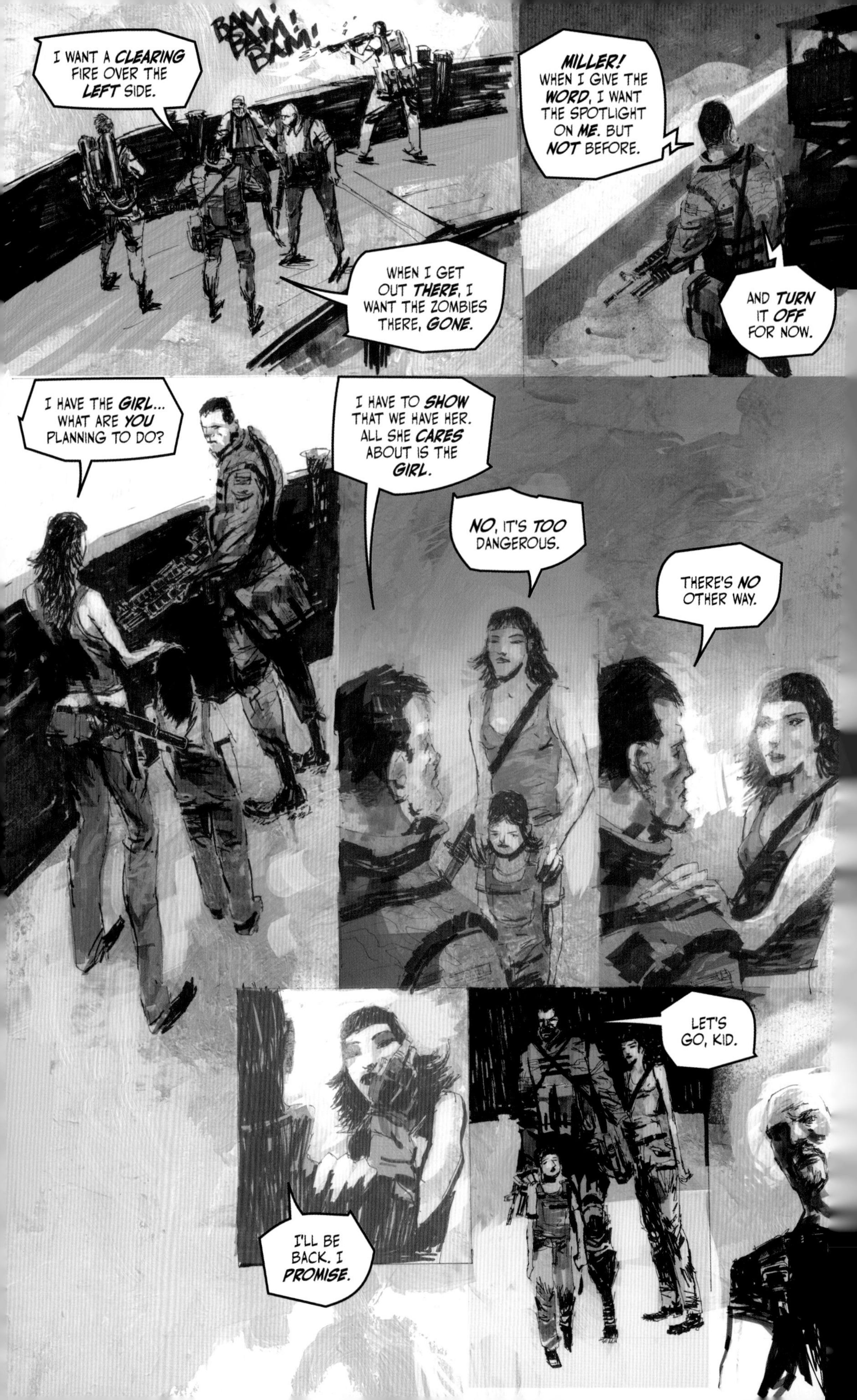
BAM! BAM! BAM!
I WANT A CLEARING FIRE OVER THE LEFT SIDE.
WHEN I GET OUT THERE, I WANT THE ZOMBIES THERE, GONE.
MILLER! WHEN I GIVE THE WORD, I WANT THE SPOTLIGHT ON ME. BUT NOT BEFORE.
AND TURN IT OFF FOR NOW.
I HAVE THE GIRL... WHAT ARE YOU PLANNING TO DO?
I HAVE TO SHOW THAT WE HAVE HER. ALL SHE CARES ABOUT IS THE GIRL.
NO, IT'S TOO DANGEROUS.
THERE'S NO OTHER WAY.
I'LL BE BACK. I PROMISE.
LET'S GO, KID.

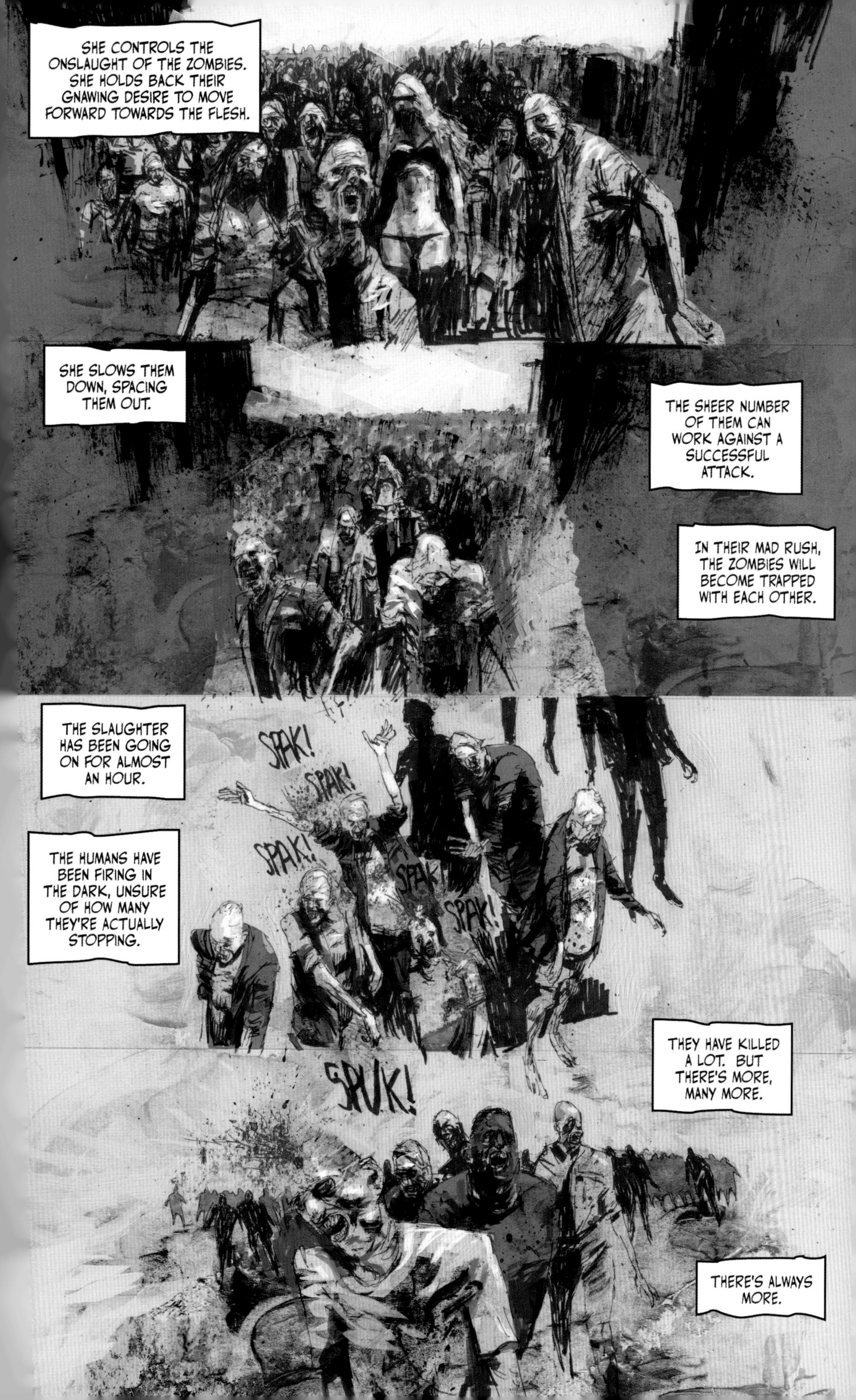
SHE CONTROLS THE ONSLAUGHT OF THE ZOMBIES. SHE HOLDS BACK THEIR GNAWING DESIRE TO MOVE FORWARD TOWARDS THE FLESH.
SHE SLOWS THEM DOWN, SPACING THEM OUT.
THE SHEER NUMBER OF THEM CAN WORK AGAINST A SUCCESSFUL ATTACK.
IN THEIR MAD RUSH, THE ZOMBIES WILL BECOME TRAPPED WITH EACH OTHER.
THE SLAUGHTER HAS BEEN GOING ON FOR ALMOST AN HOUR.
SPAK!
SPAK!
THE HUMANS HAVE BEEN FIRING IN THE DARK, UNSURE OF HOW MANY THEY'RE ACTUALLY STOPPING.
SPAK!
SPAK
SPAK!
THEY HAVE KILLED A LOT. BUT THERE'S MORE, MANY MORE.
SPUK!
THERE'S ALWAYS MORE.

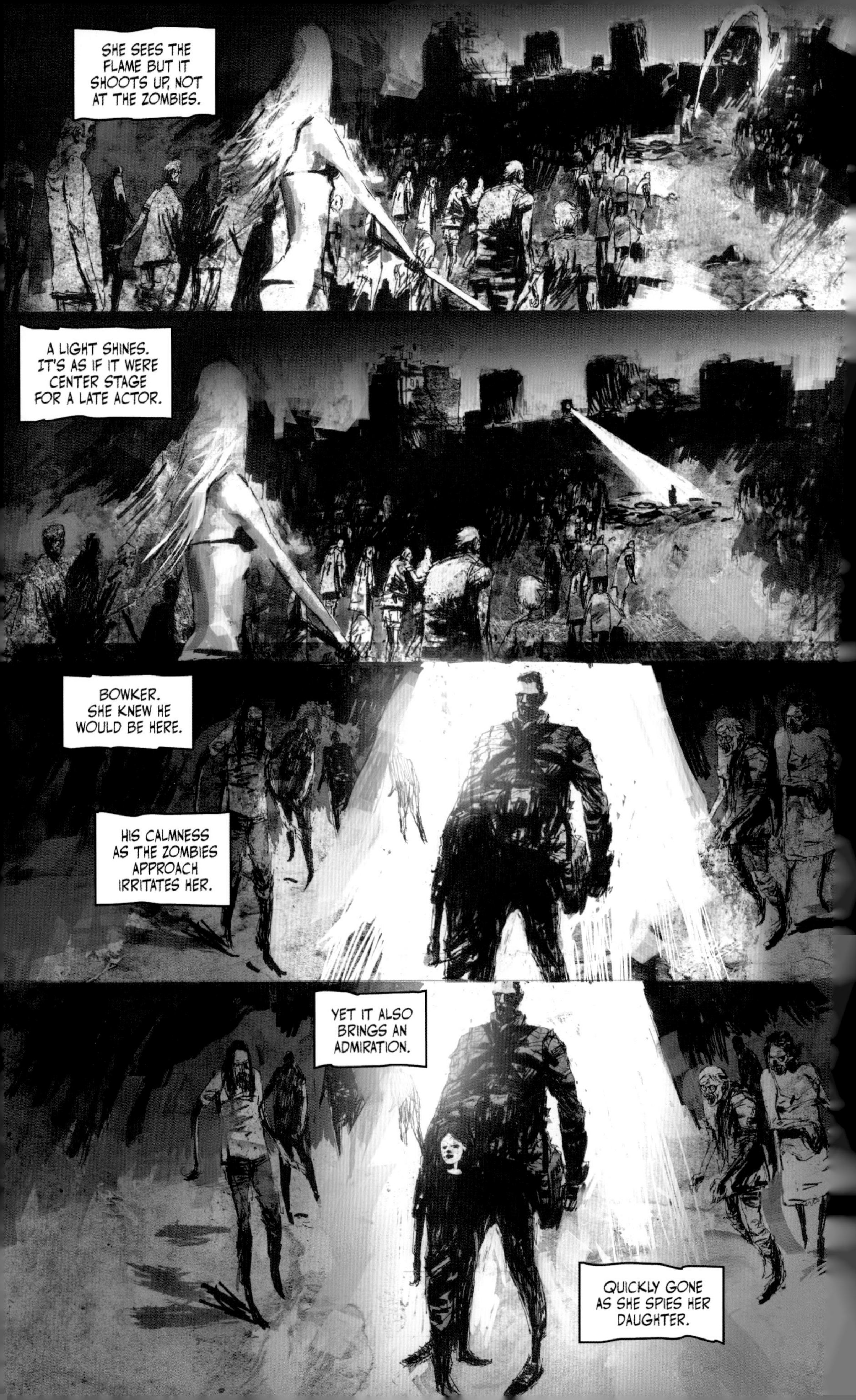
SHE SEES THE FLAME BUT IT SHOOTS UP, NOT AT THE ZOMBIES.
A LIGHT SHINES. IT'S AS IF IT WERE CENTER STAGE FOR A LATE ACTOR.
BOWKER. SHE KNEW HE WOULD BE HERE.
HIS CALMNESS AS THE ZOMBIES APPROACH IRRITATES HER.
YET IT ALSO BRINGS AN ADMIRATION.
QUICKLY GONE AS SHE SPIES HER DAUGHTER.

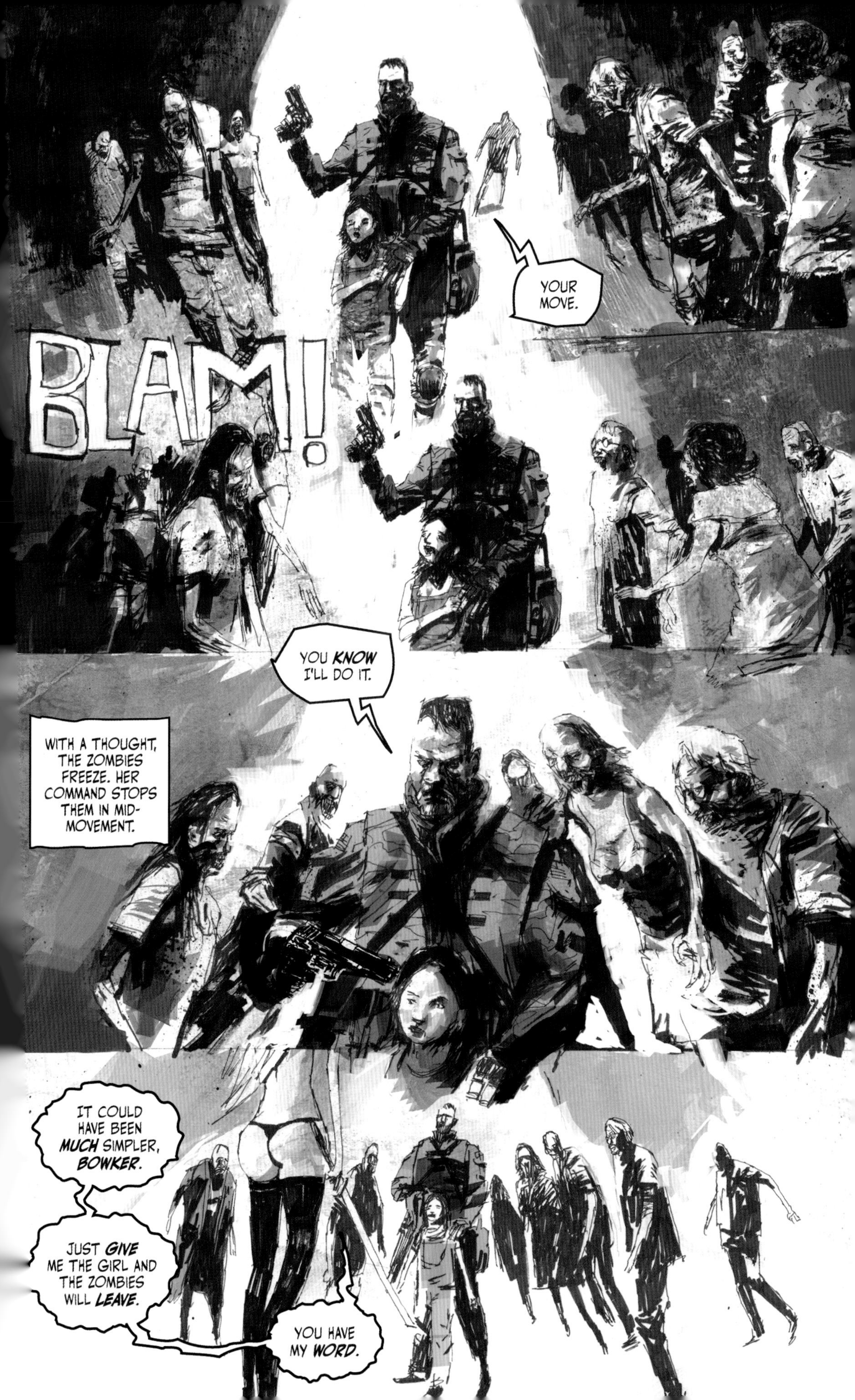
YOUR MOVE.
BLAM!
YOU KNOW I'LL DO IT.
WITH A THOUGHT, THE ZOMBIES FREEZE. HER COMMAND STOPS THEM IN MID-MOVEMENT.
IT COULD HAVE BEEN MUCH SIMPLER, BOWKER.
JUST GIVE ME THE GIRL AND THE ZOMBIES WILL LEAVE.
YOU HAVE MY WORD.

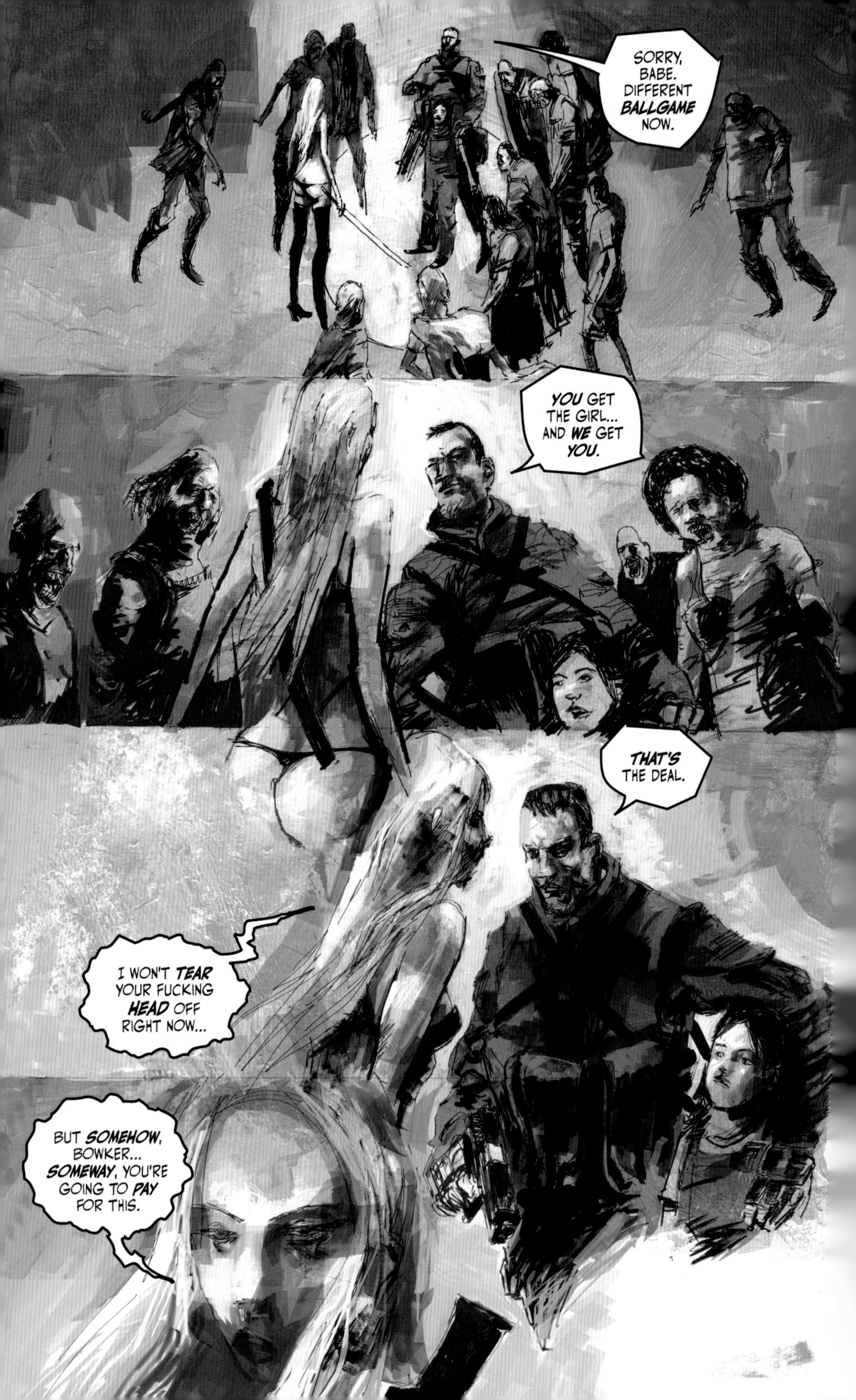
SORRY, BABE. DIFFERENT BALLGAME NOW.
YOU GET THE GIRL... AND WE GET YOU.
THAT'S THE DEAL.
I WON'T TEAR YOUR FUCKING HEAD OFF RIGHT NOW...
BUT SOMEHOW, BOWKER... SOMEWAY, YOU'RE GOING TO PAY FOR THIS.

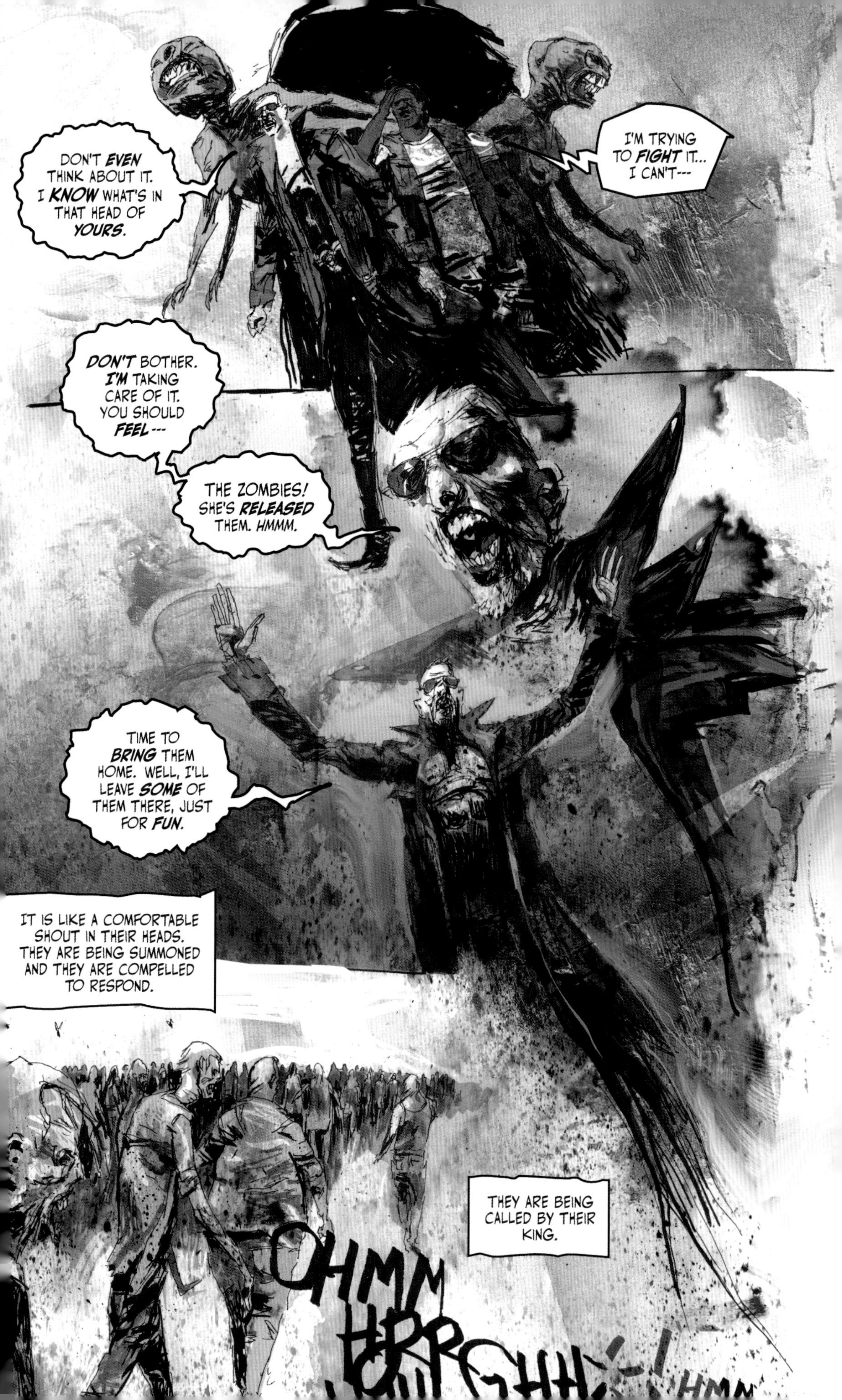
DON'T EVEN THINK ABOUT IT. I KNOW WHAT'S IN THAT HEAD OF YOURS.
I'M TRYING TO FIGHT IT... I CAN'T---
DON'T BOTHER. I'M TAKING CARE OF IT. YOU SHOULD FEEL---
THE ZOMBIES! SHE'S RELEASED THEM. HMMM.
TIME TO BRING THEM HOME. WELL, I'LL LEAVE SOME OF THEM THERE, JUST FOR FUN.
IT IS LIKE A COMFORTABLE SHOUT IN THEIR HEADS. THEY ARE BEING SUMMONED AND THEY ARE COMPELLED TO RESPOND.
THEY ARE BEING CALLED BY THEIR KING.
OHMM

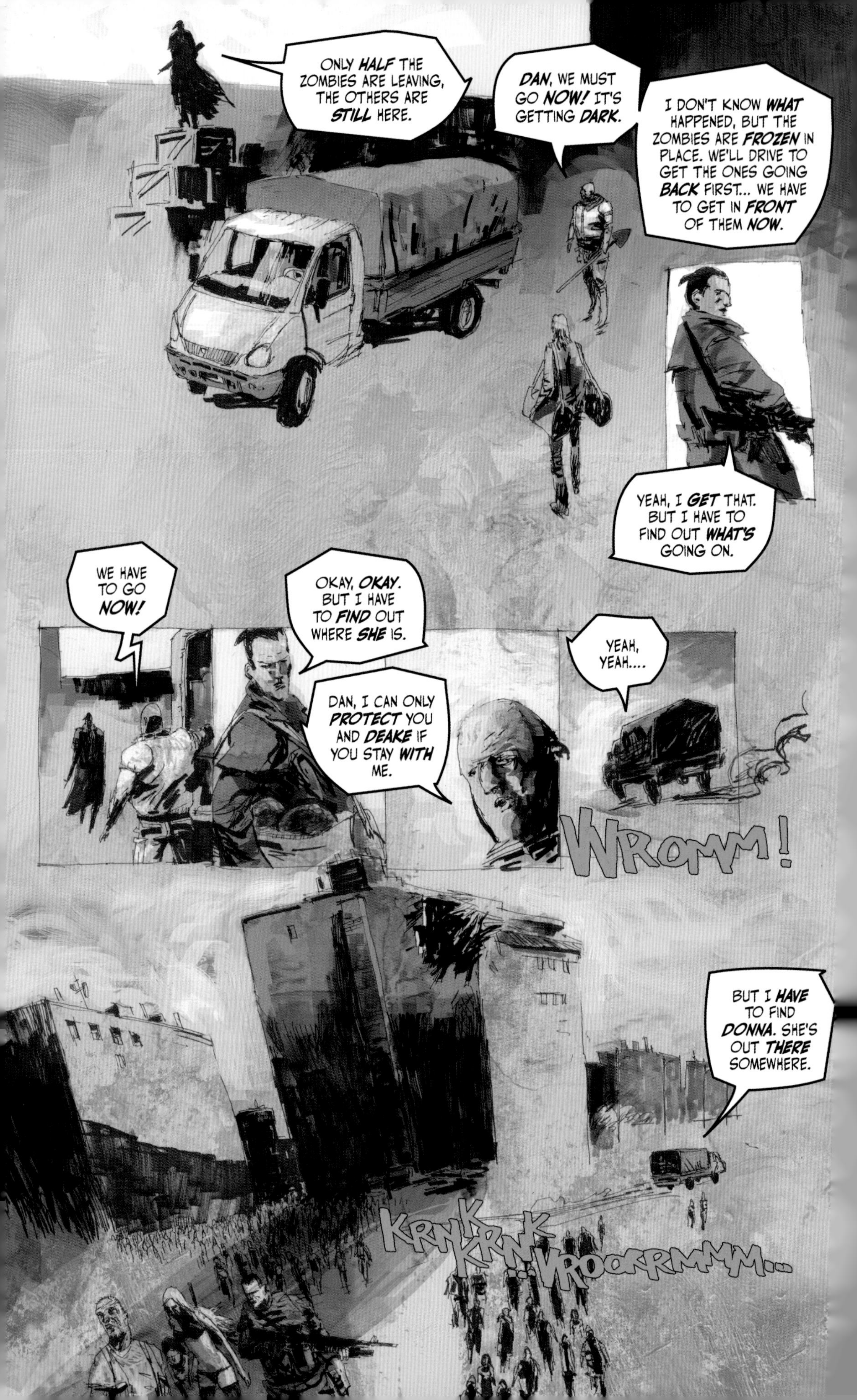
ONLY HALF THE ZOMBIES ARE LEAVING, THE OTHERS ARE STILL HERE.
DAN, WE MUST GO NOW! IT'S GETTING DARK.
I DON'T KNOW WHAT HAPPENED, BUT THE ZOMBIES ARE FROZEN IN PLACE. WE'LL DRIVE TO GET THE ONES GOING BACK FIRST... WE HAVE TO GET IN FRONT OF THEM NOW.
YEAH, I GET THAT. BUT I HAVE TO FIND OUT WHAT'S GOING ON.
WE HAVE TO GO NOW!
OKAY, OKAY. BUT I HAVE TO FIND OUT WHERE SHE IS.
DAN, I CAN ONLY PROTECT YOU AND DEAKE IF YOU STAY WITH ME.
YEAH, YEAH....
WROMM!
BUT I HAVE TO FIND DONNA. SHE'S OUT THERE SOMEWHERE.
KRNK KRNK KRNK VROORRMMM...

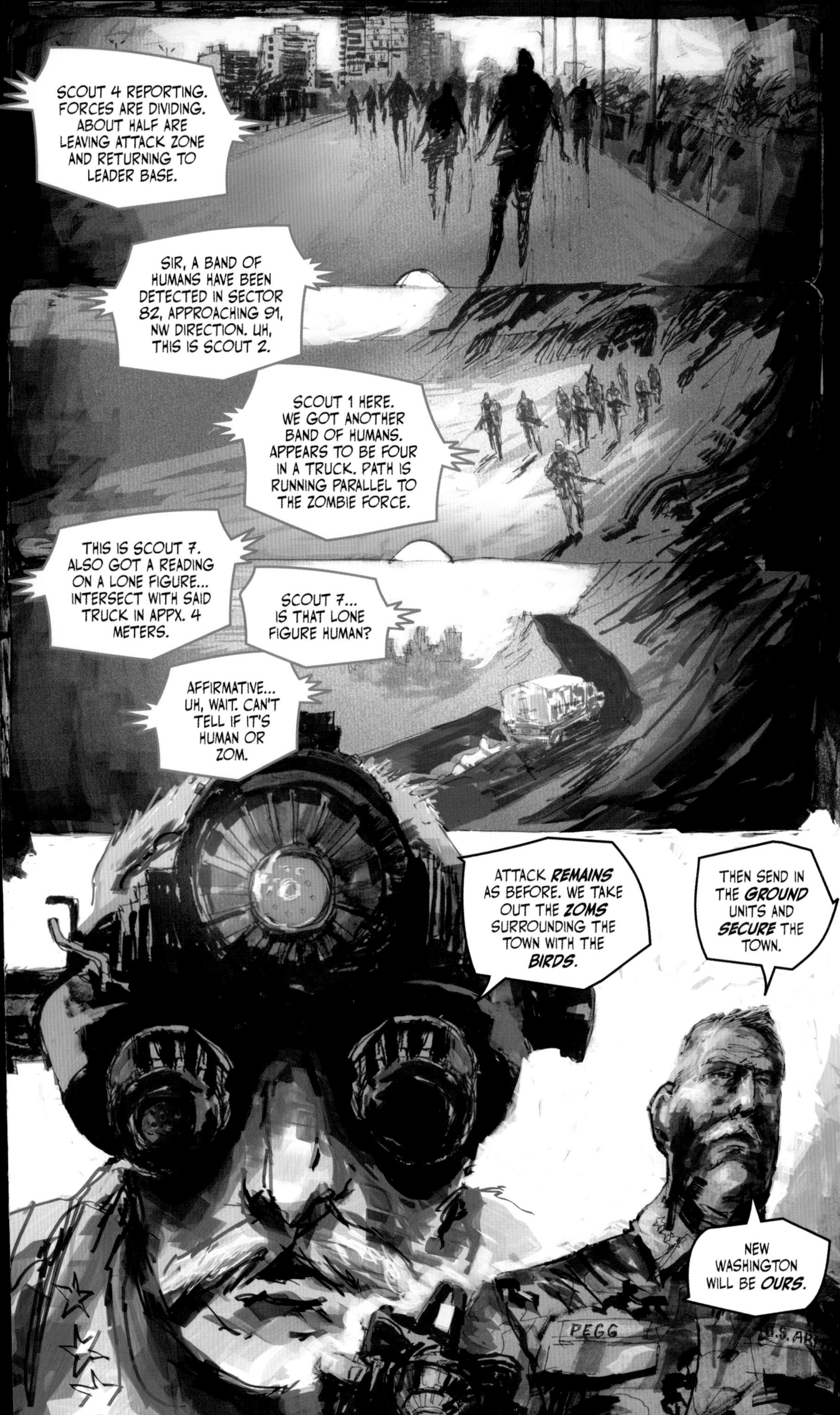
SCOUT 4 REPORTING. FORCES ARE DIVIDING. ABOUT HALF ARE LEAVING ATTACK ZONE AND RETURNING TO LEADER BASE.
SIR, A BAND OF HUMANS HAVE BEEN DETECTED IN SECTOR 82, APPROACHING 91, NW DIRECTION. UH, THIS IS SCOUT 2.
SCOUT 1 HERE. WE GOT ANOTHER BAND OF HUMANS. APPEARS TO BE FOUR IN A TRUCK. PATH IS RUNNING PARALLEL TO THE ZOMBIE FORCE.
THIS IS SCOUT 7. ALSO GOT A READING ON A LONE FIGURE... INTERSECT WITH SAID TRUCK IN APPX. 4 METERS.
SCOUT 7... IS THAT LONE FIGURE HUMAN?
AFFIRMATIVE... UH, WAIT. CAN'T TELL IF IT'S HUMAN OR ZOM.
ATTACK *REMAINS* AS BEFORE. WE TAKE OUT THE *ZOMS* SURROUNDING THE TOWN WITH THE *BIRDS*.
THEN SEND IN THE *GROUND* UNITS AND *SECURE* THE TOWN.
NEW WASHINGTON WILL BE *OURS*.
PEGG

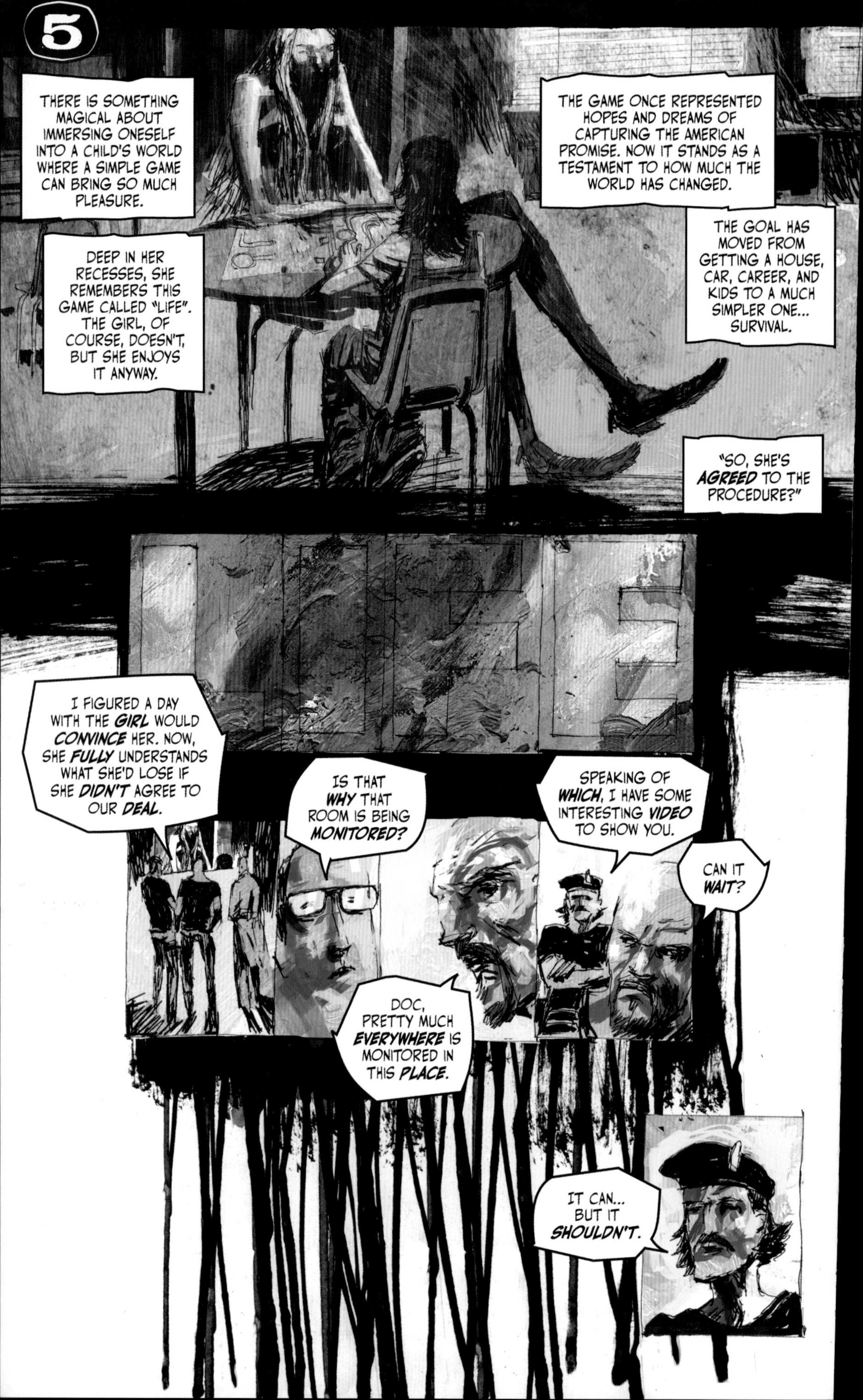
5
THERE IS SOMETHING MAGICAL ABOUT IMMERSING ONESELF INTO A CHILD'S WORLD WHERE A SIMPLE GAME CAN BRING SO MUCH PLEASURE.
DEEP IN HER RECESSES, SHE REMEMBERS THIS GAME CALLED "LIFE". THE GIRL, OF COURSE, DOESN'T, BUT SHE ENJOYS IT ANYWAY.
THE GAME ONCE REPRESENTED HOPES AND DREAMS OF CAPTURING THE AMERICAN PROMISE. NOW IT STANDS AS A TESTAMENT TO HOW MUCH THE WORLD HAS CHANGED.
THE GOAL HAS MOVED FROM GETTING A HOUSE, CAR, CAREER, AND KIDS TO A MUCH SIMPLER ONE... SURVIVAL.
"SO, SHE'S AGREED TO THE PROCEDURE?"
I FIGURED A DAY WITH THE GIRL WOULD CONVINCE HER. NOW, SHE FULLY UNDERSTANDS WHAT SHE'D LOSE IF SHE DIDN'T AGREE TO OUR DEAL.
IS THAT WHY THAT ROOM IS BEING MONITORED?
DOC, PRETTY MUCH EVERYWHERE IS MONITORED IN THIS PLACE.
SPEAKING OF WHICH, I HAVE SOME INTERESTING VIDEO TO SHOW YOU.
CAN IT WAIT?
IT CAN... BUT IT SHOULDN'T.

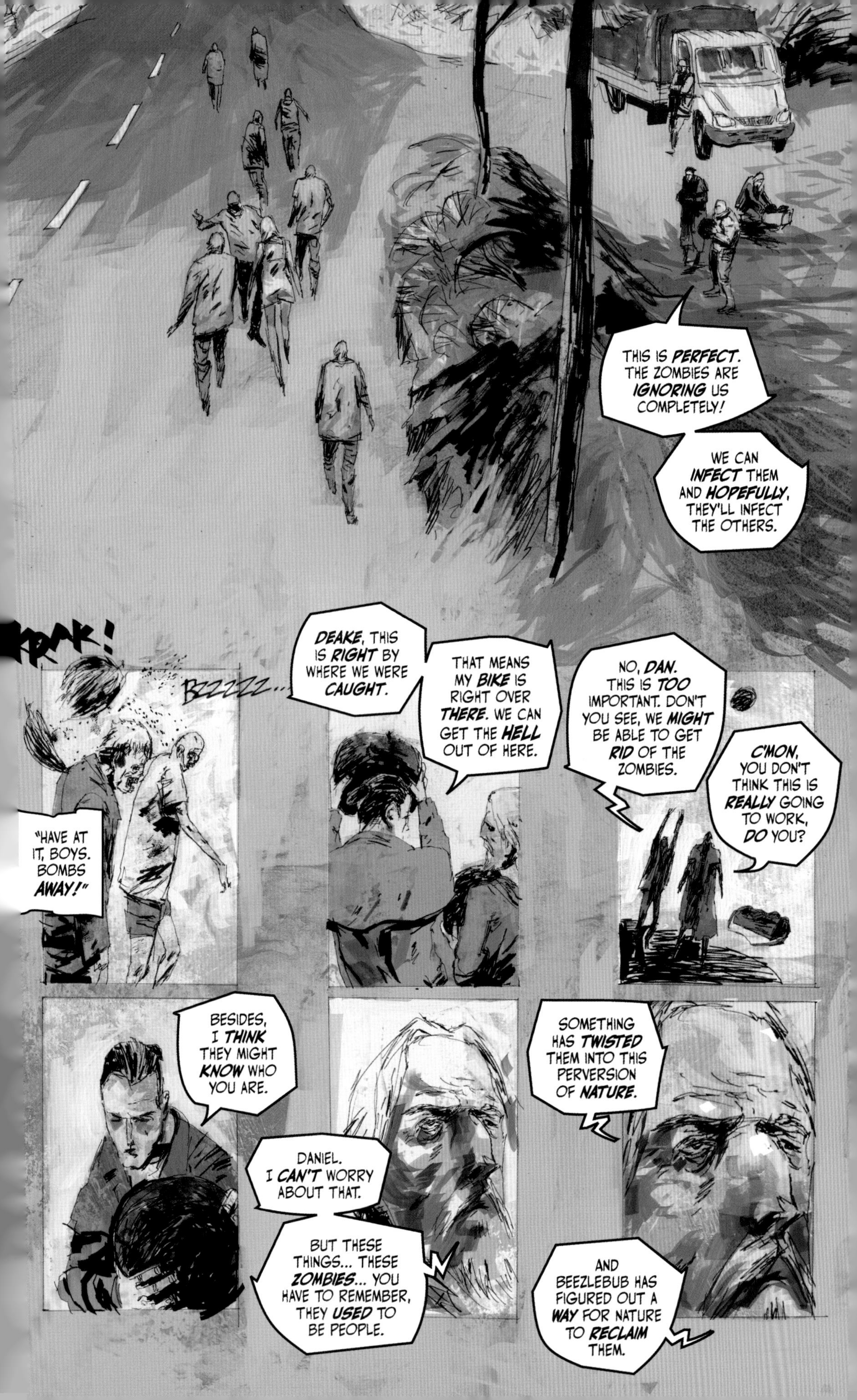
THIS IS PERFECT. THE ZOMBIES ARE IGNORING US COMPLETELY!
WE CAN INFECT THEM AND HOPEFULLY, THEY'LL INFECT THE OTHERS.
KRAK!
BZZZZZ...
"HAVE AT IT, BOYS. BOMBS AWAY!"
DEAKE, THIS IS RIGHT BY WHERE WE WERE CAUGHT.
THAT MEANS MY BIKE IS RIGHT OVER THERE. WE CAN GET THE HELL OUT OF HERE.
NO, DAN. THIS IS TOO IMPORTANT. DON'T YOU SEE, WE MIGHT BE ABLE TO GET RID OF THE ZOMBIES.
C'MON, YOU DON'T THINK THIS IS REALLY GOING TO WORK, DO YOU?
BESIDES, I THINK THEY MIGHT KNOW WHO YOU ARE.
DANIEL. I CAN'T WORRY ABOUT THAT.
BUT THESE THINGS... THESE ZOMBIES... YOU HAVE TO REMEMBER, THEY USED TO BE PEOPLE.
SOMETHING HAS TWISTED THEM INTO THIS PERVERSION OF NATURE.
AND BEEZLEBUB HAS FIGURED OUT A WAY FOR NATURE TO RECLAIM THEM.

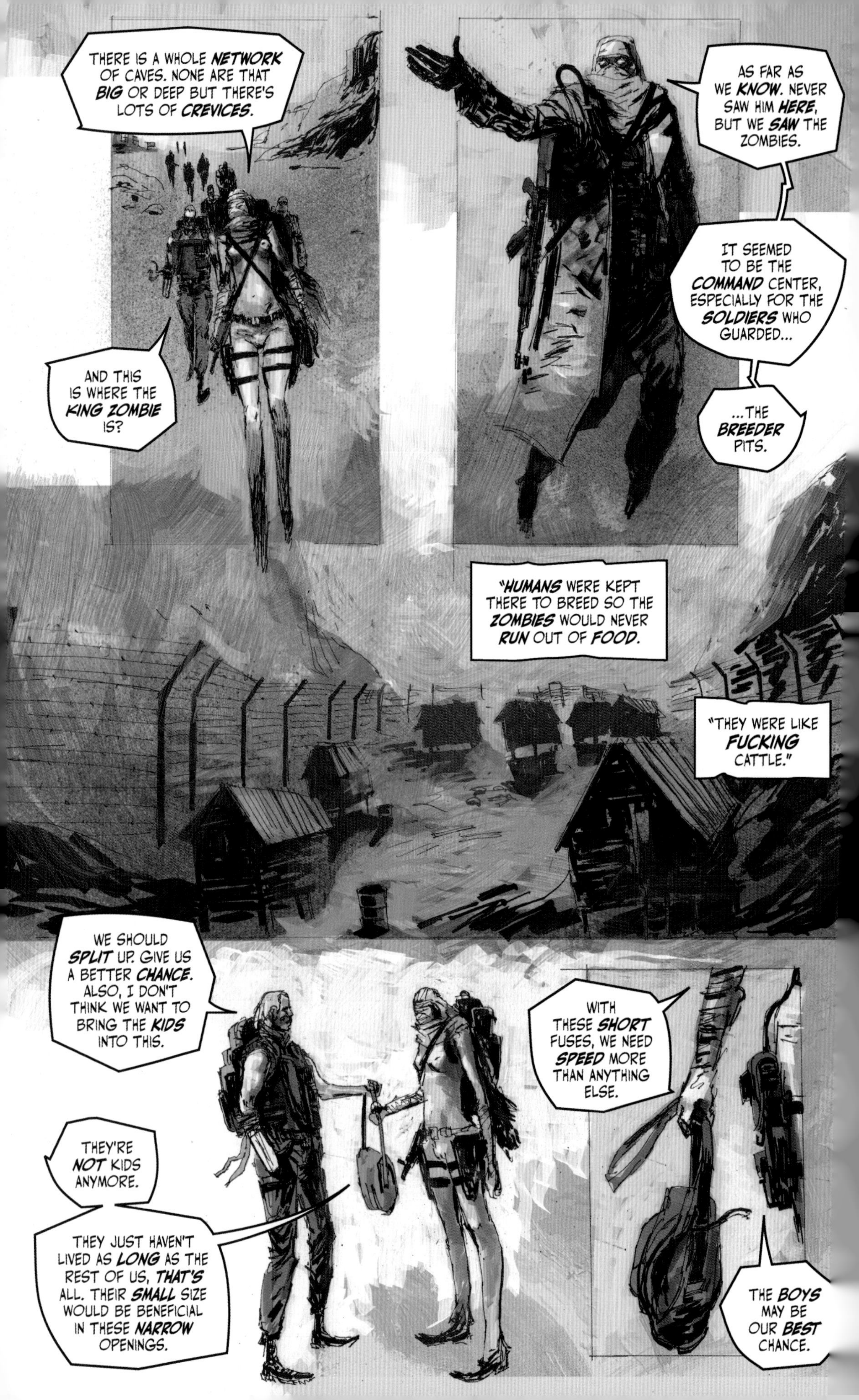
THERE IS A WHOLE NETWORK OF CAVES. NONE ARE THAT BIG OR DEEP BUT THERE'S LOTS OF CREVICES.
AND THIS IS WHERE THE KING ZOMBIE IS?
AS FAR AS WE KNOW. NEVER SAW HIM HERE, BUT WE SAW THE ZOMBIES.
IT SEEMED TO BE THE COMMAND CENTER, ESPECIALLY FOR THE SOLDIERS WHO GUARDED...
...THE BREEDER PITS.
"HUMANS WERE KEPT THERE TO BREED SO THE ZOMBIES WOULD NEVER RUN OUT OF FOOD.
"THEY WERE LIKE FUCKING CATTLE."
WE SHOULD SPLIT UP. GIVE US A BETTER CHANCE. ALSO, I DON'T THINK WE WANT TO BRING THE KIDS INTO THIS.
THEY'RE NOT KIDS ANYMORE.
THEY JUST HAVEN'T LIVED AS LONG AS THE REST OF US, THAT'S ALL. THEIR SMALL SIZE WOULD BE BENEFICIAL IN THESE NARROW OPENINGS.
WITH THESE SHORT FUSES, WE NEED SPEED MORE THAN ANYTHING ELSE.
THE BOYS MAY BE OUR BEST CHANCE.

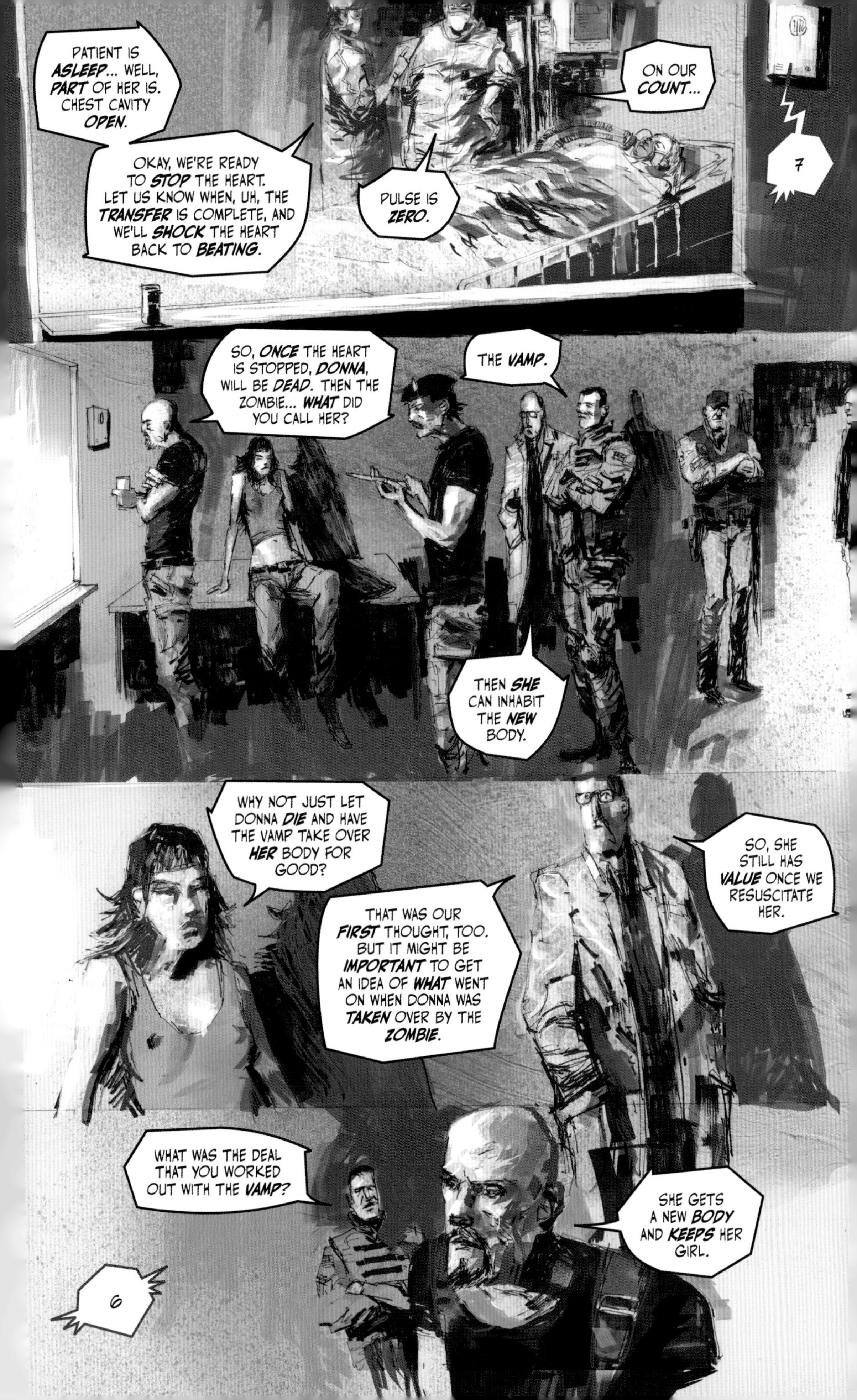
PATIENT IS ASLEEP... WELL, PART OF HER IS. CHEST CAVITY OPEN.
OKAY, WE'RE READY TO STOP THE HEART. LET US KNOW WHEN, UH, THE TRANSFER IS COMPLETE, AND WE'LL SHOCK THE HEART BACK TO BEATING.
PULSE IS ZERO.
ON OUR COUNT...
7
SO, ONCE THE HEART IS STOPPED, DONNA, WILL BE DEAD. THEN THE ZOMBIE... WHAT DID YOU CALL HER?
THE VAMP.
THEN SHE CAN INHABIT THE NEW BODY.
WHY NOT JUST LET DONNA DIE AND HAVE THE VAMP TAKE OVER HER BODY FOR GOOD?
THAT WAS OUR FIRST THOUGHT, TOO. BUT IT MIGHT BE IMPORTANT TO GET AN IDEA OF WHAT WENT ON WHEN DONNA WAS TAKEN OVER BY THE ZOMBIE.
SO, SHE STILL HAS VALUE ONCE WE RESUSCITATE HER.
WHAT WAS THE DEAL THAT YOU WORKED OUT WITH THE VAMP?
SHE GETS A NEW BODY AND KEEPS HER GIRL.
6

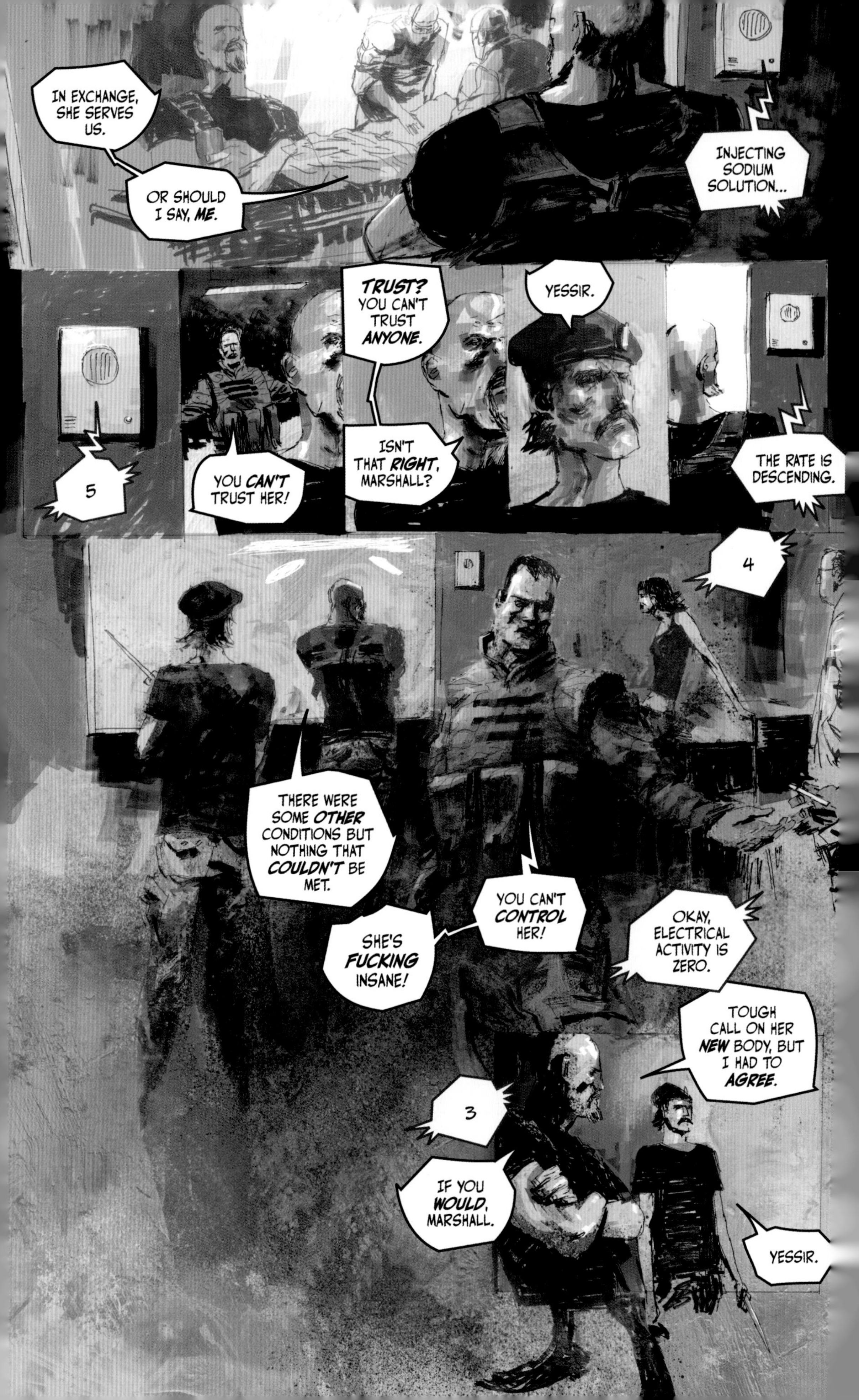
IN EXCHANGE, SHE SERVES US.
OR SHOULD I SAY, ME.
INJECTING SODIUM SOLUTION...
5
YOU CAN'T TRUST HER!
TRUST? YOU CAN'T TRUST ANYONE.
ISN'T THAT RIGHT, MARSHALL?
YESSIR.
THE RATE IS DESCENDING.
4
THERE WERE SOME OTHER CONDITIONS BUT NOTHING THAT COULDN'T BE MET.
YOU CAN'T CONTROL HER!
SHE'S FUCKING INSANE!
OKAY, ELECTRICAL ACTIVITY IS ZERO.
TOUGH CALL ON HER NEW BODY, BUT I HAD TO AGREE.
3
IF YOU WOULD, MARSHALL.
YESSIR.

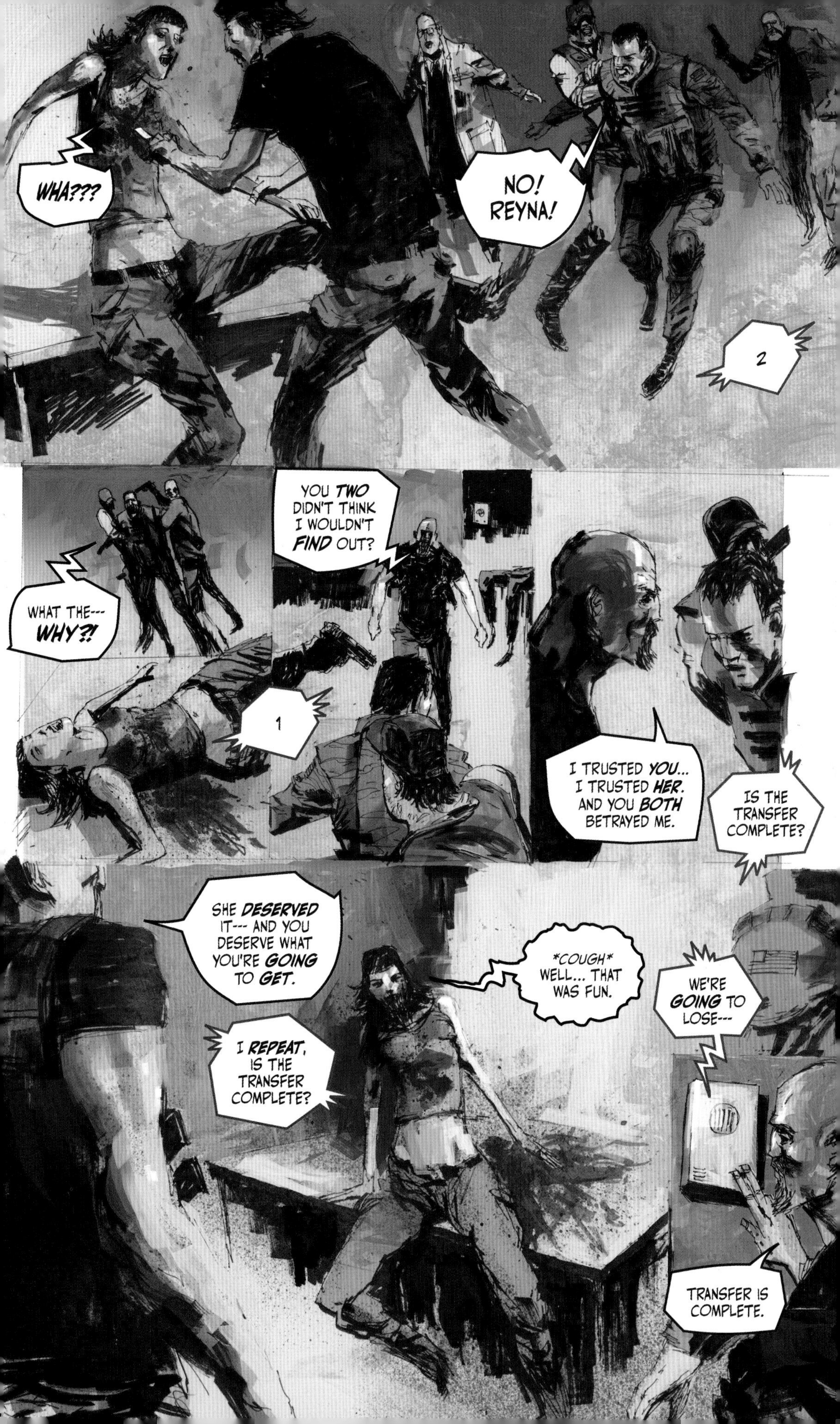
WHA???
NO! REYNA!
2
WHAT THE--- WHY?!
YOU TWO DIDN'T THINK I WOULDN'T FIND OUT?
1
I TRUSTED YOU... I TRUSTED HER. AND YOU BOTH BETRAYED ME.
IS THE TRANSFER COMPLETE?
SHE DESERVED IT--- AND YOU DESERVE WHAT YOU'RE GOING TO GET.
COUGH WELL... THAT WAS FUN.
WE'RE GOING TO LOSE---
I REPEAT, IS THE TRANSFER COMPLETE?
TRANSFER IS COMPLETE.

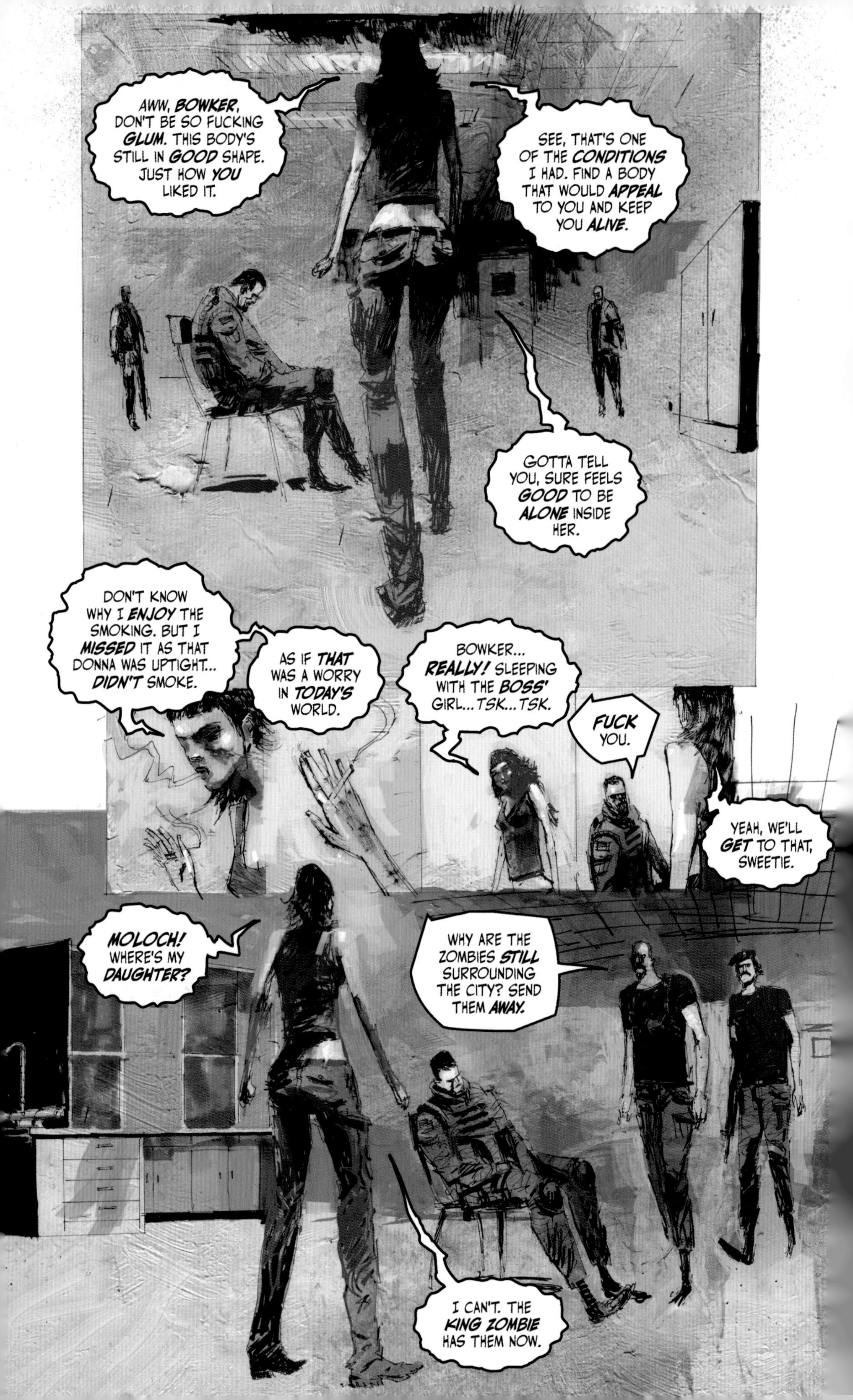
AWW, BOWKER, DON'T BE SO FUCKING GLUM. THIS BODY'S STILL IN GOOD SHAPE. JUST HOW YOU LIKED IT.
SEE, THAT'S ONE OF THE CONDITIONS I HAD. FIND A BODY THAT WOULD APPEAL TO YOU AND KEEP YOU ALIVE.
GOTTA TELL YOU, SURE FEELS GOOD TO BE ALONE INSIDE HER.
DON'T KNOW WHY I ENJOY THE SMOKING. BUT I MISSED IT AS THAT DONNA WAS UPTIGHT... DIDN'T SMOKE.
AS IF THAT WAS A WORRY IN TODAY'S WORLD.
BOWKER... REALLY! SLEEPING WITH THE BOSS' GIRL...TSK...TSK.
FUCK YOU.
YEAH, WE'LL GET TO THAT, SWEETIE.
MOLOCH! WHERE'S MY DAUGHTER?
WHY ARE THE ZOMBIES STILL SURROUNDING THE CITY? SEND THEM AWAY.
I CAN'T. THE KING ZOMBIE HAS THEM NOW.

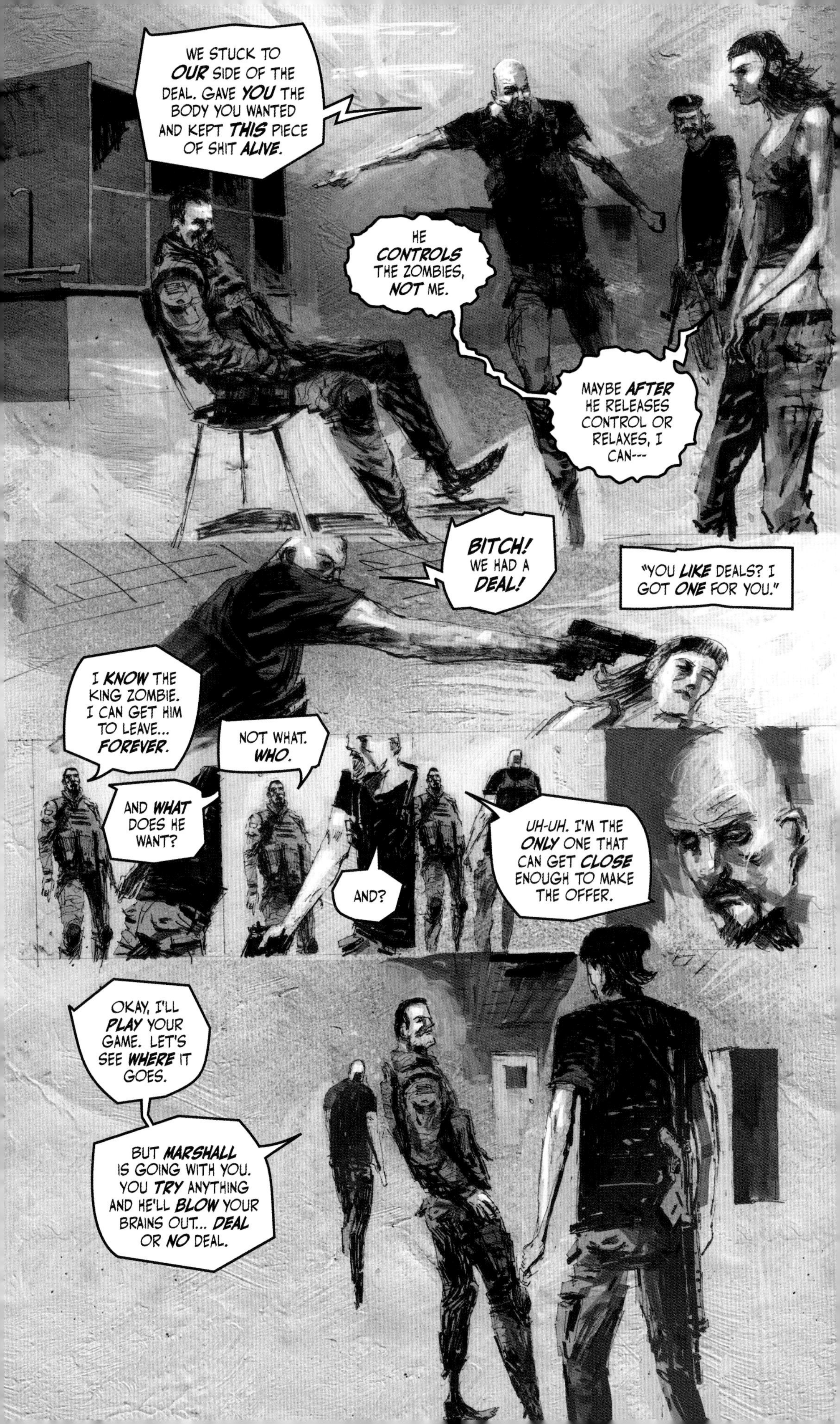
WE STUCK TO OUR SIDE OF THE DEAL. GAVE YOU THE BODY YOU WANTED AND KEPT THIS PIECE OF SHIT ALIVE.
HE CONTROLS THE ZOMBIES, NOT ME.
MAYBE AFTER HE RELEASES CONTROL OR RELAXES, I CAN---
BITCH! WE HAD A DEAL!
"YOU LIKE DEALS? I GOT ONE FOR YOU."
I KNOW THE KING ZOMBIE. I CAN GET HIM TO LEAVE... FOREVER.
AND WHAT DOES HE WANT?
NOT WHAT. WHO.
AND?
UH-UH. I'M THE ONLY ONE THAT CAN GET CLOSE ENOUGH TO MAKE THE OFFER.
OKAY, I'LL PLAY YOUR GAME. LET'S SEE WHERE IT GOES.
BUT MARSHALL IS GOING WITH YOU. YOU TRY ANYTHING AND HE'LL BLOW YOUR BRAINS OUT... DEAL OR NO DEAL.

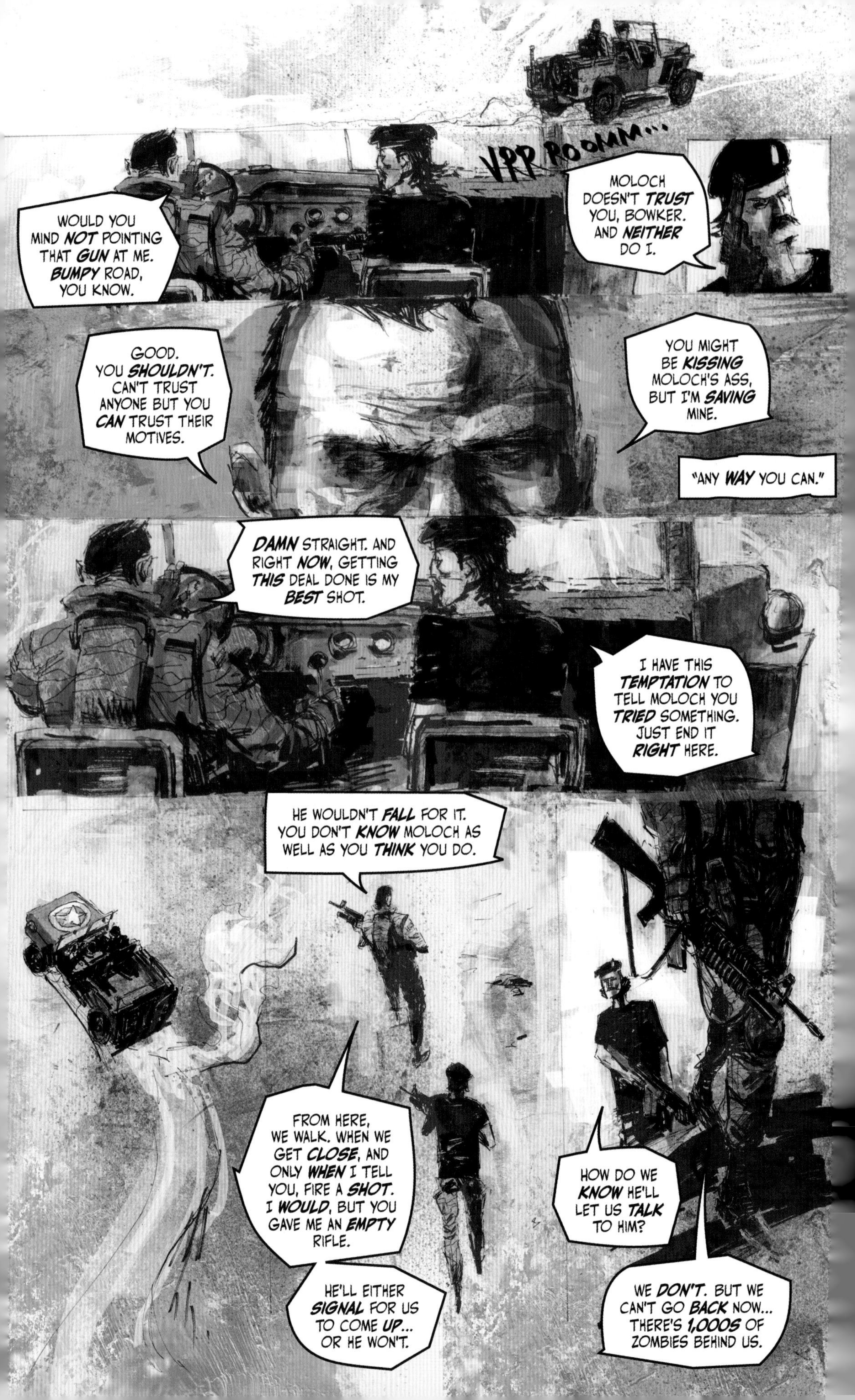

VPP ROOMM...
WOULD YOU MIND NOT POINTING THAT GUN AT ME. BUMPY ROAD, YOU KNOW.
MOLOCH DOESN'T TRUST YOU, BOWKER. AND NEITHER DO I.
GOOD. YOU SHOULDN'T. CAN'T TRUST ANYONE BUT YOU CAN TRUST THEIR MOTIVES.
YOU MIGHT BE KISSING MOLOCH'S ASS, BUT I'M SAVING MINE.
"ANY WAY YOU CAN."
DAMN STRAIGHT. AND RIGHT NOW, GETTING THIS DEAL DONE IS MY BEST SHOT.
I HAVE THIS TEMPTATION TO TELL MOLOCH YOU TRIED SOMETHING. JUST END IT RIGHT HERE.
HE WOULDN'T FALL FOR IT. YOU DON'T KNOW MOLOCH AS WELL AS YOU THINK YOU DO.
FROM HERE, WE WALK. WHEN WE GET CLOSE, AND ONLY WHEN I TELL YOU, FIRE A SHOT. I WOULD, BUT YOU GAVE ME AN EMPTY RIFLE.
HE'LL EITHER SIGNAL FOR US TO COME UP... OR HE WON'T.
HOW DO WE KNOW HE'LL LET US TALK TO HIM?
WE DON'T. BUT WE CAN'T GO BACK NOW... THERE'S 1,000S OF ZOMBIES BEHIND US.

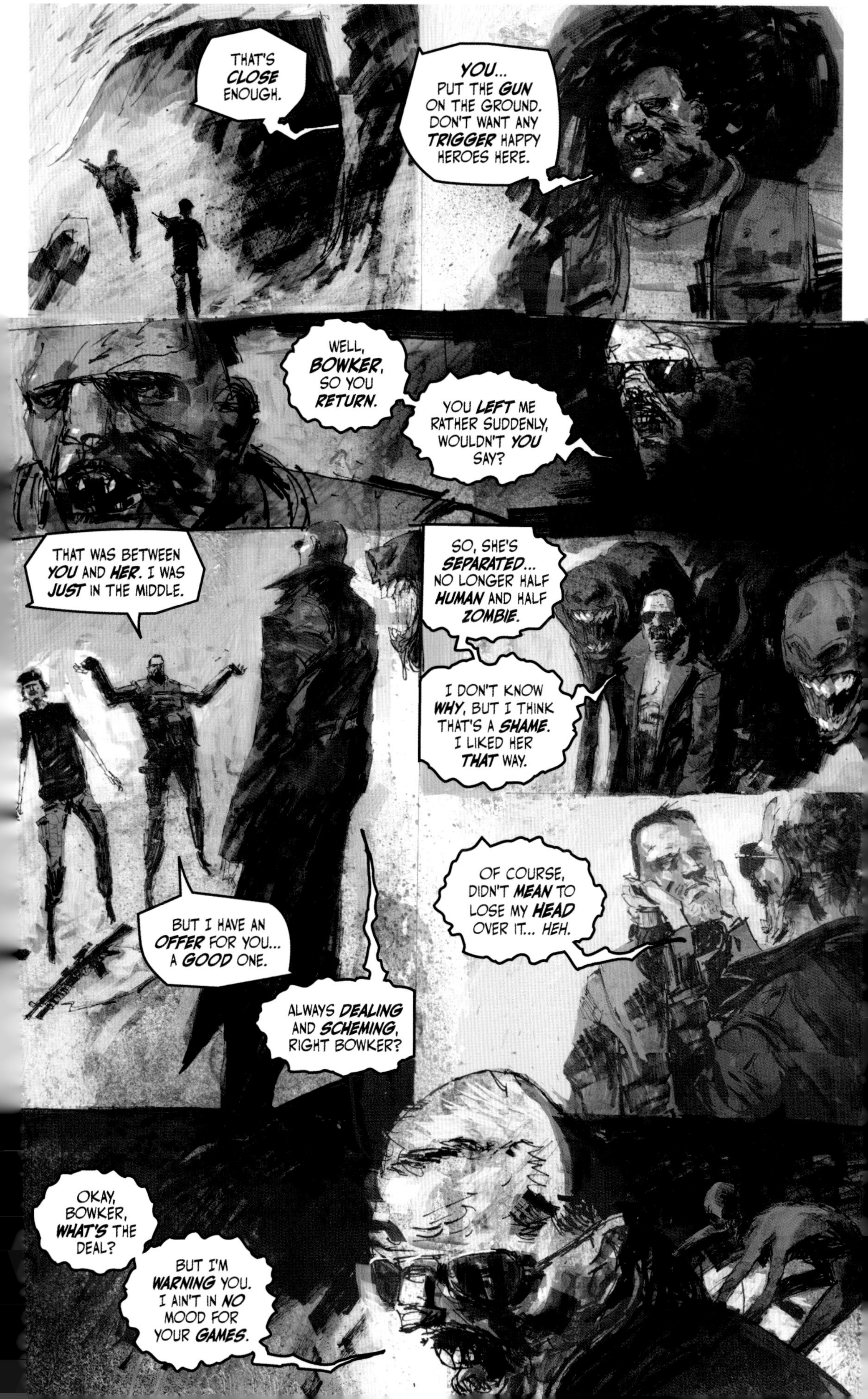

THAT'S CLOSE ENOUGH.
YOU... PUT THE GUN ON THE GROUND. DON'T WANT ANY TRIGGER HAPPY HEROES HERE.
WELL, BOWKER, SO YOU RETURN.
YOU LEFT ME RATHER SUDDENLY, WOULDN'T YOU SAY?
THAT WAS BETWEEN YOU AND HER. I WAS JUST IN THE MIDDLE.
BUT I HAVE AN OFFER FOR YOU... A GOOD ONE.
ALWAYS DEALING AND SCHEMING, RIGHT BOWKER?
SO, SHE'S SEPARATED... NO LONGER HALF HUMAN AND HALF ZOMBIE.
I DON'T KNOW WHY, BUT I THINK THAT'S A SHAME. I LIKED HER THAT WAY.
OF COURSE, DIDN'T MEAN TO LOSE MY HEAD OVER IT... HEH.
OKAY, BOWKER, WHAT'S THE DEAL?
BUT I'M WARNING YOU. I AIN'T IN NO MOOD FOR YOUR GAMES.

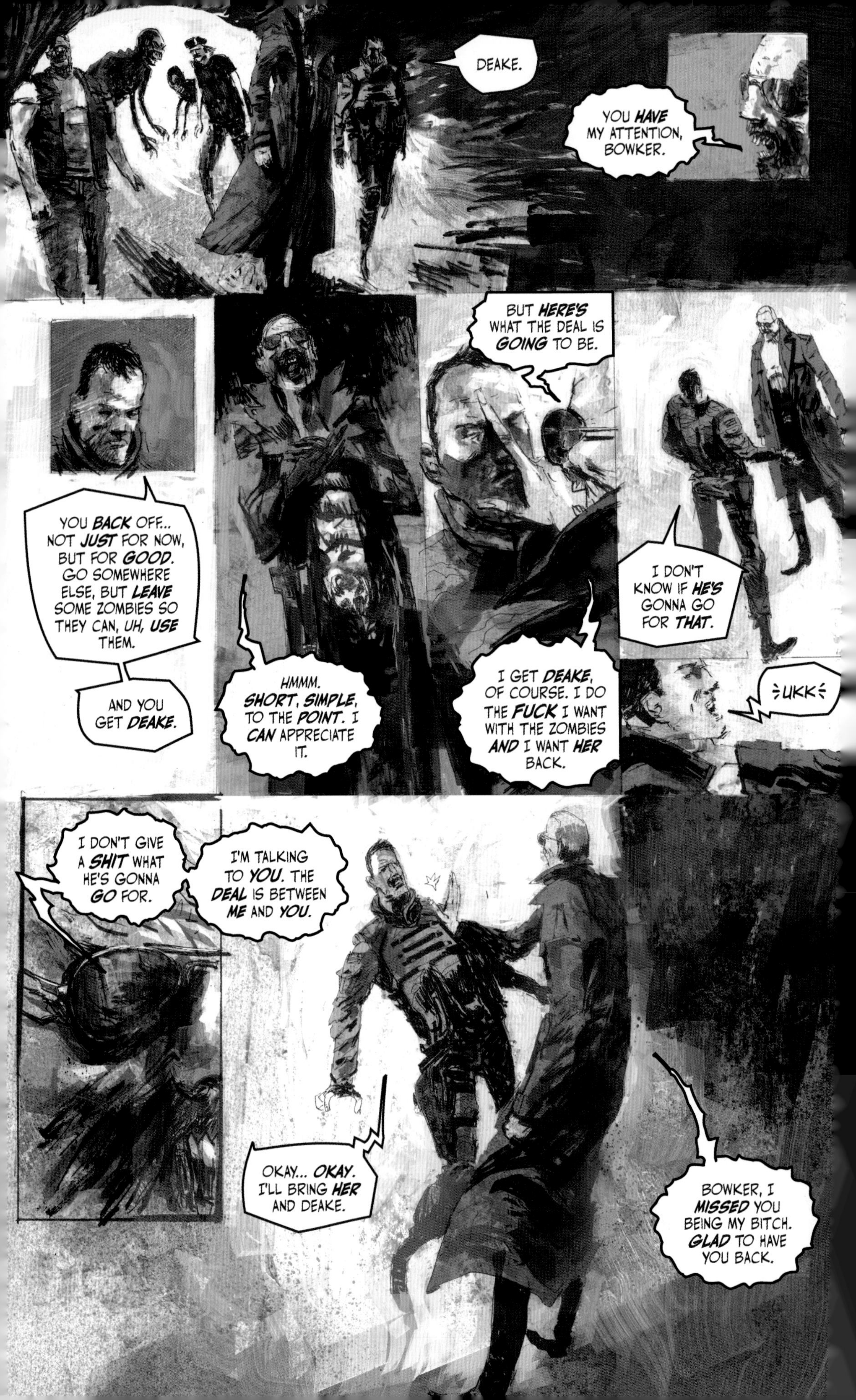
DEAKE.
YOU HAVE MY ATTENTION, BOWKER.
YOU BACK OFF... NOT JUST FOR NOW, BUT FOR GOOD. GO SOMEWHERE ELSE, BUT LEAVE SOME ZOMBIES SO THEY CAN, UH, USE THEM.
AND YOU GET DEAKE.
HMMM. SHORT, SIMPLE, TO THE POINT. I CAN APPRECIATE IT.
BUT HERE'S WHAT THE DEAL IS GOING TO BE.
I GET DEAKE, OF COURSE. I DO THE FUCK I WANT WITH THE ZOMBIES AND I WANT HER BACK.
I DON'T KNOW IF HE'S GONNA GO FOR THAT.
UKK
I DON'T GIVE A SHIT WHAT HE'S GONNA GO FOR.
I'M TALKING TO YOU. THE DEAL IS BETWEEN ME AND YOU.
OKAY... OKAY. I'LL BRING HER AND DEAKE.
BOWKER, I MISSED YOU BEING MY BITCH. GLAD TO HAVE YOU BACK.

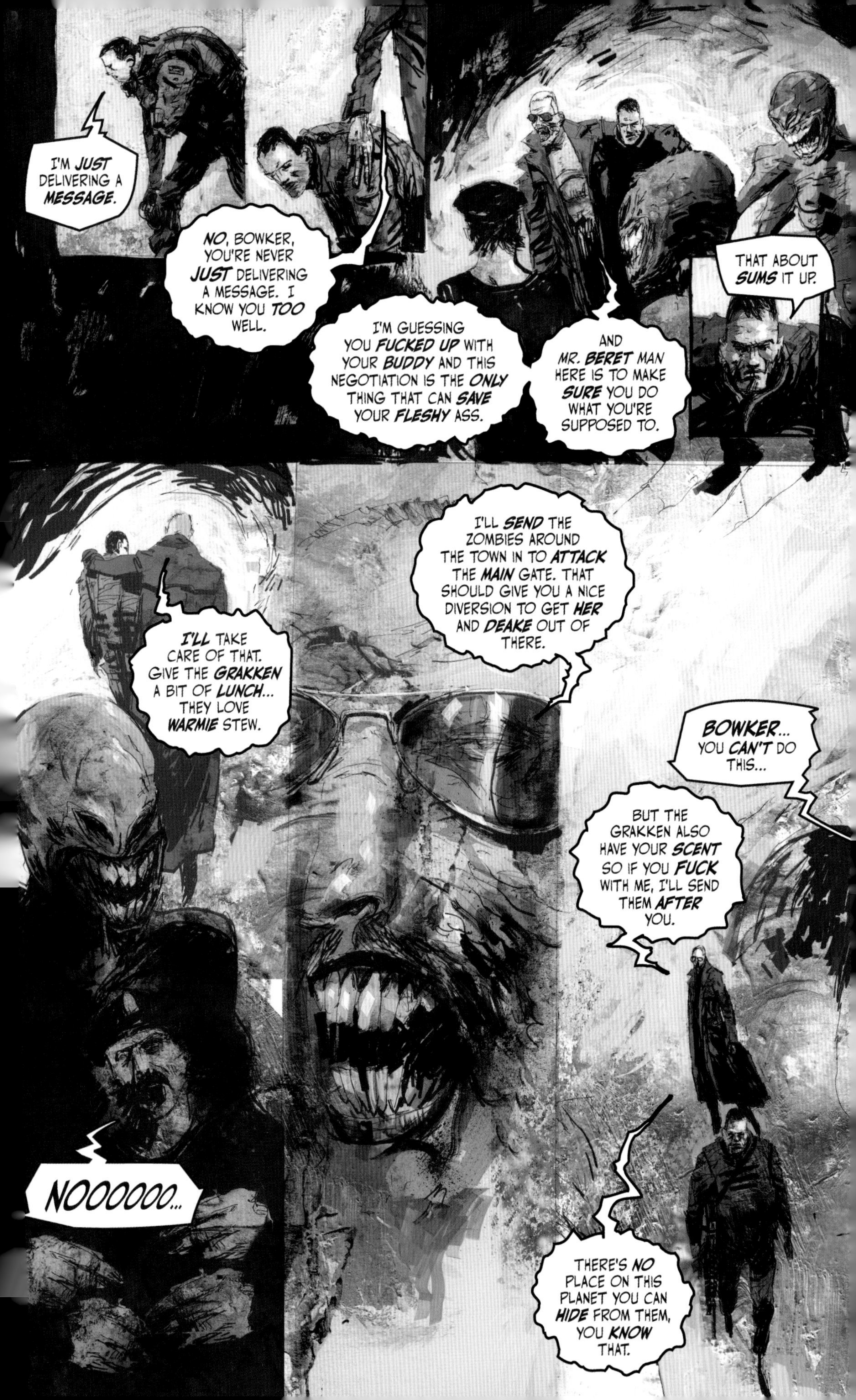
I'M JUST DELIVERING A MESSAGE.
NO, BOWKER, YOU'RE NEVER JUST DELIVERING A MESSAGE. I KNOW YOU TOO WELL.
I'M GUESSING YOU FUCKED UP WITH YOUR BUDDY AND THIS NEGOTIATION IS THE ONLY THING THAT CAN SAVE YOUR FLESHY ASS.
AND MR. BERET MAN HERE IS TO MAKE SURE YOU DO WHAT YOU'RE SUPPOSED TO.
THAT ABOUT SUMS IT UP.
I'LL SEND THE ZOMBIES AROUND THE TOWN IN TO ATTACK THE MAIN GATE. THAT SHOULD GIVE YOU A NICE DIVERSION TO GET HER AND DEAKE OUT OF THERE.
I'LL TAKE CARE OF THAT. GIVE THE GRAKKEN A BIT OF LUNCH... THEY LOVE WARMIE STEW.
BOWKER... YOU CAN'T DO THIS...
BUT THE GRAKKEN ALSO HAVE YOUR SCENT SO IF YOU FUCK WITH ME, I'LL SEND THEM AFTER YOU.
NOOOOOO...
THERE'S NO PLACE ON THIS PLANET YOU CAN HIDE FROM THEM, YOU KNOW THAT.

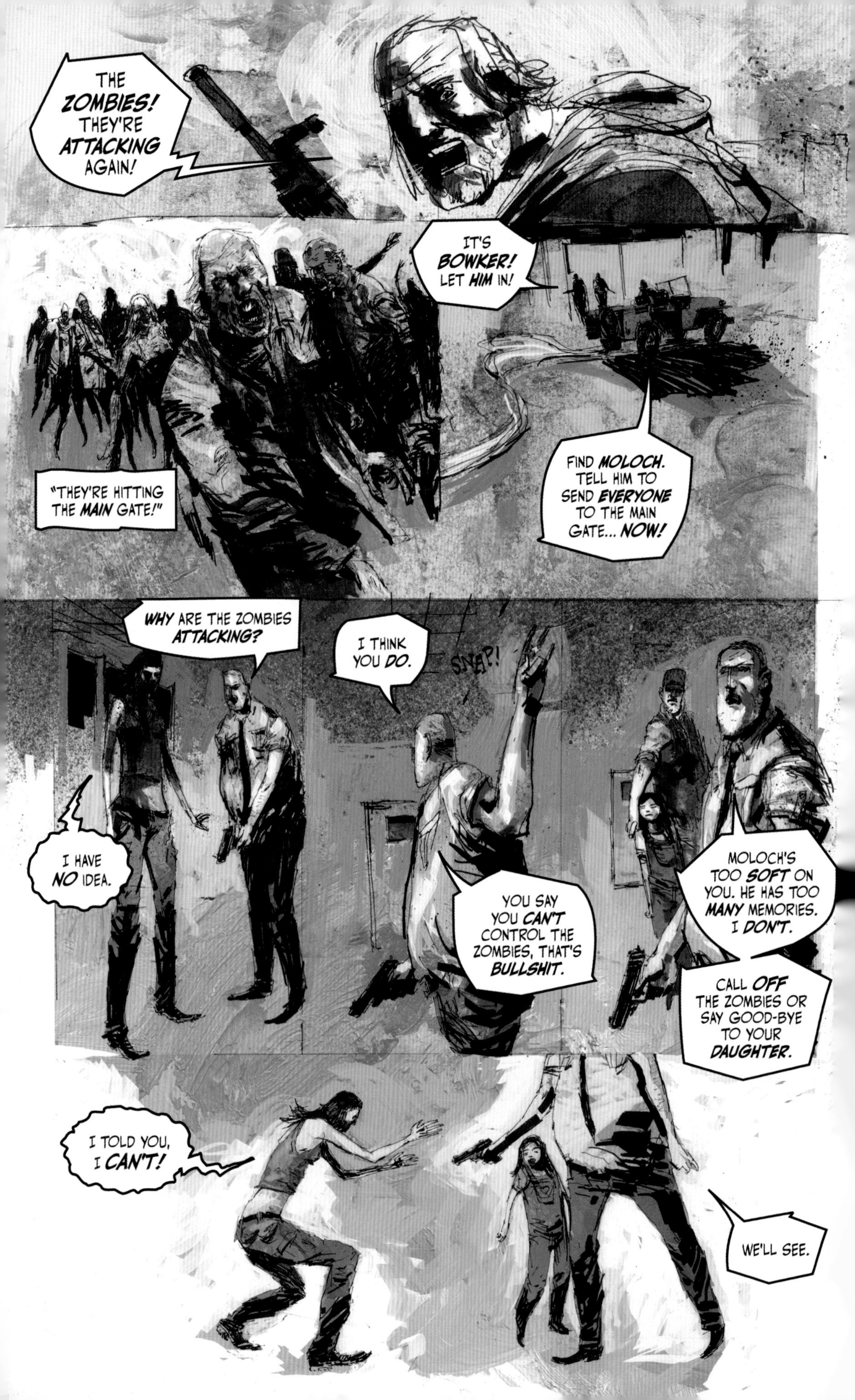

THE ZOMBIES! THEY'RE ATTACKING AGAIN!
IT'S BOWKER! LET HIM IN!
"THEY'RE HITTING THE MAIN GATE!"
FIND MOLOCH. TELL HIM TO SEND EVERYONE TO THE MAIN GATE... NOW!
WHY ARE THE ZOMBIES ATTACKING?
I HAVE NO IDEA.
I THINK YOU DO.
SNAP!
YOU SAY YOU CAN'T CONTROL THE ZOMBIES, THAT'S BULLSHIT.
MOLOCH'S TOO SOFT ON YOU. HE HAS TOO MANY MEMORIES. I DON'T.
CALL OFF THE ZOMBIES OR SAY GOOD-BYE TO YOUR DAUGHTER.
I TOLD YOU, I CAN'T!
WE'LL SEE.

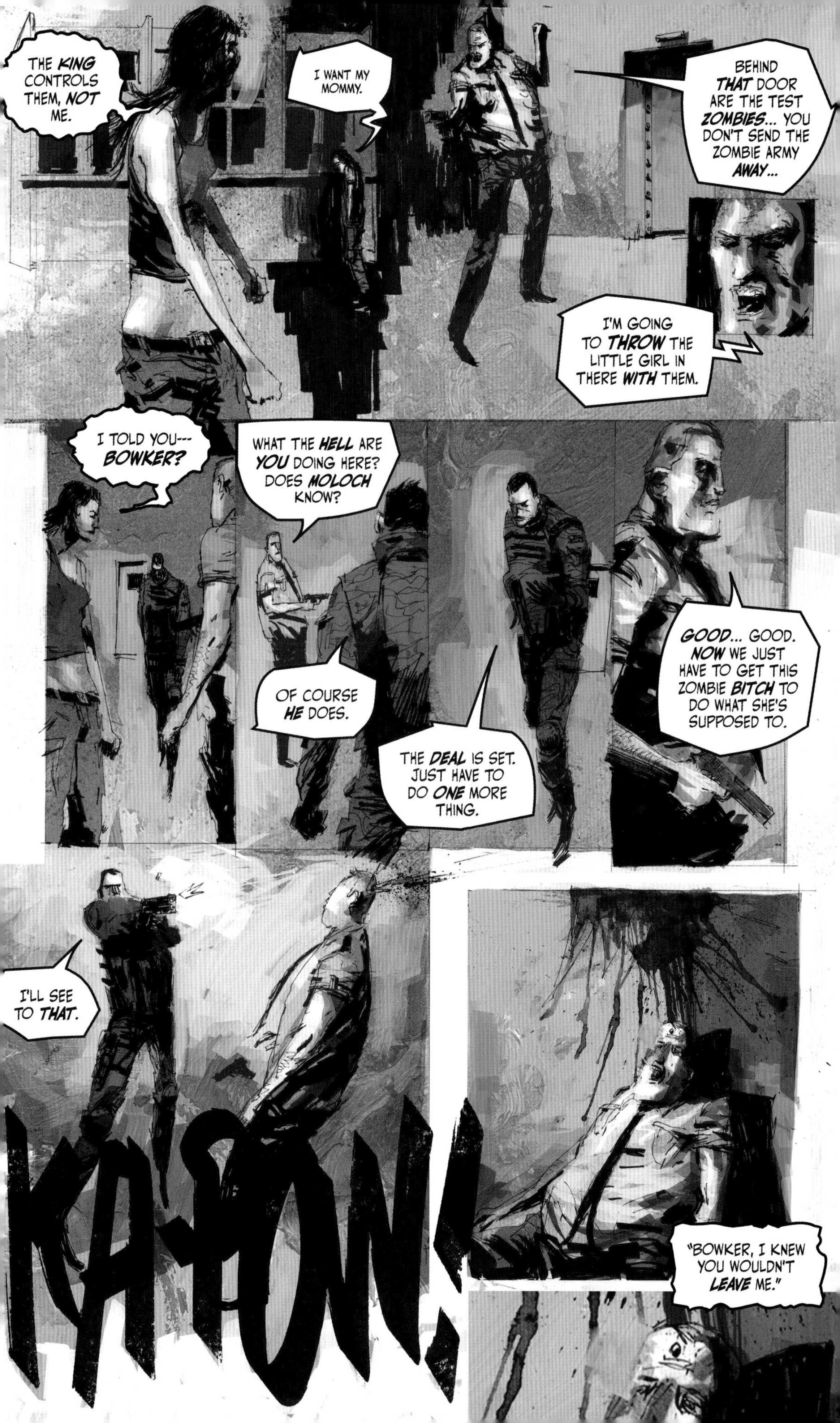
THE KING CONTROLS THEM, NOT ME.
I WANT MY MOMMY.
BEHIND THAT DOOR ARE THE TEST ZOMBIES... YOU DON'T SEND THE ZOMBIE ARMY AWAY...
I'M GOING TO THROW THE LITTLE GIRL IN THERE WITH THEM.
I TOLD YOU--- BOWKER?
WHAT THE HELL ARE YOU DOING HERE? DOES MOLOCH KNOW?
OF COURSE HE DOES.
THE DEAL IS SET. JUST HAVE TO DO ONE MORE THING.
GOOD... GOOD. NOW WE JUST HAVE TO GET THIS ZOMBIE BITCH TO DO WHAT SHE'S SUPPOSED TO.
I'LL SEE TO THAT.
KA-POW!
"BOWKER, I KNEW YOU WOULDN'T LEAVE ME."

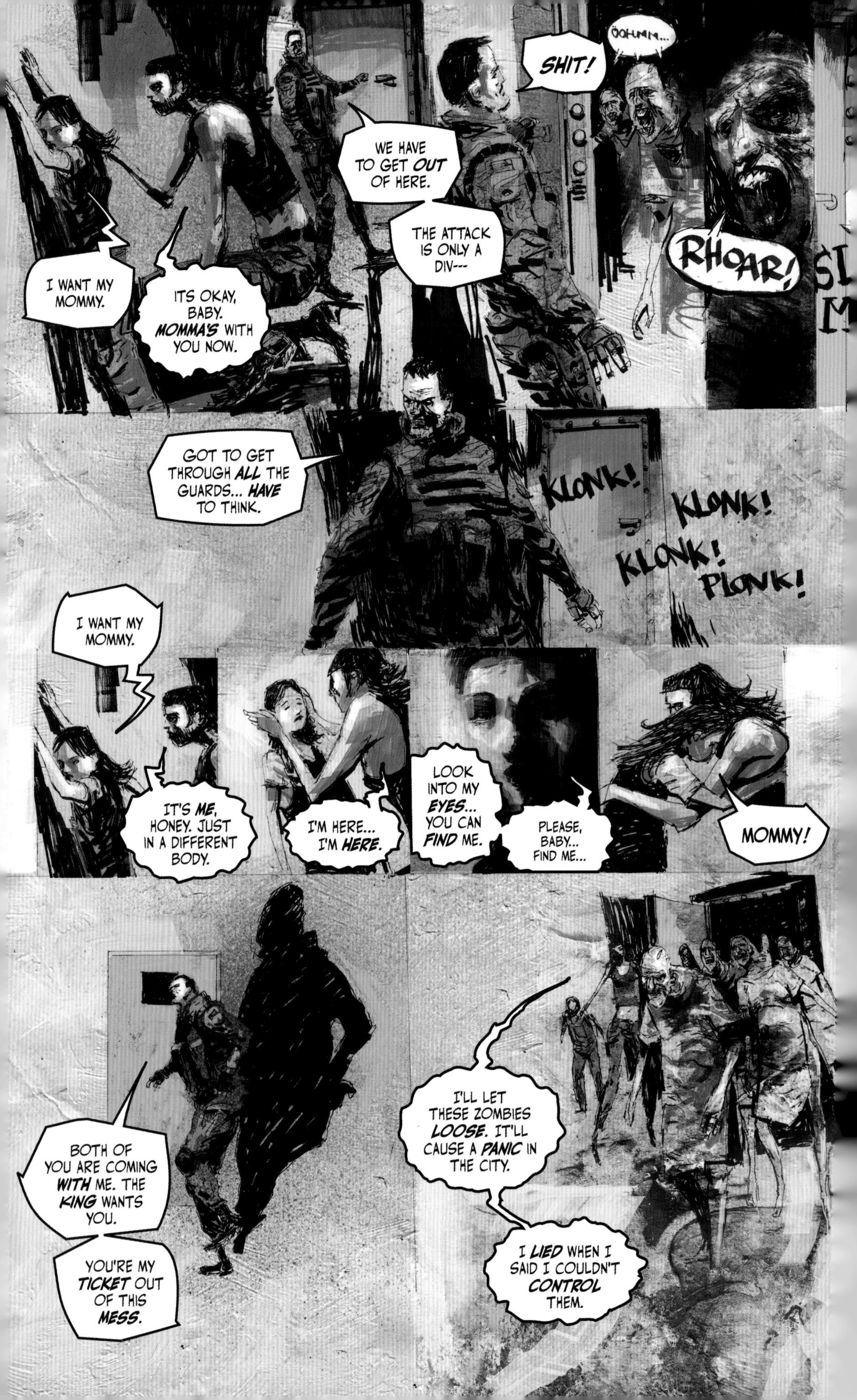
SHIT!
ÖOH-MM...
WE HAVE TO GET OUT OF HERE.
THE ATTACK IS ONLY A DIV---
RHOAR!
I WANT MY MOMMY.
ITS OKAY, BABY. MOMMA'S WITH YOU NOW.
GOT TO GET THROUGH ALL THE GUARDS... HAVE TO THINK.
KLONK!
KLONK!
KLONK!
PLONK!
I WANT MY MOMMY.
IT'S ME, HONEY. JUST IN A DIFFERENT BODY.
I'M HERE... I'M HERE.
LOOK INTO MY EYES... YOU CAN FIND ME.
PLEASE, BABY... FIND ME...
MOMMY!
BOTH OF YOU ARE COMING WITH ME. THE KING WANTS YOU.
YOU'RE MY TICKET OUT OF THIS MESS.
I'LL LET THESE ZOMBIES LOOSE. IT'LL CAUSE A PANIC IN THE CITY.
I LIED WHEN I SAID I COULDN'T CONTROL THEM.

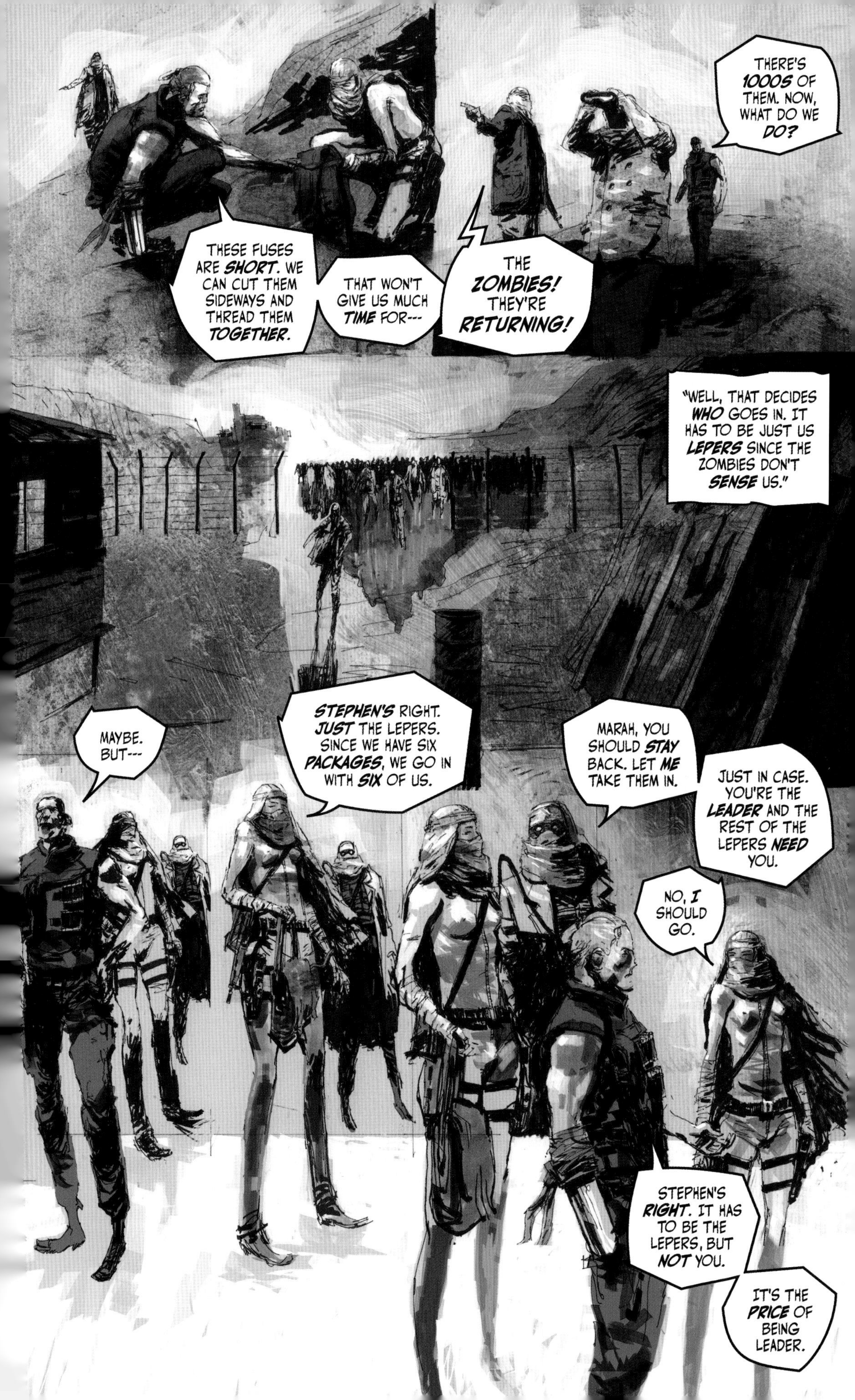
THESE FUSES ARE SHORT. WE CAN CUT THEM SIDEWAYS AND THREAD THEM TOGETHER.
THAT WON'T GIVE US MUCH TIME FOR---
THE ZOMBIES! THEY'RE RETURNING!
THERE'S 1000S OF THEM. NOW, WHAT DO WE DO?
"WELL, THAT DECIDES WHO GOES IN. IT HAS TO BE JUST US LEPERS SINCE THE ZOMBIES DON'T SENSE US."
MAYBE. BUT---
STEPHEN'S RIGHT. JUST THE LEPERS. SINCE WE HAVE SIX PACKAGES, WE GO IN WITH SIX OF US.
MARAH, YOU SHOULD STAY BACK. LET ME TAKE THEM IN.
JUST IN CASE. YOU'RE THE LEADER AND THE REST OF THE LEPERS NEED YOU.
NO, I SHOULD GO.
STEPHEN'S RIGHT. IT HAS TO BE THE LEPERS, BUT NOT YOU.
IT'S THE PRICE OF BEING LEADER.

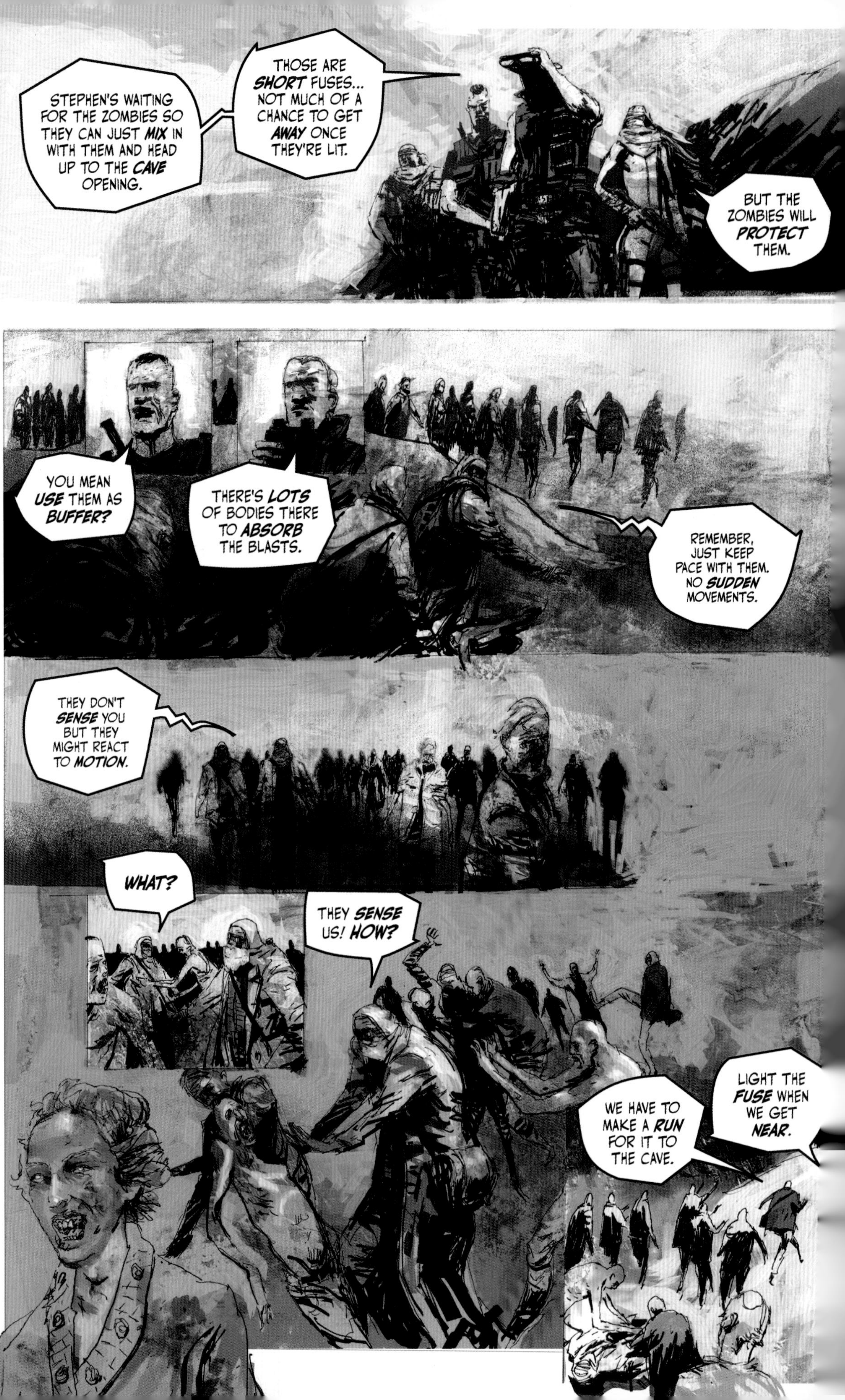
STEPHEN'S WAITING FOR THE ZOMBIES SO THEY CAN JUST MIX IN WITH THEM AND HEAD UP TO THE CAVE OPENING.
THOSE ARE SHORT FUSES... NOT MUCH OF A CHANCE TO GET AWAY ONCE THEY'RE LIT.
BUT THE ZOMBIES WILL PROTECT THEM.
YOU MEAN USE THEM AS BUFFER?
THERE'S LOTS OF BODIES THERE TO ABSORB THE BLASTS.
REMEMBER, JUST KEEP PACE WITH THEM. NO SUDDEN MOVEMENTS.
THEY DON'T SENSE YOU BUT THEY MIGHT REACT TO MOTION.
WHAT?
THEY SENSE US! HOW?
WE HAVE TO MAKE A RUN FOR IT TO THE CAVE.
LIGHT THE FUSE WHEN WE GET NEAR.

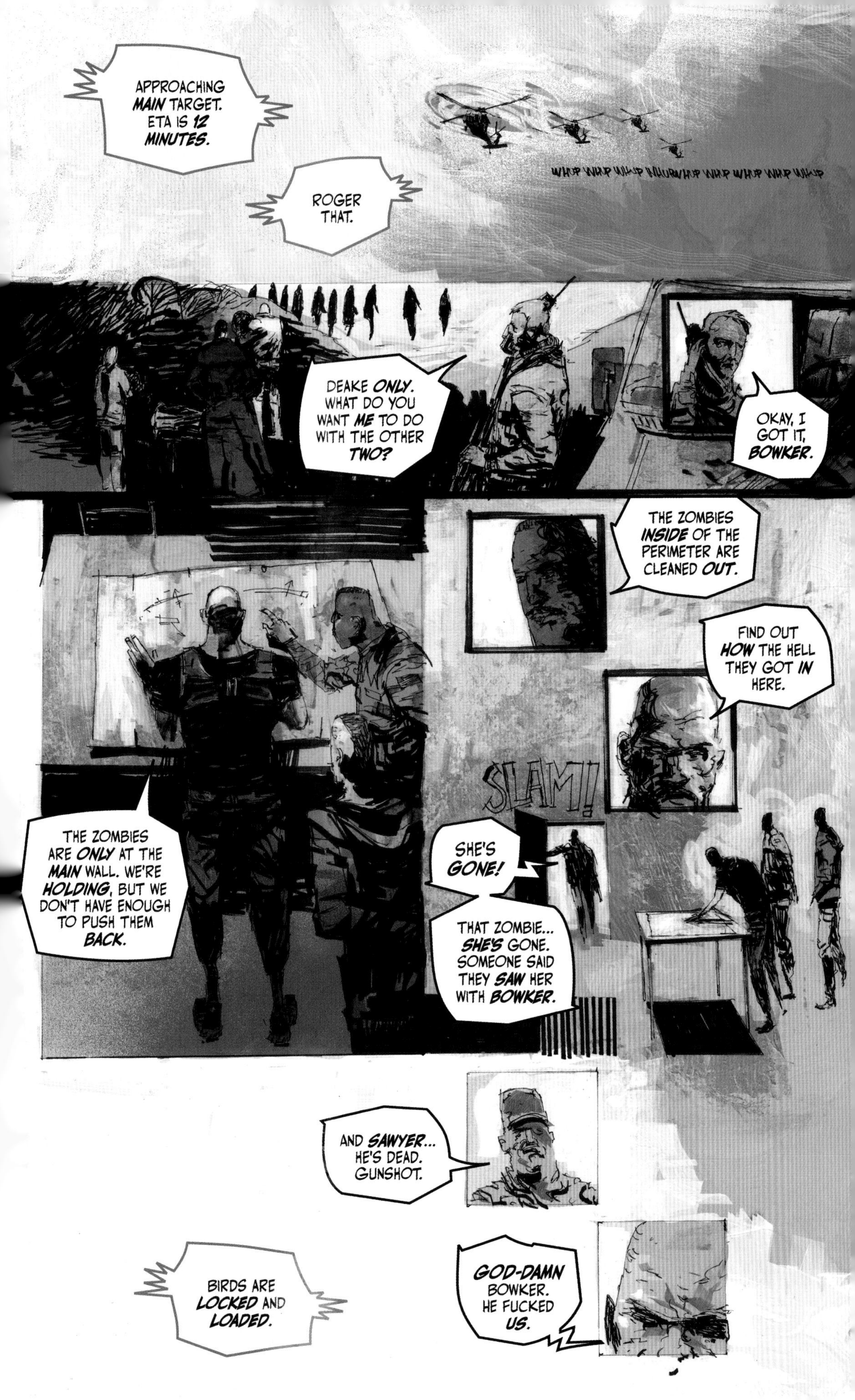

APPROACHING MAIN TARGET. ETA IS 12 MINUTES.
WHUP WHUP WHUP WHUPWHUP WHUP WHUP WHUP WHUP
ROGER THAT.
DEAKE ONLY. WHAT DO YOU WANT ME TO DO WITH THE OTHER TWO?
OKAY, I GOT IT, BOWKER.
THE ZOMBIES INSIDE OF THE PERIMETER ARE CLEANED OUT.
FIND OUT HOW THE HELL THEY GOT IN HERE.
THE ZOMBIES ARE ONLY AT THE MAIN WALL. WE'RE HOLDING, BUT WE DON'T HAVE ENOUGH TO PUSH THEM BACK.
SLAM!
SHE'S GONE!
THAT ZOMBIE... SHE'S GONE. SOMEONE SAID THEY SAW HER WITH BOWKER.
AND SAWYER... HE'S DEAD. GUNSHOT.
BIRDS ARE LOCKED AND LOADED.
GOD-DAMN BOWKER. HE FUCKED US.

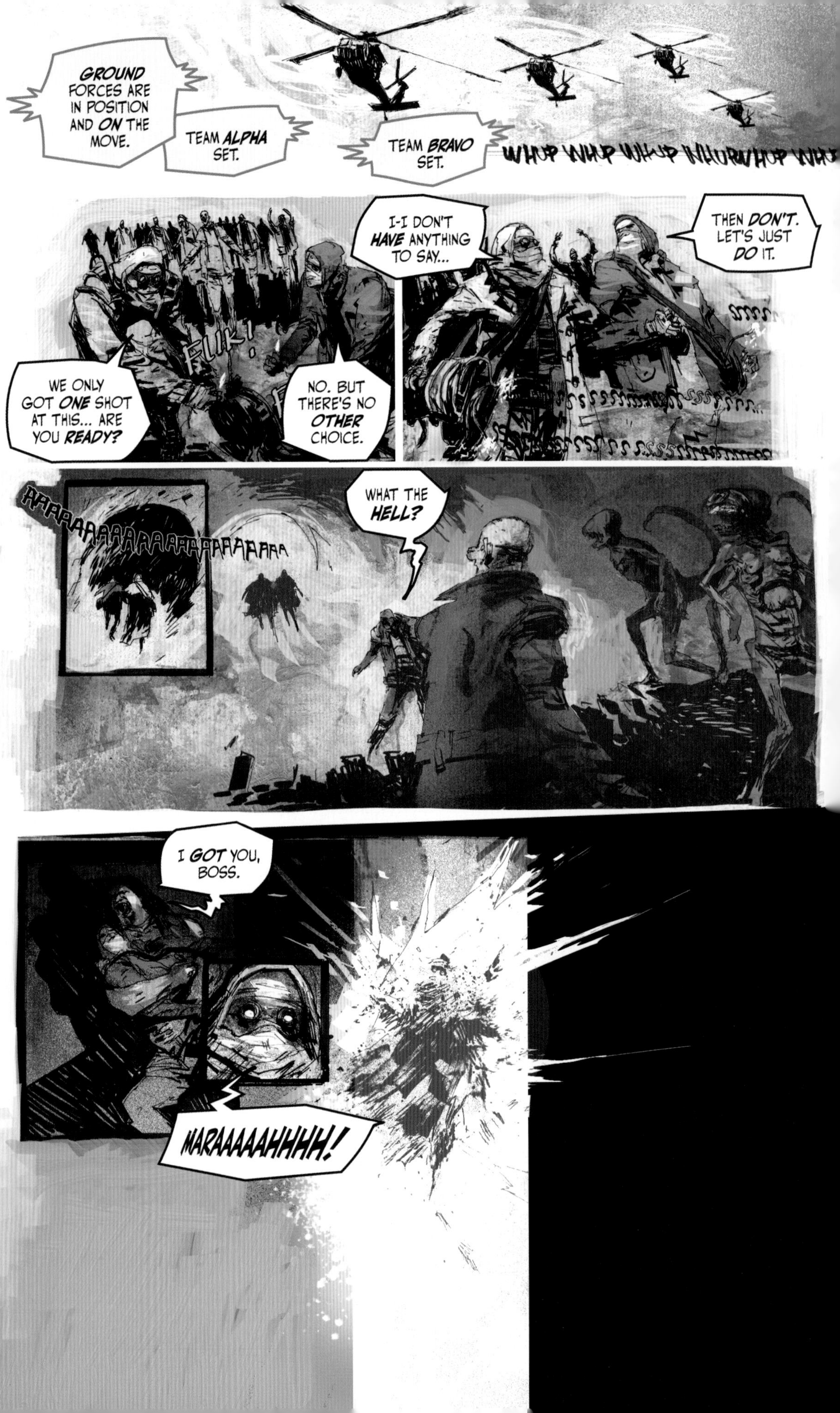
GROUND FORCES ARE IN POSITION AND ON THE MOVE.
TEAM ALPHA SET.
TEAM BRAVO SET.
WHUP WHUP WHUP WHUP WHUP WHU
FLIK!
WE ONLY GOT ONE SHOT AT THIS... ARE YOU READY?
NO. BUT THERE'S NO OTHER CHOICE.
I-I DON'T HAVE ANYTHING TO SAY...
THEN DON'T. LET'S JUST DO IT.
AAAAAAAAAAAAAAAAAAAAAAAA
WHAT THE HELL?
I GOT YOU, BOSS.
MARAAAAAHHHH!

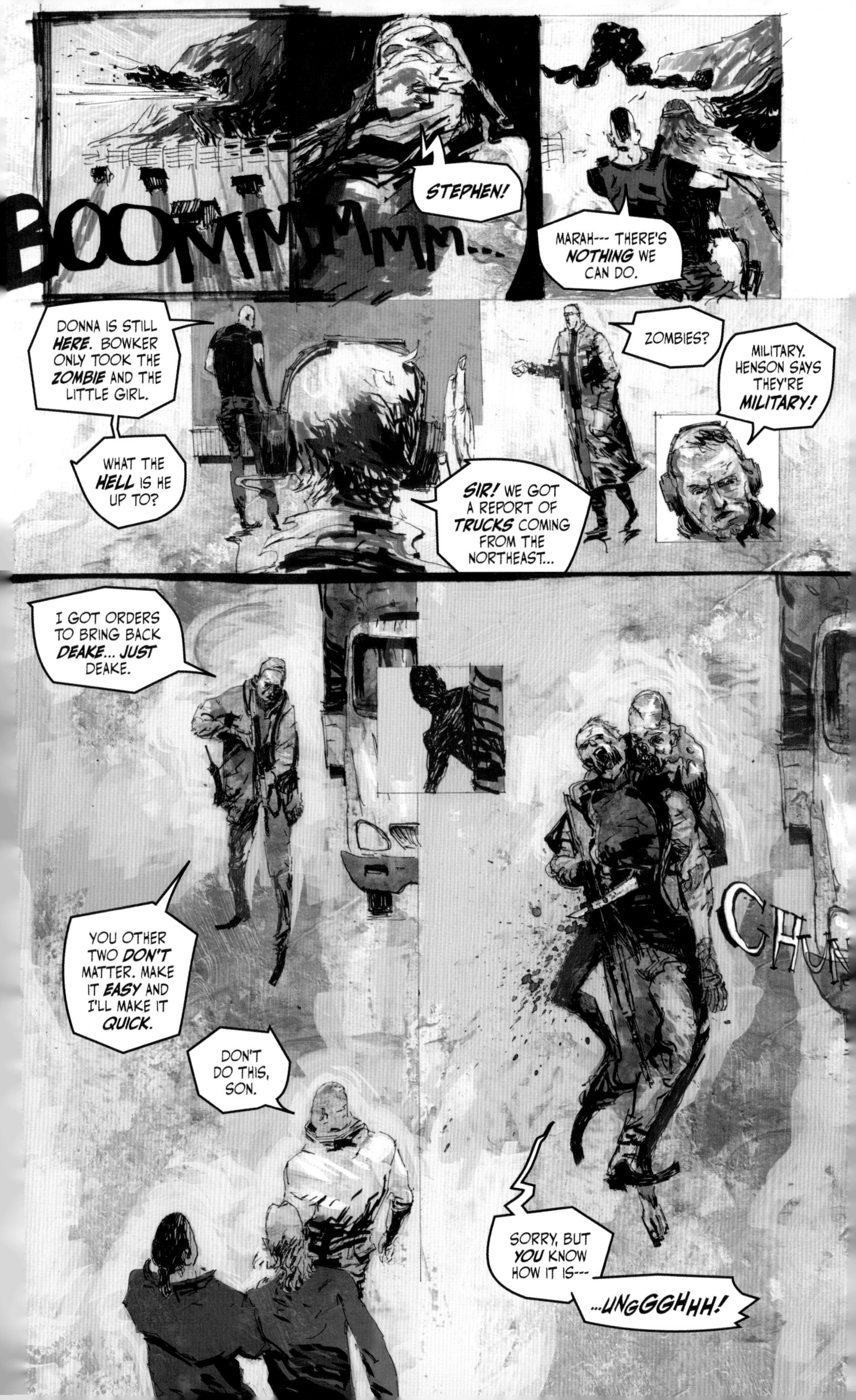
BOOMMMMMM...
STEPHEN!
MARAH--- THERE'S NOTHING WE CAN DO.
DONNA IS STILL HERE. BOWKER ONLY TOOK THE ZOMBIE AND THE LITTLE GIRL.
WHAT THE HELL IS HE UP TO?
SIR! WE GOT A REPORT OF TRUCKS COMING FROM THE NORTHEAST...
ZOMBIES?
MILITARY. HENSON SAYS THEY'RE MILITARY!
I GOT ORDERS TO BRING BACK DEAKE... JUST DEAKE.
YOU OTHER TWO DON'T MATTER. MAKE IT EASY AND I'LL MAKE IT QUICK.
DON'T DO THIS, SON.
SORRY, BUT YOU KNOW HOW IT IS---
...UNGGGHHH!

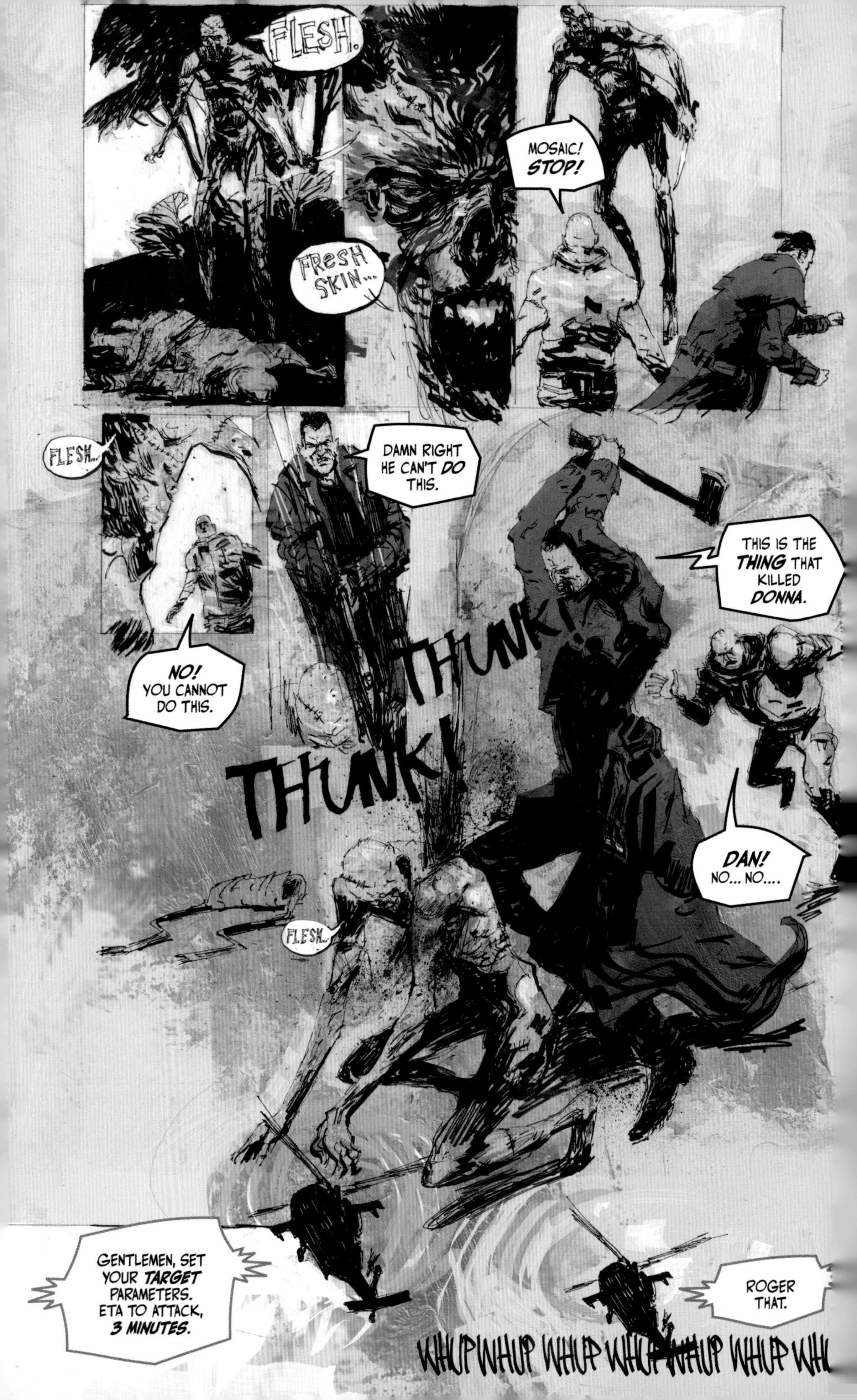
FLESH.
FRESH SKIN...
MOSAIC! STOP!
FLESH...
DAMN RIGHT HE CAN'T DO THIS.
NO! YOU CANNOT DO THIS.
THIS IS THE THING THAT KILLED DONNA.
THUNK!
THUNK!
DAN! NO... NO....
FLESH...
GENTLEMEN, SET YOUR TARGET PARAMETERS. ETA TO ATTACK, 3 MINUTES.
ROGER THAT.
WHUP WHUP WHUP WHUP WHUP WHUP WHU

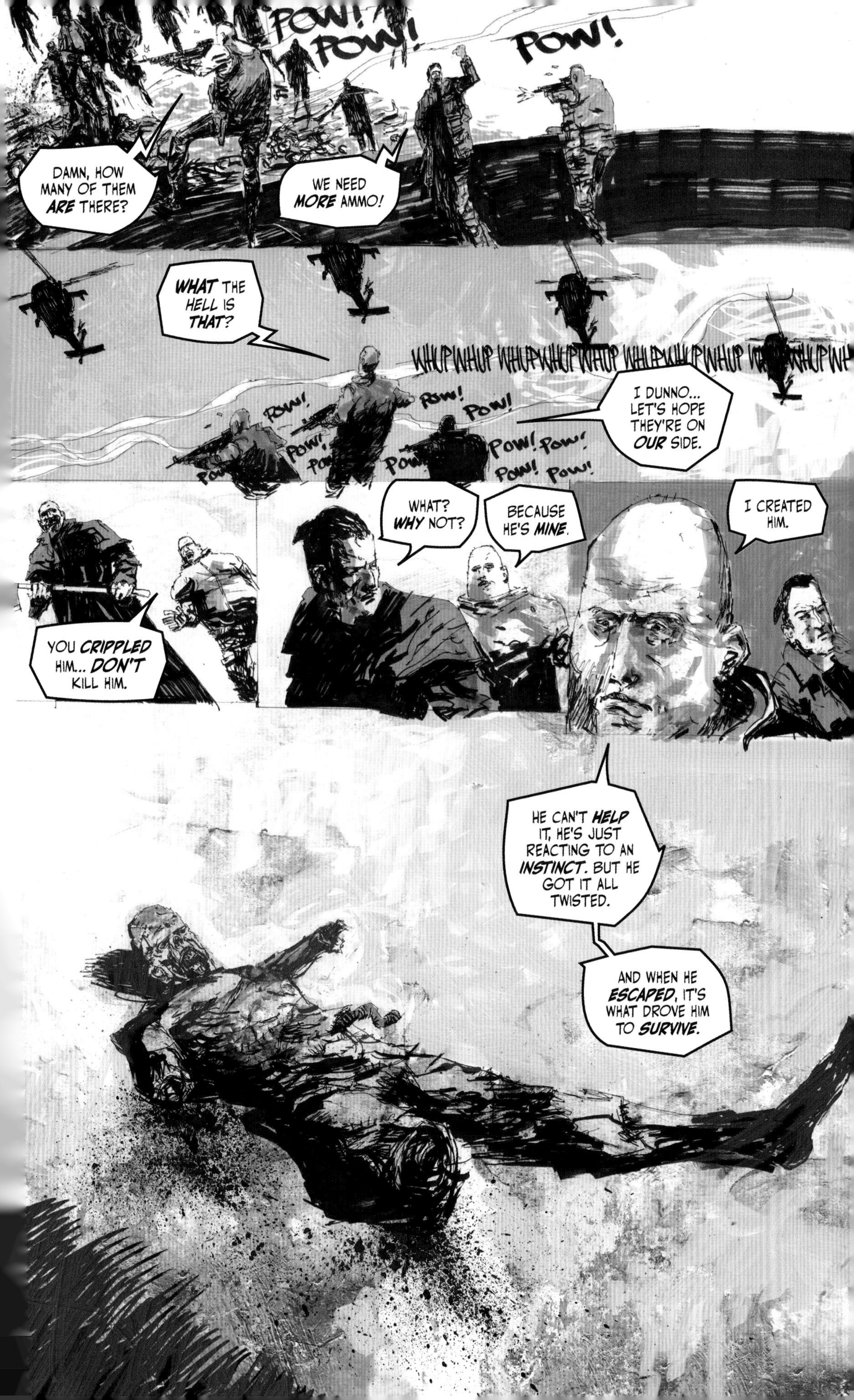
POW! POW!
POW!
DAMN, HOW MANY OF THEM ARE THERE?
WE NEED MORE AMMO!
WHAT THE HELL IS THAT?
WHUPWHUP WHUPWHUPWHUP WHUPWHUPWHUP WHUPWHUP
POW! POW! POW! POW! POW! POW! POW! POW! POW! POW! POW!
I DUNNO... LET'S HOPE THEY'RE ON OUR SIDE.
YOU CRIPPLED HIM... DON'T KILL HIM.
WHAT? WHY NOT?
BECAUSE HE'S MINE.
I CREATED HIM.
HE CAN'T HELP IT, HE'S JUST REACTING TO AN INSTINCT. BUT HE GOT IT ALL TWISTED.
AND WHEN HE ESCAPED, IT'S WHAT DROVE HIM TO SURVIVE.

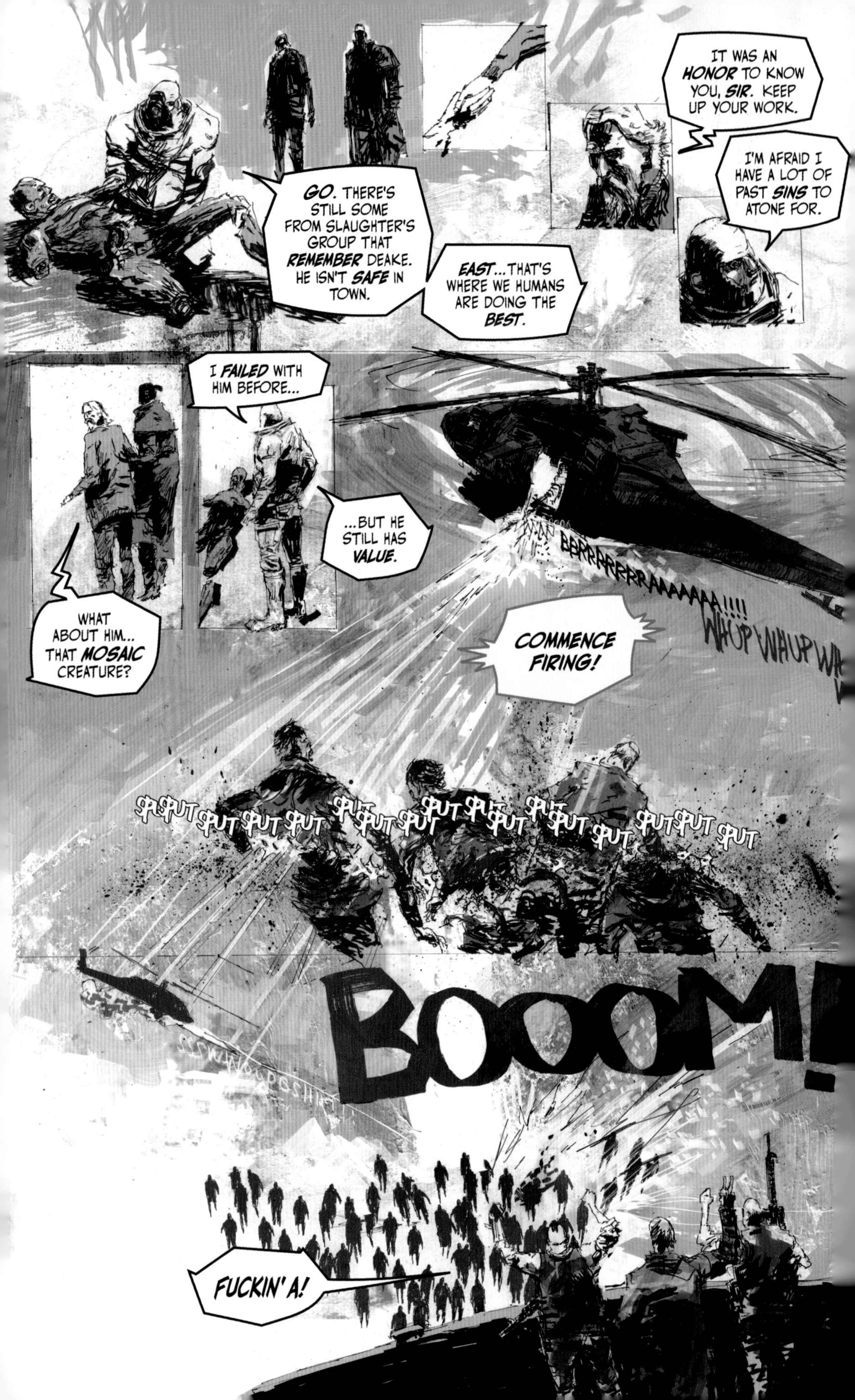
GO. THERE'S STILL SOME FROM SLAUGHTER'S GROUP THAT REMEMBER DEAKE. HE ISN'T SAFE IN TOWN.
EAST...THAT'S WHERE WE HUMANS ARE DOING THE BEST.
IT WAS AN HONOR TO KNOW YOU, SIR. KEEP UP YOUR WORK.
I'M AFRAID I HAVE A LOT OF PAST SINS TO ATONE FOR.
WHAT ABOUT HIM... THAT MOSAIC CREATURE?
I FAILED WITH HIM BEFORE...
...BUT HE STILL HAS VALUE.
BBRRRRRRRRAAAAAAA!!!!
WHUP WHUP
COMMENCE FIRING!
SPUT SPUT SPUT SPUT SPUT SPUT SPUT SPUT SPUT SPUT SPUT SPUT SPUT SPUT SPUT SPUT SPUT SPUT
BOOOM!
FUCKIN' A!

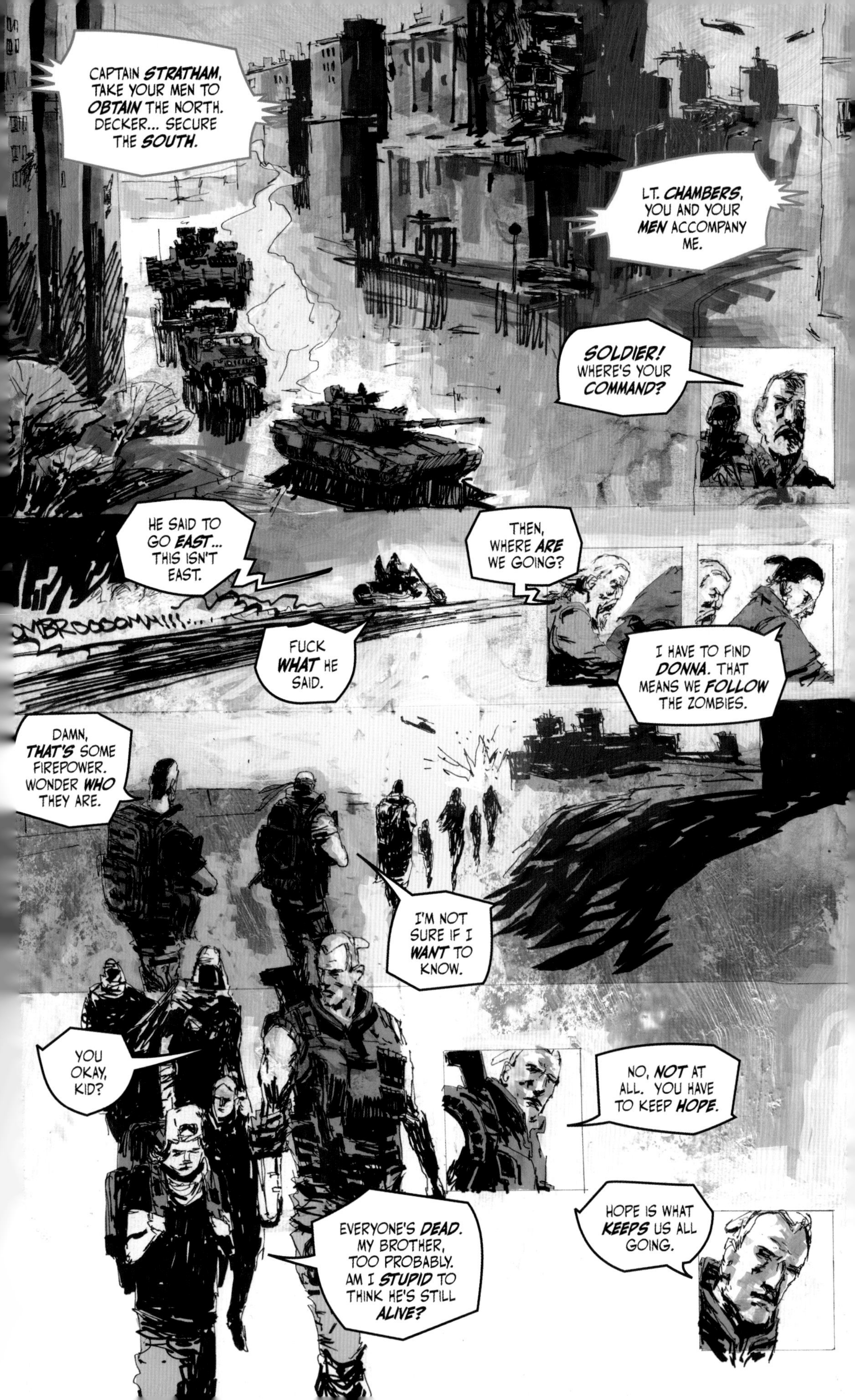
CAPTAIN STRATHAM, TAKE YOUR MEN TO OBTAIN THE NORTH. DECKER... SECURE THE SOUTH.
LT. CHAMBERS, YOU AND YOUR MEN ACCOMPANY ME.
SOLDIER! WHERE'S YOUR COMMAND?
HE SAID TO GO EAST... THIS ISN'T EAST.
THEN, WHERE ARE WE GOING?
FUCK WHAT HE SAID.
I HAVE TO FIND DONNA. THAT MEANS WE FOLLOW THE ZOMBIES.
DAMN, THAT'S SOME FIREPOWER. WONDER WHO THEY ARE.
I'M NOT SURE IF I WANT TO KNOW.
YOU OKAY, KID?
NO, NOT AT ALL. YOU HAVE TO KEEP HOPE.
EVERYONE'S DEAD. MY BROTHER, TOO PROBABLY. AM I STUPID TO THINK HE'S STILL ALIVE?
HOPE IS WHAT KEEPS US ALL GOING.

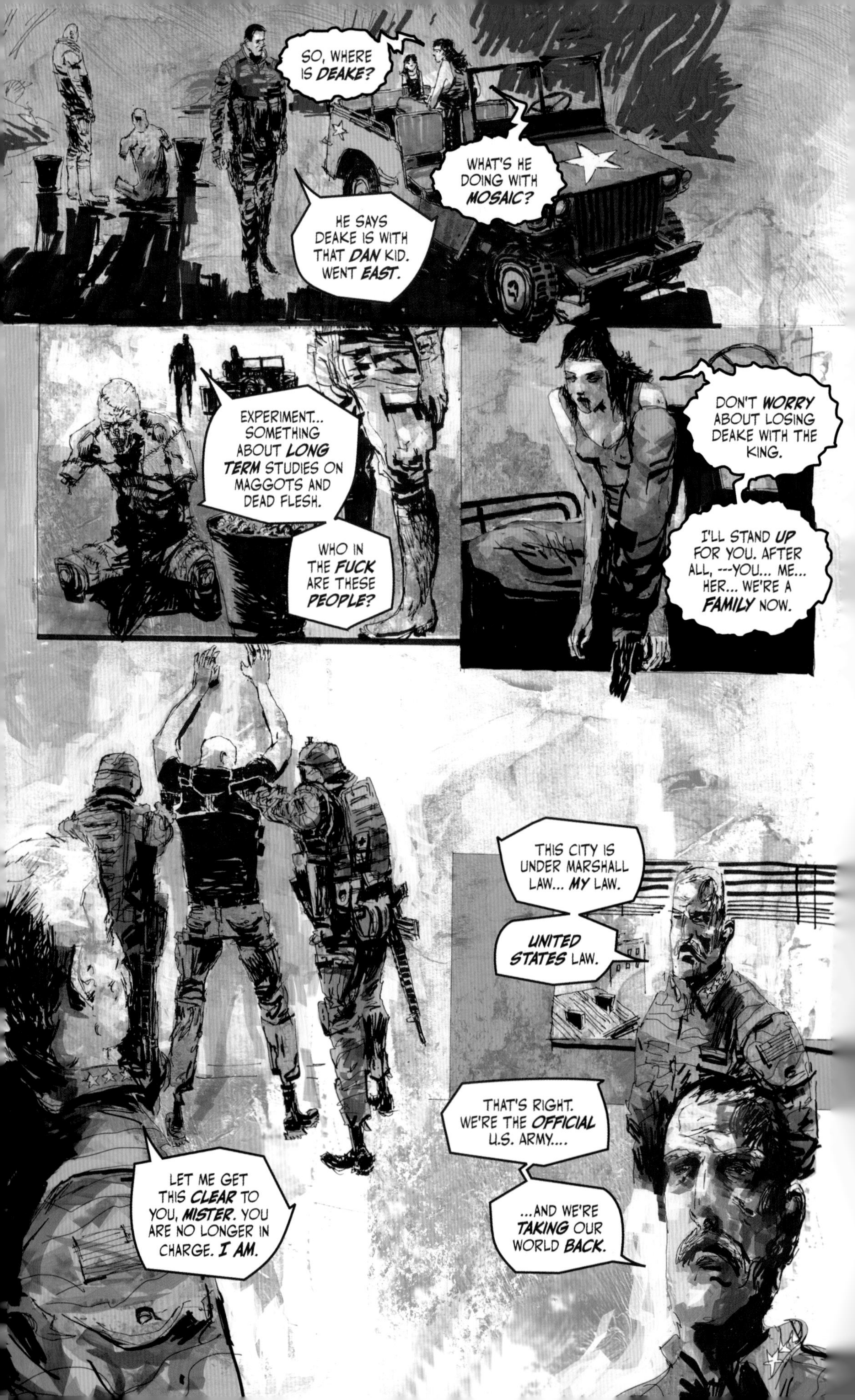
SO, WHERE IS DEAKE?
WHAT'S HE DOING WITH MOSAIC?
HE SAYS DEAKE IS WITH THAT DAN KID. WENT EAST.
EXPERIMENT... SOMETHING ABOUT LONG TERM STUDIES ON MAGGOTS AND DEAD FLESH.
WHO IN THE FUCK ARE THESE PEOPLE?
DON'T WORRY ABOUT LOSING DEAKE WITH THE KING.
I'LL STAND UP FOR YOU. AFTER ALL, ---YOU... ME... HER... WE'RE A FAMILY NOW.
THIS CITY IS UNDER MARSHALL LAW... MY LAW.
UNITED STATES LAW.
LET ME GET THIS CLEAR TO YOU, MISTER. YOU ARE NO LONGER IN CHARGE. I AM.
THAT'S RIGHT. WE'RE THE OFFICIAL U.S. ARMY....
...AND WE'RE TAKING OUR WORLD BACK.

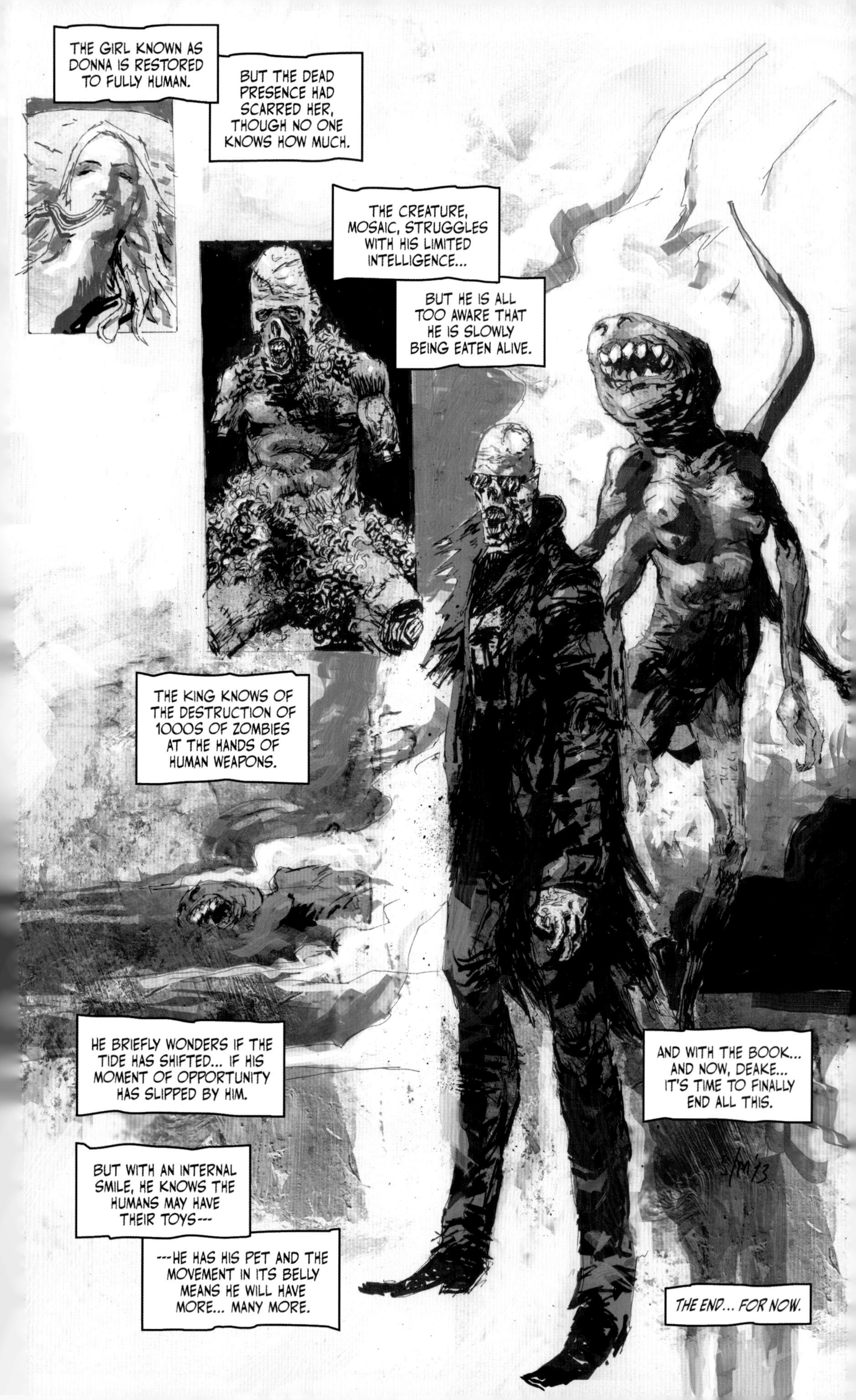
THE GIRL KNOWN AS DONNA IS RESTORED TO FULLY HUMAN.
BUT THE DEAD PRESENCE HAD SCARRED HER, THOUGH NO ONE KNOWS HOW MUCH.
THE CREATURE, MOSAIC, STRUGGLES WITH HIS LIMITED INTELLIGENCE...
BUT HE IS ALL TOO AWARE THAT HE IS SLOWLY BEING EATEN ALIVE.
THE KING KNOWS OF THE DESTRUCTION OF 1000S OF ZOMBIES AT THE HANDS OF HUMAN WEAPONS.
HE BRIEFLY WONDERS IF THE TIDE HAS SHIFTED... IF HIS MOMENT OF OPPORTUNITY HAS SLIPPED BY HIM.
BUT WITH AN INTERNAL SMILE, HE KNOWS THE HUMANS MAY HAVE THEIR TOYS---
---HE HAS HIS PET AND THE MOVEMENT IN ITS BELLY MEANS HE WILL HAVE MORE... MANY MORE.
AND WITH THE BOOK... AND NOW, DEAKE... IT'S TIME TO FINALLY END ALL THIS.
THE END... FOR NOW.

AFTERWORD

Usually the afterword is reserved for a peek at what might be up-coming. When I did the afterword for *War of the Dead*, I said at that time that I really didn't know what was coming next. Of course, "next" was *Restoration*. So, now what?

Again, I really don't know. Sure, I have some ideas and a certain path that I want to travel with the series but I like to step away a bit and let things run through my head.

What I did want to bring up here is the artist, Sami Makkonen. Sami first came on board with the original graphic novel, *Slaughterhouse*, which is the first part of a trilogy (so far) of *Slaughterhouse*, *War of the Dead*, and now *Restoration*.

When I was formulating *Slaughterhouse*, I wanted it to be dark. It needed to convey a sense of hopelessness and be something that struck at the core of humanity. I wanted to reach deep into mankind's attempt to deal with this plague and what humans were capable of in order to survive. I hoped I got the idea that almost everyone's actions were based on what they thought would help man best survive.

That's why I needed a specific artist. When I saw Sami's art, I saw that it was moody and edgy and there was a frantic sensibility about it. Instantly, I knew I found the artist I was looking for. I loved what he did with *Slaughterhouse* and then when we switched to color with *War of the Dead*, I was blown away.

As a writer in comics, you're always tied in with your artist on any project. When I look back on this trilogy, I always think of the books that I did with Sami. He elevated the darkness more than I thought possible yet also knew when to pull back and let the art fade into the story.

I wanted to express my deepest thanks for Sami for what he brought to *Deadworld*. Even though, as a writer, every project is special, I think he elevated it even beyond what I hoped for.

So, to Sami... you have my utmost respect and my most heartfelt thanks.

Gary Reed

SAMI MAKKONEN ART GALLERY

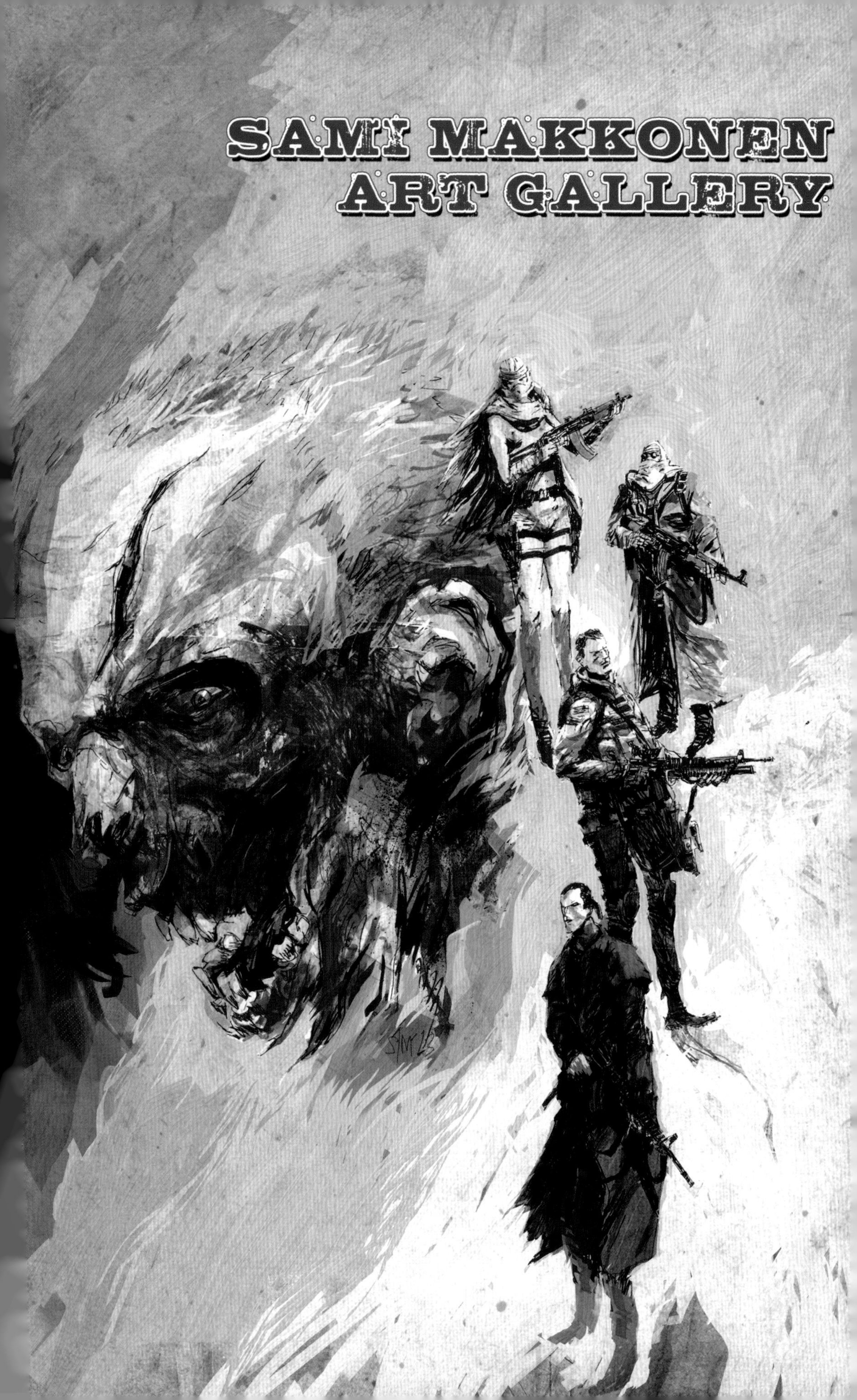

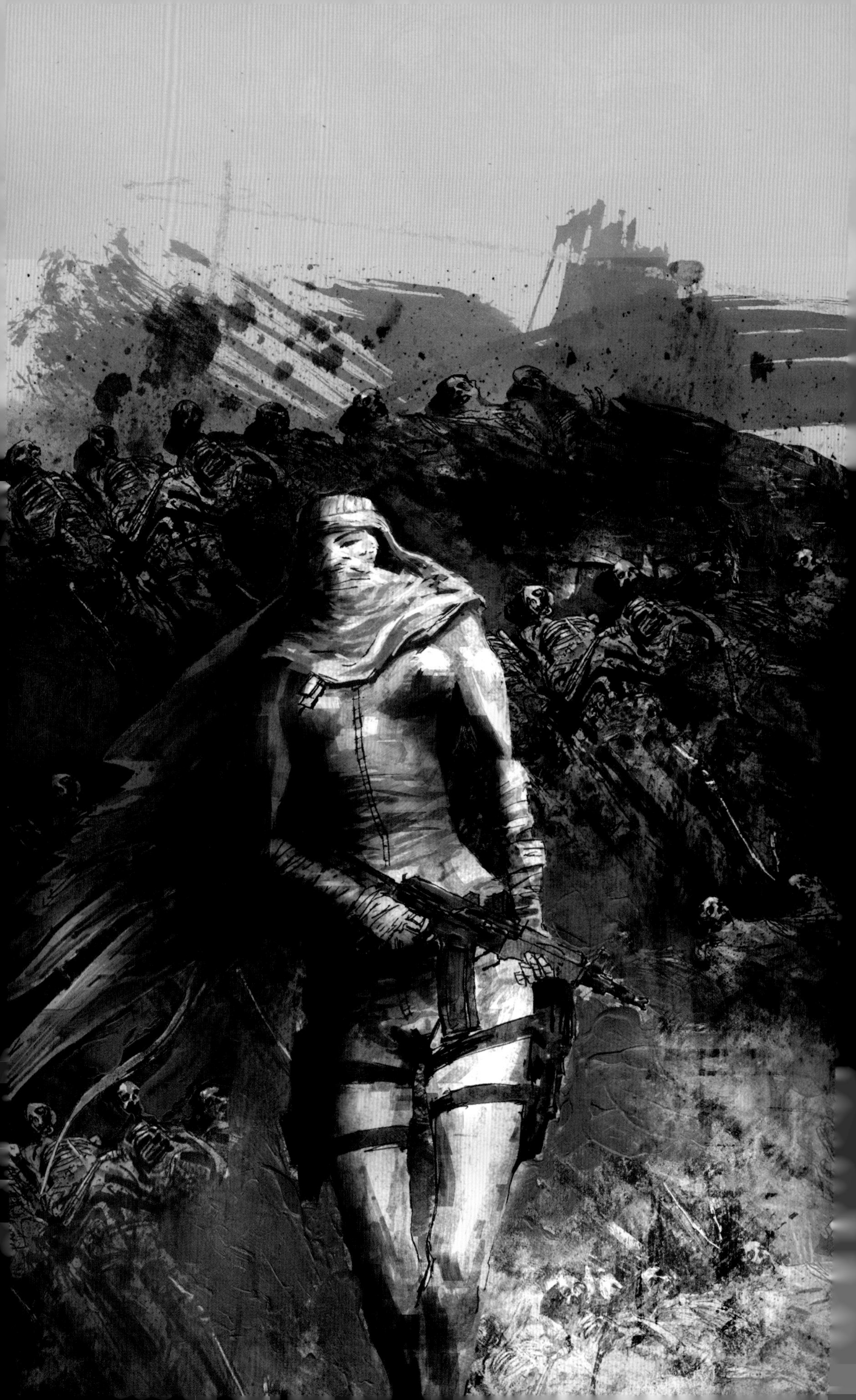

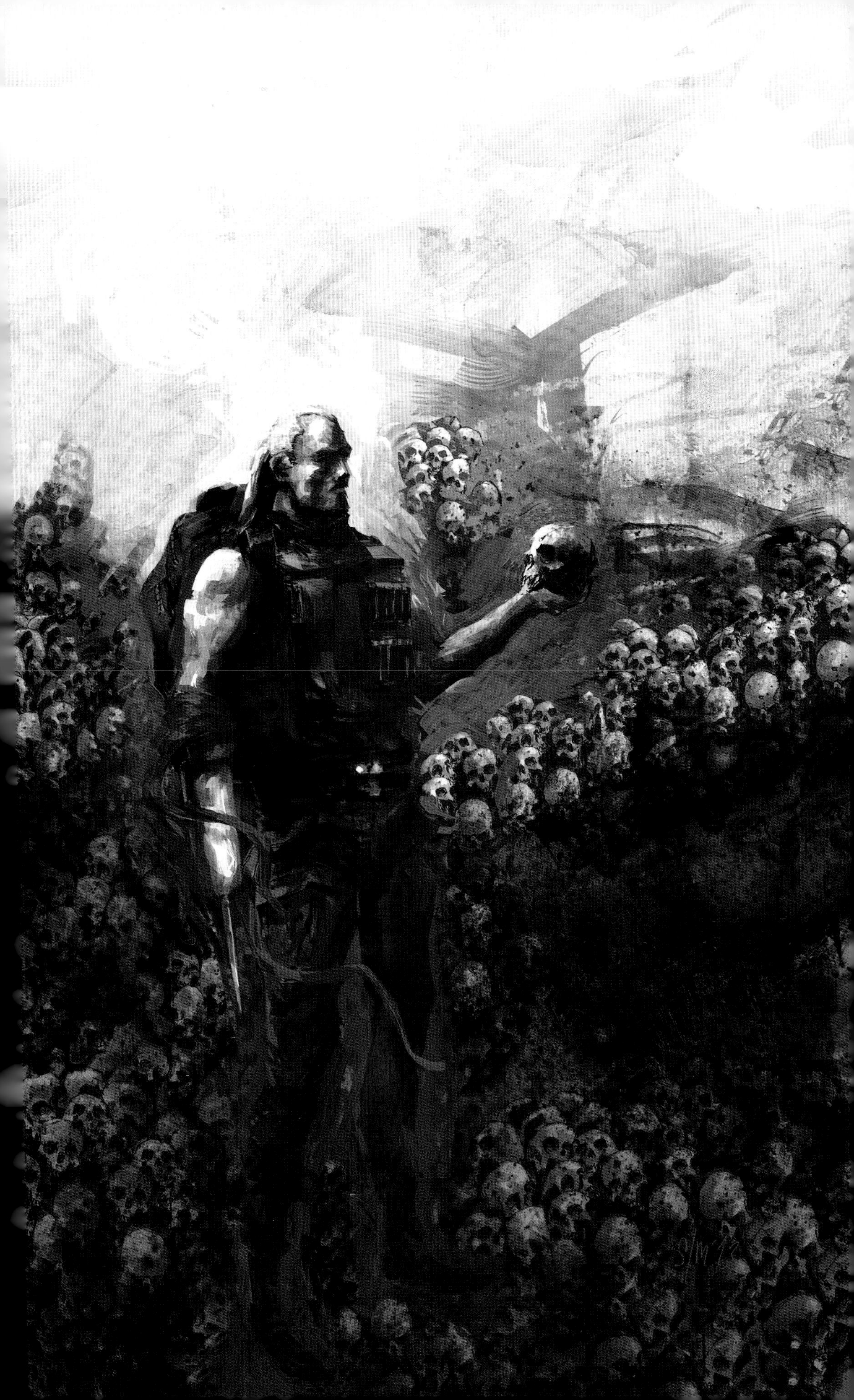

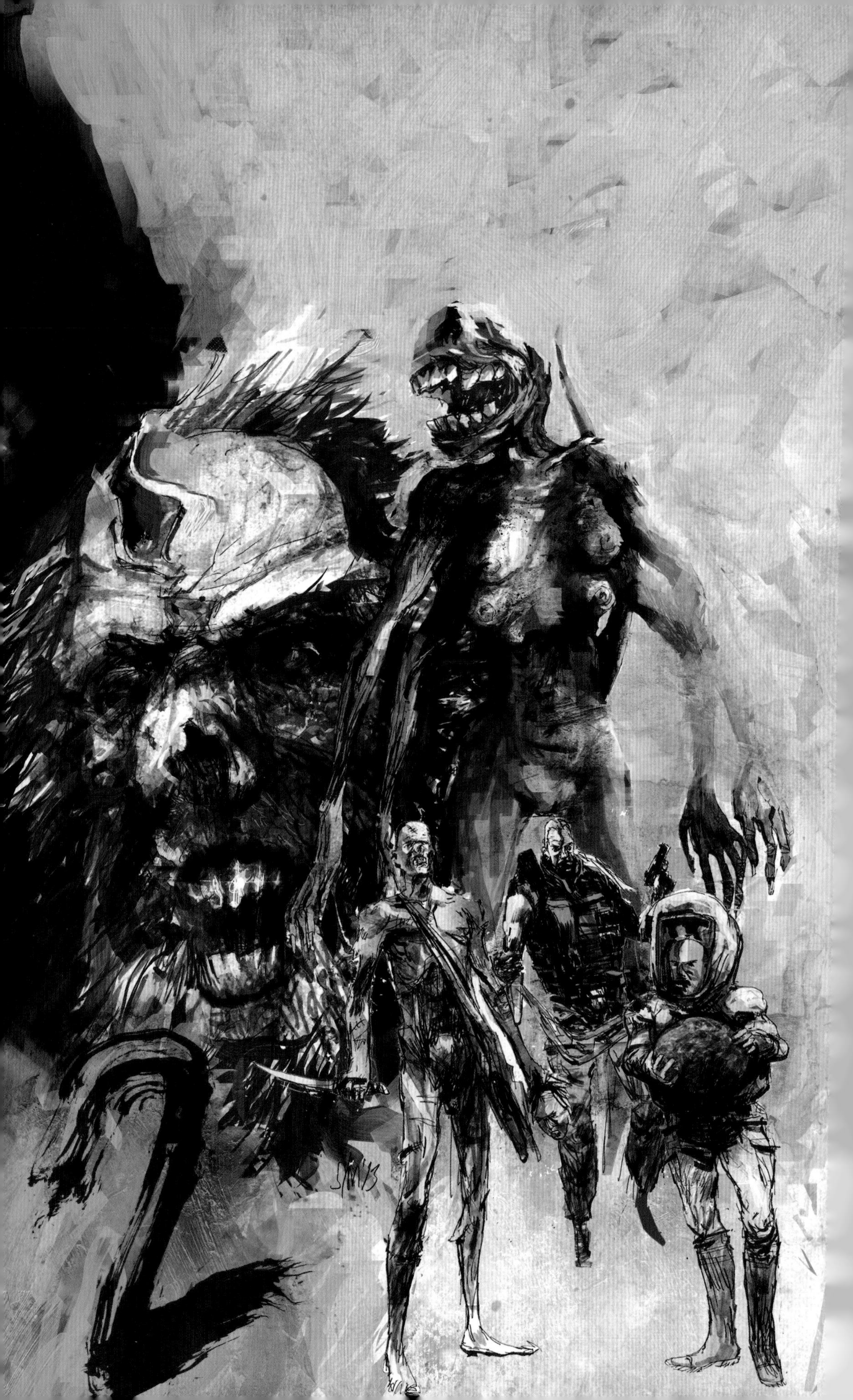

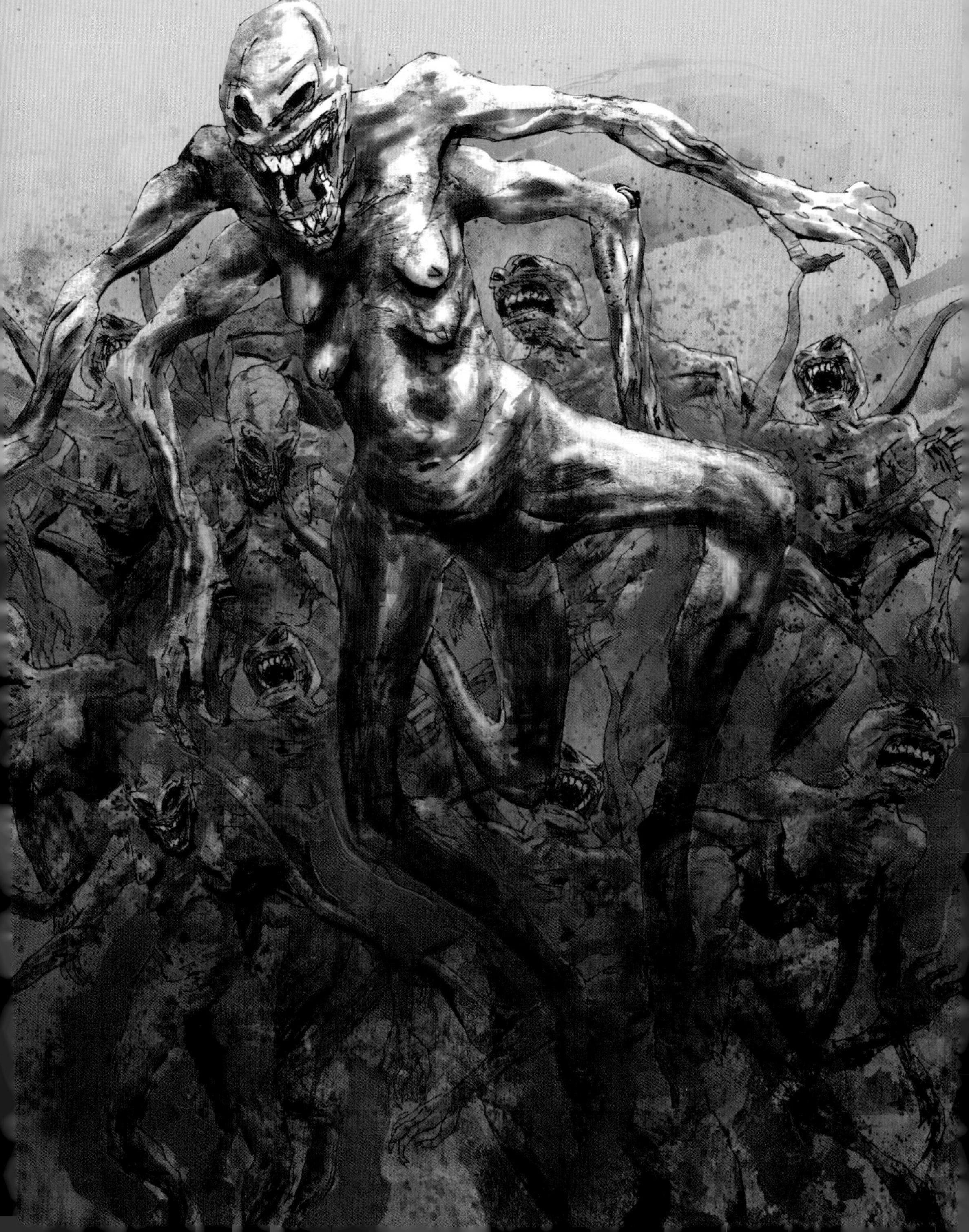

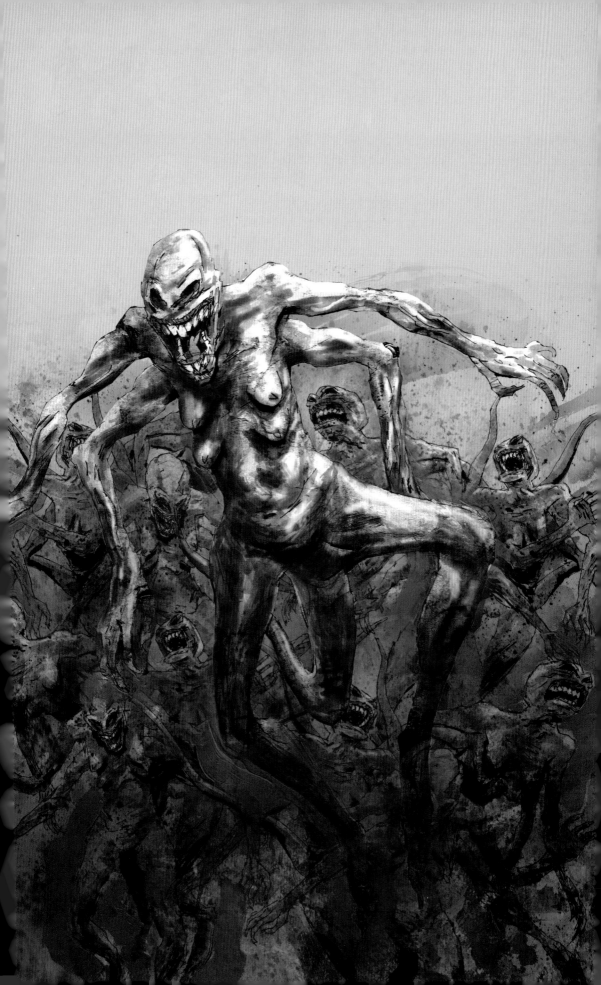

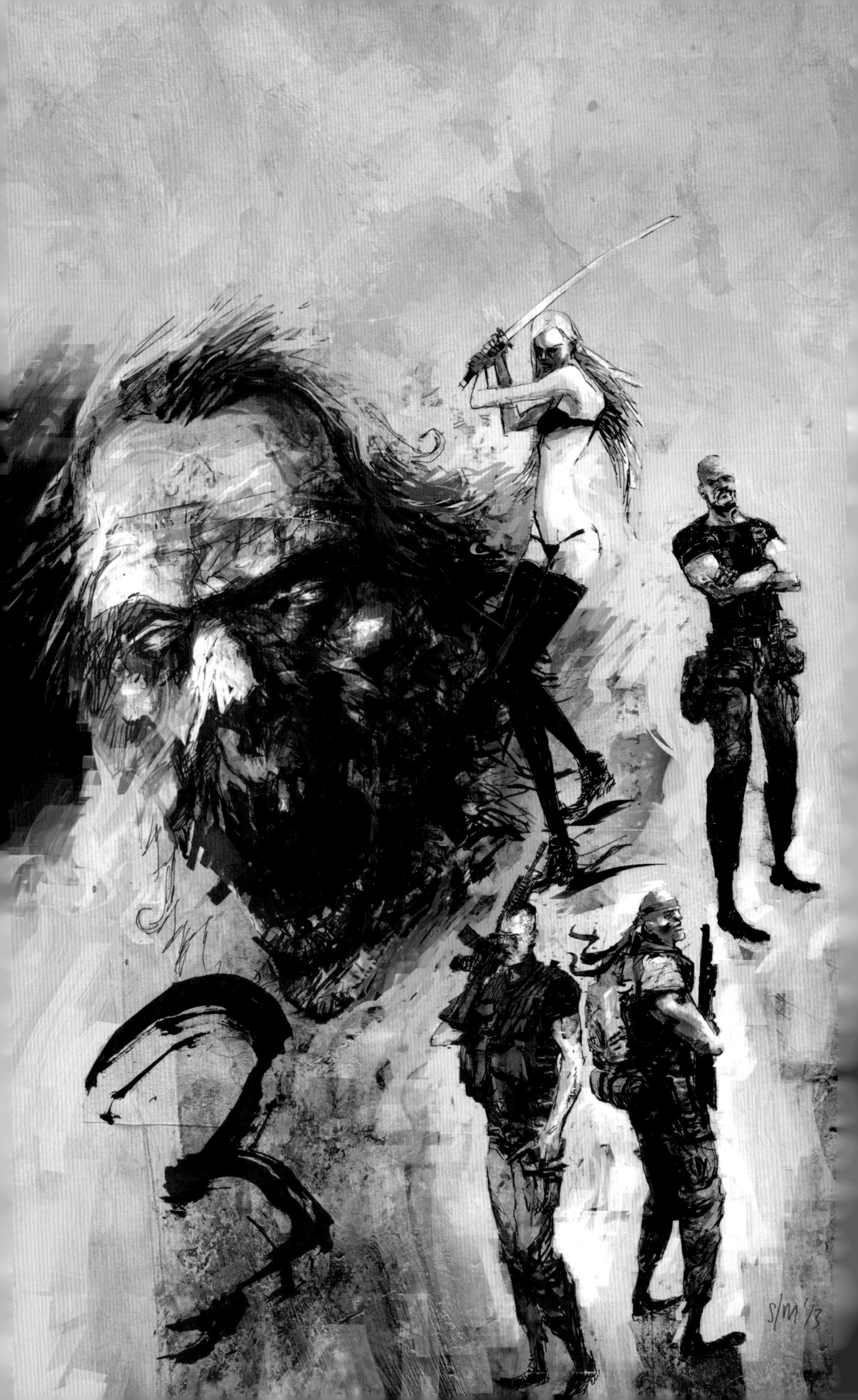
3